CASS SERIES: ST
(Series Edito

SIR FREDERICK SYKES AND
THE AIR REVOLUTION
1912–1918

CASS SERIES: STUDIES IN AIR POWER
(Series Editor: Sebastian Cox)
ISSN 1368-5597

1. *A Forgotten Offensive*
Royal Air Force Coastal Command's Anti-Shipping Campaign, 1940–1945
by CHRISTINA J. M. GOULTER

2. *Courage and Air Warfare*
The Allied Aircrew Experience in the Second World War
by MARK K. WELLS

3. *Despatch on War Operations*
by SIR ARTHUR T. 'BOMBER' HARRIS

4. *The Strategic Air War Against Germany, 1939–1945*
Report of the BRITISH BOMBING SURVEY UNIT

5. *Industry and Air Power*
The Expansion of British Aircraft Production, 1935–41
by SEBASTIAN RITCHIE

6. *Air Power at the Battlefront*
Allied Close Air Support in Europe, 1943–45
by IAN GOODERSON

7. *Russian Aviation and Air Power in the Twentieth Century*
edited by ROBIN HIGHAM, JOHN T. GREENWOOD AND VON HARDESTY

8. *Sir Frederick Sykes and the Air Revolution 1912–1918*
ERIC ASH

SIR FREDERICK SYKES
AND THE
AIR REVOLUTION
1912–1918

ERIC ASH
United States Air Force Academy

FRANK CASS
LONDON • PORTLAND, OR

First published in 1999 in Great Britain by
FRANK CASS PUBLISHERS.
2 Park Square, Milton Park, Abingdon, Oxon, OX14 4RN

and in the United States of America by
FRANK CASS PUBLISHERS
270 Madison Ave, New York NY 10016

Transferred to Digital Printing 2005

Website http://www.frankcass.com

Copyright © 1999 Eric Ash

British Library Cataloguing in Publication Data

Ash, Eric
  Sir Frederick Sykes and the air revolution, 1912–1918. –
  (Cass series. Studies in air power)
  1. Sykes, Sir Frederick   2. World War, 1914–1918 – Aerial
  operations, British
  I. Title
  940.4'4'091

ISBN 0-7146-4828-0 (cloth)
ISBN 0-7146-4382-3 (paper)
ISSN 1368-5597

Library of Congress Cataloging-in-Publication Data

Ash, Eric, 1957–
  Sir Frederick Sykes and the air revolution, 1912–1918 / Eric Ash.
    p.   cm. – (Cass series – studies in air power; 7)
  Includes bibliographical references and index.
  ISBN 0-7146-4828-0 (cloth). – ISBN 0-7146-4382-3 (pbk)
  1. Sykes, Frederick Hugh, Sir, 1877–1954.   2. World War,
  1914–1918–Aerial operations, British.   3. Great Britain. Royal Air
  Force–Biography.   I. Title.   II. Series.
  D786.A77   1998
  940.54'4941–dc21   98-22294
                                                                  CIP

Typeset by Regent Typesetting, London

Printed and bound by Antony Rowe Ltd, Eastbourne

To Dawn, Austin and Andy

Contents

List of Illustrations   ix

Foreword by General Ronald R. Fogelman   xi

Editor's Preface   xiii

Acknowledgements   xv

Abbreviations   xvii

Introduction   1

1 Casting the Net   9

2 Into Air Power: 1912–14   22

3 The Great War   50

4 Maritime Air Power: Gallipoli to 1916   75

5 Manpower and Morale: 1916–18   92

6 Chief of the Air Staff: Administrative Turbulence,
   April–August 1918   112

7 The Air War Finale: Supply, Bombing and Tactics,
   August–December 1918   155

8 To Reconnoiter the Enigma: Sykes and his Environment   187

9 The Forgotten Theorist and Air Power Leader   216

Epilogue   231

Appendices   249

Select Bibliography   255

Index   263

List of Illustrations

Between pages 174 and 175

1. Sykes mounted as a trooper in the Boer War

2. Sykes as a prisoner of the Boers

3. Sykes in the dress uniform of the 15th Hussars

4. Aerial photographs from Sykes' personal album, probably of the airfield and harbor at Imbros

5. Wing camp and aerodrome during the Gallipoli campaign, 1915

6. Sykes as Chief of the Air Staff, 1918

7. Sykes and colleagues from the British Air Section at the Paris Peace Conference, February 1919

8. Sykes and Bonar Law in 1920 at the Air Conference, Croydon

9. Sykes as Governor of Bombay, 1932

10. Sykes in later life, *c.* 1940

11. Lord Trenchard, Marshal of the Royal Air Force

12. Henri Farman biplane

13. Sopwith Camel

14. Fokker D VII

15. DH9 bomber aircraft

16. BE2c

17. Handley Page and Vickers Vimy

Foreword

In the history of air power forward-looking airmen have often become victims of bureaucracies, and Sir Frederick Sykes was just such a person. Even among scholars of air power Sykes has never enjoyed the recognition of his more famous contemporaries such as Lord Trenchard, Giulio Douhet, and General Billy Mitchell. He fell instead into obscurity, even though his work in organizing, training and equipping the Royal Flying Corps and the Royal Air Force was crucial to the birth and development of military flying. He had greater vision than many of his colleagues, whose ideas proved more acceptable to the establishment at the time. Sykes, in contrast, never received proper recognition for his seminal accomplishments owing to politics and prejudice. He should have been recognized for the depth and breadth of his conceptual thinking on air power, which led to unique advances in military thinking. He refused to give up in the face of entrenched opposition, and even after he was removed from the center of the military aviation arena he continued to serve in a variety of public positions unrelated to military aviation.

The world's air forces were able to grow into the powerful independent services they are today because of staunchly committed airmen such as Sykes. At long last this study of Sykes brings to light important aspects of air power that had previously been overlooked. Serious students of aviation history should read this book, and I recommend it to all airmen who wish to learn more about their heritage.

GENERAL RONALD R. FOGELMAN
July, 1998

Editor's Preface

The impact of the First World War on the development of air power has long been recognized. There have also been biographical studies of many of the airmen who played leading roles in the rise of British military aviation and the creation of the world's first independent air force, including Lord Trenchard, Sir Sefton Brancker and Sir John Salmond.[1] All these studies were, however, written more than 30 years ago, before the major official papers relating to the Royal Flying Corps (RFC), Royal Naval Air Service and the Royal Air Force (RAF) in the First World War were made available. Largely based on the memories and personal papers of the protagonists, these works were more than usually partial. Therefore, not only does this study of Major-General Sir Frederick Sykes represent the first proper assessment of his life and contribution to military aviation, but it is also the first biographical study of a senior First World War British airman to make use of the full range of official material now available to scholars. In so doing, it not only offers us new and important insights into Sykes himself, but also throws new light on the relationships in the high command of the RFC and then the RAF, and improves our understanding of other important figures involved, especially Lord Trenchard and Sir David Henderson.

There is little doubt that the part played by Sykes in the early years of British aviation has been eclipsed, partly as a result of aspects of his own character, and partly because, ultimately, he lost out in the bureaucratic battle to head the Royal Air Force in the post-war era. Eric Ash succeeds in demonstrating both the originality of Sykes' thinking and the practical contribution he made to the eventual success of the RAF in battle. The analysis is also sufficiently dispassionate and penetrating to reveal the weaknesses in Sykes' personal make-up which so bedevilled his relations with others, and which were to prove a significant factor in preventing his achieving all that he sought for the Royal Air Force and British aviation. At the same time, it reveals the degree to which some facets of Sykes' character have been exaggerated, notably his supposed taste for intrigue.

As students of air power increasingly recognize, the achievements of military aviation in 1914–18 have too often been viewed through the distorting prism of the later experience of 1939–45. Eric Ash's study is a valuable contribution to the growing body of scholarship devoted to analyzing the policies and thinking of the era in a more objective fashion.

SEBASTIAN COX

NOTE

1. The major biographies are: Andrew Boyle, *Trenchard* (London: Collins, 1962); Norman MacMillan, *Sir Sefton Brancker* (London: William Heinemann, 1935); Basil Collier, *Heavenly Adventurer: Sefton Brancker and the Dawn of British Aviation* (London: Martin Secker & Warburg, 1959); John Laffin, *Swifter than Eagles: The Biography of Marshal of the RAF Sir John Maitland Salmond* (Edinburgh: Blackwood, 1964).

Acknowledgements

This study would have been impossible without God's grace and my family's patience, as well as generous help from friends and esteemed historians. Dr Tim Travers was a superb academic advisor, and the helpful suggestions and support from Professor Holger H. Herwig, Head of the Department of History, University of Calgary, were sustaining during difficult moments. I also appreciated assistance from the following people: Dr John Ferris, Dr James Titus, Dr Harold Winton, Dr Robin Higham, Lord Blake, Mr Sebastian Cox, Wing Commander Peter Dixon; Mr Chris Hobson, Major James Hogan, and Brigadier General Philip Caine, who launched me into this endeavor. I was sustained by the memory of my father, Dr Rodney P. Ash, and by my mother Mrs Anne Ash, who followed me to London as editor and research assistant. I was inspired by my grandfather, Mr Frank Abbott, who fought with the American Expeditionary Force, 42nd Infantry 'Rainbow' Division, at Château-Thierry in 1918. Finally, I especially thank Bonar, Mary and Hugh Sykes for their valuable assistance and warm hospitality at Conock Manor. I appreciated my sponsorship from the United States Air Force Academy and the Air Force Institute of Technology; this study reflects my personal opinions rather than the views of the United States Air Force.

Abbreviations

Adm	Admiralty Files, PRO
ADL	Admiralty Letters, NMM
AHB	Air Historical Branch
Air	Air Files, PRO
BEF	British Expeditionary Force
CAB	Cabinet Office Paper, PRO
CAS	Chief of the Air Staff
CAT	Civil Air Transport (Committee)
CFS	Central Flying School
CGCA	Controller General of Civil Aviation
CGE	Controller General of Equipment
CID	Committee of Imperial Defence
CIGS	Chief of the Imperial General Staff
DGAP	Director General of Aircraft Production
DGMA	Director General of Military Aeronautics
GHQ	General Headquarters
GOC	General Officer Commanding
IAF	Independent Air Force of the RAF
IF	Independent Force of the Allied Air Forces
IFF	Indentification Friend or Foe
IWM	Imperial War Museum
LADA	London Air Defence Area
MEF	Mediterranean Expeditionary Force
MGP	Master General of Personnel
NMM	National Maritime Museum
OHL	Oberste Heeresleitung (Supreme Army Command)
PRO	Public Record Office
RAF	Royal Air Force
RAFM	Royal Air Force Museum
RES	Royal Empire Society
RFC	Royal Flying Corps
RN	Royal Navy
RNAS	Royal Naval Air Service
WAAC	Women's Army Auxiliary Corps
WLMD	Women's Legion Motor Drivers
WO	War Office Files, PRO
WRAF	Women's Royal Air Force

Introduction

On 10 October 1954 a famous flyer wrote to a grieving widow:

> I was deeply touched by your husband's wish that I should scatter the ashes over Salisbury Plain. I will, of course, do so . . . I always had admiration and affection for your husband and will always remember his kindness and help in the early days at Farnborough.

Yours Very Sincerely
Geoffrey de Havilland

Later de Havilland wrote, 'Yes, of course it will be a Secret and I would hate to have the slightest publicity made out of what is such a private and personal matter.'[1] The founding Chief of the Air Staff (CAS) of Britain's Royal Air Force (RAF) had died. Why such mystery surrounding the final tribute to Sir Frederick Sykes?[2]

Many air power enthusiasts, military historians and active-duty RAF members have never heard of Sykes and would argue that Lord Trenchard was the founding father of the RAF as its first Chief of Staff.[3] This is understandable considering that the Trenchard legend has dominated the air force history of the First World War and that few scholars have written about Sykes. Yet Trenchard demanded the acceptance of his resignation as CAS 12 days before 1 April 1918, the birthdate of the RAF, and Sykes was called in to salvage a tenuous situation as the new CAS of the world's first independent air force. While Trenchard's tenure as the first CAS lasted a few days, Sykes held the position for nearly a year – during some of the most critical moments of the war leading up to the victorious climax for the Allied nations. Nevertheless, in most histories of the First World War Sykes is an unimportant participant, and in many he is never even mentioned.

In 1966 the historian Robin Higham noted Sykes' anonymity and remarked that he should receive more attention, particularly since he played significant roles in the leadership of the Royal Flying Corps (RFC) and the RAF.[4] Recently a few scholars, such as Michael Paris, have begun to recognize Sykes' achievements and influence. Paris concluded that Sykes, not Trenchard, initiated the concept of air power as a means of imperial control and suggested that, compared with Trenchard, Sykes had been treated unjustly in history: 'Considering the rivalry and mutual dislike of the two men, it was ironic that, although Trenchard became the dominant figure in RAF hagiography ("the Father of the RAF"), it was Sykes' theoretical basis which ensured the continued independence of the RAF.'[5] In addition, Air Vice-Marshal Tony Mason, in *Air Power: A Centennial Appraisal*, supports the interpretation that Sykes was perhaps more responsible than Trenchard for what evolved into the RAF's costly strategic bombing doctrine of the Second World War.[6] The majority of air histories, however, starting with the official history by Sir Walter Raleigh and H. A. Jones, *The War in the Air*, have generally omitted Sykes from the story of early air power.[7] Perhaps this is because histories of First World War aviation started during Trenchard's firm reign as the head of the RAF.

A friend of Sykes once wrote, 'In no country is lionizing more difficult than in England.'[8] That statement has remained valid for some British airmen more than for others. It is sardonic that the two front pews of the RAF church in London are side-by-side memorials of two enemies – Sykes and Trenchard. The left pew is practically the only dedication to Sykes to be found in Great Britain, while across from it lies one of many tributes to Lord Trenchard – legendary 'Father of the RAF'.[9] The 'Trenchard school' has dominated the story of early British air power, while Sykes has been labeled both insignificant and a 'scheming intriguer', driven by personal ambition to maneuver his way into positions of leadership. This study will show clearly that Sykes' influence in the air war was significant and that he was not an intriguer.

Sykes was, however, partly responsible for his own historical demise. He accepted loss of popularity among his peers by fighting for overly ambitious air programs, and even when in positions of authority from which he could have ensured proper recognition for his accomplishments, he was reticent to speak up. It was beneath him to ask for accolades, and later, he simply did not desire to re-engage with Trenchard. Because he rejected the rank of Air Vice-Marshal in 1926, on the basis that it would be embarrassing so many years after he had left the RAF, Sykes' rank of Major-General remains somewhat of an anomaly in RAF history, as it became customary for the CAS to be promoted to at least an honorary Marshal of the RAF.[10] Hence, in some ways he deserved his rejection by the RAF and his reward of relative anonymity, which has hardly been an oversight. During the twenty-fifth anniversary of the RAF, for example, an official Air Ministry publication stated: 'Honour to the pioneers of military flying – Henderson, Longcroft and Brancker, Sueter, Samson and Lamb, and to that towering martial figure, Lord Trenchard, whose genius, foresight, leadership and driving force fused the naval and military elements of air power into one mighty service, the Royal Air Force.'[11] Sykes was easy prey for demigods with less humility.

When Sykes was given posthumous credit for his accomplishments in a London *Times* obituary, the anti-Sykes and pro-Trenchard/ Henderson (Director General of Military Aviation) cause was heralded by Edward Ellington, who attacked the story as improperly crediting Sykes with achievements belonging to others.[12] Ironically, Ellington was writing from the United Services Institute in Whitehall, where Sykes first presented his visionary talks to the Royal Aeronautical Society in 1912. Perhaps the one exception to the RAF's general abandonment of Sykes came from Sir Robert Saundby in 1954, when his article in *The Aeroplane* acknowledged Sykes' unmerited anonymity: 'Though but little known to the modern generation of airmen, Sykes must be counted among the few, those very few, who shaped and guided the early growth of British air power, and he deserves an honourable place in the history of the Royal Air Force.'[13]

The only other places where Sykes received any credit in aviation histories were in his own autobiography, *From Many Angles*, and in his earlier work, *Aviation in Peace and War*.[14] Sykes' autobiography is more a collection of ideas than a chronology of events. A major focus is British survival during the Second World War, when the book was published, as Sykes takes ample opportunity to suggest that, had the military and political authorities listened to him earlier, Britain might not be in such a difficult situation. As for the First World War and Sykes' role with the RFC and the RAF, not surprisingly, in both books he has a positive perspective on his influence and the effectiveness of the air service.

The air power story has moved with the ebb and flow of historiographical trends. Initially, in works such as the official history, the RFC and the RAF were lauded as effective organizations that 'saved the British Expeditionary Force [BEF] at Mons', and then went on to capture air supremacy and help the Allied war effort indirectly – by dislocating German war-making. Exciting stories and airmen's personal accounts accompanied the positivist approach as exemplified by L. A. Strange's *Recollections of an Airman*, and Gwilym Lewis' *Wings over the Somme*.[15] Focusing on 'everyman's war', historians portrayed the romantic image of Trenchard's heroic flyers and their superhuman efforts, and 'blood and guts' depictions that bordered at times on the mythical. Histories such as H. R. Allen's *The Legacy of Lord Trenchard*, P. R. C. Groves' *Behind the Smoke Screen* and David Divine's *The Broken Wing* reversed course to condemn air force leaders whose stubborn commitment to offensive doctrine cost the lives of many young flyers.[16] Recently, with the growth of war and society studies, air histories have focused more on social issues, politics and strategies than on individuals. Contemporary scholars, such as John Morrow, in *German Air Power in World War I* and *The Great War in the Air*, have concentrated on the aircraft production battle, technologies and doctrines.[17] The increasingly structuralist histories by Michael Paris, Denis Winter, Alfred Gollin, B. D. Powers, Malcolm Cooper and Lee Kennett have discussed air power in the context of its social environment: command structures, political agendas, media campaigns and public influence.[18] The role of Sykes throughout these trends has been similar – he has been seen as a tangential issue to the air power story. As this study of Sykes will show, however, he was more than a merely peripheral figure in the history of the British air service.

That Sykes has been overlooked is obvious; less apparent is the slanted approach used when historians have discussed him: Sykes' antagonistic relationships with other airmen, particularly Trenchard; Sykes' supposed 'intrigue' against Henderson; and Sykes' notorious 'secretive personality'. These themes provide interesting reading, and Sykes' apparent inability to get along with other airmen may have influenced the British air effort to some extent; but there are more important topics in the story of Sykes: his visionary theories and significant achievements as policy maker, organizer and leader. Contrasting personalities contributed less to the animosities than Sykes' deliberate fight to achieve goals and help in winning the war with air machines.

What follows is not a biography but an analysis of Sykes' theories, influence and leadership in various positions in the RFC, the Royal Naval Air Service (RNAS) and the RAF before and during the First World War. It focuses on his achievements: organizing, mobilizing and commanding the Military Wing of the RFC that went to war in 1914; reorganizing maritime air power at Gallipoli in 1915; commanding the Air Staff of the RAF in 1918; and helping to create strategic bombing prior to the Armistice on 11 November 1918. This study will show that Sykes was a key player in establishing British aviation and fighting the first air war, and that his influence helped to revolutionize warfare by promoting a relatively quick and fundamental change in the way armed forces fought which had a lasting effect on the conduct of warfare. This occurred during the First World War, despite the fact that air power was in its infancy and its destructive effect was marginal compared with that caused by the much larger ground forces.

Sykes helped to lead a revolution in warfare, brought about by the scientific application of air power. People and their ideas create revolutions; machines do not. The conventional air history of the First

World War has portrayed the developments in aviation incorrectly as ineffective, *ad hoc* reactions to external pressures: German bombing, public demands, economic forces and politics. As Morrow recognized recently, there was an enormous growth of aerial fighting and of the aviation industries during the war, and air power was a top priority of governments.[19] He is correct that the air arm – in particular the embryonic strategic bombing arm – did not determine the outcome of the war, but its impact was more than most authors have perceived. Although British air forces in the first air war struggled against a steep learning curve and, like the other services, often failed to live up to expectations with the brutal use of infant technologies, Sykes and some fellow air-minded disciples promoted a new dimension of warfare that was not only an essential aspect of the Allied victory but changed the way armed forces fight.

It is difficult to convince some academic historians that an aerial revolution has ever taken effect, much less during the First World War, particularly when scholars insist on looking only at the meagre damage caused by long-range bombing in comparison with that resulting from artillery. What many recent historians have failed to acknowledge is that the many facets of air power, in addition to strategic bombing, worked synergistically to change the face of battle. Historians may be blind to this reality, but combatants in the First World War certainly were not. German war diaries from the Somme in 1916 focused primarily on artillery; however, during and after the German spring offensives in 1918 German soldiers expressed one complaint above all others – aircraft . . . aircraft . . . aircraft! British aerial attacks stopped their movement, killed troops and horses, cut off supplies and prevented sleep. The soldiers were completely exhausted and their morale was low. They were convinced that warfare had changed.

The administrative and logistical developments to bring about such a change also point toward a revolution. The RFC entered the war in 1914 with fewer than 50 airworthy machines and the industrial and organizational infrastructure to replace those aircraft was practically non-existent.[20] By the Armistice, however, the RAF had 22,000 aircraft, coming from a supply system that could replace thousands per month. In terms of squadrons, the quantum leap in four years was over tenfold, going from fewer than ten squadrons in 1914 to almost one hundred in 1918. The RFC and the RNAS entered World War I with 276 officers and 1,797 men of other ranks. The RAF ended the war in 1918 with 27,333 officers and 263,837 other ranks.[21] Finally – fundamental to revolutions – there was a change in organization. To support such an air service and to pursue new thinking in terms of warfare with aircraft, a new Air Ministry was created and the RAF was separated from the other two services. And although the focus of this study is on Sykes and his air service, the revolution was not limited to British aerial warfare as similar developments and changes in fighting were taking place in other countries as well.

In addition, Sykes' work and influence did not die after the war. His exhausting struggle against his opponents, including Trenchard, to establish organizational structures and make seminal changes in aerial doctrine and strategy have endured to the present. As this study will show, Sykes helped to create new thinking about the application of technologies in modern war. Most notably, he was a paramount influence in the implementation of the long-range bombing force, the Independent Air Force (IAF). His visions of aerial warfare in strategic and tactical arenas, combining air power with military and naval efforts – using wide-ranging innovations varying from aircraft carriers, to aerial routes, to civil reserve fleets – were decades ahead of their time. His prediction of the dominant role air power would play in war and peace has become reality.

The story of Sykes begins with his challenging formative years, which tempered an independent character and an immured personality. Sykes constantly tested himself and rarely sought an easy path. He had great ambition and continually sought adventure, which became manifest in flying. As the First World War loomed on the horizon, Sykes promoted British aviation development, organized military flying and commanded the wing that would enter the war. During the war he orchestrated numerous developments in army and navy aviation and ended his participation as CAS of the new RAF.

It is argued that although Sykes was not involved in the conception of the RAF and the IAF, he had to direct their delivery and nurse them to fighting stature. Sykes assumes command as the Air Staff is in chaos over Trenchard's resignation and the RAF is fighting for its life against the most threatening German offensive of the war, Operation Michael in spring 1918. After establishing administrative stability at the top of the air hierarchy, Sykes fights other services, fellow airmen and foreign governments, to create the IAF – his crowning achievement – which had the capability and the intent to bomb Berlin as the war ended.

This study then involves a retrospective analysis of Sykes' personality and difficult relationships with key leaders and with the air service in general. It concludes with an assessment of his theories, the air revolution in warfare and a brief look at his post-war years. Sykes thought strategically and technically, motivated by the desire to wage war by the most efficient manner possible. His ideas were to promote and exploit technologies by applying them scientifically; to support the army and navy with air power, but to use it as a separate arm; and to bomb strategically. These ideas were contrary to military traditions and ahead of their time. Sykes fought those traditions to implement his ideas and contribute to the air revolution, which was just beginning to take hold when the Armistice was declared.

Throughout his life, Sykes remained staunchly devoted to his country, and he struggled against people, traditions and institutions to promote his visions and goals. At times his perspective was too far ahead of its time, clouded by idealism, and seen by military and political bureaucrats as foolish. This led to his estrangement from RAF circles and air power history. Yet, driven by an insatiable work ethic, Sykes was haunted more by his desire to help the British Empire prosper than by his disappointing lack of recognition as a founder of British flying.

Surprisingly, this is the first study of the founding CAS of the RAF. It is not intended to elevate Sykes at the expense of others for his achievements stand on their own. This story must, however, correct historical misperceptions and is bound to spark controversy in its conclusion that Sykes was a paramount influence behind the rise of air power during the First World War.

NOTES

1. De Havilland to Lady Sykes, 10 October and 28 October 1954, Sykes Private Papers, Conock Manor, Devizes, England. The famous De Havilland had started as the Assistant Designer at the Royal Aircraft Factory in 1910.
2. The Sykes family's desire for privacy is understandable, but the lack of public recognition at the passing of such an influential and significant actor in the formation of the RAF is indicative of Sykes' depreciation in the RAF during the latter half of his life and his relative anonymity in British air power history.
3. Air Commodore Henry Probert, author of *High Commanders of the Royal Air Force* (London: Her Majesty's Stationery Office, 1991), spoke to an audience of air power enthusiasts in spring 1994. A member of that audience (a retired RAF officer) mentioned in a telephone interview, 25 May 1994, that when a picture of Major-General Sykes was shown, no one admitted recognizing the face.
4. Robin Higham, *The Military Intellectuals in Britain: 1918–1939* (New Brunswick, NJ: Rutgers University Press, 1966), 120–1.
5. Michael Paris, *Winged Warfare: The Literature and Theory of Aerial Warfare in Britain, 1859–1917* (Manchester: Manchester University Press, 1992), 39, 214, 241–2.
6. Tony Mason, *Air Power: A Centennial Appraisal* (London: Brassey's, 1994), 34, 42. Mason states that after the First World War Trenchard was against the strategic bombing doctrine in concept but inherited it nevertheless.
7. Walter Raleigh and H. A. Jones, *The War in the Air* (London: Hamish Hamilton, 1922). There are numerous histories, such as Basil Collier's *A History of Air Power* (London: Weidenfeld & Nicolson, 1974) and Richard P. Hallion's *Rise of the Fighter Aircraft 1914–1918* (Annapolis, MD: Nautical & Aviation Publishing Co., 1984), that make no reference to Sykes. David MacIsaac, 'Voices from the

Central Blue: The Air Power Theorists', in Peter Paret (ed.), *Makers of Modern Strategy* (Princeton, NJ: Princeton University Press, 1986), 624–47, failed to attribute Trenchard's post-war theories to their originator, Sykes. MacIsaac did not even mention Sykes as a theorist, which is surprising, considering that Sykes' air power theories were published as the Lees-Knowles Lectures on aeronautics at Cambridge University in 1921 and were contemporary with those of Giulio Douhet. In Myron Smith's *World War I in the Air: A Bibliography and Chronology* (Metuchen, NJ: Scarecrow Press, 1977), only two books out of 2,000 on air power are about Sykes – both written by Sykes!

8. Lord Sempill to Lady Sykes, 4 October 1954, Sykes Private Papers.

9. The RAF Church of St Clement Danes, also known as the 'Oranges and Lemons Church', was consecrated in 1958 as the RAF's Central Church.

10. Sykes to Samuel Hoare (Air Minister), 18 January 1926, Sykes Private Papers; and Probert, 99–141. Sykes rejected the offer on the basis that it was not a promotion at all, but a lateral rank change, as Major-General and Air Vice-Marshal were equivalent ranks.

11. Air Ministry Broadcast, 0900 hours, 28 March 1943, Trenchard Papers, MFC 76/1/411, Royal Air Force Museum (RAFM), Hendon. Sykes was mentioned only once in the program notes, and he was omitted from the Reception Committee and the historical synopsis, 'RFC and R.N.A.S. Family Tree'.

12. Sir Robert Inaswell and F. H. Brown, 'Sir Frederick Sykes, A Many-Sided Career', *The Times*, London, 2 October 1954. Undated letter to *The Times* by Edward L. Ellington in Sykes Private Papers.

13. Robert Saundby, 'Sir Frederick Sykes', *The Aeroplane*, 15 October 1954.

14. Sykes, *From Many Angles* (London: Harrap, 1942); and *Aviation in Peace and War* (London: Edward Arnold, 1922). Although the latter was published as Sykes' Lees-Knowles Lectures, which he gave at Cambridge University in February and March 1921, Sykes had contracted with Edward Arnold in 1916 to write the book.

15. L. A. Strange, *Recollections of an Airman* (London: Greenhill Books, 1989; first published in 1933); and Gwilym H. Lewis, *Wings over the Somme 1916–1918*, ed. Chas Bowyer (London: William Kimber, 1976).

16. H. R. Allen, *The Legacy of Lord Trenchard* (London: Cassell, 1972); P. R. C. Groves, *Behind the Smoke Screen* (London: Faber, 1934); and David Divine, *The Broken Wing* (London: Hutchinson, 1966).

17. John H. Morrow, *German Air Power in World War I* (Lincoln: University of Nebraska Press, 1982). Morrow, *The Great War in the Air, Military Aviation from 1909 to 1921* (Washington, DC: Smithsonian Institution Press, 1993), p. xiv. Morrow stated that, while the stories of famous flyers and their machines are popular, the studies of doctrine, politics and industry are the subjects of scholarship.

18. Denis Winter, *The First of the Few* (London: Allen Lane, 1982); B. D. Powers, *Strategy without Slide-Rule: British Air Strategy 1914–1939* (London: Croom-Helm, 1976); Alfred Gollin, *The Impact of Air Power on the British People and Their Government, 1909–1914* (London: Macmillan, 1989); Lee Kennett, *The First Air War 1914–1918* (New York: Free Press, 1991); Malcolm Cooper, *The Birth of Independent Air Power* (London: Allen & Unwin, 1986).

19. Morrow, *The Great War in the Air*, 364.

20. In 1914 the RFC and the RNAS had a combined total of 218 aircraft, 52 seaplanes and 7 airships. Yet many of these were in poor condition to fly, much less fight. See Mason, 18.

21. Ibid.

1

Casting the Net

At a young age Frederick Sykes began making his own way through life. He was born in 1877 to two Sykeses, distant cousins from Yorkshire who lived in Western Villas, North Park, Croydon, south of London. Frederick was the youngest of seven children: three brothers Henry (called Guy), Godfrey and Frederick; and four sisters Edith, Hilda Mary, Lilian (called Loly) and Ethel. Ethel, whom Frederick referred to as 'Number 2', was Frederick's closest sibling, and the one with whom he corresponded the most.[1] His father Henry Sykes was a mechanical engineer and successful businessman; however, his parental influence on Frederick was negligible, as he died two years after Frederick's birth.[2] His mother Mary Sykes had an indomitable spirit and, although she suffered from ill health, was able to keep the family going as well as enter into her husband's business as a partner following his death. Frederick was quite close to his mother and admired her ambitious and courageous attitude. He also had a fondness for his older sisters, who raised him until he was sent off to boarding school at age seven. This was not unusually early to be departing for boarding school and it most likely suited Frederick's adventurous spirit. It established a pattern early on of self-reliance that would last throughout his life.

Sykes' education was chequered as he moved from one school to another. He corresponded regularly with his mother, but he lacked a father-figure to emulate or to ask for advice. Sykes first attended a boarding school in Brighton that was run by a Mrs Hodges and another lady, and he then transferred to the Whitgift School, an old and well-established public school, which he attended from 1889–91.[3] Whitgift may have been a difficult social adjustment for Sykes, but it prepared him well academically and marked the end of his formal education.[4] When he was nearly 15 he left for Paris to learn French and German. There a succession of widows taught him and for a time he worked in various jobs to support himself. Sykes took education seriously and received a firm enough scholastic foundation so that he had little difficulty in demonstrating his intellectual abilities later in life.

While in Paris, Sykes first began to exhibit traits which would mark his personality. To satisfy an inner drive to explore the unfamiliar and to challenge himself, he set goals to test his limitations and determine his level of endurance.[5] Perhaps this was because he was physically smaller than most of his peers and felt the need to match them (which he certainly did). Sykes was not only self-reliant but self-confident – carrying himself with an erect posture, eyes straight ahead, as if posed to challenge any obstacles than might appear in his path. At the age of 16 Sykes dared to traverse potentially dangerous areas of Paris, walking, during one particular adventure, over 60 miles in a day.[6] He was undaunted by the fact that he was a boy of slight build, living in a foreign country and without much family support. His ambition at that time to serve in the Diplomatic Corps was both idealistic and unrealistic for he had no finances. After visiting Switzerland as part of his education, Sykes returned to London to work temporarily in a shipping firm before launching another quest, this time to the island then known as Ceylon.

Still in his teens, Sykes had chosen a rather ambitious and exotic adventure to learn the business of tea planting in the hope of working his way up the system to become a successful plantation owner. A hard worker, the actual labor involved in farming tea was not difficult for Sykes, even though the geography and especially the climate of Ceylon were quite different from those of London or Paris. Writing home about the thick jungle, infernal dampness and lack of floors or running water in his bungalow, Sykes stated, 'It is an awful life for any one but I think if I were a woman out here I would shoot myself straight off.'[7] He challenged himself, gained respect from fellow workers and plantation owners who thought he would never last in the environment, and was offered the position of assistant manager of an estate. Nevertheless, after working in the tea industry for a time he noticed that most of his fellow workers wished to leave but stayed because of indebtedness. Sykes surmised that his prospects for great success were dim and decided that a better quest might be in Africa.

The opportunity to leave did not come quickly, however. Sykes endured his situation and adjusted to the different life by socializing and seeking new physical and intellectual challenges. For Sykes, trying to mix with a crowd was much more difficult than climbing a mountain or learning a new language. He proudly wrote home of his accomplishments at a local dance – that he had danced and had actually enjoyed himself, quickly reassuring his mother that he had not become drunk like the other men.[8] He tried to improve his accommodation in case a member of the family came for a visit, and he explored the island in his free time. Perhaps his most ambitious endeavor was a 40-mile journey in the dark through thick jungle up steep mountain slopes to the Temple of Buddha's Footstep.[9] Despite having tried to embrace the culture by learning Tamil and exploring the teachings of Buddhism, Sykes became frustrated with his surroundings. He relayed to his mother his regret that he had felt animosity toward some of the local people who had taken advantage of his innocence and inexperience.

Thus in Ceylon Sykes first exhibited his preference for proper society and his utter distaste for injustice and laziness. He wrote in a fit of frustration, 'I do hate these natives more and more the longer I stay amongst them I think. Cowardly, mean, despicable, villainous, beasts, there – that ought to have done me good.'[10] In contrast to them, he found the theosophist Mrs Besant, who had an Ashram in Madras, to have been charming and wonderfully eloquent.[11] Ceylon was an important ingredient in Sykes' early years, as it reinforced his determination to work hard to achieve a satisfactory position in life.

His return to England also was not without adventure, as he took a circuitous route through the Orient and North America. Just as the English had decided that China, Burma and Japan were the 'Far East', Sykes held similarly ethnocentric attitudes during his youth. During his trip around the world he was impressed by all the contributions his British ancestors had made. This impression remained with him for life, as he envisioned the English-speaking peoples to be the hope of the future for world peace and endeavored to help the Empire in that noble quest.[12]

When the long-brewing hostilities in the Orange Free State and the Transvaal erupted into war, Sykes finally saw an opportunity to satisfy his zeal for Africa and serve the Queen at the same time. This change of direction toward the military would transform his life. He sailed for South Africa and upon his arrival in Cape Town enlisted with the Imperial Yeomanry Scouts and was soon on a train to Bloemfontein. Although in the bottom ranks, Sykes took notice of different commanders' leadership styles and approaches to combat. He appreciated Lord Roberts's 'great forbearance' with the Boers, but acknowledged that it was less successful than that of his successor Lord Kitchener, who pursued a more ruthless policy of search and destroy. Sykes most admired the leadership of the enemy – particularly of the commanders Christian De Wet and Louis Botha – and their use of irregular warfare. He also appreciated the response of the British colonies, who strongly supported Britain's side in the conflict by sending troops immediately.[13]

Sykes was not impressed with the British military. He stated that they were 'caught napping', had poor intelligence, were outnumbered, and fought unsuccessfully against an unconventional army. After an all-night march to reinforce the poorly-defended post at Roodevall,

Sykes' unit encountered the enemy from all directions. Without any artillery to counter enemy shelling, the traditional British tactics in battle failed under fire. They argued heroically against the thought of surrender but surrendered nevertheless.

Sykes' experiences as De Wet's prisoner of war constituted his most significant memories of the Boer War. Used to long marches under difficult conditions, Sykes again proved his remarkable endurance by outlasting the enemy. The Boers were unable to keep their prisoners any longer and freed Sykes, who made another long walk over the pass to Ladysmith, where he caught a ride to Cape Town. Yet his impressions of the enemy lasted. He respected the way they treated their horses, and he admired their organizational system. Against the poorly prepared British forces they were efficient and effective.

Back at Cape Town, Sykes did not arrive with pomp and circumstance as the survivor of a great ordeal. Instead, the Imperial Yeomanry Scouts were disbanded and Sykes had to seek new employment. He joined the bodyguard of Lord Roberts, who would later play a significant part in Sykes' military career by supporting his endeavors in air power.[14] After six months of duty, Sykes experienced his second significant event of the war. His unit, out on patrol, was ordered to ride to a particular location to reinforce a town. Because they had seen the enemy earlier and had been deceived into thinking the Boers were fleeing, Sykes' cavalry column moved vulnerably up a valley where they soon encountered their forward scouts returning under fire. It was too late to avoid envelopment as the enemy had established a successful ambush. In the fray Sykes was knocked off his horse by a Henri-Martini bullet that passed through his chest.

He was once again at the mercy of the enemy. While lying on the ground and unable to move, he realized that enemy raiders were stripping his body of uniform items and equipment that the Boers badly needed. Fortunately, Louis Botha's brother, one of the enemy commanders, intervened to stop the plunder. Soon British reinforcements arrived to chase off the enemy, and a field ambulance rescued Sykes.

One bullet had entered his lower right side, shattered ribs, pierced his liver and traveled through his lung before exiting at his shoulder. Another had hit his arm. Once in the hospital, Sykes complained of 'beastly aggravating' living conditions and of his difficulty in breathing, but he was optimistic that soon the unpleasant holes would close up, allowing him to return to his men. For some time, however, he remained bent over, could not move his right arm and could hardly walk. He was convalescing from his wounds at the time Queen Victoria died.[15]

Sykes was unable to return to the war, and his recovery from the ordeal gave him an opportunity to reflect on his recent military experiences. He had been part of a poorly prepared army that had been steeped in traditional methodologies that were both inefficient and ineffective. The Staff College emphasis on morale and the castigation of independent thinking had not ensured victory in battle, and now the British Army was entering a new century of warfare where old systems, principles and time-honored tactics might not prove success-ful.[16] Sykes had witnessed war from some of its worst perspectives: – as a line soldier, as a prisoner, and as a casualty. Yet he embraced those experiences as valuable lessons in life, and they would shape his character and approach to a future war. His adventure in South Africa complete, Sykes returned to England.

He also returned to the military. Ten months after having lain near death on a dusty battleground, Sykes eagerly accepted a reward for his brave and sacrificial service to the Queen: a commission in the Regular Army as a second lieutenant with the 15th Hussars.[17] This formal step into a military career established the course of Sykes' life for the next two decades, but it also created within him a self-image he maintained for the rest of his life. Although educated on the battlefield during war, he had not received his commission in the British Army through the proper channels of Sandhurst and therefore lagged behind his contemporaries in the profession of arms.[18] Throughout his military career Sykes would feel the need to better himself to catch up with others. He would be driven to prove his abilities to his superiors, to his peers and to himself.

Regardless of his circumstances, Sykes drove himself to the limits to demonstrate his professionalism. His first assignment was with the depot of the 15th Hussars in Ireland, where he perfected his riding skills and practiced drill. Then he left for Meerut to begin his next posting as a soldier for the Empire. In India Sykes earned a reputation as a selfless, tireless worker with an obsession for propriety. A friend said that Sykes 'had the highest sense of duty and right and wrong of any man I ever met'.[19] He once returned from Simla to Muttra during the hot season just to pay back a debt immediately. His astonished friend stated that 999 out of a thousand would have been content to offer an apology at a later time, 'But that would not do for him.'[20] Sykes was most impressed by the character traits of a Major Peyton (later Lieutenant-General Sir William Peyton), who exhibited great courage but stressed practicality, initiative and efficiency.[21] Perhaps owing to this influence, Sykes promoted the same goals years later in the First World War.

He was spring-loaded to discover, serve and learn. He kept his kit prepared so that he was constantly ready to embark on any missions that might arise. During his spare time he studied Hindustani and gained practical colonial experience by attending diplomatic events as a representative of the King.[22] When hostilities broke out in northern Nigeria Sykes was eager to return to action. He was sent to Sierra Leone, however, a trip that was significant for one reason – he met there his life-long and closest friend P. R. C. Groves. Sykes served for one year in West Africa as a supply officer at headquarters. He endured inhospitable living conditions and, as in previous adventures, once again began to appreciate the amenities afforded back in England.

His next quest was one that would change the course of Sykes' military career for life. He still felt compelled to improve his qualifications as an officer and in 1904, while in England on leave from Sierra Leone, rested very little before enrolling on a number of courses to enhance his military status. Sykes took instruction in rifle and machine-gun firing and excelled in a signalling course. He also completed courses on transport, topographical mapping and veterinary medicine, and at Aldershot passed his examination for captain. Yet the most significant experience in 1904 came in ballooning. Colonel John Capper, in charge of the Field Balloon Factory at Farnborough, attached Sykes to the Balloon Section of the Royal Engineers.[23] Sykes weighed less than most men and had courage, which made him a highly recruitable volunteer for balloon tests, some of which involved harrowing experiences, but all of which triggered enthusiasm in him.[24] In going aloft, he had finally found a way to satisfy his adventurous spirit.

In his diary of the balloon course, Sykes revealed a great deal about his interests and personality at the time. It is full of detailed drawings of the mechanics and principles of ballooning, keying on the technical details and contemplating how to make the systems of production more efficient (see Appendix 1).[25] At the same time, it is militarily oriented, as Sykes continually envisioned ballooning in terms of tactical capabilities and vulnerabilities. He admired the 'by-numbers' process the *Manual of Military Ballooning* established for launching and controlling balloons. Sykes experimented with signalling, reconnaissance, photography, stability and mapping. He helped to launch balloons in foul weather and at night. One experiment must have been particularly humorous, as it involved testing the maximum height at which the human voice could still be heard from the ground.[26]

Sykes' eagerness to go up surpassed all other considerations – perhaps even those for his own safety – and, at times, he became frustrated. As was to be expected in England, rain, wind, and fog constantly hampered the sorties. On occasion, when a good day came along, he could not understand why the section would shut down simply to observe a Sunday or a Bank Holiday. To improve ballooning capabilities, Sykes studied wind patterns to try to predict balloon performance aloft.

Despite his preoccupation with the fact that he was taking a military course, Sykes did appreciate the opportunity to make unscheduled flights and said that those sorties were the most enjoyable, even though they were also the most dangerous. On one occasion, after launching from Beacon Hill and changing direction and altitude several times owing to extreme temperature variations, Sykes and his companion were forced to make a hard landing. They had flown 30 miles, but because their grapnel would not catch, the trip was not complete. They bumped and tumbled for some time and distance until the balloon had dumped much of its gas.[27]

Sykes somehow survived his leave in England during the summer of 1904, and after receiving his ballooning certificate he returned to the Hussars in India as a more experienced and better-trained officer. He was posted to Muttra and there first met Sir Douglas Haig, the Inspector-General of Cavalry. Unlike Lord Roberts, Haig left no appreciable impression on Sykes, who stated that Haig did not utter a word of praise or correction, but simply 'galloped off in a cloud of dust to another victim'.[28]

A few months later Sykes was transferred from Muttra to the Frontier Section of the Intelligence Department, stationed with the Military Headquarters at Simla. There he met another high-ranking officer – Lord Kitchener, the Commander-in-Chief, who was having difficulty working under the Viceroy Lord Curzon. Although such upper-level political problems had little to do with a low-ranking intelligence officer, Sykes would remember this situation many years later when he assumed the position of Governor of Bombay. According to Sykes, Kitchener was a complete autocrat and hard worker, but not unapproachable.[29] More significantly, however, Sykes deplored the fact that Kitchener's Chief of Staff, Beauchamp Duff, was not very practical. Practicality, efficiency and effectiveness were becoming the hallmarks of Sykes' thinking.

Simla provided him with many opportunities to expand his knowledge of India and continue his quest for self-improvement and adventure. He learned more Hindustani, demonstrating proficiency in several examinations; participated in many of the local sporting traditions; and joined several social clubs.[30] He again exercised his penchant for hardening himself, and on one occasion won 1,000 rupees in a wager that he could not walk the 60 miles from Kalka to Simla in 24 hours. Sykes arrived seven hours early. His paramount military accomplishment was to write the handbook on India produced by the Intelligence Branch.[31] This extensive work was read by incoming officers to familiarize themselves with India.

Because Sykes had written such an impressive work that far exceeded the normal staff products, he was identified as a potential candidate for the Staff College. He therefore transferred to Quetta to work under Sir Horace Smith-Dorrien, the Chief of Staff under the Western Command GOC, General Sir Archibald Hunter. Sykes' introduction to the staff was inauspicious: he had broken his cheekbone when kicked by his horse, hence his face had to be bandaged, and he was housed in Smith-Dorrien's quarters while the rest of the staff were on maneuvers. This notwithstanding, he recovered quickly and thoroughly impressed his commander.[32]

The preparatory staff education Sykes received at Quetta was certainly as beneficial as that he would receive later at the Staff College. Sykes had tutors and essay assignments that challenged his thinking and literary abilities; in terms of military strategy and operations, he studied supply, training and morale; and on the tactical level he analyzed terrain and always included the detailed maps he drew to illustrate his concepts and ideas.[33] Since Sykes had already completed an exhaustive study of India, his tasks at Quetta were manageable. He received high marks for analysis, but in terms of his ability to put together a staff package he was perhaps a little verbose and came across as too 'intellectual' (with the military's negative connotations of that term).[34] Having excelled in his preparatory training, he was eager to improve himself once again. In April 1907 Sykes obtained leave to return to England for the Staff College examination.

He failed it. Although this was not an unusual outcome for aspiring staff officers on their first attempt – Haig and Trenchard also failed – to Sykes it was another hint that even though he had great abilities he was an outsider. When he did eventually pass the next year, it was for a new staff college just opened in India rather than the traditional one at Camberley. Twenty years earlier India had attracted the best and the brightest in uniform, but by 1907 its luster was fading as Germany began to loom on the horizon as a growing economic and military threat.

When the War Office ordered Sykes to Germany to observe the military maneuvers in 1907, he recovered his good spirits. Sykes was attached to the German XVIII Army Corps while the manuevers took place in Ober-Hessen and Hessen-Nassau between 6 and 18 September 1907.[35] Proudly wearing a German medal he had earned earlier in India, Sykes reported to the commander of the German 'blue force'.[36] He was received warmly and introduced to the entire staff but, as the only foreign officer present, he felt slightly intimidated by the situation. The Germans found Sykes' Indian Khaki uniform humorous; he found their drunken festivities 'particularly trying'. Throughout the military exercises, Sykes increasingly sensed the

German animosity toward England and observed the maneuvers as if scouting the enemy.

In typical fashion, Sykes took his job seriously. His focus was broad and his assessment exhaustive, as he looked at everything from latrines, to tactics, to pay. The Germans demonstrated their traditional particularism, which Sykes condemned as inefficient. Yet he suspected that it would evaporate in time of war. Overall, he criticized most of the maneuvers, implying that the British system was superior.[37] Sykes noted the German propensity to over-control events, to fabricate unrealistic scenarios, and to allow too many orderlies and civilians to interrupt the actual conduct of operations. German cavalry tactics were sloppy, fire discipline was poor, and communication techniques were unsophisticated in terms of the newest signals technology.[38]

Sykes also noted the German emphasis on offensive doctrine. Although he had not yet been through the Staff College, Sykes was already familiar with the concepts and supposed universal principles of war that dominated military theory at the time, such as offense, offensive–defensive, initiative, counterattack, and concentration. He agreed with the Germans' approach that the offensive was the key to victory and appreciated their opinion that it was easier to learn prudence than dash on the battlefield. The Germans liked to quote the German military revisionist Scharnhorst: 'Victory is won by teaching soldiers how to die, not how to avoid dying.' Sykes was a prudent man, but he was writing a report for the War Office and still trying to get into the Staff College. Therefore, whether he sincerely believed it or not, he concurred with the German approach to (offensive) doctrine and the emphasis on teaching and training.[39]

Sykes passed the Staff College entrance examination on his second attempt and in February 1908 joined the staff at Quetta under Major-General Sir Thomas Capper. For the next two years Sykes perfected his staff abilities while becoming officially indoctrinated into the accepted contemporary military theory of the European powers during the pre-war years. Sykes found that the Staff College curriculum clearly focused on Clausewitz. As part of their study of strategy in preparation for their essays, Sykes and his fellow students were supplied with a copy of the Staff College's 'Notes on War', a collection of excerpts from the writings of Clausewitz and other military theorists. Sykes' essay, a detailed analysis of ten previous wars, with an emphasis on Clausewitz and Napoleon I, was a typical submission.[40]

Unlike some of his fellow students, Sykes had expertly reflected the commandant's theoretical emphasis at the staff college. In a lecture to Sykes' class, Capper criticized his pupils' preoccupation with details and their lack of understanding of the basic principles of war –

primarily the importance of moral over physical force.[41] Capper's ideas all related to what Clausewitz had written, but some involved questionable interpretation:

> After all is said and done, the art of war consists almost entirely in the application of one principle. That principle never changes. It is the principle that determination to conquer or die must pervade all ranks . . . Let, then your guiding light in Strategy be – the concentration of all the efforts you can possibly command on the decisive point, having first carefully distinguished what that point is; the preservation of the idea that will lead you to do this through all the varying fortunes of war by a bold initiative preserved under all conditions, and by an uncompromising offensive.[42]

Capper continued by arguing that the enemy would impose his will upon the army that failed to keep the offensive, and then noted that a cautious spirit was 'most un-English'. He quoted Clausewitz: 'Even foolhardiness, that is boldness without an object, is not to be despised.'[43]

Analyzing the battle at Mukden in 1905, Capper credited the Japanese victory to their being better men because their hearts were in the right place – they had obtained the necessary 'organized abnegation of self'.[44] He never mentioned the fact that such blind obedience to this moral foundation led to heavy casualties in 1905 as men tried to charge machine-guns. Thus, the highly sought Staff College into which Sykes had finally gained entrance demanded acceptance of several supposed fundamental truths that would create severe problems in 1914.

Sykes was persuaded of the need to become one of the insiders, and at the Staff College he demonstrated his excellent student abilities by embracing Staff College teachings.[45] Capper had stated that England was used to small wars and that in the event of a large one it would have to enter battle with every atom available. Sykes remembered this in August 1914 when he took all available air resources to France. In addition, the analysis of Sykes' essays indicates that in 1908 he had an excellent knowledge of military history, a veritable mastery of approved strategic and tactical concepts, and a deep appreciation of technology in warfare.[46] His essays, like most of his writings, were illustrated with many detailed drawings, which not only demonstrated his freehand talent, but indicated his preference for visual conceptualization.[47] Finally, the Staff College left Sykes more a strategic and operational thinker than a tactician. His visual focus was on campaigns and wars rather than battles, and he maintained this theoretical orientation in the First World War, where he fought against short-sighted conventional habits in the use of air power and constantly tried to implement new technologies into war-winning strategies.

Sykes' Staff College experience involved more than just the class-room. While at Quetta he purchased his first automobile, one of the first in India. Since no one in the town knew anything about repairs, Sykes had to take a course in motor engineering while on leave.[48] Such a course certainly paid off handsomely later, as aircraft were fitted with whatever automobile engines were available, and pilots had to know a great deal about their engines in order to keep them running. Although increasingly a technologist, Sykes was a cavalry man who maintained his admiration and deep affection for horses, a trait for which he was well known at the college. In and out of the classroom, Sykes impressed instructors and comrades with his abilities and with his dedication. He was willing to spread his talents and help others, and he made several life-long acquaintances. One friend wrote: 'We all loved Sykie and admired his sterling character. His wonderful power of work and his courage.'[49] After completing the Staff College, Sykes left for South Africa where he commanded a machine-gun training camp at Bloemfontein. This was a significant assignment, as he would later call upon his experience with machine-guns to help in organizing a corps for the War Office in 1916. More important in terms of his mili-tary career and future, however, was the time he spent on leave in England, when he persuaded Captain H. Wood to arrange a ride for him in a Farman boxkite (biplane) at Brooklands. Following this seminal incident, Sykes returned to South Africa where he continued to receive letters from friends in India who missed him and urged his quick return.[50]

He did return to India, but not until many years and a world war had passed. Sykes' adventure in ballooning and his recent flight in a heavier-than-air machine had sparked in him an enthusiasm which would not die. Upon arriving back in England to work in the War Office, Sykes was preoccupied with thoughts of flying. Aware that flying in the early 1900s was one of the most dangerous exploits man had invented, he cast aside fears and disregarded warnings from suspicious soldiers that the pursuit of such a novelty was equally dangerous to one's professional career. Flying required a spirit of adventure, courage, physical stamina and the conviction to cast a larger net than it might be possible to retrieve. It suited Sykes perfectly.

NOTES

1. Croydon Census Return, Sykes Private Papers.
2. Sykes had no ambition to follow his father's footsteps, but his older brother Henry did become an engineer, as did Sykes' cousin Stanley (son of Godfrey). Stanley Sykes moved to the United States in 1882 and designed the light-measuring instrument that helped astronomers discover the planet Pluto.
3. F. H. G. Percy (Whitgift archivist) to Bonar Sykes, 24 January 1991, Sykes Private Papers.
4. The fact that Sykes never mentioned Whitgift to anyone throughout his life might suggest that he lacked fond memories of the school.
5. Address by the Bishop of Salisbury at St John the Baptist Church, 3 November 1957, Sykes Private Papers.
6. Sykes, *From Many Angles*, 17.
7. Sykes to mother, 13 February 1895, Sykes Private Papers.
8. Ibid. Sykes' letter contains detailed illustrations of his lodge and various people. Sykes calculated that he had danced two-thirds of the time, between 2130 and 0300 hours.
9. Sykes to mother, 9 March 1896, Sykes Private Papers.
10. Ibid.
11. Sykes, *From Many Angles*, 19.
12. Ibid., 20.
13. Ibid., 22. Sykes was impressed by allied teamwork, and he remembered it during the next war when he pushed for an inter-Allied bombing force.
14. Ibid., 151. Lord Roberts helped to promote British air power and the formation of the RFC and boosted Sykes' morale in 1914 when he visited him at RFC HQ in France.
15. Sykes to mother, 9 January 1901, Sykes Private Papers; and Mary to Mrs Carr (Hilda Mary), 15 April 1901, Sykes Private Papers.
16. P. R. C. Groves, 'This Air Business', 36, box 3, Groves Papers, Liddell Hart Centre for Military Archives, King's College, University of London. Also Capper Papers, II/4/1a, Liddell Hart Centre.
17. Sykes Papers, MFC 77/13, RAFM. Sykes' commission was dated 2 October 1901. Today there are a few of Sykes' items on display at the 15th King's Royal Hussars Regimental Museum at Newcastle.
18. Interview with Bonar Sykes, 17 July 1994; and James, 26.
19. John Goodman (comrade of Sykes in 15th Hussars) to Lady Sykes, 3 October 1954, Sykes Private Papers.
20. Ibid.
21. Sykes, *From Many Angles*, 40. Two years later at Simla this same man's dog ate a portion of Sykes' manuscript on India.
22. Ibid., 41–2. Sykes escorted the Grand Duke of Hesse at the Proclamation Durbar in 1903, celebrating the accession of Edward VII.
23. 'Diary and Notebook of Work with Balloon Section', Sykes Papers, MFC 77/13/2. The balloon course at Aldershot lasted from 22 July until 1 September 1904. See also Raleigh and Jones, 1:200.
24. Ibid.
25. Ibid., 23 July 1904. On 25 July he mentioned the value of reconnaissance: from an altitude of 1,300 ft he saw Salisbury 12 miles away.
26. Ibid., 3 August 1904. Sykes did not mention who were the best screechers, but it was unfortunate 'Boom' Trenchard was not present to demonstrate his natural calling.

27. Ibid., 10 August 1904.
28. Sykes, *From Many Angles*, 51.
29. Ibid., 55.
30. Membership certificates, Sykes Papers, MFC 77/13/3. From 1904 to 1906 Sykes was a member of three masonic lodges.
31. Frederick H. Sykes, *Military Handbook of General Information on India* (Simla: Intelligence Branch, 1908). See British Library, India and Oriental Office, L/Mil/17/12/2. This work, which was later revised by two attachés in the Intelligence Branch, was an extensive look at the history, physical geography and political administration of India.
32. Sykes Papers, MFC 77/13/4. Smith-Dorrien apologized for having kept Sykes' essay so long; however, he found it most interesting and added: 'I hope the day may yet come when I may be fortunate enough to have you on my staff.'
33. Sykes Papers, MFC 77/13/4, p. 15.
34. Ibid., p. 14. Obviously the most gifted intellectuals are concise. Sykes' knowledge of India was extensive, and his essay was, nevertheless, in a league of its own compared with those of other students.
35. 'Report on Foreign Manoeuvres', Sykes Papers, AC 73/35.
36. Sykes, *From Many Angles*, 42. In 1903 at the Proclamation Durbar in Delhi, the Grand Duke of Hesse had presented Sykes with the Cross of the Order of St Philip.
37. 'Report of German XVIII Army Corps', Sykes Papers, MFC 77/13/5.
38. Ibid., 5.
39. Ibid., 7. Also Sykes, *From Many Angles*, 68. 'The German soldier was an automaton.'
40. 'Outlines of Strategy', Sykes Papers, MFC 77/13/5.
41. Staff College notes, Capper Papers, II/4/1b, Liddell Hart Centre. Responding to claims that the moral–physical relationship ranged from 3 to 1, to 10 to 1 (Trenchard later claimed 20 to 1), Capper emphasized that it was not just a 'claptrap expression!' War was an art, not a science.
42. Capper lecture at Quetta, Capper Papers, II/4/1a and II/4/1b.
43. Ibid. Also Peter Paret, 'Clausewitz', in Paret (ed.), *Makers of Modern Strategy* (Princeton, NJ: Princeton University Press, 1986), 201. Much of Clausewitz's ingenious analysis of warfare did apply to the British pre-war military situation and, in particular, would apply to the future air war. Properly applied, his paradigm of a trinity in war, and matching purpose, objective and means, was a valuable insight into the link between politics and war. Yet, misinterpreted as a prescription for blind enthusiasm for offensive initiative rather than a description of warfare, Clausewitz's ideas had a disastrous potential. Many historians have erred in making too much of Clausewitz's influence in the First World War, especially in regard to Germany. German losses in 1914 were terrible, but not as attributable to Clausewitz as some writers have implied.
44. Ibid.
45. Capper's official report on Sykes, Sykes Papers, MFC 77/13/5; and Capper to Sykes, 1 December 1909, Sykes Restricted Papers, 1:16. Capper praised Sykes for his 'highly' satisfactory work: 'He is very conscientious and is inclined to overwork himself.'
46. Staff College essays, Sykes Papers, MFC 77/13/5.
47. Ibid.
48. Sykes, *From Many Angles*, 72.
49. General Sir Harry H. S. Knox to Lady Sykes, 4 October, 1954, Sykes Private Papers.
50. Groves to Sykes, 31 January 1910, Sykes Papers, MFC 77/13/6.

2

Into Air Power: 1912–14

Sykes' early work in military flying was seminal in establishing British air power. He was one of Britain's most prophetic champions of air power and the fundamental leader of a revolution in warfare involving aircraft. Sykes' revolutionary movement began in 1911.

Once Sykes had gone aloft, he immediately embraced the military advantages of being airborne and envisioned an air service that would play a critical role in the next war. From 1912 until August 1914 Sykes was an organizer, an oracle and a mobilizer. He organized the air service as commander of the Military Wing of the Royal Flying Corps (RFC) and as its spokesman predicted the future of air power. Anticipating the need to mobilize for war, Sykes trained and equipped his force so that it would be prepared. After war broke out, he commanded the staff and, intermittently, the air force. Sykes was the main reason the RFC was able to enter the First World War in August 1914 and participate as a viable military force during the first months of the war.

Sykes' enthusiasm for flying had begun before Staff College, but his major launch into the air was while he was assigned as a staff officer in the War Office Directorate under General Sir Henry Wilson.[1] There Sykes made some valuable contacts, working with people such as Lieutenant-Colonel George Macdonogh, the future Chief of Intelligence of the British Expeditionary Force (BEF), and Colonel J. E. 'Archimedes' Edmonds, the future official historian for the War Office. Sykes occupied every spare moment studying aerodynamics and aerial navigation and, during the early morning hours, in learning to fly. After four weeks in several types of machine, he attempted to qualify, but failed when a near mid-air collision forced him to crash land.[2] As a result, by the end of 1910 Sykes was temporarily grounded.

Wilson had supported Sykes' flying ambitions, but he was more interested in his abilities and value as an intelligence officer. Since the growing threat of Germany was a pre-eminent concern, Wilson wanted Sykes to be more proficient in German and sent him to Hanover to refresh his linguistic abilities. Sykes improved his German enough to pass the interpreter's proficiency examination upon his return, but his focus in Germany was more on aviation than language. The Germans were ahead of the British, and that worried him.

Once back in England, however, Sykes again flew during his free time to regain proficiency and make a successful attempt at gaining his license. Although he loved the excitement of becoming airborne, he did not enjoy the early hours nor the damp, cold weather. In the air his greatest annoyances were the unpredictable ones: mechanical failures and the downdrafts then called 'gaps in space'. On 20 June 1911 he was ready, and this time he passed, flying a Bristol Biplane at Brooklands aerodrome.[3] His aviator's certificate was No. 95, making Sykes the sixth British officer to have earned one and the only qualified pilot on Wilson's staff.

Sykes was enamored with flying even though aviation offered poor career prospects. While most pilots saw the dangerous novelty in terms of a thrill, Sykes was preoccupied with thoughts of air power. Yet so far aviators had demonstrated very little 'power', and British aeronautics progressed slowly through 1911. When Army aircraft failed to arrive at the annual maneuvers because four of the five available aircraft crashed, they demonstrated their susceptibility to poor weather and mechanical breakdowns. Such questionable reliability had caused the Committee of Imperial Defence (CID) to decide that technological development should be left to private industry. Yet the War Office recognized the potential advantages of air power and instituted military aviation. The Army's air service was known, however, as an unprofessional and undisciplined group of radicals.[4] Sykes wanted respect for his flyers and fought this anti-aviation tide by instilling discipline and organizing the new air arm into a viable military element.

Although the 1911 Army maneuvers were disastrous, a private demonstration in May at Hendon airfield was not. With Cabinet Ministers, Members of Parliament and military officers in attendance, Sykes rode as an observer in a Henri Farman 'boxkite'. His task was to find and report the location of a small Army unit hidden a few miles away. After a harrowing flight in an ill-trimmed machine that constantly pitched up, Sykes successfully reported the location to the Director of Military Training.[5]

Despite its laborious and overdue birth compared with other European air services, British military aviation was not the *ad hoc* reaction to events that many historians have portrayed, and it was not just a product of war. In 1912 the War Office estimated that it would take four years to form and organize the RFC; yet Sykes and his fellow air advocates created air power in just two peacetime years.[6] As Divine stated,

> Though he found it more difficult to discover people who shared his
> views on the military importance of the aeroplane, Sykes was practically
> equipped for the task which he was given and he was, in addition, a
> trained staff officer accustomed to the procedures and, probably more
> important, to the delicate and ever changing climate of opinion in the
> War Office.[7]

Sykes did not achieve all his objectives. But many he did, and it
appears reasonable to conclude that the end result was intended and
not simply a product of chance.

General Wilson recognized Sykes' interest in military aviation and
sent him to Spain, Italy and France to practice flying and to observe
flying operations. Hence Sykes was in Italy at the same time Giulio
Douhet began to speak out on behalf of air power. Although Sykes did
not mention Douhet in his memoirs, he did credit his trip to Italy as an
important influence in his own convictions about air power: 'My
Italian experiences confirmed me in the opinion that the aeroplane was
going to play a decisive role in the coming struggle, but I could find
hardly anyone to share this view.'[8] Because Sykes spoke French he was
the natural choice to attend the aeroplane competitions in Rheims in
autumn 1911. He traveled to France with Captain J. D. B. Fulton,
Commander of No. 2 Company of the RFC's Air Battalion at Larkhill.
Since Sykes had already studied engine technology, he chose to report
on the details of motors and machines, while Fulton concentrated
on the trials themselves.[9] During October and November 1911 the
two men visited the Concours Militaire d'Aviation de Rheims and
numerous other aerodromes, and Sykes' report, 'Notes on Aviation in
France', helped to awaken the military and political elite to the fact
that British aviation and air power lagged behind much of those of
Europe. It also made Sykes one of Britain's most acknowledged
experts on flying, types of aircraft, training and flying organization.

Sykes noted that the French trials were 'considerably in advance
of anything yet attempted [in Britain]'.[10] He studied in detail the
different machines and their capabilities in flight, and he analyzed the
French flying organization and system of training.[11] He agreed with
France's recent organization into smaller units as well as their slower,
methodical training method – compared with the German haste that
appeared to have a higher 'wastage' rate. At the same time, he recognized that Britain could not simply copy French methods. In England
there was less land, different topography, different weather patterns
and fewer flyers.[12]

Sykes' analysis of French flying led directly to the organization of
British squadrons and aerodromes in the RFC.[13] His report to the War
Office advocated the building of facilities close to each other so that
flying training could include cross-country flights via hops from one

aerodrome to another. He also urged that airfields be near Army units so that the troops would get used to seeing and working with aircraft. After studying the French training system as well as their medical requirements and flying limitations for airmen, Sykes advocated training that had pilots and observers flying together regularly to become familiar with each others' habits and abilities.[14] In addition, he recommended the formation and the size of the squadron.[15] In all, the organizational process he recommended in 1911 was precisely the one the RFC implemented in 1914: 'Aeroplane sections will, as a rule, be under the direct orders of the General Officer Commanding, Army Corps, but when several Army Corps are operating together the sections will be massed under the General Commanding-in-Chief or distributed to Army Corps as required.'[16] Before the war, France was the recognized world leader in flying, and hence Sykes' report from France could be considered one of the most important pre-war organizational influences on British aviation.

1912

In 1912 Sykes took control as organizer of military aviation. He assumed command of the Military Wing of the RFC, and it was his organization that went to war two years later. Yet the RFC Sykes helped to direct was a product of committee confusion. War Secretary Lord Haldane's standing Sub-Committee, the CID, appointed a Technical Sub-Committee to study military aviation and the possibilities of a more extensive organization than the Royal Engineers' Air Battalion, which had grown out of the Balloon School.[17]

Colonel J. E. B. Seeley was Chairman of the Sub-Committee, which consisted of the following members: Brigadier-General G. K. Scott-Moncrieff, Brigadier-General David Henderson, Commander C. R. Samson, RN, Lieutenant R. Gregory, RN, and Mr Mervyn O'Gorman. Rear-Admiral Sir C. L. Ottley and Captain Maurice Hankey were appointed secretaries.[18] Henderson can be credited with the effort that led to the RFC.

Henderson recognized the potential of military aviation, but he was one of few who had any significant power and influence. He had written *The Art of Reconnaissance* in 1907 and was the Army's acknowledged expert on the subject.[19] Since early air power was limited to the reconnaissance role, and because Henderson was one of the oldest qualified pilots, he was the Army's logical choice for RFC Commander. He pleased the Army hierarchy because he was not a radical air power advocate; in particular, he refused to claim that aeroplanes made the cavalry obsolete, which was a decisive and emotional issue.[20] Seeley knew Henderson was the committee member who could work out the specific and necessary details of organization and gave Henderson that task.

Henderson sought help from experts, particularly ones who had been to France and knew flying organizations and the types of aircraft. Hence Henderson established another committee consisting of himself, Colonel Macdonogh, Major Duncan Sayre MacInnes (a Signals Staff Officer) and Sykes. As a result, Sykes ended up on an informal sub-committee of the Technical Sub-Committee of the Standing Sub-Committee. Even though this committee system has a confusing historical record, it was at the individual level (with Sykes) that the work was accomplished. Even the basically *sans*-Sykes official history has recorded that he was largely responsible for organizing the RFC.[21] He had already worked out the details in his report from France. Thus when Haldane pressed Seeley for a quick decision, plans to form an RFC were ready.[22]

After Sykes' and Henderson's ideas were approved up the chain of sub-committees, a White Paper announced the new air organization on 11 April 1912.[23] The RFC was established by Royal Warrant the following month. A Military Training Directorate replaced Henderson's informal committee and he assumed command as Director of Training.[24] The Directorate was to report to an Air Committee, which had replaced Seeley's Technical Sub-Committee. Owing to traditional War Office–Admiralty competition for resources, the CID realized that the fledgling air service would need an advisory body. Sykes sat on that ill-fated committee.[25]

The RFC consisted of a Military Wing, a Naval Wing, a Central Flying School (CFS), a Reserve and a Royal Aircraft Factory; Henderson asked Sykes to command the Military Wing. This aroused envy when Sykes was promoted immediately to major.[26] Trenchard complained 20 years later that Sykes had maneuvered to achieve the command which Trenchard believed should have gone to the commander of the Air Battalion's First Wing, Sir Alexander Bannerman.[27] There is no evidence that Sykes did this other than in Trenchard's recollection, and clearly Sykes' expertise and organizational abilities made him a top contender for the job.

Trenchard may have learned from Sykes how to build monuments out of piles of rubble. When Sykes assumed command of the Military Wing in 1912, he started without a brick. There were no manuals, no training texts, no regulations; he was the only expert. He had no precedent other than sister-service organizations and what he had seen in France, Germany and Italy. Now that he was the commander, Sykes was responsible for implementing the plan he had given to Henderson.

Sykes' vision had been to establish a corps of seven squadrons of 13 aircraft each, with two pilots for each aircraft and two in reserve. In addition, his plan called for an airship and kite squadron, as well as an aircraft park for supply and repair. He therefore needed 364 trained pilots, half of whom were to be officers, but in May 1912 he had a total of 11 flyers, still three more than were available in the Naval Wing, but far short of France's 263.[28] Sykes not only had to organize, he also needed to recruit.

All of this required a staff, and he established a cadre made up of an able adjutant, Lieutenant B. H. Barrington-Kennett, and four squadron commanders: Majors C. J. Burke and H. R. M. Brooke-Popham for aircraft, Major E. Maitland for airships and Major A. D. Carden to head the Aircraft Park.[29] With Sykes at the helm of the Military Wing, that core of flyers was the genesis of the RFC.

After the RFC had been in existence only ten days, King George V and Queen Mary came to Aldershot for a visit, and the impact of their interest in military aviation was felt all the way up to the Cabinet. Sykes remembered the royal couple's strong support during a time when established military institutions viewed air power with skepticism.[30] Sir Douglas Haig had taken over the command of Aldershot and, although he was more cordial to Sykes than he had been in India, he nevertheless complained about RFC infringement upon Army space.[31] Sykes understood that public image and military co-operation were vital to the effectiveness, if not the very survival, of the new air service, and he embraced public relations duties as part of the job. As a popular spokesman for air power, he presented numerous lectures to societies interested in flight and he constantly championed air power as a necessity for the British Empire in the expected continental conflict.[32] While Italy was using aircraft to fight in Tripoli, and France had employed 50 machines in the annual maneuvers the previous year, Britain was probably in last place among the major European powers in terms of air capability.

Because he was flying blind in many areas of organization, the work was largely done by trial and error. Sykes and his men had to develop transport systems and proper procedures for night and bad weather flying. They needed to experiment with fatigue and establish flying limits for men and machines. Organizationally, the squadrons were designed as homogeneous and self-supporting units, with autonomous flights to enhance flexibility and mobility. Close to the initial plan of 13 aircraft, squadrons were composed of three flights of four aircraft each.[33]

Sykes' primary goal was to build an effective force. Bad weather and mechanical failures hampered flying, and he did not want to add to his problems by creating organizational problems. He had learned at Quetta that *esprit de corps* was critical to victory, so this was particularly applicable to the RFC which had no traditions nor history. Therefore it was up to the commander to inculcate pride, confidence and discipline within the unit, and Sykes was determined to make his men and the rest of the British military system understand that the Military Wing was to be a serious and professional organization. On 5 July 1912, when two of his airmen were killed in a flying accident near Stonehenge, Sykes established one of many precedents – he ordered flying to continue as usual.[34] He also pushed for a new uniform that was both distinctive and practical for flying.[35] In addition, he obtained the King's sanction for pilot wings and approved the Corps motto that one of his officers had suggested: *Per ardua ad astra* (with effort to the stars). It was particularly fitting for their arduous task.

Sykes was a staunch disciplinarian who promoted a military atmosphere among the troops from the moment they volunteered to serve. His emphasis in recruiting was to select soldiers, not people looking for fun and adventure. New personnel were to look to the senior-ranking members as examples of discipline and professionalism. Sykes' training standards were strict; he demanded both consistency and continuity and paid close attention to details because he knew the smallest of them could lead to disaster in the air. His three key words were 'loyalty', 'efficiency', and 'keenness', and he urged people to remember them.[36] Sykes wanted 'efficiency in every branch', and would not allow show-flying, known as 'stunting', because it involved selfish pleasure and unnecessary risks. The only way to work on Sykes' team was through individual self-sacrifice. He condemned the use of alcohol and tobacco, and ordered all members of the Wing to wear revolvers and to practise with them for proficiency. Sykes knew that if his flyers were to survive the adversities of war, they needed more 'seasoning' during peacetime.[37]

The two important aerial tests of 1912 were the aeroplane competition from 1–25 August and the annual Army maneuvers the following month. Sykes was a key player in both as judge and participant. Military flying in 1912 was limited to reconnaissance, and Sykes and Henderson organized the trials and competitions with that role in mind.[38] Their goal was to find the aircraft–engine combination with the best downward visibility, stability and loitering ability. Sykes established demanding standards, and only three machines met all the requirements of the competition.[39]

The designer Geoffrey de Havilland of the Royal Aircraft Factory at Farnborough produced the top entry among 24 competitors in the aeroplane competition. Called the BE2 (Bleriot Experimental), it had to remain the unofficial winner, however, since it was Government-sponsored and O'Gorman was one of the judges.[40] Sykes and his fellow judges awarded S. F. Cody £5,000 for his biplane; second place went to a monoplane built by A. Deperdussin, which crashed and killed its occupants less than a month later.[41] Most likely Sykes' primary motive for the competition was to compare RFC products with those coming from private enterprise. If he had to go to war in the near future, he needed to know how best to equip the Military Wing.

In order to make the best possible decision, Sykes flew with many of the competitors, including de Havilland and Cody, and he joined Henderson in testing cockpit visibility in a shed that had a floor marked with squares. Sykes remained sensitive to the dangers of flying and refused to climb aboard any machine that had not met pre-trial specifications or appeared less than airworthy.[42] When the weather presented danger, Sykes and his men stayed on the ground and passed the time playing cricket. The morning of 12 August was beautiful, however, and Sykes and de Havilland broke the British altitude record by climbing to 9,500 feet.[43] This achievement made Sykes a public celebrity and enhanced his position as an advocate of air power.[44] The 1912 competition showed that the Factory produced the best product, but that British military air power was still quite technologically limited.

The 1912 Army maneuvers in August and September were more promising but led to hostility from the Army. Sykes was commandant of the RFC in the defending 'Red' camp under General James Grierson, while Haig led the attacking force.[45] Sykes recalled that Haig, who was convinced their aircraft would not replace the cavalry as the primary means of reconnaissance, instructed one of his majors to 'tell Sykes he is wasting his time; flying can never be of any use to the Army'. Later in 1914 Haig apparently mentioned in a speech that 'I hope none of you gentlemen is so foolish as to think that aeroplanes will be able to be usefully employed for reconnaissance purposes in war. There is only one way for a commander to get information by reconnaissance, and that is by use of cavalry.'[46] According to Sykes, even in 1926 Haig maintained animosity toward air power, claiming that it was auxiliary to the Army and that the horse would have as much use in the future as it ever had in the past.[47] Sykes may have overstated his recollection of Haig, but he correctly noted his bias in favor of the cavalry and that air power threatened not only the cavalry's role but the cavalry itself, since horses were vulnerable targets. Yet, in Haig's defense, it must be admitted that before the 1912 maneuvers and aeroplane competition the cavalry maneuvers had claimed the lives of several airmen and proved disastrous for aeroplanes.[48]

During the Army maneuvers, however, Grierson became an air power convert.[49] The cavalry under General Briggs failed to gather intelligence for Grierson, while Brooke-Popham's aircraft provided the necessary reconnaissance.[50] Grierson embraced the concept of air power: 'It is impossible to carry on warfare unless we have mastery of the air.'[51] Talking with reporters, Sykes was not satisfied with the simple reconnaissance success. He championed the true air power cause, claiming that the best plan was 'not to spend money on elaborate air-targets for the artillery, but to spend it on them.'[52] The maneuvers had convinced at least some within military circles that air power could provide help to the ground mission and therefore needed more support and mutual co-operation between the services. Unfortunately for the airmen, however, their support from Grierson did not last long. He died on the way to war in 1914.

A disturbing series of accidents during the last months of 1912 caught Sykes' attention and raised concern about monoplane technology. Amid speculation and rumor that monoplanes were inherently dangerous, the War Office ordered the RFC to stop flying them.[53] Sykes was appointed to the accident investigation committee, known as 'The Monoplane Committee', which finally determined that there was 'no reason to recommend prohibition of the use of monoplanes'.[54] The report, however, was not issued until 3 December 1912 and not released to the public until 8 February 1913. The War Office action and the consequent delay in testing monoplanes may have thwarted a technological development that could have competed against the Fokker *Eindecker* in late 1915. Yet there was a positive outcome for the RFC when Sykes recognized the need for a permanent inspecting staff to test machines periodically and to investigate accidents in order to prevent future ones.[55]

Sykes had many organizational successes as a Wing Commander, but the battle he entered in 1912 over airships was one he eventually lost in 1913. He had experienced parochial infighting at the outset of his command, but the Admiralty soon expressed it in terms of a proposal that airships should belong exclusively to the Navy.[56] Sykes disagreed. Airships were more expensive and vulnerable than aeroplanes, but they were producing valuable experiments in wireless technology and showed promise as a weapon of war.[57] He argued that the transfer would be a 'gross injustice' that would ruin Army morale and would set airship development back a decade by replacing his existing efficient unit with 'an utterly untrained and embryonic organization'.[58] He claimed that the Navy's only rationale for their proposal was that 'ship' was part of the name and that if the Navy took airships, then the Army should take all aeroplanes. His bottom line was that both the Navy and the Army should have them, and that the Navy should build their own. Nevertheless, the No. 1 Airship Squadron of the RFC, which had descended from the Balloon School, was handed over to the Navy in 1913.

1913

The organizational difficulties Sykes experienced in 1912 were minor compared with the bureaucratic morass that enveloped him in 1913. Against looming interservice friction and public reluctance to invest heavily in a novelty, Sykes risked creating enemies on all fronts to promote his vision of British air power. He realistically recognized the limits of military aviation – tactical and operational reconnaissance for the Army – but he also knew that flying would soon expand beyond such roles and that Britain would need to have competitive air power to survive the next war.

Sykes' ideas about aerial defense seem obvious today, but they ran contrary to British tradition in 1913. He had a dilemma: whether to promote development by publicizing British accomplishments or to keep them secret from potential enemies. In a series of articles and speeches advocating an aerial program that could compete with the rest of Europe economically and militarily, Sykes stepped across the line that Navy and Army traditionalists had drawn around air power to keep it in its place. On 11 February and again on 26 February 1913 he spoke to the Aeronautical Society of Great Britain at the Royal United Services Institute. 'I think that a little fighting in the air will have a far-reaching deterrent effect on the moral[e] of the aerial forces of the losing side.'[59] He urged that in the future war 'initial success will mean an enormous advantage' and that such success would go to the side 'imbued with greater staying powers, greater determination to fight'.[60] He knew that air power would play a key part and repeated Grierson's comments that war was impossible without command of the air. In order to obtain such a command, Britain needed courageous airmen with high morale and skill, as well as capable machines for them to fly. That required effective training, an efficient organization and support. Sykes' vision of air power in 1913 did not contain specific details about types of aerial combat, policy or doctrine; he was more concerned about support. His message was simple and clear – British complacency was deplorable.[61]

Sykes' conviction in 1913 about the need to enter war fully armed helps explain the controversial action he took in 1914 when he sent all resources to France, leaving Trenchard and Brancker empty-handed at home. Sykes preached:

> The attempt to obtain command of the air will take place during the strategical concentration and before land hostilities have commenced. It is improbable that superiority once gained will be much affected by fresh machines being sent to the front. The moral effect accruing from original physical success in the air will be too great. The side which loses

command of the air will labour under all the disadvantages of defensive action.[62]

His short-sighted approach was a product of Staff College teaching: what applied to the Army was necessary for the air service as well. Many of his concepts of the future of aerial warfare were far from naive, however, and remained consistent throughout the war: the morale effect of flyers being overhead, the separation of air into geographic areas, air supremacy, the scientific application of aerial technologies, the imperative for efficiency gained through interservice cohesion rather than competition, and the necessity for offensive aerial action. Sykes' vision of air power matured between 1913 and 1919 in that he witnessed aerial capabilities and limitations and was able to modify his ideas accordingly. Most of his concepts, however, moved from dream to reality in the war, which simply confirmed his prognostications.

Air power was a popular topic in 1913, and Sykes was not alone in pronouncing the threat of war and the need to develop British flying. The April issue of the *Aeronautical Journal*, for example, listed 44 new books on flying. Sykes also received helpful advice and support from other air enthusiasts. General Sir John French, Chairman of the Aeronautical Society and future GOC of the BEF, commented on Sykes' address to the Aeronautical Society on the necessity for command of the air. According to French, it was 'profoundly interesting' and the best one they had heard in the hall to date. Both Henderson and Captain Godfrey Paine agreed with most of Sykes' opinions as well.[63] In writing to Sykes, Thomas Capper concurred that air power would relieve the cavalry of some of its role, but he reminded him that aerial capabilities did not yet exist, whereas a capable cavalry did. Capper continued, 'at present, our General Staff here have put nothing much [of air] into concrete form.'[64] Capper's brother John, who was more intimately involved with air power, repeated Sykes' message about the future roles of aircraft and the necessity for Great Britain to pursue their development.[65]

Sykes recognized, however, the potential for a pyrrhic victory in promoting air power to an extreme. He recalled various Staff College immutables and maintained that aviation would never eliminate war nor change its fundamental principles. O'Gorman took a more radical approach, implying that air power would fundamentally revolutionize warfare, changing it from 'a war of blind man's buff in a fog into a war like chess in the sunshine'.[66] To O'Gorman, Sykes' opinion that war's fundamental principles would remain was familiar dogma.[67] Sykes had maintained that aircraft would help clear the fog of war by making hidden movements impossible and eliminate old situations where smaller forces could defeat larger ones. O'Gorman, however, proposed that aircraft would do much more than aid reconnaissance and through aerial transport would help to even the odds by contributing to the rapid movement of smaller forces. Ultimately, O'Gorman wanted Britain to seize the initiative in aircraft development.

While O'Gorman, who had a strong financial interest in increasing aircraft production, may have had ulterior motives behind his prophecy, Sykes was spurred primarily by one objective – to create an effective air force. That meant not overreacting nor jumping into poorly planned schemes. Only through a careful and systematic process could the science and technology of aeronautics be exploited properly:

> Aeronautics are destined to become an ever larger feature and more decisive element in peace and war. It is of the utmost importance that the science should be developed on logical and predetermined lines. It is insufficient to do what has so frequently been done in the past, that is merely to carve some niche in the military organization into which to fit inventions.[68]

Although many air advocates seemed to agree ideologically, the *realpolitik* of how to organize the air service soon had many at odds with each other. Sykes' position and expertise gave his statements political clout, and he was elected an Associate Fellow of the Aeronautical Society at a time when others had barely learned to fly. With such authority, Sykes may have been over zealous in pursuing the type of air organization he desired. He ended up fighting both people and institutions, including Henderson, Trenchard, Paine, Brancker, the CFS, the Royal Aircraft Factory and the Navy.

Sykes' difficulties began when Henderson chose a reorganizational scheme that gave half of Sykes' duties to the CFS. As the Director General of Military Aeronautics of the new Directorate, Henderson determined that a decentralization of the flying organization was necessary because Sykes had been given too much authority and responsibility under the previous system. Now that there were more officers available, Henderson wanted a change:

> By degrees the Officer Commanding the Military Wing must be relieved of all duties except those which he will perform in war, and those which it is necessary that he should carry out in order to prepare and train the squadrons of the Royal Flying Corps (Military Wing) for war; the multifarious duties in connection with experiments, recruiting, recruit training, supply and repair of material (beyond repairs such as could be carried out in the field), records, etc., etc., must be placed under responsible officers dealing direct with the Directorate of Aeronautics at Army Headquarters, as is done in the case of other arms.[69]

The plan was eventually published in November.

Specifically, Henderson wanted to divide the RFC into two branches; a Combat Branch, to be headed by Sykes, and an Administrative Branch, which would include the Aircraft Depot, the Flying Depot, the CFS, Inspection Branch, Records Branch, Experimental Branch and the Royal Aircraft Factory. Sykes was to have only one duty – the 'command and training of the flying squadrons'.[70]

Henderson's concepts were far more realistic than Sykes'. Once the RFC had gained critical mass, Sykes could not have accomplished all his tasks, regardless of his unique abilities. Henderson knew that in time of war Sykes would be consumed by the business of directing aeroplanes in support of the Army. Sykes, however, perceived some salient organizational problems with Henderson's plan, and he was sufficiently upset by Henderson to respond immediately, before he had a chance to think and report more fully.[71]

Sykes was convinced that Henderson's proposal would undermine the effectiveness of military flying by divorcing peacetime operations from those of combat. He believed it would lead to scientific stagnation and ruin morale. From a maintenance standpoint, it would be disastrous: an 'offshoot from the workshop section of an Aircraft Depot rigidly divorced from the Military Wing in peace' simply could not repair aircraft with the same standards as people working directly with flyers. According to Sykes, it was the scientific and technical nature of flying that made it unique and necessitated a different type of organization from that required by the other services.

Henderson's plan gave much of the experimentation and quality control directly to the Royal Aircraft Factory, to which Sykes objected strongly. He liked the Factory's BE2 aircraft, but he accused O'Gorman's system of dealing in military matters that were the responsibility of soldiers. He also attacked the Factory's processes as inefficient due to lack of staff, stating that they caused acute congestion: 'mistakes, bad workmanship passed, slowness in building airships and aeroplanes, [and] slowness in execution of repairs'.[72] Sykes suggested a total reorganization of the Factory and developed a detailed plan that he believed would promote efficiency, help meet demand and keep the Factory working on tasks appropriate to its civilian status. He desired a production system that would cater to military needs, rather than a military system that was obliged to conform its operations and tactics with production capabilities.

Sykes suspected that Henderson's plan had been influenced by the Navy.[73] The Admiralty had already taken his airship squadron, and now the main beneficiary of the newest proposal was the CFS, which was headed by Godfrey Paine, a Navy captain. Sykes had stood against the Navy previously, and one of his main arguments was that its contribution toward aviation development had been minimal compared with the Army's.[74] 'What service aeronautical progress has been made in this country has been done by the Army which has made greater efforts, greater sacrifices, has shewn greater perseverance and achieved greater success.'[75] Sykes desired autonomous flying units responsible for specific geographical areas; hence the only way to organize functionally was along geographical lines, so that Navy flying would be over water and Army flying over land.

Sykes' antagonism toward naval flying was not paranoid and went deeper than the traditional anti-Navy attitude of his Army background. The Navy's entire approach to flying ran contrary to Sykes' vision and jeopardized his work in the Military Wing. The Navy stressed individualism. Sykes wanted cohesion.[76] To him, naval flyers were disorganized and inefficient.[77] They lacked discipline.[78] Hence they wasted valuable resources, which the Military Wing could use.

Up to September 1914 the Navy and the Army fought for the role that neither could perform – aerial home defense. In some ways the rivalry was a continuation of an old argument between 'blue water' theorists in the Admiralty, who wanted a large navy to defend the country and 'bolt from the blue' Army strategists, who wanted a coastal Army to defend the island in case an enemy slipped past the Navy. As First Lord of the Admiralty in 1913, Churchill placed home defense as a top priority and publicly guaranteed the Navy's performance against aerial attack.[79] The War Office was more realistic, however, and admitted its inability to make such claims.[80] A committee formed by Asquith reported in April 1914 that naval flying would be best suited for home defense, and one month after war broke out the War Office released home defense to the Navy, which pleased Sykes. He had fought for airships, not home defense. He wanted to protect the homeland by fighting the enemy in Europe, not over England.[81] At the outbreak of war when the RFC sent No. 4 Squadron to Eastchurch to reinforce the RNAS, Sykes believed it was a waste of resources.[82]

To a large extent the traditional interservice rivalry involved resources, and Sykes naturally tried to protect his own against a Naval Wing that was better than the Army at procuring supplies and equipment.[83] He disliked working with the Navy and wanted the competition for resources and the entire organizational problem to be handled at the highest levels. Sykes was plagued with administrative confusion over naval and military roles and argued for definitive guidelines.[84] He reminded Henderson that the CID had established the RFC on the understanding that there be two separate wings – one military and one naval. The Navy simply could not support Army needs effectively because it did not understand how to conduct land warfare. In the same way, the Navy was to provide its own air support. In Sykes' opinion, one service was cramping the development of the other.[85]

Meanwhile, naval influence dominated the Air Committee and little had been done to alleviate administrative problems and interservice competition.[86] From Sykes' point of view, the Military Wing was being short-changed, and he suggested the transfer of personnel and equipment between the services until an equitable arrangement could be achieved. Henderson agreed that there was a problem, but disagreed with the solution. He wanted time to let the situation resolve itself. Sykes was in a hurry.[87]

Still upset with the CFS, he wrote to Henderson: 'the character of the CFS remains amphibious [naval] . . . I think it is quite unsound.'[88] He was convinced that it was usurping his power by draining his resources, and he knew that Paine was trying to take over additional responsibilities within the RFC. The following statement from Paine to Henderson substantiates Sykes' opinion: 'In conclusion I would submit that unless the CFS is to be responsible for more than mere training of pilots, it seems that its existence is hardly worth the cost.'[89] Sykes had agreed to the initial plan that the CFS be given top priority with the idea that it would supply the Military Wing. As a result, many resources were siphoned from the flying squadrons to supply the CFS. By the end of 1913, however, Sykes felt the effects of such depletion: 'The time has now come for the School to take up its proper role of assistance to the Wing instead of the Wing giving the best of itself for the School.'[90] He still linked the CFS to the Navy, saw such resources going to the Navy via the CFS, and maintained that practical difficulties between the divergent services rendered 'common training unsuitable'.[91] Therefore Sykes' solution to the problem of the CFS was the one that was implemented within a year – Navy flying training split off with its own school at Eastchurch.[92]

Sykes may have been more responsible than any other man for the Navy's decision to organize independently from the RFC. Since 1912 he had argued for separate flying services, and he repeatedly reminded Henderson that his soldiers simply did not like working with sailors – that it ruined their morale. For that reason alone, he was convinced that the CFS could not teach flying to both the Navy and the Army. In the end, the RNAS did not break away from the RFC; it was compelled to leave.[93] Sykes approved of the departure, and it is ironic that he would be sent to command the RNAS at Gallipoli within a year.

Trenchard had not expressed such anti-Navy biases and, as a member of the first graduating class of CFS pilots, he had remained at the school as an instructor and number-two man behind Paine. There they apparently talked about Sykes, for Trenchard recalled Paine's opinion of Sykes as 'an "intriguer" with too fine a conceit of himself . . . unpopular with his subordinates at Netheravon, most of whom thought him "a cold fish".'[94] The accuracy of Trenchard's recollections aside, Sykes probably had few friends within the Navy or the CFS.

One of Sykes' overriding administrative concepts was that the peacetime air organization should match the one that would go to war. This meant linking maintenance, training and experimentation to the combat wing to support the needs of soldiers flying the aircraft. In this regard, Sykes' fears about the CFS were legitimate. Paine, in a letter to Henderson, stated his belief that experimentation should simply vanish if they went to war.[95] Sykes was trying to protect his authority, but much of his rationale was sound that experiment and technological development would be necessary during the war and would need to be linked to the flyers who knew what kinds of development were needed.

He presented extensive organizational plans with detailed charts and at the same time urged general restraint in making changes. He wrote to Henderson in December: 'No organization, military or civil, can hope to make much progress towards efficiency so long as it is subjected to frequent changes of organization and policy.'[96] Sykes was most concerned with mobilization. He believed the flying service that mobilized first would gain command of the air, and he feared that all the changes that separated peacetime and wartime organizations would jeopardize his ability to mobilize. Sykes used some of the suggestions of his adjutant Barrington-Kennett, but generally fought alone during the organizational struggles. It was his style which set in motion the personal alienation that would haunt him for the rest of his career and life.

At the same time as Sykes was entering the reorganizational debate, he was planning the RFC's participation in the annual military maneuvers. Intent on demonstrating the quantum leap his wing had made since the 1912 exercises, Sykes published detailed operations orders and training manuals a month and a half in advance.[97] He maintained tight control of the air forces and ordered his troops to use common sense in finding the best solutions to problems. They were to keep him well informed and were not to question his process or arrangements. All actions affecting other units were to go through Sykes first.

He attempted to cover all possible contingencies. He worked out an identification system of flight patterns, lights and paint schemes on aircraft so the 'brown force' under Field Marshal Sir John French and the 'white force' under Major-General Charles Monro could determine which aircraft were theirs.[98] Sykes anticipated the problems of friendly fire against the vulnerable aircraft, and this precursor of a modern 'identification friend or foe' (IFF) system should have reduced the wastage from friendly fire during the war. Sykes observed, supervised and flew several missions, including a record-setting preliminary demonstration flight with Captain Charles Longcroft.[99]

The military exercises were successful on paper due largely to Sykes' extensive preparation. Almost the only detail he had not settled was the supply of beer to the troops – low priority to Sykes but most likely not to them.[100] He understood the importance of the exercises to the future of his air service, and he ensured that the demonstration proved the value of aircraft for tactical and strategic reconnaissance as well as intercommunication. That effort may have been counter-productive. The fact that the forces moved no field bases during the exercise, for example, was poor preparation for the retreat from Mons in 1914. In addition, the RFC flew 'free' preliminary reconnaissance missions to obtain information on the enemy. This cheating during the exercise was unrealistic and may have provided false impressions and expectations. Few enemies would be so kind as to allow the other side safe overflights to obtain any initial reconnaissance information.

Although most of Sykes' struggles in 1913 were organizational, his final difficulty was technological. He and Major (later Air Marshal) Sir W. Brancker, a staff officer in the Air Section of the War Office, dis-agreed on what type of aircraft to build for the RFC. Sykes correctly based his arguments on exercises and competitions which had shown the BE2 to be the best reconnaissance machine.[101] The Henri Farman aircraft was too difficult to fly, the Maurice Farman was too slow, and Sykes wanted the standardization and consistency that the Factory could provide.[102]

Brancker, on the other hand, wanted individual competition to produce superior aircraft – fighting platforms as well as those for observation. The BE2 was too small to carry guns; therefore Brancker wanted the Farmans until a better machine could be developed. Both men were correct in their judgements – Sykes focused on reconnaissance and Brancker on fighting – but their debate lasted into 1914 and eventually ended in compromise. Nos. 2 and 4 Squadrons were equipped with the BE2, No. 3 Squadron had Blériots and Henri Farmans, and No. 5 Squadron received Henri Farmans, Avros, and BE8s.[103] Sykes had once again alienated a fellow airman by fighting hard for his vision of British air power.

1914

The funding shortages that inhibited Sykes' desires for organization and technological development in 1914 were his ball and chain for life. His grand vision was always too expensive for the realities of fiscal restraint. The reality of 1914, however, was the impending war, and

Sykes believed that money was less important than survival. His struggles to train and equip the air force were as difficult as anything he would face during war itself, and he recalled that the only change in the strain was an occasional period of further increased strain.[104]

The organizational debate continued. Sykes knew that he had some time until the Directorate could affect changes and implemented his own in the interim. To ensure that his supply people knew the unique air business before they experienced the demands of war, he pressed for the new Aeronautical Ordnance Depot to be manned by Army Ordnance personnel immediately.[105] Sykes created an Experimental Flight within each squadron as well as a Headquarters Experimental Section headed by Major Musgrave.[106] To foster squadron autonomy, he established sections to handle various duties: meteorology, maintenance, transport, supply and administration. When the Navy took the airships in May, Sykes had to reorganize No. 1 Squadron as an aeroplane squadron. That same month Henderson published his revised reorganization scheme.

Sykes' struggle had not been in vain. The new plan called for a Headquarters Military Wing to consist of a Headquarters Section, a Kite Section, a Records Office and a Depot. In peacetime, the HQ Military Wing would be attached to the Depot, but in time of war it would become the HQ RFC and accompany the BEF overseas, leaving the Depot and Records Office behind at Farnborough. Sykes wanted little organizational change when going from peace to war, and he wanted to be able to react immediately, arriving in Europe with all possible resources to throw against the enemy. The modified plan involved much less transitional change than the original one and half of the new emphasis dealt with the ability to mobilize quickly.[107] Owing to Sykes' insistence, Henderson had reduced his number of reserve squadrons from two to one.[108] Overall, the reorganization shifted men in time of war from administrative sections to the RFC Military Wing. Hence Sykes' depletion of Trenchard's and Brancker's resources in August was something he had planned, and clearly reflected Staff College influence.

Although Henderson's plan appeased most of Sykes' desires, one aspect was upsetting. Henderson had failed to keep his word and allow Sykes to command the RFC.[109] According to Sykes, Henderson had promised him that position if war broke out, and Henderson's plan in May 1914 provides strong support to Sykes' claim. Sykes was the commander of the HQ Military Wing and nowhere does the plan call for the DGMA to replace him in time of war. Just the opposite – it stipulates that the Military Wing Commander becomes the RFC commander in the field.[110] On the other hand, it is perfectly reasonable that once war broke out Henderson reconsidered the situation and concluded that Sykes was too junior to command the RFC. Regardless of Sykes' abilities or experience, the implications of junior rank at the top would have hurt the fledgling force's image and ability to function.

Another point of contention had to do with the delineation of duties. According to the revised reorganization, in time of war the Depot was to handle all administrative issues, including military pay and accounts. In peacetime, however, the Depot was under the HQ.[111] Hence when the RFC departed for France, Trenchard was saddled with numerous outstanding accounts, for which he held Sykes responsible. Sykes was busy fighting a war and dismissed the issue, which no doubt contributed to further friction between the two men.

Henderson's plan provided one of the greatest testimonies to Sykes' influence when it noted the responsibilites of the Military Wing HQ: 'command, training, and administration of the Corps. The duties of the Headquarters Section in war will be defined in RFC. Training Manual Part II, Chapter 1, Para. 6.'[112] Sykes had produced and personally written much of that manual during the winter of 1913–14.[113] Sykes saw a direct link between training and organization; a well-trained unit could be well organized and, consequently, effectively employed against an enemy. Training needed to be realistic and standardized and hence the manual was not just a training manual but an all-encompassing, regulations manual for the RFC. It was a typical Sykes product – massive in size, detailed and focused entirely on the goal of achieving organizational efficiency.

The size of the manual and the areas it covered are less important than its influence. It was the air power bible the RFC carried into battle. In addition to great technical detail on aspects of aircraft and engine assembly and repair, it included the RFC regulations on instrumentation, navigation, meteorology, transport and flight training. It outlined the RFC organization and established administrative guidelines. More significantly, it was the RFC's published statement on doctrine in which Sykes set down the strategic and tactical concepts the RFC was to follow in time of war. RFC flyers and commanders entered the conflict with established guidance, which documentary evidence shows they used.[114] In short, even before the war Sykes had basically written the book on British air power.[115]

Throughout the manual Sykes emphasized the ideas he had promoted the previous year: discipline, efficiency and effectiveness. He desired experimentation along the lines that RFC flyers wanted, and he demanded planning and proper preparation. Above all, he required professionalism. Sykes stated that RFC efficiency depended on rapid and clear communication and he required proper paperwork with precise reporting rather than deduction.[116] Since the primary air role was reconnaissance, the key to aerial effectiveness lay in establishing a system that processed information accurately and quickly, ensuring that it reached the people who needed it.[117] At the same time, Sykes wanted to keep tight control over air resources. The Army's need for reconnaissance information could be limitless, but the Army did not understand the unique dangers and limitations of flying. All aerial activities were to go up through the RFC commander (Sykes) and requests from the Army for air support were to be co-ordinated through him as well. To facilitate the whole process, the RFC HQ in the field was to be co-located with the Army's General Headquarters (GHQ).

Some scholars have questioned the official historians' claim that RFC reconnaissance saved the BEF during the first two months of the war. The argument to the contrary is that flyers incorrectly reconnoitered and that even their occasional correct information did not reach decision-makers or have any effect.[118] Sykes' pre-war developments, however, provide at least indirect support to the official history. He had established in detail a reconnaissance system designed to work in the fog of war, and before the war the RFC trained with Sykes' manual, which gave specific guidance regarding how to provide information to the Army during a retirement and how to move aerodromes during battle. At Mons the RFC simply undertook what Sykes had called 'protective reconnaissance'.[119]

While the manual attests to the impact Sykes had on early air activities in the war, it convicts him in retrospect for making some costly mistakes. In the modern sense of the term, a training manual would involve flight training; however, Sykes' book contained only five pages on the subject. At the time, flight training still remained an unpolished process left largely up to instructors and their individual techniques.[120] Sykes tried to obtain some type of training standardization, hoping that it would reduce the danger and death toll. Yet his manual did not emphasize an adequate training program, and British trainees had to endure a poor methodology during the first years of the war.

Sykes' oversight in not establishing an effective IFF system also contributed to British wastage. He had worked on aircraft identification during exercises, so it is surprising that he simply dismissed the subject in the manual by stating that identification was ineffective and only to be done by trained observers, as ships were identified in the Navy.[121]

In addition, Sykes fully embraced the costly 'cult of the offensive' and applied it to aviation. He wanted to throw all air assets against the enemy as soon as possible. Courageous flying would reign supreme:

> It must be borne in mind that the side whose aircraft show the greater determination to fight on every opportunity will rapidly gain a moral ascendency which will largely contribute to obtaining the command of the air.[122]

Historians have condemned Trenchard's offensive policy from 1915 to 1917, but he merely maintained the policy Sykes had established before the war. While Trenchard was a line instructor at the CFS, Sykes wrote that aircraft limitations would prevent much material damage to the enemy, but that the effect on morale would be 'very considerable'.[123]

Doctrinally, therefore, Sykes' offensive simply mirrored that of the BEF, which was appropriate since the RFC belonged to the BEF. His air policy was to fly aggressively – even in reconnaissance – to take advantage of aircraft speed and flexibility in providing intelligence to the army. In addition, the RFC was to deny such aerial intelligence gathering by the enemy.[124] In other words, the goal was to obtain mastery of the air. The two primary roles were reconnaissance (including artillery spotting and co-ordination) and ground protection, but specific tactics involved in those roles were not delineated in the manual. In air-to-air combat, however, the aim was to disable the enemy pilot rather than his aircraft. In all, Sykes was guilty of letting his enthusiasm for morale blind him to the realities of modern warfare.[125] He expected the RFC to join the Army in a great moral victory. He did not predict trench warfare. He did not prepare for the stalemate.[126]

On the positive side, Sykes' prior planning contributed immeasurably to the initial performance of the RFC in battle. As the historian Robin Higham wrote recently, 'The creation and employment of air power in the Great War was a matter of management – a form of command, control and communications.'[127] Without a doubt, Sykes was the RFC's leading manager. His manual contained codified technical details of artillery observation and established parameters of flight for several aircraft. It defined types of reconnaissance and the duties of aircraft, airships and kites, and listed job descriptions for various command positions. The key to effectiveness was in having good repair and supply, and the specifics of those duties were listed as well.

During the same winter that he wrote the manual, Sykes also compiled the 'RFC Standing Orders'. Not published until 1915, they were originally designed just for the Military Wing. Once the RNAS split from the RFC, however, the orders applied to the RFC in general. The Standing Orders comprised another set of regulations that duplicated those in the training manual, but the primary focus of the orders was discipline.[128] Sykes wanted discipline – discipline in the air – which many flyers lacked.[129] Therefore the regulations established rules of flight and approved procedures for the several phases of a mission, from pre-flight planning to post-flight critiques. Although as impressive in scope as the Training Manual, the Standing Orders did not have as large an impact on RFC operations because they were published long after the first few months of war when they had been most needed.

By summer 1914 the RFC was an established organization with published procedures, but the threat of war made Sykes anxious to test the system. Half of Henderson's reorganization had dealt with mobilization, but the plan was complex and confusing and Sykes doubted its potential success.[130] He decided to exercise RFC mobilization with a peacetime camp at Netheravon during June. Historians are unanimous in crediting Sykes with the initiative and direction of the 'Netheravon Concentration Camp', perhaps the single most important step in the RFC's preparation to fight in the First World War.[131]

Netheravon was both a system self-test and a public demonstration that the RFC was a legitimate part of the Army and ready to help in defending the Empire. Recent 'Zeppelinitis' panics and Parliamentary debates questioning the air service's ability and organization had damaged the RFC's reputation. Valuing morale as he did, Sykes was determined to rectify the situation. His public relations campaign was impressive, and by the end of June most literate Englishmen must have known about Netheravon and the RFC.[132] Since Sykes orchestrated the media coverage, it is not surprising that he personally received recognition.[133] He entertained visiting dignitaries and placated reporters with the impressive statistics and aerial photographs they eagerly published.[134] Sykes even allowed journalists to join some phases of the exercise.

His pleas for support had produced few results, so at Netheravon he turned his attention to an area where he could have an impact – his organization.[135] A superior organization with good flying skills, effective maintenance and motivated troops could overcome backwardness in machines. To boost morale he appeased the troops with inter-squadron athletic games and other competitions. He recognized the advantages of integral crews and encouraged the same people to fly with each other for familiarity. He also tried to link pilots with aircraft, so that they would feel a sense of ownership and confidence in specific machines. Sykes' efforts appear to have been successful, as reporters consistently noted the cheerful and positive attitude in the camp.[136]

Sykes exercised all RFC functions under realistic conditions. Anticipating ground fire, for example, reconnaissance missions were flown above 2,000 feet, and at night. The camp ran day and night for 30 days, testing photography, bombing, supply, maintenance, meteorology, wireless communication, day and night flying and transport. In the evenings personnel attended lectures where they reviewed daily performance and assessed their progress. Netheravon also successfully concentrated the RFC's resources and tested Henderson's mobilization plan, which underwent some revision once the camp was over.[137] Thus, when Britain went to war less than two months later, the RFC was relatively well prepared.

The threat from the east was not a mirage, and Sykes' two-year rush to build a military flying organization was not a wasted effort. He had been instrumental in establishing British air power and taking the first steps toward a military aerial revolution. Sykes was an empire builder – motivated by his vision of an aerial empire benefiting the British Empire. Fearing the impending war's threat to that empire, he had battled against individuals and bureaucracies to orchestrate many developments from recruitment and training schemes, to experimentation, to aerial procedures, policy and doctrine. Air power was to be used offensively, efficiently and scientifically to enhance ground operations. It was not to be a separate arm which could work alone to achieve victory, but was to enhance combined-arms action against the enemy by maintaining mastery of the air. Sykes, then, not only officially published RFC regulations and policy, but tested them under the RFC's practice mobilization before the fateful 'July days' of 1914. That the RFC was prepared for war in August is largely a testimony to Sykes' foresight and initiative.

NOTES

1. Sykes, *Aviation in Peace and War*, 20, 26. He stated that his Boer War experience had incited his initial interest in air power. In South Africa in 1904 he had seen the British Army demonstrate its scientific superiority over the enemy through the use of balloons. At the same time, the Boers had shown the value of mobility in war. Sykes put the two lessons together and recognized aerial technology as a means for the Empire to stay ahead in the world.
2. *Royal Aero Club Year Book, 1915–1916* (London: Royal Aero Club of the United Kingdom, 1916), 131. Also, Flight Lieutenant D. W. Clappen sound recording, Reel No. 1, IWM sound recordings. The final portion of the examination was to land within 50m of the evaluator after having cut the engine at altitude. Gliding without engine power, Sykes had no chance to recover after turning to avoid a mid-air collision. The decision of the Committee of the Royal Aero Club was final and without appeal, so when Sykes crashed in 1910, he had no choice but to wait until 1911 to reattempt the examination.
3. Aviator's Certificate, Sykes Papers, MFC 77/13/7.
4. Raleigh and Jones, 1:189.
5. Sykes, *Aviation in Peace and War*, 17–18.
6. Sykes, Henderson and MacInnes comprised the first technical sub-committee that created the RFC organization.
7. Divine, 37.

8. Sykes, *From Many Angles*, 80.
9. 'Notes on Aviation in France', 16 December 1911. Sykes Papers, MFC 77/13/8, RAFM.
10. 'Notes on Trials' (no date), Sykes Private Papers.
11. 'Notes on Organization and Training' (no date), Sykes Private Papers.
12. 'Notes on Aviation in France', 16 December 1911, 44, Sykes Papers, MFC 77/13/8.
13. Raleigh and Jones, 1:179; and 'Aviation in France', 45, Sykes Papers, MFC 77/13/8.
14. Ibid., 46.
15. Sykes, *Aviation in Peace and War*, 28. In 1912 Sykes deliberately chose the size of the squadron to be larger than French or German units, because he knew Britain did not have many officers available to assume command positions. The French *escadrille* was about one-third the size of the British RFC squadron, or the size of an RFC flight.
16. 'Notes on Organization and Training', Sykes Private Papers.
17. Public Record Office (PRO) WO 132/6936/42 gives the organization of the Balloon School and formation of the Air Corps.
18. Raleigh and Jones, 1:198–9. Seeley became Secretary of State for War and Chairman of the first Air Committee until an incident in Parliament over numbers of aircraft available led to his dismissal immediately before the war. Samson became the commander of the RNAS during the war, and Mr Mervyn O'Gorman was Superintendent of the Royal Aircraft Factory.
19. Brigadier-General Sir David Henderson, *The Art of Reconnaissance*, 3rd edn (London: John Murray, 1914). The first edition contained not a word about aerial reconnaissance and in the 1914 edition Henderson acknowledged that aircraft were an essential part of reconnaissance, but stated that their use was still limited.
20. Henderson, preface and 181.
21. Raleigh and Jones, 1:200; James, 38; and Sykes, *From Many Angles*, 94–5.
22. Raleigh and Jones, 1:202.
23. Gollin, 190. The White Paper was entitled 'Memorandum on Naval and Military Aviation'.
24. Within a year, the War Office replaced the Training Directorate with a Military Aeronautics Directorate so that Henderson, the Director General of Military Aeronautics (DGMA), could report directly to the Secretary of State for War. See Raleigh and Jones, 1:416.
25. Sykes, *From Many Angles*, 95.
26. Ibid.
27. Autobiographical notes, Trenchard Papers, MFC 76/1/61, RAFM.
28. Raleigh and Jones, 1:202–6. The general opinion was that officers made better flyers than NCOs, but the most important factor was that they were all of a 'superior race' (i.e. British).
29. Barrington-Kennett remained with Sykes until spring 1915 when doctors recommended that he leave staff work. He transferred back to the Army and was killed in May. See Baring, 90.
30. Sykes Restricted Papers, vol. I, p. 10, RAFM.
31. Sykes, *From Many Angles*, 99.
32. Lectures, Sykes Papers, MFC 77/13/17 and MFC 77/13/10. The *Quarterly Review* and *Army Review* published several of Sykes' lectures, as well as his translation of a French document on air power, 'Report of the Chamber Deputies Budget Commission upon the Aeronautical Section, French Budget 1912.'
33. Sykes, *From Many Angles*, 95.

34. Sykes Papers, MFC 77/13/12; and Raleigh and Jones, 1:234. Those killed were Captain Eustace B. Loraine and Staff Sergeant R. H. V. Wilson.
35. The double-breasted khaki uniform, which represented Lancers (cavalry) in the air, lasted until 1918 when Sykes brought in a new RAF uniform.
36. Speech given to Officers and Men following the Army Maneuvers of 1912, 23 September 1912, Sykes Papers, MFC 77/13/12.
37. Ibid.
38. 'RAF Staff College 2nd Course', RAFM, Accession No. C/5/1/1; and Raleigh, 1:213.
39. Sykes, *From Many Angles*, 101. Aircraft had to remain aloft for three hours, climb to 4,500 ft, and fly fully loaded at 80 kph.
40. Morrow, *The Great War in the Air*, 41.
41. 'Editorial Comment', *Flight*, 31 August 1912, 786.
42. 'Military Aeroplane Trials and some side Issues', press clipping *Flight*, 23 August 1912, 795, Sykes Papers, MFC 77/13/11.
43. *The Aeroplane*, 22 August 1912, cover article.
44. For months Sykes' fame was spread in *The Aero, The Aeroplane* and *Flight*.
45. Press clipping from *Flight*, 31 August 1912, 802, Sykes Papers, MFC 77/13/11.
46. Sykes, *From Many Angles*, 105.
47. Ibid.
48. 'RAF Staff College 2nd Course', RAFM, Accession No. C/5/1/1.
49. Norman Macmillan, *Sir Sefton Brancker* (London: Heinemann, 1935), 29.
50. Raleigh and Jones, 1:243.
51. 'Guns versus Aeroplane', *Flight*, 7 December 1912, editorial comment, 1, Sykes Papers, MFC 77/13/13.
52. Ibid.
53. Raleigh and Jones, 1:235–6.
54. Salmond Papers, B 2658, RAFM; and C. F. Snowden Gamble, *The Air Weapon* (London: Oxford University Press, 1931), 1:192.
55. Sykes, *From Many Angles*, 100.
56. Robin Higham, *The British Rigid Airship, 1908–1931: A Study in Weapons Policy* (Westport, CT: Greenwood Press), 160–73, mentioned no particular interservice rivalries, but that a CID sub-committee decided that large airships were inappropriate for the Army due to the lack of large transportable sheds.
57. Raleigh and Jones, 1:224. General Grierson had stated that airships had 'revolutionized the art of war'.
58. 'Memorandum on Proposal that Navy should take over Airships, 1912', p. 3, Sykes Papers, MFC 77/13/9.
59. Speech to Aero Society, February 1913, Sykes Papers, MFC 77/13/13.
60. Ibid.
61. Sykes Papers, MFC 77/13/13, MFC 77/13/14. Sykes' speech was published in *Army Review*, July 1913, and *Morning Post*, 12 February 1913.
62. *Aeronautical Journal*, July 1913, 136–7.
63. Ibid., 137–8.
64. Capper to Sykes, 20 March 1913, Sykes Papers, MFC 77/13/14.
65. 'Effect of Air Craft on War', Capper Papers, III/2/2b, Liddell Hart Centre.
66. *Aeronautical Journal*, July 1913, 137.
67. Ibid.
68. Sykes Memorandum, 8 September 1913, PRO, Air 1 757/204/4/100.
69. DGMA Letter 20 Royal Flying Corps/38. M.A.1., 10 November, 1913, Air 1 780/204/4/477.
70. 'Royal Flying Corps Organization Notes', Air 1 780/204/4/477.
71. Sykes to DGMA, 17 November 1913, Air 1 780/204/4/477.

72. Sykes Memorandum, 8 September 1913, Air 1 757/204/4/100.
73. Ibid.
74. Speech to Aeronautical Society, p. 138, Sykes Papers, MFC 77/13/14.
75. Sykes Memorandum, 8 September 1913, Air 1 757/204/4/100.
76. Sykes, *Aviation in Peace and War*, 34.
77. Ibid., 32; and Chamier, 6.
78. Captain F. D. H. Bremner, RNAS, sound recording, Reel No. 9, IWM sound recordings.
79. PRO, Adm 1/8549 and CAB 37/121/125; Gollin, *Impact of Air Power*, 294; and Boyle, 122.
80. Gollin, 201–3.
81. H. R. Allen, *The Legacy of Lord Trenchard* (London: Cassell, 1972), 12; and Gollin, 201.
82. Gollin, 296.
83. Higham, *Air Power*, 43.
84. Ibid.
85. Ibid.
86. First Annual Report of the Air Committee, 7 June 1913, CAB 38/24/21, PRO.
87. Henderson to Sykes, 16 October 1913, Air 1 757/204/4/100.
88. Sykes to DGMA, 16 December 1913, Air 1 780/204/4/477.
89. Paine to DGMA, 26 November 1913, Air 1 118/115/40/56. This section of the letter has been pasted over, evidently, so that it would not be read.
90. Sykes Memorandum, 8 September 1913, Air 1 757/204/4/100.
91. Ibid.
92. Conference on 8 January 1914, National Maritime Museum (NMM), ADL/2 /1/5. The Admiralty first considered a separate naval flying school at this conference.
93. Henderson to Sykes, 16 October 1913, Air 1 757/204/4/100. Henderson tried to placate Sykes' impatience by stating that the Navy had promised they would leave 'almost at once'.
94. Boyle, 109.
95. Paine to DGMA, 26 November 1913, Air 1 118/15/40/56.
96. Sykes to DGMA, 16 December 1913, Air 1 780/204/4/477.
97. 'Instructions for the Participation of Royal Flying Corps, Military Wing, in the Army Manoeuvres and the Divisional Operations Preceding them', 8 August 1913, Sykes Papers, MFC 77/13/15.
98. Ibid.
99. Raleigh and Jones, 1:256. To demonstrate range, Longcroft and Sykes flew from Farnborough to Montrose during a 7-hour 40-minute flight which involved one landing.
100. 'Instructions for Units of RFC (M./W.) taking part in Army Exercise 1913 with the White Force', 2, Sykes Papers, MFC 77/13/15.
101. Higham, *Military Intellectuals*, 129; Sykes, *From Many Angles*, 111; and Raleigh and Jones, 1:292–3.
102. Morrow, *German Air Power in World War I*, 188, maintained that Britain's aerial victory over Germany was due in part to standardization that helped them to mobilize.
103. Raleigh and Jones, 1:293.
104. Sykes, *Aviation in Peace and War*, 29.
105. 'Some Notes on Supply', Brancker Papers, 73/183/1, IWM.
106. Sykes, *Aviation in Peace and War*, 29; and Sykes, *From Many Angles*, 112.
107. DGMA to Sykes, May 1914 [no day listed, but must have been after 10 May], Air 1 118/115/40/56.

108. Sykes to DGMA, 9 May 1914, Air 1 118/115/40/56.
109. Sykes, *Aviation in Peace and War*, 27.
110. DGMA to Sykes, May 1914, Air 1 118/115/40/56.
111. Ibid.
112. Ibid.
113. 'Training Manual, Royal Flying Corps', RAFM, Accession No. 001287. The manual was published in two parts, the first (provisional) part 15 May 1914 by the War Office General Staff and His Majesty's Stationery Office.
114. RAF Staff College lecture by Brooke-Popham, March 1924, RAFM, Accession No. C/5/1/1.
115. 'Training Manual, Royal Flying Corps, Part II', Air Publication 144, RAFM, Accession No. 001289. This second volume was published on 3 June 1914. Sykes undoubtedly had help producing the manual and the final product had to go through the War Office for approval before publication.
116. 'Training Manual, Royal Flying Corps, Part II', 43.
117. Ibid., 35, 39; and see I. B. Holley, *Ideas and Weapons* (Hamden, CT: Archon Books, 1971), 176. Holley's argument was that American systems in the First World War failed in many respects due to breakdowns in the flow of information. 'The war showed the necessity of organizations at all echelons for making authoritative decisions based upon information systematically, objectively, and continuously accumulated by responsible and effective organizations especially created to gather data . . . decisions based upon opinion, memory, a limited range of personal experience, or emotional bias led only to failure.' Sykes anticipated Holley's argument before the war.
118. Divine, 50–2; Malcolm Cooper, *Birth of Independent Air Power*, 18.
119. 'Training Manual, Royal Flying Corps, Part II', 30–3.
120. Kennett, *The First Air War*, 122–4.
121. 'Training Manual, Royal Flying Corps, Part II', 60.
122. Ibid., 41.
123. Ibid., 23, 49.
124. Ibid., 24–6. RFC pilots were to have 'a fixed determination to attack and win'. That would be the surest road to victory.
125. Sykes' approach to war was typical of the time. See Douglas Porch, 'Bugeaud, Gallieni, Lyautey: The Development of French Colonial Warfare', in Paret, 407; and Michael Howard, 'Men against Fire: the Doctrine of the Offensive', in Paret, 523.
126. Anticipating trench warfare might not have changed aerial tactics or strategy, but foreknowledge of the stalemate would have placed greater emphasis on keeping more reserves initially to build a long-term air service.
127. Higham, 'Air Power in World War One, 1914–18', in *The War in the Air 1914–1994* (Canberra: RAAF Air Power Studies Centre, 1994), 31.
128. 'Standing Orders. Royal Flying Corps, Military Wing', Sykes Restricted Papers, vol. I, item 31; and Sykes Papers, MFC 77/13/16.
129. Sergeant Cecil Reginald King and Walter G. Ostler, sound recordings, IWM.
130. DGMA [Henderson] to Sykes, May 1914, Air 1 118/115/40/56.
131. Raleigh and Jones, 1:259.
132. Numerous newspaper clippings, June 1914, Sykes Papers, MFC 77/13/18.
133. London *Daily Telegraph*, 3 July 1914, Sykes Papers, MFC 77/13/18. Lieutenant Colonel Sykes was 'an extremely popular officer' who performed 'in a masterly manner'.
134. During the camp, which lasted from 2 June to 3 July, the RFC flew 630 flights, 21,210 miles and 336 hours. In three months the air service had flown a distance equivalent to three times around the world, or 79,708 miles.

135. Article in *Flight*, 26 June 1914, Sykes Papers, MFC 77/13/18.
136. Articles from *Flight*, 26 June 1914 and 3 July 1914, Sykes Papers, MFC 77/13/18; Sykes, *From Many Angles*, 118; and Sykes, *Aviation in Peace and War*, 30.
137. DGMA to Sykes, 20 July and 29 July 1914, Air 1 118/115/40/56.

3

The Great War

A lion has come out of his lair;
   a destroyer of nations has set out.
He has left his place
   to lay waste to your land.
Your towns will lie in ruins
   without inhabitant.
Jeremiah 4:7

Sykes' enthusiasm to engage the enemy matched his belief in the offensive doctrine. He knew that Britain's air service was out-numbered yet he was convinced that the RFC's superior organization and efficiency would provide a counterbalance. He wrote to his sister that the war he had expected for years had arrived and reminded her that he was an experienced soldier who knew the war would mean death and destruction – something excited civilians did not appreciate. He was content, however, with the government's decision to fight and confident that the struggle would be quick.[1] As for the RFC, he said that the most difficult time of peacetime preparation was over. It would be easier during the glamor of war.[2]

On 5 August 1914 Henderson notified Sykes that the RFC would be redistributed in two days. Trenchard would replace Sykes as commander of the Military Wing, and Sykes and Brooke-Popham would proceed to the War Office to direct the RFC Headquarters Staff.[3] Sykes had thought that a lieutenant-colonel should lead the air force into war, if that man had organized and trained the force during peacetime. That had been the plan, but now Henderson had different ideas. No doubt Sykes was hurt emotionally but surely must have recognized the need for higher rank to command the air service.[4]

Henderson may have demonstrated keen logic in taking over from Sykes, but his decision also hints at personal ambition clouding his judgement about what was best for the RFC. As a senior brigadier general, he had the necessary rank, but no one could perform the two most important jobs in the air service at the same time: General Officer Commanding (GOC) in the Field and DGMA. Henderson kept both, and his poor health prevented him from performing either task adequately.

Sykes and Henderson tried not to let Henderson's late assumption of command interfere with the mission. Writing to his family, Sykes mentioned no animosity toward Henderson nor dissatisfaction about his loss of command, and Henderson's correspondence is similarly positive: 'I have a delightful lot of officers to deal with, all as keen as is expected, and up to their work.'[5] As his chief of staff, Sykes would have been the person working the closest with Henderson.

Trenchard, on the other hand, was disappointed about his being left in England. His desire to go to France outweighed any loyalty to the air service, and he immediately applied to return to his old regiment.[6] Henderson rejected the request, but Trenchard continued to make his dissatisfaction known, which may have paid him dividends with Kitchener.[7] The RFC's departure exacerbated Trenchard's resentment when Henderson and Sykes, anticipating a short war, took most of the RFC to France.[8] According to Sykes, he knew from Staff College courses that the German thrust would come through Belgium. Surmising that cavalry would have difficulty in 'the enclosed nature of the country,' he deduced that air reconnaissance would be vital and took all that he had.[9] Trenchard did not have Kitchener's insight as to the length of the war and the need to sustain building programs at home; he simply resented being left in England in charge of a depleted force and blamed Sykes and Wilson for the situation.[10]

Trenchard was not completely abandoned, and his complaints were extreme. The RFC took 105 officers, 755 personnel of other ranks, 63 aircraft and 95 transport vehicles to France. Left behind were 41 officers, 116 aircraft and 23 vehicles. Even though many of those remaining aircraft were old or unserviceable, approximately one-third of the RFC's strength stayed in England.[11] Hence, the Trenchard–Sykes hostility that grew in August 1914 was mainly a product of Trenchard's envy and Sykes' lack of sympathy. From 6 until 12 August neither man slept much, and the stress of mobilization, combined with the anxiety of war, contributed to short tempers. Trenchard resented Sykes' abilities to speak and write; his own communication skills were limited to disconnected fortissimo phrases. Furthermore, Sykes was preoccupied with things other than Trenchard's damaged ego.

The circumstances surrounding the change of command and Sykes' departure are confusing, and Trenchard's recollection is suspicious. What is certain is that an incident occurred that fueled Trenchard's animosity toward Sykes, which became mutual within a few years. Trenchard recalled that Sykes' departure was discourteous and shortsighted:

I remember being told by Major [*sic*] Sykes that all my duty would be [*sic*] to send a few new machines and a few more men to re-inforce the four squadrons in France, and that there would be no necessity for any new squadrons nor were they to be raised. I informed him it was nothing to do with him what we did in England and I proposed to begin to raise twelve squadrons at once.[12]

Boyle recorded the incident as a heated argument that Trenchard finally terminated by telling Sykes that his ideas were 'damned rubbish'.[13] Part of the episode involved a confidential box with a key, which Trenchard remembered receiving from Sykes.[14] Sykes supposedly told him it contained all the defensive plans for a possible invasion by German airships. Trenchard kept the key, but he apparently arrived the next morning to find Major Brooke-Popham and an open box with nothing in it but a pair of old shoes.[15] He concluded, that 'there was nothing left at Farnborough bar one clerk and one orderly'.[16] To Trenchard, Sykes had added insult to injury.

Sykes' account is quite different. He mentioned the box but claimed that it contained detailed records of the formation of the RFC's Military Wing. Writing years later, he stated that it was unfortunate that someone had hidden or destroyed those accounts while he was away.[17] If Trenchard's recollection is accurate, how did Brooke-Popham open the box? It is surprising that Trenchard would not have secured the box, if it had indeed contained confidential plans. Most likely, it never did. Sykes had already demonstrated that he was not concerned about the aerial defense of England, a role that was being taken over by the Navy. Hence why give Trenchard such plans if they did exist? Interestingly, Brooke-Popham, who could have substantiated Trenchard's story, failed to record anything about the box incident and also kept no information on Sykes' departure from France in 1915, when he took over from him.[18] There is little possibility that Sykes simply played a heartless joke on Trenchard. At the time Sykes was exhausted and in a hurry to get to war, and he did not particulary enjoy humor. Trenchard's perception of Sykes' insensitivity was probably accurate, however. Under the unrelenting pressure of war preparations Sykes had his sights set on loftier targets than the emotions of fellow airmen.

On 8 August 1914 the RFC's four aeroplane squadrons and the aircraft park were ordered to fly from their locations to Dover and from there to France.[19] The objective was Maubeuge (see Appendices for a map of France). The size of the RFC was noticeably small compared with the other branches of the Army, and the only mention of the RFC in the BEF standing orders was that Army personnel should avoid getting in the way of aircraft that were attempting to land![20] Sykes arrived at Dover at midnight on 12 August and issued orders and maps for the flight across the Channel scheduled for 0600 hours the next morning.[21]

The movement to Dover cost the RFC its first casualties, but the cross-Channel flight went without mishap.[22] One of the intriguing issues of this embarkation was that neither Henderson nor Sykes led the RFC flight across the channel. Henderson did not have the flying skills, or the proficiency. As chief of staff rather than commander, Sykes may have considered it inappropriate, or he may have been compelled to handle other duties. Nevertheless, this was consistent with a trend that lasted throughout the air war, where top-level leaders did not fly into combat.[23]

Sykes arrived at Amiens on 13 August with Henderson, Barrington-Kennett and Brooke-Popham. After moving into the Hotel Belfort, they spent the rest of the day setting up an office and searching for missing cases of oil. The next day Sykes organized staff duties, entertained visitors, including Sir John French, and listened to dire predictions from French locals.[24] Meanwhile, the squadrons had established a temporary airfield and were preparing for the next leg of the journey. On a rainy 15 August the RFC departed for the French headquarters at Maubeuge.[25] Sykes arrived there on 17 August, four days ahead of the aircraft park, which took three days to unload. By this time the squadrons were already flying reconnaissance missions, and the hot weather was good for flying. The only real threat to airmen was ground fire half of which came from French and British troops.[26]

Sykes spent the next week trying to make sense out of confusing reconnaissance reports and attempting to get information to an ever-moving GHQ. The RFC staff was constantly on the move as well, which added to their duties. From 24 to 26 August, they moved three times, ending up at La Fère, the very ground German troops would occupy during their eastward swing five days later, which, ironically, RFC reconnaissance would report. The news on the 26th that Cambrai had fallen had everyone but Henderson gloomy. He remained calm, trying to raise others' spirits.[27] The staff's attention quickly shifted to another concern, however, when it had to pursue a reputed local spy.[28] The staff often heard German guns in the distance, and reports of Germans in the immediate vicinity kept the RFC vigilant.

As a result of one of these reports on 27 August, Sykes joined the rest of the staff in setting up a defensive perimeter around a turnip field. No Germans. After spending the night in a château, against the objections of the caretaker, they departed for Compiègne at 0400 hours on 28 August, where the staff were billeted in a school. In terms of air power history, Compiègne was important because it was at that airfield that the Germans first dropped a bomb from the air.[29] It did little damage, but the aerial attack proved to be more real than anything British airmen had experienced from German ground forces, and it reminded RFC HQ that they were entering an air war.

After two more moves, the RFC located in Juilly, where another rumor of German envelopment created panic. Sykes and Barrington-Kennett were a few miles away in Dammartin having dinner. Upon hearing that their HQ had been cut off, they grabbed Henderson's equipment and loaded it into their car. Barrington-Kennett delayed the departure when he went back for some 'important dispatches' that turned out to be tins of meat and jam, and once again, they established a defense around the airfield and spent a sleepless night waiting for Germans who never appeared.[30] Sykes' chaotic experience during the first few weeks of the war was almost humorous when compared with the fierce fighting between German, French and British soldiers.

The stresses of the retreat, false alarms and ground fire from friendly soldiers created resentment between the RFC and the BEF.[31] According to the official history, soldiers simply did not appreciate RFC flyers who tried to boost Army morale by flying overhead and dropping leaflets to warn troops of danger in their area. The infantry did not like anyone being above them, regardless of nationality, and ground fire from the BEF continued.[32] Despite such hostility from friendly forces, the RFC continued its primary mission of reconnaissance.

The story of early RFC reconnaissance is one of the most contentious issues in the history of the First World War. According to Sykes and the official history, RFC reconnaissance helped to save the BEF from destruction by preventing its envelopment from the north. It also kept the BEF in communication with itself during the retreat from Mons, and it helped to set up the successful Battle of the Marne.[33] Recently historians have attacked this record as fallacious, claiming that RFC reconnaissance was inaccurate, that information gained from it was ineffectively presented to GHQ, and that as a result the RFC had little influence on the course of events.[34] As Morrow has inferred, however, the recent condemnation of RFC reconnaissance is extreme.[35]

There is evidence that RFC reconnaissance performed as generally depicted by the official historians, even though it was at times chaotic.[36] Sykes and the official history may be in error, however, regarding how RFC intelligence was used by GHQ. While BEF Intelligence (I Branch) was organized to use RFC reconnaissance, and Sir John French had recognized such information-gathering as the principal role of his air service, French and I Branch used aircraft in a confirmatory role rather than as the primary information source implied by Sykes and Raleigh.[37]

Sykes recorded that aerial reconnaissance began from Maubeuge on 19 August; it was not an outstanding beginning. The two pilots were from different squadrons and had separate objectives, but they planned to fly together for the first phase of the mission, approximately 17 miles from Maubeuge to Nivelles. After losing each other and their own ways, independently, they flew by compass and ground navigation. One flew 90 degrees off course and ended up 15 miles from his objective; the other flew 125 degrees off course and landed over 35 miles away from his desired destination.[38] This was more fiasco than success.

According to Sykes, however, within three days of the first mission, RFC reconnaissance was vital to the BEF. A sortie apparently spotted approximately 5,000 German troops in Grammont and more heading south-west.[39] Sykes and Henderson determined that the information was important and personally drove to GHQ to notify Sir John French. Such action was according to the system Sykes had established and published in the training manual. Over a year before war was declared, Sykes had predicted in the *Army Review* exactly what occurred in late August and early September 1914:

> Owing to the fear of moving troops in a wrong direction and having to countermarch them, there will, I think, be a tendency both in the strategical and tactical stages for commanders to await the reports of their aerial reconnoitres before deciding what to do. Preliminary orders will be issued and confirmed or altered in accordance with the results of reconnaissances.[40]

Although Sykes' system had called for co-locating of RFC HQ and GHQ to facilitate communication, Sykes and Henderson had to drive 25 miles to Le Cateau. The official history records that, based on this reconnaissance information, Sir John French terminated the offensive and ordered a retreat. When General Charles Lanrezac, Commander of the French 5th Army, asked for help during his retreat, Sir John grudgingly agreed to hold his position on 24 August.[41]

During the retreat from Mons, the RFC HQ moved ten times in its attempt to keep up with GHQ. Returning from reconnaissance missions, flyers had difficulty in locating their home field.[42] Yet they had anticipated the situation and had practiced the contingency system, which, fortunately, was not hampered by poor weather. Hence, according to the official history, this episode was the first effective use of air power.

Sykes not only supported the official history that RFC information thwarted the German surprise and thus saved the BEF, but he used that account to justify his August departure from England with most of the RFC's machines and personnel. He confirmed the famous record of the retreat from Mons when RFC flyers were sent 'to find Sir Douglas Haig' and helped to co-ordinate the BEF's retirement.[43] In addition, he recorded that once the German 1st and 2nd Armies were correctly identified, aerial reconnaissance tracked their movements and showed that their commanders, Kluck and General Karl von Bülow, were not well co-ordinated. As Sykes noted the enemy's vulnerability, created by Kluck's march across the front ahead of Bülow, he urged Henderson to suggest a BEF offensive.[44] The German High Command, however, also aware of their predicament, ordered 1st and 2nd Armies to position for battle to the south-west, which forced Kluck to perform a difficult 'backward wheel'.[45] The Battle of the Marne began two days later. The RFC had played an important part in setting up this critical battle by exposing enemy movements and reducing the German advantage of interior lines.

After the Allied success on the Marne, the RFC was less decisive during the 'race to the sea', when poor weather hampered flying operations.[46] In particular, aerial contributions during the first Battle of Ypres were minimal, as pilots and observers had difficulty seeing and identifying ground subjects. Trying to combat the problem, Sykes ordered continuous missions in an attempt to track the enemy and avoid the misidentifying of enemy units. Weather plagued the process; yet any knowledge at all was helpful in eliminating the element of surprise, which could mean the difference between victory and defeat.

In assessing the official history of early RFC reconnaissance, one must note a couple of questionable areas. First, that the BEF was 'saved' is a counterfactual argument – historians cannot assume that the Germans would have destroyed the BEF, had such aerial information not reached GHQ. Therefore the primary question is whether that information influenced Sir John French's decision-making, which in turn may or may not have led to the BEF's survival. This leads to the second consideration.

Army dispatches were the main evidence Sykes and the official historians used to justify the RFC's effectiveness. French appeared to substantiate that he used RFC information:

> It was the timely warning aircraft gave which chiefly enabled me to make speedy dispositions to avert danger and disaster. There can be no doubt . . . aircraft saved the very frequent use of cavalry patrols and detailed supports.[47]

Yet in this same dispatch from French to Secretary of State for War Kitchener on 7 September 1914, French failed to mention that RFC intelligence information specifically warned him of impending envelopment by army-sized enemy forces, or that he used aircraft reconnaissance to make the specific decision to retire from Mons.[48]

The French commander General Joseph Joffre, wrote praises as well: 'The precision, exactitude and regularity of the news brought in are evidence of the perfect training of pilots and observers.'[49] These statements were not intended to depict what had occurred within army decision-making circles; rather they were simply to encourage the air services by applauding the heroic efforts of flyers. More importantly, French and Joffre sought to increase the size of their air services, and the best argument for more air support was to note how valuable it had been.

The best indication that the RFC had, in fact, proved its worth was, therefore, an indirect one. Had aircraft been a failure, the Army would not have fought for a more extensive flying organization. French wrote to Kitchener that tactical reconnaissance 'has proved so valuable' and stated that the RFC was barely able to meet demands.[50] At the same time Rawlinson wrote to Kitchener that the RFC would continue to be 'of the utmost assistance to us', and that the aircraft 'are doing first class work'.[51]

Reconnaissance effectiveness was influenced by the errors of individual flyers and by problems with the whole intelligence system. System ineffectiveness was not within the RFC, but within the Army – between the intelligence and the operations branch. Intelligence personnel under Lieutenant-Colonel George M. Macdonogh were eager to acquire and process all possible pieces of information, including that gained from the air. Yet tactical and operational decisions were made in Operations Branch, where planners viewed aerial reconnaissance with some skepticism. Their jaundiced perspective that RFC flyers were crying wolf was warranted, as many reports were in error and detracted from the overall credibility of the RFC.[52] In addition, GHQ planners were aware that the flyers presented a threat to BEF security. It was a downed British aircraft, after all, that first revealed to the Germans the presence of British soldiers on their front.[53] The attitude of suspicion toward the RFC did change, but not until after the late August and early September battles.[54]

Overall, the reconnaissance story was a mixed success involving chaotic inexperience, fortunate circumstance and determination. The fog and friction of war can smile favorably on lucky soldiers as well as on strong or intelligent ones, however, and perhaps the RFC experienced some beginner's luck in August 1914. Even though the first RFC missions were anything but smooth operations, a few flyers did stumble across some critical information, and the RFC system got that information to GHQ. Air power's effectiveness should not be measured by what GHQ then did with it.

Sir John French was impressed, during the Battle of the Marne when the RFC flew tactically for Haig and Horace Smith-Dorrien, the two BEF Corps commanders.[55] Subsequently, when the fighting stale-mated into trench warfare, this required tactical trench recon-naissance. Up to this point, Henderson had tried to maintain fairly tight control of air resources by keeping all reconnaissance 'strategic' at GHQ.[56] Now Sir John French wanted to detach RFC units from their strategic role at GHQ and attach them directly to Army corps.[57] The Army initiative to disperse the flying service threatened the RFC's autonomy and thus evolved into a large reorganizational effort later in November 1914.[58]

The more immediate RFC struggle following the Battle of the Marne, however, was September weather. Sykes was at Saponay with the RFC HQ and all the squadrons. They still had no sheds for their aircraft, and when a fierce storm hit northern France on 12 September it destroyed all but ten of the RFC's aircraft.[59] Consequently, the RFC was ineffective during the Battle of the Aisne, which lasted from 12 to 15 September.[60] Flyers tried to help where they could by lending vehicles to the Army and by helping to transport the wounded. Seeing the results of the battle reminded Sykes and the staff that their less than favorable circumstances were still far better than the situation of those at the front.

Sykes' staff work continued as he arranged boxes into makeshift desks and chairs. The food deteriorated to the point that Henderson fired the cook and ordered Barrington-Kennett to wear the chef's hat. Complaints from French locals became common and part of Sykes' responsibility. When the mayor of Saponay claimed their airmen had stolen fruit, the RFC settled the incident with a half-serious threat to the mayor's title and life.[61] Sykes also had to deal with administrative problems back home. The same day as the violent September storm, 'Boom' Trenchard sent word that individual accounts from Nether-avon were outstanding and that Sykes needed to acquire the money. Sykes responded that such debts were to be covered by squadron mess funds, but had Barrington-Kennett send a balance sheet which showed that Trenchard's figures did not match those Sykes had on record.[62] The incident was resolved without further debate, but both men probably assumed that the other was inaccurate and irresponsible.[63]

Sykes' underlying message to Trenchard was that outstanding accounts were less important than the reinforcements he needed in France. Boyle claimed that part of the Trenchard–Sykes disagreement was over the issue of replacements – that Trenchard wanted to replace entire squadrons, while Sykes wanted RFC reinforcements to come on an individual basis.[64] After one month of war, Sykes wrote:

> I am anxious to get Squadrons on to their correct estabt. basis. But it is

difficult as you can imagine. As a matter of fact all squadrons are still short of their estabt. of officers. We have been extraordinarily lucky as regards not losing personnel: but it is not possible that times can be so for ever. We have had some wonderful escapes as it is. Officers and men are all working splendidly.[65]

Sykes now realized the war might turn into a longer affair than expected, and he was eager for Trenchard and Brancker to get the supply system into gear. The key to victory had just changed from winning the mobilization battle to winning the production–training–technology battle.[66]

The RFC's role was changing as well. Besides tactical reconnaissance, pilots were starting to fight. Hence Henderson sent a request to England for grenades, bombs and some aircraft that could carry machine-guns.[67] At this point, the RFC was reacting to the situation – inventions in offensive aerial fighting and tactical bombing were being driven by necessity.

When German forces began a siege of Antwerp on 28 September, the BEF's attention shifted to Belgium and the RFC was called upon for reconnaissance and communication assistance.[68] Sykes was to make contact with the Belgian commander and relay to GHQ the situation at Antwerp; hence on 3 October Sykes flew as an observer in a modified BE with extra fuel capacity. He landed in a muddy field four miles south of Bruges and attempted to ride a bicycle to the town – until he crashed into a tree, injuring his shoulder. After obtaining a car and driver from the commandant at Bruges, Sykes reached Antwerp at midnight and by 0600 hours was again airborne and soon in contact with Sir John French.[69]

Morale within the RFC rose once the retreat ended, and gradually British forces were able to move northward. RFC headquarters moved from Fère-en-Tardenois to Abbeville, where they stayed from 8 to 12 October, and then to St Omer. The RFC had finally found a home – it would remain at St Omer for the next two years. The staff started receiving mail and settling into a daily routine that involved more than moving. Sykes' office and quarters were in a red and white château located on a hill between the town and the aerodrome.[70] When the First Battle of Ypres started on 19 October the RFC was ready to help. Poor weather hampered flying, however, and thwarted the RFC's contribution.[71] The air power failure during this battle, which lasted until 21 November, demonstrated the need for RFC reconnaissance as much as success had in September.

Back in England, flying training and resupply were chaotic, a result of marginal resources and the courageous enthusiasm of prospective flyers who accepted dangers from poor equipment and inconsistent training standards as simply part of war.[72] To Trenchard's credit, he objected to the situation. Sir John French had been impressed by the RFC's results and told Kitchener that he wanted the same product to come to France in the future: 'It is therefore most desirable that any reinforcements should be organized, trained, and equipped in exactly the same manner as the squadrons now in the field.'[73] Yet, when Kitchener placed heavy demands on Trenchard and Brancker, Trenchard complained bitterly.[74]

The RFC organization back in England was plagued with problems. Brancker was out-ranked at the War Office and unable to compete successfully on behalf of the RFC. Complaining that the other high-ranking officers did not take him seriously, he wrote: 'We must make up in the senior officer line or get left behind'.[75] The stressful situation led to friction between Trenchard and Brancker. Trenchard complained about Brancker, and Brancker wrote to Henderson about Trenchard's shortfalls as an administrator: 'Already Trenchard is finding that much of his valuable time and energy, which should be devoted to bigger things, is being absorbed by petty details which could be delegated to subordinate commanders.'[76]

Henderson and Sykes tried to rectify the situation by shifting personnel in France and releasing others for duties back in England. Although the decision to send flyers home was unpopular among the squadrons, it did improve RFC training.[77] A new training scheme developed which matched Sykes' 1911 plans from France.[78] Trenchard proposed raising 12 new squadrons, which Brancker believed would be insufficient and changed the total to 30.[79] That figure was the one that eventually went before Kitchener, where it received the famous 'double this' response.[80] Although historians have credited Trenchard with the expansion, he had been in France six months by the time the War Secretary doubled Brancker's plan.[81]

The major RFC concern was how to build and reorganize so that air power could help in the future. Sir John French wanted more tactical reconnaissance, but he followed Sykes' desires not to use naval flyers.[82] Henderson had decided to decentralize the RFC by splitting it into wings and attaching them to Army corps. This matched what Sykes had predicted a year earlier:

> As the strategical merges into the tactical phase, so the character of the reconnaissance work will be modified. Certain long distance flights will still be advisable to discover possible flanking and reserve movements, but the greater number will consist of short flights to ascertain the tactical position and place the information immediately in the hands of the commander.[83]

Sykes drafted Henderson's reorganization plan in October, while Brancker and Trenchard submitted ideas of their own.[84]

Henderson's primary objective was to enhance the flow of information from the RFC to the BEF, and he agreed with Sykes that the RFC needed to remain an autonomous corps under central control by an RFC general officer.[85] It was too specialized a service to be handed over to Army corps commanders who did not understand air power capabilities or appreciate the risks of flying.[86] Hence the reorganization needed to maintain uniformity in all flying operations, which would be ensured by maintaining an RFC HQ and commanding RFC wings with colonels.[87] Henderson submitted his plan to the War Office for Army Council approval on 1 November and talked with Kitchener two days later for his concurrence.[88]

Trenchard and Brancker viewed the necessary reorganization from a logistical rather than a command point of view.[89] To facilitate maintenance and supply, Brancker proposed abolishing the GOC RFC position and advocated total decentralization of the air force.[90] Trenchard agreed that the RFC HQ only interrupted supply channels, and he voiced Army Council opinion that the leadership of the RFC was to be advisory only and not to direct flying operations.

Henderson disagreed and underscored Sykes' criticisms of the Brancker and Trenchard proposals.[91] The only reorganizational area where Henderson and Sykes disagreed was operational command. Henderson believed that RFC wings could do strategic as well as tactical reconnaissance, while Sykes wanted strategic missions left solely to the prerogative and direction of RFC HQ. Henderson's plan was finally accepted by the Army and published on 15 January 1915 as 'Organization of the Royal Flying Corps in the Field' by Lieutenant-General A.J. Murray, the Chief of the General Staff.[92] The RFC was decentralized into wings for tactical work but maintained its autonomy as an air service. Aircraft were to be flown only on missions suited to their type; there was to be no duplication of effort; and reconnaissance was not to be requested if not vitally necessary. The reorganization was profoundly significant for the future air force as it provided an organizational framework for growth and established a definitive separation from naval flying. Henderson and Sykes had ensured that the RFC did not lose control of its mission.

The reorganization had underlying effects, however, on the relationships between Sykes, Trenchard, Brancker and Henderson. Henderson had not fallen for Brancker's ploy to establish a higher rank for his position, and Sykes had noticed Trenchard's proposal to eliminate Sykes' role.[93] When Henderson notified Trenchard that the RFC was to be divided into wings and that he needed a commander, Trenchard was concerned about having to serve under Sykes.[94] Henderson and Sykes had worked harmoniously to recreate the new RFC and Henderson expressed his satisfaction with Sykes in an

official dispatch.[95] Sykes, on the other hand, did not feel such content-
ment in return and noted Brancker's difficulties as the deputy DGMA,
as well as the strain upon Henderson, which were caused by
Henderson's dual-hatted position. Sykes wrote a memorandum that
inferred that many of the reorganizational problems were due to
Henderson's inability to be both GOC in the field and DGMA: 'In the
strained and abnormal conditions of war, the weight of control would
seem to be even more essential. But, as a fact, the Directorate of
Military Aeronautics has been heavily weakened by the services of the
Director General himself being required in the field.'[96] Sykes was
merely trying to help the RFC, and Henderson should have acknowledged his own limits; however, his thoughts were in a different direction as he requested a transfer back to the Army.

On 22 November 1914 Henderson eagerly replaced the injured
Major-General H. J. S. Landon as Commander of 1st Infantry
Division.[97] Sykes was placed in command of the RFC the same day and
promoted to temporary colonel.[98] Henderson's move demonstrated
two things: Sykes' role in RFC reorganization and Henderson's preoccupation with personal aspirations. Sykes was excited to obtain the
position he had anticipated before the war, and he eagerly implemented the reorganization by publishing his first set of Routine Orders
as well as the 'Memorandum on new organization of the Royal Flying
Corps' that he and Henderson had completed.[99] Now that Sykes was in
command, however, his orders reflected his own desires regarding
tactical and strategic reconnaissance.[100]

Trenchard recalled that when he arrived in Flanders on 18
November to find out that Henderson was being replaced by Sykes, he
exploded, stating that he would rather return to the Royal Scots
Fusiliers. Under Sykes, Trenchard was an insubordinate wing
commander. He wrote disrespectfully to Sykes and fought to implement the reorganization that he had wanted – the one Sykes and
Henderson had rejected.[101] Historians have written that Trenchard
approached Kitchener to complain about having to work under
Sykes and that such intrigue on Trenchard's part led to Henderson's
transfer back to the RFC in December 1914.[102] It is true that Sir John
French, not Kitchener, had sanctioned Henderson's transfer to 1st
Division; however, there is no available evidence of underhanded
correspondence between Trenchard and Kitchener.[103] Nevertheless,
on 21 December 1914, an unhappy Henderson received orders to
report back to the RFC, which undoubtedly disappointed Sykes, who
was demoted to lieutenant-colonel.[104]

Sykes was also concerned that the RFC should maintain strong
leadership: the principle Henderson had promoted on paper but was
not following in practice, as he demonstrated by his desire to leave the

RFC but then return, keeping both DGMA and GOC commands. Hence Sykes' memorandum was again valid, expressing his concern that the RFC was dependent on reinforcements, but facing an extended war with a 'depleted Directorate at the War Office for guidance and control'.[105] He suggested that the Directorate needed someone with experience in the field as well as 'responsible and adequate authority', implying that Henderson might best serve in that capacity.

Sykes was not alone in noticing Brancker's problems at the War Office and John Salmond's administrative difficulties at Farnborough.[106] In addition, Henderson's poor health was obvious.[107] For the good of the RFC, Henderson should have offered to return as DGMA – the position he did assume once Sykes left for Gallipoli.[108] Instead, Henderson took offense at Sykes' suggestion and, in a service consumed with rumors, Henderson's animosity against Sykes became well known. Whether Trenchard had contributed to the rift or not, he quickly sided with the stronger party: Henderson. The incident became important three years later when the Air Minister, Lord Rothermere, considered Sykes for the CAS position and General Jan Christian Smuts confirmed that Sykes had done nothing improper to warrant Henderson's wrath.[109]

The practice of attaching flying units to Army corps had occurred during the Battles of the Marne and First Ypres, but the formal implementation of RFC reorganization into wings occurred under Sykes' temporary tenure as commander. On 29 November 1st Wing, under the command of Trenchard and consisting of Nos 2 and 3 Squadrons, was assigned to IV and Indian Corps. Under Lieutenant-Colonel C. J. Burke, Nos 5 and 6 Squadrons comprised 2nd Wing, which was assigned to II and III Corps. The wireless squadron (No. 4), RFC HQ and one strategic reconnaissance squadron were stationed with GHQ.[110]

Some of the flying reorganization progressed without much influence from Sykes. While Sykes was concentrating on the Western Front, the predecessor of the RFC's Middle East Brigade was sent to Egypt to defend the Suez Canal against Turkish attack.[111] In addition, although Sykes had been a major force behind keeping the RFC and the RNAS separate, the RNAS reorganized at the same time and in the same manner that the RFC did.[112] A primary RNAS focus was on bombing, but Sykes kept the RFC mainly involved in reconnaissance. Although the enemy air service was organized independently of any British influence, the Germans studied the British system, just as the RFC was aware of the German organizational structure.[113]

In addition to his reorganizational efforts, Sykes performed familiar roles, hosting King George V, the Prince of Wales and a Russian general, who insisted on receiving a flight over the line in full uniform (including spurs).[114] Sykes wrote to his sister that the weather had turned cold and snowy and that the roads around St Omer were 'appalling'. Although they had seen many German aeroplanes earlier, by December there were very few.[115] Unfortunately, however, the RFC could not enjoy a reprieve – a winter storm hit northern France and destroyed 16 aircraft and damaged 30 more.[116]

Weather permitting, Sykes kept his aircraft on constant patrol at the request of Sir John French. Sykes also pushed hard for more developments in wireless communication, bombing, air-to-air fighting and photography.[117] Murray's new delineation of RFC duties would be entitled 'Notes on Air Reconnaissance', but it pointed the way toward expanding the offensive roles into which reconnaissance had evolved.[118]

Sykes recognized that the key to successful trench reconnaissance was photography. With aircraft having to fly higher to avoid ground fire, it became impossible for observers to locate the intricate details of gun emplacements, railheads, supply depots and trenches with the naked eye.[119] The one flyer who was more responsible than any other for advancing British aerial photography was Lieutenant John T. C. Moore-Brabazon.[120] As Lord Brabazon of Tara he wrote in 1954 to Lady Sykes about her husband:

> To me personally he was a very dear friend. I knew him in the far off days of the birth of the RFC, and it was due to him I was put in charge of photography in the RFC in 1914. This action of his had great repercussions in my life and I have been eternally grateful to him for his kindness. The more you got to know him the more you loved him and valued him. I consider it one of the privileges given to me in my life to have come in contact with him and to have been his friend.[121]

Sykes had advocated aerial photography in his pre-war Training Manual, and he recognized shortly after the war began that the French were ahead of the British in this field. Hence he sent Major Geoffrey Salmond to study their methods and bring back information to Major H. Musgrave of the (No. 9) Experimental Squadron.[122] Upon learning that one of his ambulance drivers – Moore-Brabazon – was an experienced photographer, Sykes assigned him to the same unit and ordered him to build an aerial camera.[123] Aerial photography improved RFC reconnaissance safety and performance as observers were motivated to take good photographs so that they would not have to repeat their missions. In February 1915 Rawlinson explained to Kitchener about the benefits of RFC photography.[124]

Because of the shortage of ammunition, the second most important RFC role at the end of 1914 was artillery spotting.[125] The RFC had devised a clock-face system of codes, using Verey lights to communicate to the ground, but the co-ordination was poor and demanded effective wireless communication.[126] On 8 December 1914 Sykes formed a wireless squadron with a flight allotted to each wing. Most of the initial difficulties with wireless were technological, stemming from the size and the weight of airborne transmitters, but another problem was due to hostility from airmen who considered technical work contemptible.[127] Against this attitude Sykes pushed for more experimentation. According to Brooke-Popham, the technological breakthrough occurred when scientists at Brooklands and the Experimental Squadron's airmen at St Omer discovered that they needed to enhance the ground receiving capability rather than boost airborne transmission.[128] Once wireless communication was perfected to the point that it was useful, it also enhanced contact patrol work and other duties that had depended hitherto on lights and flares.

1915

Sykes had helped to reorganize and lead a new RFC whose role was expanding dramatically, but he entered 1915 under confusing circumstances. The war Sykes had predicted to be quick and decisive had stalemated, and decision-makers on both sides had few answers to the predicament. Henderson's presence was unpredictable, which was detrimental to the RFC.[129] He was back in command at the start of 1915, but as soon as the winter weather broke to allow action by the BEF and the RFC, his health once more began to deteriorate.[130] He attempted to work but often had to spend parts of the day in bed, and when doctors ordered him to take extended leave on 17 March, he did not return to the RFC until 19 April.[131] In addition, Henderson was called away for short periods to handle his duties as DGMA. For example, after returning on 19 April he left for London three days later and remained there until the 28th. In all during the first months of 1915 Sykes commanded the RFC for one-third of the time.[132]

The first major battle of 1915 was at Neuve Chapelle. Poor weather hampered flying, and Henderson was in bed. Now attached to the Army Corps, the RFC wings flew in support of the attack and according to the new procedures Sykes and Henderson had established.[133] Flyers had to cope with fog and rain as well as personnel in the BEF who were unaccustomed to an attached wing.[134] Interservice friction grew, incidents of friendly fire against airmen continued, and artillery spotting failed due to battery commanders' reluctance to co-operate with the RFC.[135] RFC leadership was also erratic, as apparently

Trenchard did not even realize that Henderson had left Sykes in command until Sykes criticized him for a high casualty rate.[136]

Sykes' record of aerial activity was more positive. He noted that, before the battle, Trenchard's wing had supplied Haig with 1,500 maps of the terrain. Sykes looked beyond the immediate results of March, noting that the RFC had demonstrated new developments in air power, including bombing. The RFC War Diary recorded the first night-bombing sortie against railway stations at Courtrai, Menin and Lille.[137] Sykes also noted that Sir John French had praised the RFC move toward more offensive activity.[138]

Although the RNAS had bombed systematically from the air, RFC bombing before spring 1915 was sporadic. RFC flyers had experimented with various types of aerial weapon, from grenades to flechettes to leaflets, but bombing had been left largely to individual initiative against targets of opportunity. On 15 February Sykes presented a memorandum at RFC HQ advocating a formal move toward planned, systematic bombing.[139] He argued that bombing should not be done except by trained specialists and according to established procedures to ensure accuracy. His approach to bombing was seminal in establishing an effective bombing force, but that would not occur until 1918, when he returned to the RAF as CAS.[140]

In April the French and British learned that the Germans were planning to use poisonous gas, and the RFC was ordered to reconnoiter German trenches in search of cylinders.[141] They spotted nothing until 22 April, the outbreak of the Second Battle of Ypres. RFC flyers reported seeing gas clouds streaming westward, and Sykes carried the message to GHQ. He recalled that he then broke custom by personally flying over the battlefield to ascertain the exact location of the gas attack.[142]

In May, when Henderson returned once again from sick leave, it was the last time that he and Sykes changed positions. The War Office notified Sykes that they had released him to the Admiralty for work in the Dardanelles. Trenchard recalled that Henderson had finally listened to him and realized that Sykes needed to be fired. Trenchard further stated that he refused to assume Sykes' position as Chief of Staff and recommended Brooke-Popham for the job.[143] Trenchard was in no position to make such a recommendation, but Brooke-Popham did replace Sykes.[144] Trenchard's 20-year-old recollection of Sykes' 'exile' is questionable. Sykes certainly did not confirm the interpretation, but stated merely that he was sad to leave France when ordered to investigate RNAS flying at Gallipoli.[145]

Most likely, an exhausted Henderson had become envious of Sykes' abilities and endurance, and, like Trenchard in 1914, resented Sykes' extreme focus on the mission. In addition, however, Henderson was suspicious of Trenchard and tired of his complaints. Hence, Henderson simply solved both issues by making Sykes a Wing Commander. Sykes would get the command he wanted, and Trenchard would not have to work under Sykes. When Sueter convinced the Admiralty that they needed Sykes' expertise, however, Henderson did not object to releasing Sykes. Hence Sykes' move to Gallipoli was not an exile and not a demotion but a promotion. It had resulted from RNAS problems in the Dardanelles – specifically, the command of Wing Commander C. R. Samson – and Sykes was the man who could correct the situation. The 'Easterners' saw in the Dardanelles an opportunity to break the trench deadlock that had developed in the west, and Sykes joined some of Britain's most capable and politically connected officers in his journey to Gallipoli.

The primary problem with the 'exile' interpretation of Sykes' departure is the issue of Henderson's command and influence. Although Sykes clearly had a quarrel with his superior officer, any attempt on Henderson's part to ruin Sykes was thwarted by his popularity and support from the Army, the Navy, and the political hierarchy. As the diary of Lady Hamilton (wife of the Anglo-French Army commander at Gallipoli Sir Ian Hamilton) demonstrates, Sykes was held in as high esteem as Henderson. Within her influential circle, Sykes was considered 'concentrated and reliable', and she was pleased that he was going to Gallipoli to help her husband. As for Henderson, she wondered whether he was really as well liked as people seemed to think.[146] It seems that the popular interpretation of Sykes' downfall in 1915 is erroneous.

Although Henderson had taken over Sykes' command of the Military Wing in August 1914, it was Sykes' air service and intelligence system that had survived the initial tests of war. Sykes' wartime management and intermittent leadership helped the RFC to more than double in size, and during the first six months of war Sykes continued the organizational tasks that he had begun two years earlier. Operationally, RFC reconnaissance contributed to the BEF's successful retreat from Mons, which set up the Battle of the Marne and most likely blocked a quick German victory. Sykes helped to instigate significant technological developments, such as aerial photography and wireless communication, and he established the foundation for systematic bombing. Due principally to Sykes' efforts, half of which were during Henderson's absence, the RFC adapted to changing conditions with a complete organizational transformation. Part of that reorganization was Sykes' firm stand to keep naval and military flying separate. Ironically, in May 1915 he was to observe and report on naval flying operations in the Dardanelles.

NOTES

1. Sykes to Edie and Sykes to Guy, August 1914, Sykes Private Papers.
2. Sykes to No. 2 (Ethel), 10 August 1914, Sykes Private Papers.
3. 20/Royal Flying Corps/38 (MA1), Air 1 118/115/40/56.
4. Sykes, *From Many Angles*, 122.
5. Henderson to Lady Henderson, 18 August 1914, Henderson Papers, AC 74/ 2/5(b), RAFM.
6. Autobiographical notes, 63, Trenchard Papers, MFC 76/1/61.
7. Sir Philip Joubert de la Ferté, *The Third Service* (London: Thames & Hudson, 1955), 19. Joubert de la Ferté suggested Trenchard's promotion to brevet lieutenant-colonel was Kitchener's way of placating him by making him equal in rank to Sykes.
8. Kennett, *The First Air War*, 120. The anticipation of a sudden 'all-or-nothing' battle was universal. German Army operations called for using their reserves at once, and the Germans and French sent all air resources to the front, closing their training schools.
9. Sykes, *Aviation in Peace and War*, 45.
10. Trenchard Papers, MFC 76/1/542.
11. Raleigh and Jones, 1:411.
12. Autobiographical notes, p. 64, Trenchard Papers, MFC 76/1/61.
13. Boyle, 116.
14. Trenchard Papers, MFC 76/1/61; and Boyle, 115.
15. Major H. R. M. Brooke-Popham was leaving for France as Deputy-Assistant-Quartermaster-General.
16. Trenchard Papers, MFC 76/1/61.
17. Sykes, *Aviation in Peace and War*, 25.
18. Brooke-Popham's historical records at the Liddell Hart Centre for Military Archives contain nothing about this episode.
19. Raleigh and Jones, 1:283–6. Part of No. 4 Squadron was sent to Eastchurch.
20. 'Standing Orders for the Expeditionary Force', p. 9, Sykes Papers, MFC 77/13/ 19.
21. Norris, 52.
22. Lieutenant-Colonel L. A. Strange, *Recollections of an Airman* (London: Greenhill Books, 1989). Among the casualties, Lt S. Kene and mechanic Barlow of No. 3 Squadron crashed while flying from Netheravon to Dover.
23. RFC Diary, 10 March 1915, Air 1 1176/204/5/2595. 'Wing or Squadron Commanders will not make ascents in aeroplanes except by permission or order of RFC Headquarters.' Brancker to Henderson, 18 November 1914, Sykes Private Papers, 'it is undesirable that [training commanders] should habitually fly'.
24. Maurice Baring, *Flying Corps Headquarters 1914–1918* (London: Blackwood, 1968), 17.
25. Raleigh and Jones, 1:294. During the flight from Amiens to Maubeuge, 2nd Lt E. W. C. Perry and mechanic H. E. Parfitt crashed and were killed.
26. Ibid. When the BEF arrived at Maubeuge, de la Ferté recalled, 'We were rather sorry they had come . . . because up till that moment we had only been fired on by the French when we flew.' The RFC did not adopt its identification of blue, white and red roundels until October 1914.
27. Baring, 25.
28. Ibid. Apparently, the spy was a French woman who was caught because she twisted her ankle while fleeing.

29. Baring, 28.
30. Ibid., 31.
31. 'Per Ardua', Trenchard Papers, MFC 76/1/114. Baring's poem depicts the resentment the RFC felt toward the Army:

> At Juilly, in the evening calm and cool,
> The pilots doze in the deserted school;
> And some are bathing in a shaded pool.
> All of a sudden a scare!
> 'The Germans are here, and there and here.'
> The Commander-in-Chief must away
> As quick as he may;
> But the RFC
> Must wait patiently
> For the morning light,
> And are not to land at night.
> But the night while they stand at arms steals by,
> Without disturbance from the enemy.

32. Raleigh and Jones, 1:334, 348.
33. Sykes, *Aviation in Peace and War*, 46. Sykes claimed that GHQ listened to RFC reconnaissance reports because the head of the intelligence section, Colonel Macdonogh, 'was our firm ally'. Also, Raleigh and Jones, 1:316–22. The RAF's first official account of the war was the 'Synopsis of British Air Effort During the War', a document written by Sykes' Air Staff immediately after the Armistice and sanctioned by him. It states, 'These squadrons played their part in the retreat from Mons and suffered heavy casualties both in personnel and machines . . .', 'Synopsis of British Air Effort During the War', April 1919, Air 8/13. According to the official history, flyers from No. 4 Squadron spotted Kluck's 1st Army swinging to the south-east on 31 August. Having engaged the Germans and now aware of their strength, the BEF commander Sir John French ordered a retreat until 3 September, when he decided to hold fast. Aerial observations on 4 September revealed that Kluck had changed direction and was marching into a gap between the French Fifth and newly formed Sixth Armies.
34. Morrow, *The Great War in the Air*, 76. Morrow noted the reconnaissance debate between air power historians. Cooper, *Birth of Independent Air Power*, 18, concluded, 'There is little justification for believing that the air arm "had saved the army" at Mons, or "directly led to the victory of the Marne".' Divine, 50–2, stated the BEF took no action due to RFC reports, claiming that Sir John French's decision not to attack was based purely on the French retreat and that the staff at GHQ considered the RFC report 'to be somewhat exaggerated'. Collier, 50, stated that although the army did not depend upon RFC reports, those reports 'provided vital confirmation'.
35. Morrow, *The Great War in the Air*, 76. Morrow noted, 'It is ironic that Divine and Cooper give the RFC less credit for its performance than did the BEF command.'
36. 'Marches of German Troops, August 30 and September 2nd', RAF Staff College 2nd Course, RAFM, Accession No. C/5/1/1. The RAF Staff College compared RFC tracings of 1914 visual reconnaissances against actual known locations of German forces. Although sizes and compositions of forces often did not match, locations were accurate. Maps of 30 August recorded German forces moving south-westerly from Guise toward La Fère and from Peronne toward Montdidier. Maps of 31 August showed those same troops then swinging to the east above the Aisne. The enemy was not identified as to size, but flyers noted

whether they were infantry or cavalry, and whether they had heavy guns. The German IX and VII Corps, between La Fère and Noyon along the Oise, remained undetected because the RFC sent no missions to that area.

37. RFC War Diary, 4 March 1915, Air 1 1176/204/5/2595.
38. Raleigh and Jones, 1:298–99. The two pilots were Lieutenant Mapplebeck and Captain de la Ferté.
39. Sykes, *From Many Angles*, 127.
40. 'Military Aviation', Sykes Papers, MFC 77/13/14, a lecture presented to the Aeronautical Society, 26 February 1913, published in *Army Review*, July 1913, 129.
41. Raleigh and Jones, 1:303.
42. Norris, 56; and Sykes, *From Many Angles*, 125. Sykes recalled the RFC 'circus train', and the famous 'World's Best Appetizer' red van pilots used as a landing beacon.
43. Raleigh and Jones, 1:313; and Sykes, *From Many Angles*, 135.
44. Sykes, *From Many Angles*, 136.
45. Ibid.
46. Sykes, *Aviation in Peace and War*, 56; and Raleigh and Jones, 1:347.
47. Sykes, *Aviation in Peace and War*, 54. Sykes again used this same quote in *From Many Angles*, 127.
48. French's Mons despatch to Kitchener, 7 September 1914, in Cecil Chisholm, *Sir John French: An Authentic Biography* (London: Herbert Jenkins, 1915), 140–1.
49. Ibid.
50. Sir John French to K. [Kitchener], 17 October 1914, Sykes Private Papers.
51. Rawlinson to Kitchener, 17 October 1914, Kitchener Papers, PRO, 30/57/51/WB4.
52. 'RAF Staff College 2nd Course', RAFM, Accession No. C/5/1/1. On 29 August RFC reconnaissance reported the German Guard Cavalry Division as VII Corps. Two days later the German III and IV Corps were misidentified in Lassigny, and part of the BEF was reported as German troops. GHQ confirmed the errors.
53. Raleigh and Jones, 1:298. German General Hans von Zwehl, Commander of the 7th Reserve Corps, confirmed after the war that the Germans had received valuable information about the location of British forces when the aircraft flown by Lt V. Waterfall and Lt G.C.G. Bailey was shot down in German-held territory.
54. 'RAF Staff College 2nd Course', RAFM, Accession No. C/5/1/1.
55. Raleigh and Jones, 1:334.
56. Tactical reconnaissance referred to action in the local zone of the Army (i.e., along the trenches), whereas strategic reconnaissance meant sorties deeper into enemy territory. Strategic reconnaissance was initiated by GHQ through RFC HQ and flown from the HQ location. Tactical reconnaissance was initiated by the Army corps, approved by the appropriate RFC wing commander, and flown from the corps location. RFC HQ was still notified of all tactical reconnaissance missions.
57. Raleigh and Jones, 1:349. On 1 October 1914 No. 2 Squadron was ordered to attach to I Army Corps, No. 3 Squadron to II Army Corps, and No. 5 Squadron to III Army Corps. The wireless squadron, No. 4, was left at RFC HQ for strategic reconnaissance.
58. Speech to Royal Aeronautical Society, 26 February 1913, Sykes Papers, MFC 77/13/14. Divine, 55, stated that when fighting resolved into trench warfare, the RFC lost its *raison d'être* as an extension of the cavalry and had to reorganize.

Divine has overstated the impact of the trenches. Sykes did not predict a stalemated war, but in 1913 he did predict the reorganization that the RFC underwent in November 1914.

59. Sykes to Trenchard, 13 September 1914, Air 1 762/204/4/161.
60. Raleigh and Jones, 1:335–7; and Norris, 62.
61. Baring, 44.
62. Sykes to Trenchard, 13 September 1914, Air 1 762/204/4/161.
63. Barrington-Kennett to Trenchard, October 1914 (date not given), Air 1 762/204/4/161.
64. Boyle, 119.
65. Sykes to Trenchard, 13 September 1914, Air 1 762/204/4/161.
66. Raleigh and Jones, 1:407.
67. Gollin, 314; Baring, 44; and Raleigh and Jones, 1:412. Major Musgrave flew the first bombing mission on 18 September.
68. Sykes, *From Many Angles*, 142. No. 6 Squadron was mobilized in 24 hours and sent to Ostend to help the British Marine Brigade at Antwerp.
69. Raleigh and Jones, 1:347; and Sykes, *From Many Angles*, 141.
70. Baring, 53.
71. Raleigh and Jones, 1:353.
72. Ian Henderson to Lady Henderson, 5 August 1914, Henderson Papers, AC 71/12/423. Henderson's son was full of enthusiasm and oblivious of the dangers. Also, S. S. Saunders, sound recording, Reel No. 3, IWM sound recordings. Training at Brooklands was 'just a mob', with nobody in charge.
73. French to Kitchener, 17 October 1914, Sykes Private Papers.
74. Raleigh and Jones, 1:431–2; and Boyle, 121. Kitchener told Trenchard, 'When I come down to Farnborough I want to see machines flying in formation.' Trenchard responded, 'But, Sir, it cannot be done.'
75. Macmillan, 106.
76. Brancker to Henderson, 26 October 1914, Sykes Private Papers.
77. S. S. Saunders, sound recording, Reel No. 3, IWM sound recordings; and Baring, 46.
78. Raleigh and Jones, 1:430.
79. Boyle, 118.
80. Morrow, *The Great War in the Air*, 79.
81. Divine, 70.
82. French to Kitchener, 17 October 1914, Sykes Private Papers. 'Owing to the complete divergence between the methods and equipment of the Naval and Military Air Services, I do not consider that units of the Royal Naval Air Service would be suitable as reinforcements to this [RFC] Force.'
83. *Army Review*, July 1913, 129, Sykes Papers, MFC 77/13/14.
84. 'RFC 433 Organization of the Royal Flying Corps', 30 October 1914, Sykes Private Papers.
85. 'Organization of the Royal Flying Corps', Henderson Papers, AC 71/4/4. See also Cooper, 'A House Divided', 182.
86. Ibid., and Henderson to Brancker, 14 August 1914, Sykes Papers, MFC 77/13/22.
87. Henderson to Chief of the General Staff, 30 October 1914, Henderson Papers, AC 71/4/4.
88. Untitled, undated memorandum of meeting with Kitchener, where Sykes was most likely present, Sykes Private Papers. They agreed to the following plan:
    In the Field
    – Keep a GOC RFC in the field at RFC HQ

> – Keep the RFC general staff, operations and intelligence, also at RFC HQ
> – RFC to be divided into three wings with Lt-Col. Wing Commanders
>
> *In England*
> – Maintain the DGMA, colonel rank
> – One Wing at Netheravon
> – One Wing at Brooklands
> – One Wing at Farnborough.

89. Multiple reorganization letters between Henderson, Brancker, and French, Sykes Papers, MFC 77/13/22.
90. Brancker to Henderson, 26 October 1914, Sykes Papers, MFC 77/13/22.
91. Henderson to Army Council, 21 November 1914, Sykes Private Papers.
92. Sykes Private Papers; Sykes Restricted Papers, vol. 1, p. 62; and Sykes, *From Many Angles*, 525. Brancker advocated a decentralization where the commander in the field would be a staff officer rather than a director. Trenchard wanted to organize the RFC like Army or Divisional troops: 'definitely allocated to the large units of the field army, the squadron commanders being directly responsible to the high [Army] commanders.' Sykes (or possibly Henderson) wrote in the margin, 'No', 'This is unsound', and 'No, cohesion is essential still'. Murray's 'Organization' orders were published in the 'Royal Flying Corps Notes for Observers', Appendix A, and in November Sykes penned Murray's 'Notes on Air Reconnaissance'. They specifically established that air organizations might be 'temporarily allotted' or 'detached' to army units, but that final command of air resources remained with RFC HQ.
93. Brancker to Henderson, 26 October 1914, Sykes Private Papers; and Henderson to Brancker, 13 November 1914, Sykes Private Papers. Henderson bluntly informed Brancker and Trenchard that they and their associates back in England were trying to enhance their careers by recreating a peacetime air service.
94. Boyle, 123.
95. 'Dispatch from B. G. Henderson, GOC, RFC, 12 September 1914 to the Military Secretary British Army in the Field', Sykes Papers, MFC 77/13/20. Henderson was pleased with Sykes' performance:

> I have the honour to bring to the notice of the Field Marshall [*sic*]. . . . The excellent organization of the Royal Flying Corps in the field and its system of reconnaissance are largely due to Lieut. Colonel Sykes' admirable management in peace time. During the operations his knowledge, judgement and energy have been of greatest value. His rapid advancement would be for the good of the service.

96. 'Notes on the Superior Control and Coordination of the Aeronautical Services', November 1914, Sykes Restricted Papers, Vol. 1, p. 40.
97. Henderson to wife, 21 November 1914, Henderson Papers, AC 74/2/5(b). Henderson's reluctance to leave was an act. He had pushed hard for the transfer and was excited to go: 'I have got my orders and go off tomorrow to the 1st Division. Sorry to leave my baby, the Royal Flying Corps, but it can be weaned now.'
98. Telegram No. AA507 from GHQ to RFC, Sykes Restricted Papers, vol. 1. p. 54.
99. 'Routine Orders No. 90' by Col. F. H. Sykes, Commanding Royal Flying Corps In the Field, 29 November [n.d., probably 1914], Sykes Restricted Papers, vol. 1, p. 56.
100. Sykes Restricted Papers, vol. 1, p. 1 (second item 1 – these repeat at the end of the volume).
101. Trenchard to Sykes, 2 December 1914, Sykes Papers, MFC 77/13/22; and Air

Pub.956, 75, RAFM, Accession No. 001525. Trenchard wanted to be in charge of his own supplies and to be attached to the Army, not handcuffed to the RFC HQ.

102. Joubert de la Ferté, 32; and Divine, 70–1.

103. Boyle, 125, wrote that Sampson claimed that 'Trenchard had acted in accordance with the correct but violent impulse of his nature, pulling down the roof on Sykes in the process'. There is no proof of this conjecture.

104. 'Appointments List No. 7', Sykes Papers, MFC 77/13/22; and 'Army "A" Form No. 464', 21 December 1914, Sykes Restricted Papers, vol. 1, p. 57.

105. 'Notes on the superior control and co-ordination of the Aeronautical Services', Sykes Restricted Papers, vol. 1, p. 40.

106. Brancker to Admiralty, 2 December 1914, Air 1/2561. The desperate Brancker pleaded with the Admiralty for some of their equipment after already suggesting that all Navy requests be placed on hold for three months so that the Royal Aircraft Factory could supply the RFC's needs.

107. Autobiographical notes, Salmond Papers, B2621, RAFM; and Cooper, 'A House Divided', 184 and 191.

108. Boyle, 141.

109. Beaverbrook, 223–4. In a letter to Lloyd George, Smuts wrote:

> My Dear Prime Minister, Macready has been consulted about Sykes. His position as A.G. to [Sir John] French at the time when the Sykes-Henderson trouble occurred gives him authority in the matter. He has no doubt whatever that Sykes is the best man to appoint, and I have accordingly told Rothermere to have him appointed without further delay.

110. RFC War Diary, 28 November 1914 to 2 February 1915, Air 1 1176/204/5/2595; and Raleigh and Jones, 1:435. Sykes helped to establish three types of reconnaissance to correspond with the RFC reorganization: corps reconnaissance over the trenches, Army reconnaissance within a 20-mile zone of each Army, and long-range strategic reconnaissance for GHQ. See Sykes, *From Many Angels*, 145.

111. Raleigh and Jones, 1:411.

112. NMM, ADL/2/1/36.

113. 'Offence versus Defence in the Air', p. 6, Trenchard Papers, 76/1/73.

114. Sykes, *From Many Angles*, 151. Lord Roberts had also visited on 11 November, when he caught a fatal case of pneumonia.

115. Sykes to 2 [Ethel], 3 December 1914, Sykes Private Papers.

116. Sykes, *From Many Angles*, 152.

117. Ibid. The War Diary noted that the enemy 'invariably beat immediate retreat when chased'.

118. 'Notes on Air Reconnaissance', Sykes Private Papers. For example, one of the new categories was 'destructive' reconnaissance.

119. RAF Staff College 2nd Course, RAFM, Accession No. C/5/1/1, Appendix 2; and Wing Commander Sir Archibald James sound recording, Reel No. 2, IWM sound recordings, who stated visual reconnaissance 'was a pretty useless pastime'. Without cameras airmen had to fly below 1,500 ft at a time when ground fire was lethal up to 3,000 ft.

120. RFC War Diary, Air 1 1176/204/5/2595. According to the Diary, 6 March 1915, was when Lieutenants Moore-Brabazon and Campbell first used the 'special camera' they designed. Archibald James recalled a humorous incident when 'Brabs' forgot to change his film and took a double exposure of terrain and a white horse. Moore-Brabazon had been issued with Britain's first pilot's license in 1910 and a year earlier had captured public attention by carrying a live pig airborne in a Voison. After the war, Lord Brabazon became President of the Royal

Aeronautical Society.
121. Lord Brabazon to Lady Sykes, 4 October 1954, Sykes Private Papers.
122. Raleigh and Jones, 1:340. Major Musgrave's squadron, which became No. 9, was also the wireless telegraphy unit.
123. Norris, 116; Divine, 73; Boyle, 130; and Sykes, *From Many Angles*, 148–9.
124. Rawlinson to Kitchener, 12 February 1915, Kitchener Papers, PRO, 30/57/51/WB12.
125. Sykes, *From Many Angles*, 139.
126. Rawlinson to Kitchener, 25 November 1914, Kitchener Papers, 30/57/51/WB7; Raleigh and Jones, 1:350; and Bidwell and Graham, 101.
127. B. E. Smythies, 'Experiences during the War, 1914–1918', Air Pub 956, RAFM, Accession No. 001525. Smythies recalled that pilots abhorred loading their aircraft with 'gadgets'. 'An attitude of tolerant contempt was observable towards all officers engaged on technical work.' The experimental squadron was dissolved on 1 April 1915 when experimental flights were amalgamated into the Wings.
128. Commandant's lecture, RAF Staff College 2nd Course, RAFM, Accession No. C/5/1/1.
129. Baring, 87.
130. *London Gazette*, 16 February 1915; RFC War Dairy, February 1915, Air 1 1176/204/5/2595.
131. Baring, 89.
132. RFC War Diary, Air 1 1176/204/5/2595, calculations based on the number of times Sykes issued daily Operations Orders.
133. Operations Order, 1915, Sykes Papers, MFC 77/13/24; and RFC War Diary, Air 1 1176/204/5/2595. The Diary shows that air work was delegated according to Sykes' 29 November 1914 'Memorandum on new organization of the Royal Flying Corps'.
134. RFC War Diary, Air 1 1176/204/5/2595. Owing to an Icelandic storm that hit the European continent, one particular reconnaissance task took six days to complete.
135. Ibid., and 'Note for Air Committee', Montagu Papers, III/C/4, Liddell Hart Centre.
136. Boyle, 136–7. Apparently Haig mentioned to Trenchard, 'I've received a strong complaint about you. Colonel Sykes has protested to Sir John French that you incurred too many unnecessary casualties at Neuve Chapelle. I promised French I'd let you know, though this isn't a reprimand.'
137. RFC War Dairy, March 1915, Air 1 1176/204/5/2595.
138. Sykes, *From Many Angles*, 152–5.
139. 'Bomb Dropping Attacks', 15 February 1915, Air 1 921/204/5/889. Sykes divided aerial bombing into three categories: 1. 'Special missions' against vulnerable targets, 2. 'Attacks on local targets', and 3. 'Attacks on enemy communication and supply'.
140. Trenchard to Henderson; and bombing report, June 1915, Air 1 921/204/5/889.
141. B. H. Liddell Hart, *The Real War* (Boston, MA: Little, Brown, 1930), 178.
142. Sykes, *From Many Angles*, 153.
143. Trenchard Papers, MFC 76/1/61; Boyle, 139; and Norris, 140.
144. Morrow, *The Great War in the Air*, 114. Most authors have continued the story of Sykes' 'exile' without citing any source.
145. Sykes, *From Many Angles*, 155.
146. Lady Hamilton Diary, 1 August 1915, Hamilton Papers, 44, Reel No. 2, Liddell Hart Centre.

4

Maritime Air Power:
Gallipoli to 1916

Sykes' experience with naval flying in support of joint Army and Navy operations in the Dardanelles was disastrous and certainly a low point in his military career. He failed to appreciate the technological limits of air power against an overwhelming geography that made flying dangerous and only marginally helpful to military and naval operations. Sykes spent his entire Dardanelles command arguing for more support and trying to reorganize when it did not come. Early flyers had always anticipated contingencies, and western Europe provided natural landing sites that simply did not exist in the area of the Dardanelles. Flying from Imbros or Tenedos to Gallipoli was like flying across the English Channel – it was unforgiving. Sykes understood the danger but failed to appreciate that the situation led to poor aerial strategy. Aircraft were too susceptible to the harsh elements of wind, sand and heat; furthermore the RNAS was too far from Britain to be resupplied. Sykes made his first error when he was sent to the Dardanelles and argued for RNAS reorganization and more aerial support. He assumed that what was beginning to work over the Western Front should apply to maritime air power as well and, like many Dardanelles commanders, he was determined to prevent a stalemate at Gallipoli and force success. Capturing the peninsula would depend on artillery and morale, and Sykes was confident that air power could help with effective reconnaissance and gunnery spotting by courageous airmen. Sykes had not created the Gallipoli problem; it was deadlocked when he was sent there to help. Yet his contribution did not affect the outcome. Sykes experienced continual frustration, and his failure to appreciate the limits of air power contributed to the Gallipoli failure.

From July 1915 to January 1916 Sykes battled with the Admiralty, lack of supplies, harsh geography, resentment from Navy personnel and an uncooperative attitude on the part of Army and Navy gunnery officers. His trials began when he traveled to the Dardanelles in June 1915 to assess the role of air power.

When the Western Front stalled, the Asquith government decided to pursue a new strategy to attack Germany from the Mediterranean – in particular, by capturing the Gallipoli peninsula, thus enabling the bombardment of Constantinople to be carried out and, it was hoped, the surrender of Turkey to follow. Disregarding studies that had shown such an operation was unlikely to succeed, the Cabinet ordered some of Britain's top military personnel to command the campaign. That Sykes was selected to join that group indicates that he was not fired from France, as Henderson and Trenchard liked to think, but was chosen to clear up air power problems that had developed under RNAS Wing Commander C. R. Samson.

The primacy of Sykes' command is confirmed by several issues. Commodore Murray F. Sueter, Director of the Naval Air Department, wrote to inform Sykes that the First Lord of the Admiralty and the War Minister had selected Sykes to inspect naval air in the Dardanelles and to consult both General Sir Ian Hamilton, GOC Mediterranean Expeditionary Force (MEF), and Samson.[1] Someone with Sykes' abilities was needed to review the air situation at Gallipoli because fighting there was not proceeding well.[2] Naval operations on 18 March 1915 had failed to force the Straits, and the Navy had telegraphed back that they needed more aerial help to improve their shooting.[3] The Army's landings at Helles on the tip of the peninsula and Anzac (Australian and New Zealand Army Corps) Cove to the north (see Appendix 3) on 25 April 1915 had left troops stranded near the beaches.[4] Few RNAS reconnaissance or gunnery-spotting missions from February to April had been successful, and during the 25 April landings RNAS machine-gun units had helped the operation more than any aerial activity.[5] Sykes was to study air power and report by telegraph 'briefly' regarding the types of aircraft, organization and transport needed. In addition, he was to report, in person, anything of a confidential nature.[6] In other words, the Admiralty was unhappy with the aerial situation and believed that the problems might be due to poor leadership.

'Sammy' Samson was a courageous flyer, but well known for his occasional lack of tact and unco-operative attitude. When visitors, regardless of rank, would walk across the airfield at 3rd Wing to reach his office, he would yell at them with a megaphone: 'Get off my bloody aerodrome!'[7] The RNAS needed more professional command in the Dardanelles, and hence Sykes' assignment came from the highest levels. He was told that he would be given total co-operation – a promise that would be unfulfilled by Samson, the Fleet or the Admiralty.

The official request for Sykes' services came on 25 May 1915, when the Admiralty asked the War Office to release him.[8] This was at the height of Naval chaos – the famous 'departure of the titans' when Churchill and Sir John Fisher resigned their positions.[9] The War Office concurred with the Admiralty's request for Sykes and on 26 May notified him that he was at the disposal of the Lords Commissioners of the Admiralty.[10] Sykes remained a Wing Commander for a week, replaced as Chief of Staff in France by Brooke-Popham. In early June Sykes traveled from London to Marseilles, where he waited two days for a ship to Malta, and, from there, a destroyer bound for Mudros Bay on Lemnos Island.[11] His journey aboard HMS *Agamemnon* was dangerous due to the threat of German submarines, but Sykes arrived without mishap on 24 June.[12]

Sykes spent the next six days talking to Army and Navy commanders, inspecting aerial operations, and participating in aerial reconnaissance in a kite balloon flown off HMS *Manica* to support the gunnery attacks on Chanak by HMS *Lord Nelson*.[13] He visited the Army at Helles and the Anzacs and discussed their predicament with his friend, Lieutenant-General William R. Birdwood, GOC Anzac Corps.[14] On 9 July Sykes sent his assessment back to Britain: the RNAS needed to be reorganized, relocated and strengthened.[15] Sykes reported that the need for aerial reconnaissance was 'very real and urgent', and he intimated that, with adequate support, the RNAS at Gallipoli could help turn the campaign into a success.[16]

Sykes' assessment was biased by two influences: his Army background and his Western Front experiences. He requested Army aircraft rather than naval types, which predictably aroused immediate animosity from Samson and other RNAS officers who thought their service and machines were superior to anything in the RFC.[17] Sykes stated openly that he based his reorganization ideas on what he had seen in France – specifically, that the RNAS needed an HQ located as close as possible to GHQ, which was at Imbros. Just as he had designed aerial intelligence in France, Sykes wanted strategic reconnaissance requests to come from GHQ to RNAS HQ.

Sykes recognized that the air units were too separated from each other, too distant from their work areas, and lacked central control. Hence, according to Sykes, the most urgent need was to move the RNAS from Tenedos to Kephalos, on the island of Imbros, 6 miles away which would reduce the flying time to Gallipoli by one-third.[18] Sykes' recommendation made logistical sense, but it slighted Samson, who had built the aerodrome at Tenedos, most probably because of its more favorable winds.[19] Not only were Sykes' concepts of aerial reconnaissance in the Dardanelles a mirror image of what he had recently accomplished in France, many of the sentences in his report were taken direct from his earlier documents, such as 'RFC Notes for Observers'. He wanted to establish the Western Front model of an aerial intelligence system; but he had to apply it to both the Navy and the Army.

Sykes tried to eliminate the inefficiency that was hurting the RNAS's effectiveness. Joint Army–Navy aerial operations could work only with co-operation rather than through traditional competition, and hence Sykes advocated a co-ordinated effort and rejected several options: the RNAS would not be split and attached to the Army and the Navy, and an RFC wing would not be sent to work with the Army. Sykes called for the RNAS to support both services via a central RNAS HQ commanded by personnel receptive to Army and Navy needs.[20] Finally, co-operation would be impossible without standardized technologies. The RNAS had 11 seaplanes of five different types and three different engines; as well as 13 aeroplanes of five different types and six different engines.[21] This was an impossible situation, from the pilots' point of view as well as that of the mechanics. His analysis and report complete, Sykes returned to London on 12 July. His Gallipoli mission, however, had just begun.

Due to the nature of his report and his recommendation that RNAS operations required strong central leadership, Sykes had justified a position for himself at Gallipoli.[22] On 24 July the Admiralty appointed Sykes to HMS *President* as an 'additional' with the temporary rank of Colonel, 2nd Commandant, Royal Marines. Sykes' rank at this point became complex to say the least. In order to command RNAS units he was made a Wing Captain in the Royal Navy with three years seniority as a Captain. He was to assume the position held by Samson, who had been commanding No. 3 Squadron and was less than eager to see Sykes return.[23] That Sykes was placed above Samson and, as a Navy captain, ranked above all Army colonels once again shows that Sykes had not been banished from France. Yet, he was on a collision course with trouble.

Sykes departed London on 24 July for Marseilles but was detained temporarily on the way to Dover when his driver collided head-on with another automobile. The accident and subsequent late departures delayed Sykes' return to Imbros until 6 August, the day 10th and 11th Divisions landed at Suvla Bay with little aerial help. Sykes was suffering from his accident and was distressed that he had missed the opportunity to participate in one of the largest and least successful operations at Gallipoli. Forward Observing Officer K. R. Park noted that the Army was completely uninformed about air operations, as it had been throughout Samson's command. There was minimal air co-operation with infantry, artillery or naval guns at Suvla, where the attack in support of Anzac stalled.[24]

By 10 August the IX Corps Commander Lieutenant-General Frederick W. Stopford complained to Hamilton that he lacked water, that his poorly trained men were exhausted, and that artillery support had been inadequate.[25] This report matched Hamilton's similar habitual preoccupation with poor supplies of troops and ammunition.[26] It is obvious from Stopford's communications that lack of intelligence, more than lack of water, killed his mission.[27] Although the RNAS had reconnoitered the bay before the landing and had ascertained the absence of Turkish troops, Stopford did not use this information to his advantage.[28] Preoccupied with issues other than capturing Chocolate Hill (the high ground), Stopford forfeited his early opportunities, which led to later disaster.[29] The Army pattern of not properly using intelligence remained, and it contributed to the tragedy and failure at Gallipoli. Yet the Dardanelles Commission overlooked the poor use of air power – specifically of reconnaissance – as a contributory factor.[30]

Army commanders and artillery officers were reluctant to work with the RNAS even though they needed help with range and azimuth. Some gunnery officers realized that aircraft could provide assistance with difficult shooting, particularly counter-battery work, but most noted that flyers were always flying home for tea. Airmen were unable to loiter long enough for artillery and guns to establish fire and then concentrate it accurately. As Park concluded, the fighting forces at Gallipoli perceived air power as 'a ragtime show'.[31]

It was under such circumstances that Sykes entered the battle. His focus was twofold: to establish a new RNAS site at Kephalos and to support the immediate operations. Stopford's IX Corps suffered continual defeat against reinforced Turkish positions, and the final attack on 20 August was no more successful. Sykes remained aboard one of the ships that provided fire control for part of the attack, but then went ashore to try to determine how aerial support might provide assistance.[32] According to Sykes, he could do little more than observe the failure that resulted in needless sacrifice.

Sykes' organizational efforts were more successful. Before his arrival, Samson's 3rd Wing had moved from Tenedos to Imbros and was becoming operational. With much improvisation, Sykes constructed the new RNAS HQ and a second aerodrome at Imbros, which was to accommodate 2nd Wing. Sykes also established a staff, which included installing one of his most reliable friends, P. R. C. Groves, as head of operations. The Navy tried to fulfill Sykes' request for reinforcements at the end of August with the arrival of 2nd Wing, commanded by Wing Commander E. L. Gerrard. It was a poor attempt, as many of the aircraft were either unfit for service or of a different type from those Sykes had requested.[33] Furthermore, aircraft had arrived with the wrong engines, engines had arrived with the wrong propellers, and all the equipment had arrived without proper tools for its assembly. Sykes realized at this point that he was at the receiving end of a serious supply problem.

His other obstacles, in addition to lack of supplies and the enemy, were climate, geography and antagonistic individuals.[34] Sand, wind and heat destroyed the few aircraft that made it from Britain undamaged. Sheds and tents were blown to pieces and provided little protection against the elements. In addition, all flights were over water, which caused certain destruction to aircraft forced down.[35] Besides damaging machines, the harsh climate took its toll of personnel as well. The sickness rate, owing largely to an intestinal illness Sykes called 'Gallipolitis', was worse than anything Sykes had experienced in France.[36] He noted that water was always in short supply and that flies, centipedes and scorpions were a constant menace. Swarms of flies were so thick that they turned the tent poles black.[37]

Sykes' reception by the Navy was no more hospitable, particularly from the displaced Samson, who had circulated anti-Sykes propaganda. Sueter wrote to Admiral Keyes on 31 July 1915:

> I am writing a line to you to ask a favour and that it is [*sic*] to do your best to make our efforts with the air units under Col. Sykes a success. We are very lucky indeed to obtain his services, as the Navy cannot spare us any officers with organizing powers. Commander Samson is I think our bravest flyer, but he isn't much good at organizing anything big. Therefore may I suggest that you send for Samson and inform him that he has got to make the show run under Col. Sykes. We do not want any rows in the air service, all we want is to try and make ourselves useful to the Fleet and the Army. War caught us a couple of years too soon. An extra year or two would have made a lot of difference in the performance of our machines.[38]

There is no evidence that Keyes provided Sueter with the favor he had requested. Keyes and most of the other Navy personnel at Gallipoli never recognized Sykes' naval rank, and by the time he left Gallipoli, Keyes complained to his wife that RNAS air supremacy had slipped to the Germans – for which he held Sykes responsible.[39]

Shortly after Sykes' arrival at Imbros, Vice-Admiral J. M. de Robeck, Commanding Officer of the Eastern Mediterranean Squadron, wrote to Admiral Sir Henry Jackson, First Sea Lord: 'I hope [Sykes] and Samson will work together. There is rather an unfortunate publication of the Air Department which had appeared here; it contains private letters from Samson criticising Sykes.' Rear-Admiral C. L. Vaughn-Lee, who replaced Sueter as Director of Air Services, noted: 'It is unfortunate that references are made to Col. Sykes. But at that time it was not known that Col. Sykes, a Military Officer, would be placed over the head of the Senior RNAS Officer in

Mediterranean.'[40] Sykes clearly had naval guns aimed in his direction before his arrival. He had experienced such problems in the past, and it appeared that he was destined for a repeat performance at Gallipoli. He recalled that Samson was bitter about being replaced but loyal enough to the RNAS so that he provided support until the Navy recalled him from Gallipoli in November.[41]

Disregarding issues of personality, Sykes was intent on reorganization: particularly the move to Imbros and the construction of facilities. His task was similar to building a small village, complete with hospital, dining and lodging facilities, an airfield, and various huts for staff offices, as well as communication and meteorological sections.[42] The officers and men ate in the wardroom. Sykes built no bar. Captain Bremner recalled that many of the flyers lived in aircraft packing cases: wooden boxes measuring ten by seven by seven feet.[43] Although the climate was harsh, there were advantages in not being aboard ship. The discipline was less formal, and there was room to walk about.

Sykes divided the reconnaissance mission into four geographic areas: Helles, Anzac and Suvla, Dardanelles and Asiatic shore, the Gulf of Xeros and areas to the north. Functionally, he devoted half of the aerial effort to gun spotting for ships (two-thirds by land-based aircraft and one-third by seaplanes and kite balloons), and half to other work, such as mapping and tactical reconnaissance for Army operations. He chose not to separate over-water aerial operations (such as anti-submarine spotting) from those missions over land.[44] The RNAS was to co-ordinate all aerial endeavors equally in close co-operation with the Fleet and GHQ.[45] Sykes also reorganized the Royal Naval Armoured Car Division and fought to take RNAS men back from Army machine-gun duties, using them as they had been trained: as aircraft mechanics.[46]

His advantage in August 1915 was that enemy air power was negligible, so the RNAS could work as long as the weather was not prohibitive. In addition, although de Robeck was not the air power advocate his predecessor Admiral Carden had been, he did support Sykes' reorganization.[47] As Sykes built a more effective air service, however, enemy air power grew as well.[48]

As Sykes assessed his situation in autumn 1915, he identified two primary RNAS objectives: to serve as an intelligence and communication link to the Fleet and the Army, and to help prevent Turkish reinforcements from driving the MEF from the Gallipoli peninsula. His first task required an effective aerial reconnaissance system similar to the one he had developed and implemented in France. He had initiated that process with the RNAS move next to GHQ at Imbros, and he further enhanced the system by establishing a standard reporting procedure and installing telephone lines.[49] Sykes' second objective – aerial protection – was paramount, and he initiated interdiction operations against enemy railways, roads and bridges, and targeted docks to such effect that the enemy was forced to use land supply routes exclusively. Due to his limited aerial resources, he advocated multirole aircraft and missions rather than specialization, so that flyers would reconnoiter and bomb at the same time.[50]

In addition to his primary objectives, Sykes knew he had to maintain aerial supremacy. The Turks were beginning to attack GHQ from the air, and Sykes was forced to face an issue he had tried to avoid in Britain: home defense. In this case it was island defense. The MEF HQ told Kitchener that Turkish aircraft had attacked the aerodrome at night and complained that such attacks would continue 'unless Sykes in the meantime can sufficiently alarm them by retaliatory attacks to keep them off'.[51] Sykes established air-defense procedures, including an IFF system to prevent hostile fire from friendly ground and naval forces.[52] He again applied lessons he had learned in France the previous year.

Sykes understood the tactical RNAS mission at hand – to support the joint operation at Gallipoli – but in terms of air power he was thinking strategically. Hence Sykes' correspondence to the Vice-Admiral indicated his desire to build an air service in the Dardanelles that would serve as the nucleus of an entire Mediterranean air force. He advocated inter-Allied co-operation so that air power could be established at a number of strategic locations: Malta, Gibraltar, Alexandria, Cyprus and, of course, Imbros. Sykes promoted experimentation to prove air power's legitimacy in a maritime environment, and he hailed several RNAS accomplishments as aerial firsts: the first aircraft-delivered torpedo by C. H. K. Edmonds, the longest night flight by Flight Commander J. R. W. Smith-Pigott, the first demonstration of air-fleet co-operation, and the first use of an independent air arm.[53] The RNAS experimented with parachute bombs, machine-gun fire from aircraft, flechette dropping and time-fuse bombing with ten-foot cables and grapnels designed to destroy anti-submarine nets.[54]

In terms of the Gallipoli campaign, Sykes expected a fight that would last at least through to the end of 1916.[55] Hence his continual request was for more aircraft and personnel. He was trying to build a long-term air service, not one for a campaign that would terminate within four months. Part of his strategic plan was to bomb Constantinople. The Turkish capital was the objective behind the Gallipoli campaign, and damaging the city would sap Turkish morale and interdict supply lines. In addition, such a mission would demonstrate air power and promote the RNAS image throughout the Mediterranean, and, more importantly, back at the Western Front.

Sykes' plan, however, was rejected by the Navy, along with his requests for a large air force.[56]

Sykes was upset that the Admiralty would support neither his grand aspirations nor his immediate needs. He complained to the Vice-Admiral that he was being forced to fly machines in roles for which they were ill-suited, and he rationalized that lack of support was keeping short-term RNAS aerial operations from achieving success in the maritime environment.[57] In particular, the air service was inefficient, which Sykes believed was the ultimate sin in war-fighting.[58] The Admiralty sent no trained observers, so Sykes had to find volunteers and train them at Kephalos. He admitted that this system was marginal and was responsible for some of the difficulties between the RNAS and artillery officers.[59] RNAS flyers did provide valuable reconnaissance in terms of photography and in the form of maps of terrain and enemy locations. Yet this assistance arrived too late. After Suvla there were no more joint operations to capture the peninsula.

In addition, aerial bombing was insignificant and spotting for guns ineffective. Sykes fought to ease bureaucratic confusion caused by poor air-to-ground communication. He tried to quell petty inter-service animosities that detracted from effective spotting for artillery and naval guns.[60] Yet RNAS flyers, including Sykes, did not realize that many of the bombardment failures were due to the guns being technologically inadequate to destroy trenches or batteries, regardless of aerial help.[61] Sykes personally flew reconnaissance missions over the peninsula, and he recognized the difficulties flyers had in providing help to the Army and the Navy. His only answer to overcome those geographical difficulties was to create a sufficiently large and technologically capable air service, a goal the Admiralty was unwilling to pursue.[62] He was supposed to have a force of two wings, which was the equivalent of 60 aircraft, 36 pilots and 24 observers. In reality, however, his average strength was 23 aircraft capable of flying, and 17 pilots and ten observers healthy enough to fly.[63]

Week after week Sykes reminded his Navy superiors that not a single one of his requests had been fulfilled and he eventually resorted to sending a messenger in person back to London – Lieutenant L. V. Guest, his officer in charge of *matériel*.[64] Guest failed to help Sykes' supply problem, and Sykes was censured for sending him to the Admiralty without going through proper channels, even though he had received sanction from the Vice-Admiral.[65] Sueter wrote to Sykes from London that he had tried to convince the leaders in Paris that the air service was valuable in the Mediterranean, but that he faced continual obstruction. Sueter wrote, 'It is no use. They *do not* want to know how useful you and your command can be.'[66]

Increasingly frustrated with his situation, Sykes wrote to Churchill in November, again asking for supplies.[67] Churchill was displaced and relatively unemployed at the time, but he had been the primary promoter of the Gallipoli campaign and still had influence. Sykes was convinced the campaign would succeed. He wrote that 'the pendulum is about to swing this way', and he noted that he had ample evidence from photographs, enemy prisoners and his personal observations that aerial bombing was effective. Sykes emphasized that the enemy was concentrated and vulnerable, but soon the opportunity would be lost, particularly if the enemy received reinforcements before any coming to the RNAS. Sykes then jumped the chain of command, arguing that he wanted permission and supplies to be able to bomb Constantinople continuously.

He was concerned not only with the success of the campaign and the part the RNAS would play but wanted to ensure that he remained the sole commander of that air service. He told Churchill that most likely the Army would want to send out an RFC wing and asked for Churchill's help in preventing such a move, arguing that it would produce an inefficient situation of dual control. Sykes confided that before Gallipoli he had out-ranked other RFC wing commanders in France, who had been promoted since to brigadier-general rank. Hence, if brought out, they would be his superiors, which, he stated, would 'take the heart out of his unit' at Kephalos.[68] Frustration and personal ambition had clouded Sykes' judgement and breached his professionalism. In retrospect, however, the addition of an RFC wing might not have made much difference. The Gallipoli situation simply did not favor the use of aircraft with infant technological capabilities.

Winter weather arrived with blizzards of snow, hail and sand, causing considerable damage to the remaining RNAS assets. Sykes lost many of his most capable flyers and leaders, including Samson, who had been recalled to London. Parliament debated the options at Gallipoli, but few airmen, sailors or soldiers maintained Sykes' idealistic belief that the operation was about to succeed.[69] Hamilton had been ordered home in late October, and his replacement, General Sir Charles Monro, immediately recommended a withdrawal. An evacuation presented risks, but a winter at Gallipoli would be disastrous. Sykes abhorred the thought of failure, in particular, a failure of air power. He determined that the RNAS could salvage its reputation by fighting in support of the retreat. He was eager to help. Sykes notified his wings that they were to concentrate all available aircraft at Imbros to assist the evacuation and strengthen Helles at the same time.[70] The two RNAS wings would co-operate in the effort until 3rd Wing was withdrawn, leaving 2nd Wing to assume all aerial responsibilities. Aircraft were not to be abandoned and all possible equipment and supplies were to be salvaged for return to England.

General orders from the Navy for the evacuation of Suvla and Anzac on 18 and 19 December arrived at RNAS HQ on 12 December, but they contained sparse references to air operations. Only in Part IV of Appendix F was the RNAS told: 'aircraft must endeavour to keep off those of the enemy who may be reconnoitring'.[71] Sykes' flyers were to avoid their usual activities that brought out enemy airmen. Instead they were to stand ready to launch in case the enemy attacked in mass. At each of the bays Sykes was to provide only one aircraft for reconnaissance.

Sykes disagreed with the orders. He argued that the RNAS should fly normal operations before the evacuation so that the enemy would not be suspicious, and he wanted a constant patrol of aircraft over the evacuation sites. The Navy sent a message on 16 December notifying Sykes that the Vice-Admiral would compromise. The RNAS could fly continuous patrols, but Sykes had to have aircraft available to defend against a large aerial attack if it came.[72]

Sykes disseminated his own orders to the RNAS that same day. He had agreed with GHQ on 14 December that the RNAS should concentrate flying to the east and the west of the lines to prevent enemy suspicions of covering operations.[73] Sykes' orders reflected his offensive posture, as they contained instructions to fly to the east, not to the west. Pilots from 2nd and 3rd Wings were to fly the strongest patrols possible in areas well forward of the evacuation sites, so that the Turks would not focus attention on the bays. Aircraft were to carry bombs which were to be used in appropriate situations against suitable targets, and at least one wireless-capable aircraft was to be airborne at all times. Patrol aircraft were not to be drawn from their areas by enemy aircraft, and the RNAS was to ensure that no enemy flyers slipped past the patrol areas to where the Army was embarking.[74]

A German report in the *Vossische Zeitung* confirms that these RNAS operations helped the evacuation to succeed beyond all expectations. According to an enemy observer, the night of the evacuation was clear and lit by a bright moon; however, Turkish artillery camps sounded alarms all night because of RNAS bombing and patrols. Those alarms continued into the morning, even though a thick white fog obscured visibility. The few bombs that fell on the enemy camps did no damage, but the British Army had departed from the beach without incident. The enemy considered the evacuation a 'masterpiece' of retreat strategy.[75]

The escape from Helles on 11 January was equally successful. Captain Bremner recalled that a few Turkish guns fired on the departing forces, but that the high explosive shells were ineffective compared with shrapnel. Bremner attributed the miraculous evacuation to British discipline and composure under fire.[76] Sykes, however, claimed that it was due to air power: 'Never was the paramount importance of command of the air more triumphantly vindicated than on this occasion.'[77] No doubt the success was due to a combination of factors, one of which was the role of aircraft flown by Sykes' disciplined airmen.

The Navy notified Sykes that at 1000 hours, 29 January 1916, he would be transported to Mudros *en route* to London.[78] Sykes' departure was fittingly turbulent. Heavy seas prevented the use of a gangway, and after a treacherous ride in a dinghy, he was nearly tossed off the rope ladder while trying to board ship.

Sykes and the RNAS had faced insurmountable obstacles: climate, geography, technology and bureaucratic fighting within the Admiralty and the War Cabinet that had allowed the Gallipoli effort to wither on the vine.[79] Sykes had fought to make the campaign a great aerial demonstration, but in his final report he admitted that the RNAS was fortunate the evacuation had not involved a fight, owing to the few remaining RNAS resources.[80] Although the operation to capture the Gallipoli peninsula was dead, the RNAS continued bombing operations against the Turks and maritime air power remained in the Mediterranean for the remainder of the war. In April the RNAS finally realized Sykes' strategic dream when it bombed Adrianople and Constantinople.[81]

The Admiralty ended Sykes' commission as Wing Captain on 13 March 1916 and notified the War Office that he had served honorably and deserved promotion and recognition.[82] Such accolades did little to raise Sykes' spirits. His ambitions had stalled and he was unemployed. He had time to evaluate the recent disaster. Gallipoli had torn holes in Army Staff College dicta that moral courage could overcome physical obstacles. The world's most capable navy had failed to sail to its objective, and it had failed to provide adequate support to the Army. Sykes and the RNAS had failed as well. He had promised to organize a maritime air service that would provide significant help to the Army and the Navy; yet such aerial assistance never materialized due to lack of supplies and poor aircraft capability in the Gallipoli campaign.

Sykes had learned that what he did successfully in one arena might not work in another. The Dardanelles experience frustrated Sykes, for it showed that more equipment was not always the answer, particularly when war was fought where supply lines were overextended. He had learned that technology had to be adapted properly. Early aircraft were no more capable of withstanding high winds and sand than early tanks would be able to swim the deep mud of Flanders 16 months later. Revolutions often involve a process of failures and needless sacrifice, and Gallipoli was clearly a setback in the air revolution. Sykes now slipped into the obscurity of the War Office general staff for two years.

NOTES

1. Sueter to Sykes, 12 June 1915, Sykes Restricted Papers, vol. I, p. 65.
2. Sykes' earlier studies of French aviation and German maneuvers would have made him well known as a capable officer for the Gallipoli task.
3. Liddell Hart, 151; and Kennett, *The First Air War*, 181. According to Kennett, Commander of the Ottoman Air Force, Hauptmann Erich Serno spotted the Allied fleet trying to sail up the Straits on 18 March and sounded the alarm. That action may not have had much significance considering that *Bouvet, Inflexible* and *Irresistible* were lost to mines, not coastal battery fire. Following the naval failure, the British decided to pursue a ground attack on the peninsula. It was Admiral Carden who had tried to force the Straits and had called for the aerial help that eventually resulted in Sykes' assignment.
4. 'Orders for Combined Operations', 12 April 1915, Memorandum No. 49L., National Maritime Museum (NMM), HMP/3. Part of the 25 April difficulties stemmed from poor intelligence. Landing parties had few maps of the peninsula, and the ones they had were minimal. For example, there were no terrain indications on the maps except one river and one hill for the entire Gallipoli peninsula. The Turkish trench lines were simply drawn as two parallel lines from Gaba Tepe to Helles – not accurate and without detail. Orders for the landing show that the Navy tried to recognize air power by including Samson's force; yet his mission was just observation.
5. Chamier, 41–2.
6. Sueter to Sykes, 12 June 1915, Sykes Restricted Papers, vol. I, p. 65.
7. Captain F. D. H. Bremner sound recordings, Reel No. 7, IWM sound recordings.
8. Admiralty to War Office, 25 May 1915, Sykes Restricted Papers, vol. I, p. 65.
9. First Lords Churchill and Fisher resigned as a result of the Dardanelles failures and were replaced by Balfour and Sir Henry Jackson, respectively.
10. Director of Military Aeronautics to Sykes, 26 May 1915, Sykes Restricted Papers, vol. I, p. 65.
11. Orders to Mudros from Rear-Admiral Russell, Sykes Papers, MFC 77/13/27.
12. Sykes to Hamilton, summary report, 22 November 1919, Sykes Papers, MFC 77/13/48.
13. Sykes, *From Many Angles*, 159–63. General Sir Ian Hamilton was GOC of the MEF, Vice-Admiral J. M. de Robeck was the Naval Commander in Chief and his Chief of Staff was Commodore Sir Roger Keyes.
14. Sykes Diary, 26 June 1915, *From Many Angles*, 162.
15. 'Secret Report', Sykes to Admiralty, 9 July 1915, Sykes Papers, MFC 77/13/28; also Cablegram No. 825, 9 July 1915, Sykes Restricted Papers, vol. II (no page number). Sykes asked for the following:

    1. As many BE2c aircraft as possible
    2. 36 Maurice Farman aircraft with 80 to 100hp engines
    3. Spare aircraft of each type
    4. 80 aircraft mechanics
    5. 6 photographers with appropriate equipment
    6. 24 Lewis or Vickers aerial machine-guns
    7. Signal lamps, tents, and sheds

      8. 6 motor boats
      9. 8 scout seaplanes

16. 'Report on RNAS Units and the Aerial Requirements of the Naval and Military Forces at the Dardanelles', 9 July 1918. Sykes Restricted Papers, vol. II (no page number). Sykes' formal 28-page report was anything but brief.

17. Bremner sound recording, Reel No. 7, IWM sound recordings. Bremner recalled that if Samson interviewed a candidate he did not like, he would advise the candidate to join the RFC.

18. 'Summary of Events and Precis of Correspondence during the Process of Reorganization of the RNAS, EMS, 1915', Sykes Restricted Papers, vol. II. Sykes noted that the 18 miles' distance from Tenedos to Helles had plagued reconnaissance work during Army landings. Earlier, aircraft had been able to land at Helles, but once Turkish batteries were in place that option was eliminated.

19. R. D. Layman, 'Over the Wine-Dark Sea, Aerial Aspects of the Dardanelles/Gallipoli Campaign', 5–40, in *Over the Front*, Vol. 9, No. 1, Spring 1994, 28. Samson had arrived at the Dardanelles on 24 March and immediately had established an aerodrome on Tenedos. Layman noted that the winds at Kephalos were unfavorable for flying.

20. 'Report on RNAS Units and the Aerial Requirements of the Naval and Military Forces at the Dardanelles', 9 July 1915, Sykes Restricted Papers, vol. II (no page number), and Sykes Papers, MFC 77/13/28.

21. Sykes to Hamilton, summary report, 22 November 1919, Sykes Papers, MFC 77/13/48.

22. This was deliberate on the part of Sykes. Not only had he reported recommendations, he had notified the Admiralty that, due to the urgency of the situation, he had initiated changes already.

23. Admiralty to Sykes, 24 July 1915, Sykes Restricted Papers, vol. I, p. 69. A subsequent letter, 14 September, notified Sykes that, effective 24 July, he was a temporary Wing Captain in the Royal Navy. Also see Sykes, *From Many Angles*, 170; and James, 56. According to James, Samson predicted that Sykes' arrival at Gallipoli would mean simply another carbon copy of each report.

24. 'Experiences in the War, 1914–1918', Staff College Essay, Air Pub 956, RAFM, Accession No. 001525.

25. Stopford to Hamilton, 10 August 1915, Hamilton Papers, 17/7/32/6, Liddell Hart Centre for Military Archives.

26. Hamilton to Kitchener, 10 June 1915, Hamilton Papers, 5/4.

27. Stopford to Hamilton, 14 August 1915, Hamilton Papers, 17/7/32/9.

28. Sykes, *From Many Angles*, 166. Sykes stated that Capt. A. A. Walser made accurate sketches and provided aerial photographs during pre-Suvla reconnaissances.

29. Peter Meade, *The Eye in the Air* (London: HMSO, 1983), 113; and Sykes, *From Many Angles*, 167. According to many historians including Sykes, RNAS flyers warned Stopford that Turkish troops were massing on the high ground, but he disregarded that intelligence and failed to advance for 24 hours.

30. *Final Report of the Dardanelles Commission*, Cmd 371, Hamilton Papers, 16/11. The Commission noted that Field Service Regulations, 1914, Part 1, Chap. IX, placed emphasis on preliminary complete reconnaissance. Yet the fact that the Army disregarded this issue during the Suvla and Anzac attacks was rationalized on the basis that 'local conditions at Anzac and Suvla did not admit of the thorough reconnaissance prescribed in this chapter.' The Commission obviously did not consider aerial reconnaissance to be capable of determining Turkish locations.

31. 'Experiences in the War, 1914–1918', Staff College essay, Air Pub 956, RAFM, Accession Number 001525, 93; and *Final Report of the Dardanelles Commission*, Cmd 371, Hamilton Papers, 16/11.
32. Sykes, *From Many Angles*, 167.
33. Layman, 28; and Sykes, *From Many Angles*, 175. Arriving with Gerrard were 16 pilots, 200 support personnel and 22 aeroplanes. Of these aircraft 12 were Caudron biplanes or Morane Parasols, both types unsuitable for maritime aerial work.
34. Sykes to Vice-Admiral de Robeck (who replaced Admiral Carden), 21 October 1915, Sykes Private Papers. Sykes recalled his three greatest physical obstacles: climate (sand, dust, wind and heat); distance from England (difficulty keeping supplied); and over-water flying.
35. Memorandum entitled 'Résumé of Operations and Recommendations Made,' Sykes Private Papers; 'Report by Wing Commander C. R. Samson on the Work of No. 3 Wing, R. N. Air Service, 23 November 1915,' Air 1/664; and 'Standing Orders for No. 3 Wing by Wing Commander C. R. Samson', 4 December 1915, Air 1/7. Engine failures meant aircraft loss. The RNAS did not have a tug boat with a derrick, so any aircraft that survived ditching could not be lifted from the water. Any aircraft that landed on the peninsula were to be burned immediately.
36. Sykes, *From Many Angles*, 173. Owing to extreme heat, sun, lack of water and flies, the sickness rate (pilots who could not fly) was 35 per cent.
37. Kitchener Papers, Public Record Office (PRO), 30/57/63/WL/84. Most documents from the Dardanelles note that lack of water was one of the most serious problems of the Gallipoli campaign. Not only did soldiers have little water on the peninsula, but Sykes had no water source at Kephalos.
38. Sueter to Keyes, 31 July 1915, *Keyes Papers, 1914–1918*, ed. Paul G. Halpern (London: Navy Records Society, 1972), letter no. 95, 1:173.
39. Keyes to Wife, 16 January 1916, *Keyes Papers*, letter no. 143, 1:328. Keyes wrote that Colonel Sykes had failed to keep RNAS flyers from getting killed by Germans: 'The Germans were top dog. Which they never were when Davis, Samson, Marix, poor Collet, etc, were here.' This, of course, was after the evacuation, and most of Sykes' men and material, including himself, were departing the area.
40. Roskill, 223–4.
41. Sykes, *From Many Angles*, 170.
42. Sykes Papers, MFC 77/13/38. Specifically, Sykes built 2 hospitals, 4 officers' quarters, 3 quarters for other ranks, 3 supply buildings, 19 other buildings, a rail system into the water to pull aircraft and a road.
43. Bremner sound recording, Reel No. 4, IWM sound recordings.
44. Sykes Memorandum [no date], Sykes Papers, MFC 77/13/36. Sykes wrote, 'It is quite impossible to distinguish what is Naval and what is an Army question where the air service is concerned . . . it is now hard to classify any duty that the air service is capable of carrying out as belonging to either one or the other.'
45. Sykes to Vice-Admiral, Eastern Mediterranean Squadron, 15 October 1915, Sykes Private Papers.
46. GHQ to War Office, Despatch 2205, 23 October 1915, Sykes Papers, MFC 77/13/33. Sykes was battling a decision made in London when Balfour replaced Churchill. Sueter had been demoted from Director of the Air Department to Superintendent of Aircraft Construction, which seriously jeopardized Sykes' strength with the Admiralty. In addition, Balfour had given all RNAS ancillary services to the War Office, and Sykes believed that he needed those services at Gallipoli more than the Army needed them. See Admiralty Letter C.E.8423,

1 September 1915, Montagu Papers, I/C/35, Liddell Hart Centre; and Divine, 78–9.

47. Sykes Papers, MFC 77/13/33.

48. Bulgaria entered the war on the side of Germany on 6 September 1915, and by the middle of the next month Turkey had an enhanced supply line via the Berlin–Constantinople Railway.

49. Sykes Papers, MFC 77/13/33. Sykes' system involved five different reports, all to be completed in triplicate, with two copies going to himself and one to remain with the aerial unit. He personally assessed and processed the information, sending it to the Army or the Navy as he determined appropriate. Likewise, Naval Intelligence and GHQ were to supply Sykes with 'all information at their disposal which may assist the work of the RNAS'.

50. 'Precis of Memorandum on Requirements of the RNAS' (n.d.), Sykes Private Papers.

51. Col. Birdwell to Kitchener, 20 September 1915, Kitchener Papers, PRO, 30/57/ 63/WL100; and undated/untitled memorandum, Sykes Papers, MFC 77/13/36.

52. Documents from the Dardanelles, 1915, Sykes Papers, MFC 77/13/33.

53. Documents from the Dardanelles, 1915, Sykes Papers, MFC 77/13/39; Sykes, *From Many Angles*, 174, 176, and 187; Jones, 2:64; and 'Report by Squadron Commander C. L. E. Malone, Commanding, HMS *Ben-My-Chree* to Director of the Air Department', 14 August 1915, Air 1/665. Edmonds's feat was on 11 August in the Gulf of Xeros against a ship that had been torpedoed previously and was aground. Kennett, in *The First Air War*, 45, disputed the claim that Edmonds's was the first torpedo launch, noting that Capt. Alessandro Guidoni of the Italian Navy dropped an 800lb torpedo in February 1914. The long-distance flight was the marginally successful mission to bomb the Kubli Burcas bridge in November 1915.

54. Sykes to Vice-Admiral, 17 November 1915, Sykes Papers, MFC 77/13/40.

55. Sykes to Vice-Admiral, 27 October 1915, and Documents from the Dardanelles, 1915, Sykes Papers, MFC 77/13/44. All of Sykes' programs were geared for 1916, including the construction of permanent facilities that would withstand the elements.

56. J. N. de Robeck to Samson, 18 September 1915, Sykes Papers, MFC 77/13/31. The Vice-Admiral rejected the Constantinople plan on the basis that it would not be effective, that it would present too great a risk, and that it would jeopardize the valuable work the RNAS was then performing.

57. Memorandum to Vice-Admiral, 21 October 1915, Sykes Private Papers.

58. Ibid. Sykes noted that weather and the enemy had made seaplanes, kite balloons and airships ineffective tools in the Dardanelles; yet without the aeroplanes he had requested he was forced to use these naval machines.

59. 'Minutes by Mr W. A. Medrow, of the Admiralty Secretariat, on 6 January 1916', in Roskill, 277–8; and 'Résumé of Operations and Recommendations Made', Sykes Private Papers. Sykes had to fight Admiralty bureaucracy when he wanted to give his observers flight rank and incorporate them into the Intelligence Section.

60. Kennett, *The First Air War*, 200. According to Kennett, Admiral Davies acknowledged that there was Navy hostility to taking gun directions from the RNAS.

61. Tim Travers, 'When Technology and Tactics Fail: Gallipoli 1915', paper presented to the 1994 Military History Symposium, US Air Force Academy, 18, 25, and 30.

62. Deedes to Sykes (no date), Sykes Private Papers; Lt-Col. Cecil L'Estrange Malone to Lady Sykes, 14 November 1954, Sykes Private Papers; and Mrs M. L. Auldjo-Jamieson (Colonel Jamieson's wife) to Sykes, 10 January 1942, Sykes

Private Papers. Deedes, who was one of Sykes' friends and a member of Hamilton's staff at GHQ, wrote: 'Well do I remember your gallant flights in crazy aircraft over the Peninsula! But I thank God there are still a few left who have never learnt to blow their own trumpets.' Sykes had placed Jamieson in charge of the Intelligence Department at Kephalos. Malone was Squadron Commander aboard HMS *Ben-My-Chree*, an aircraft carrier in the Dardanelles.

63. Requests to the Admiralty and statistics of RNAS weekly strength, Sykes Papers, MFC 77/13/34 and MFC 77/13/35.

64. Sykes to Vice-Admiral, 21 October 1915, Sykes Papers, MFC 77/13/31; and Sykes to Vice-Admiral, 1 November 1915, Sykes Papers, MFC 77/13/30. Sykes told de Robeck that he had to have greater numbers of aircraft to respond to the enemy build-up and the expected enemy aerial offensive. Sykes argued that without a better air service he would be unable to protect the Fleet or the Army from aerial attack and that it would be impossible to carry out RNAS offensive operations, including artillery and gun co-operation.

65. Sykes, *From Many Angles*, 182.

66. Sueter to Sykes, 20 November 1915, Sykes Papers, MFC 77/13/30.

67. Sykes to Churchill, 4 November 1915, Sykes Papers, MFC 77/13/45.

68. Ibid.

69. Sir Roger Keyes wrote to his wife on 20 December 1915 that an attack would have been more successful than the 'wretched withdraw'.

70. Sykes' orders of evacuation, 12 December 1915, Sykes Papers, MFC 77/13/43.

71. 'General Orders for the Final Stage of the Evacuation of the Army from Suvla and Anzac', 12 December 1915, by R. E. Wemyss, Vice-Admiral; and evacuation correspondence, Sykes Papers, MFC 77/13/43.

72. Ibid.

73. Sykes to GHQ, 14 December 1915, Sykes Papers, MFC 77/13/43.

74. Sykes' evacuation patrol orders, 16 December 1915, Sykes Papers, MFC 77/13/43.

75. Translation from *Vossische Zeitung*, 21 January 1916, Hamilton Papers, 17/4/1/26.

76. Bremner sound recording, Reel No 3, IWM sound recordings.

77. Sykes, *From Many Angles*, 184.

78. R. A. Russell to Colonel Sykes, 28 January 1916, Sykes Restricted Papers, vol. II [no page number].

79. Sykes, *From Many Angles*, 178. He held a common assessment of Gallipoli: 'the Cabinet adhered to their policy of starving the Mediterranean Expeditionary Force in favour of the Western Front.'

80. Sykes, *From Many Angles*, 529.

81. De Robeck to Balfour, 21 April 1916, letter no. 71, in *The Royal Navy in the Mediterranean 1915–1918*, ed. Paul G. Halpern (London: Royal Navy Records Society, 1987).

82. Admiralty to Sykes, 13 March 1916, Sykes Papers, MFC 77/13/47, and Vice-Admiral to War Office (no date), Sykes Papers, MFC 77/13/33.

5

Manpower and Morale: 1916–18

From Gallipoli in 1916 until his assumption of command as CAS in 1918, Sykes struggled against air service, military and political friction to help Britain continue the fight against Germany, while trying to find an end to the stalemate through a technological victory. During this time Sykes salvaged his reputation and air force career by working for the Army; he matured as a staff officer and was able to separate old ideologies from new realities and helped to formulate much of the strategy and doctrine both the Army and the RAF would use later in 1918 to defeat Germany.

Sykes returned to England at the end of February 1916 to begin a two-year sabbatical from flying. His work remained technological, developing machine-gun and tank organizations, but his primary focus involved manpower shortages at the front and in industrial labor. Sykes joined other War Office and Cabinet members in recognizing that the two issues were interrelated – that solutions to manpower problems might lie with technology. As Sykes soon realized, however, all 'solutions' to the war effort had to be worked through the complex political and bureaucratic environment of the War Office and the Supreme War Council (SWC). By March 1918 Sykes better understood the supply system he had struggled with since 1912 and emerged a more experienced staff officer with a better idea of how to apply idealistic staff college doctrines to battlefield realities. Although his two years displaced from the air service were difficult, they prepared Sykes to carry the mantle of the Air Staff to the end of the war.

After Gallipoli, Henderson ensured that Sykes was to be an outcast from the service he had helped to create. Brancker wrote to Trenchard on 13 March 1916: 'P.S. What about Sykes as your 4th Brigadier? D.H. [David Henderson] has told me *he* won't employ him in any capacity – but we must do something with him. He is awaiting employment now.'[1] Trenchard responded the next day:

> With regard to Sykes, I am quite willing to have him to command the brigade under me provided I can see him and make him understand he has got to do what he is told and have no more of that awful intrigue which you and I know of.[2]

Trenchard then pencilled in after the last sentence, 'suffered from'. These letters show that rumors had spread while Sykes was away and his reputation had suffered. Yet within the system's propensity for gossip, the RFC's leaders acknowledged that Sykes was a valuable asset. Trenchard had gained control in France, and, provided he could keep Sykes subordinate, Trenchard, to his credit, was willing to employ him.

There is no evidence suggesting that Sykes was unwilling to serve under Trenchard, and Brancker fought to bring him back as a brigadier-general. Henderson, however, vetoed the proposal. Upset at Henderson's intransigence, Brancker complained to Trenchard on 16 March 1916: 'D.H. will not employ Sykes in any account in spite of all I have said . . .'.[3] It was ironic that part of the disagreement between Brancker and Henderson involved the size of the Air Board. Henderson was fighting to keep the Board as small as possible, but Brancker was convinced that, because Henderson was outnumbered three to one by the Navy, he needed help. In other words, Brancker believed Henderson was ineffective as the DGMA – the precise issue Sykes had raised in 1915, which led to the rumours of 'intrigue'.

Henderson had his way, however, and Sykes was forced to find employment outside the air service. Sykes' devotion to duty and desire to serve outweighed his pride. He was not willing to wait long for a position and accepted the Army's first offer – a job that was both insignificant and humiliating for a former cavalry officer. Sykes was selected as Adjutant and Quartermaster-General for 4th Mounted Division at Colchester, but the Division had no horses. Sykes was to establish a force of 'maximum mobility and fire-power', using four brigades of bicycles![4] He endured the situation but sought better opportunities at the same time. Although he had come from the air service, the courses he had taken during his leave as a lieutenant had broadened his background in different arms. In addition, he had both combat experience and a staff college education.

An opportunity arrived when the War Office's Adjutant General Sir Nevil Macready notified Sykes that help was needed in establishing a machine-gun corps. Sykes had commanded a machine-gun training camp at Bloemfontein, and he was eager to give up his bicycles and accept the new assignment. Kitchener had approved the formation of the Machine-Gun Corps on 14 December 1915 after realizing that the standard establishment of two Maxim machine-guns per battalion was insufficient in a war that had stalemated and was being dominated by firepower.[5] The Regular Army's fire rate and accuracy had nearly matched machine-guns with rifles, but Kitchener's new territorial soldiers were inexperienced and needed any technological assistance they could acquire. A machine-gun school at Grantham opened on 6 December 1915 under the directorship of Brigadier-General F. R. C. Carleton, to support a goal of eight machine-guns per battalion. After Kitchener lost his life aboard the *Hampshire*, the new Secretary of State for War, David Lloyd George, doubled Kitchener's program to 16 machine-guns per battalion.

Sykes' primary challenge in establishing the Machine-Gun Corps was to find the soldiers to man it during a time when manpower was an increasingly desperate problem. The Machine-Gun Corps had initiated recruitment from the Territorial Areas on 29 November 1915 with the following statement: 'Great care should be taken in the selection of men for training as machine gunners, as only well-educated and intelligent men are suitable for this work.'[6] By 5 February 1916 the Machine-Gun Corps had been formed into 41 companies and organized into three branches: Cavalry of the Line, Infantry of the Line and the Motor Machine-Gun Service, which was part of the Royal Field Artillery.[7] Although Haig at the start of the war had predicted that two machine-guns per battalion would suffice, he told the War Office on 3 March 1916 that he wanted one company of 16 Vickers guns for each brigade and divisional HQ, and one Lewis gun detachment assigned to each company of an infantry battalion.[8] Machine-guns had become an important issue. Yet, due to shortages of personnel in all areas and branches of the Army, 'suitable' soldiers were difficult to find. This is why Sykes was called on to help.

His initial work was reminiscent of that with the RFC Military Wing in 1912 and the RFC HQ in France in 1914. He found a vacant room at Grantham and collected a few items to establish a staff office.[9] After recruiting a typist and a number of officers, he began organizing his position within the new formation. The Machine-Gun Corps eventually evolved into a large organization with separate schools for each branch, and at that point Grantham became the Infantry Branch School. While Sykes was attached to the Corps, however, there existed only one school – at Grantham.

The Machine-Gun Record Office was at Canterbury, where Sykes spent much of summer 1916 trying to requisition supplies and personnel.[10] His struggles were endless, for while the War Office acknowledged the importance of machine-guns and other technology, Haig ensured that the Army's primary focus remained on the break-through battle, which began on the Somme on 1 July 1916. Sykes traveled to the front to assess preparations for the Somme and to try to determine how the Machine-Gun Corps could best support the battle.[11]

In addition, Sykes attempted to keep Army personnel rosters aligned by recruiting men from the branches to which they would return as machine-gunners, and he urged Carleton to allow them to transfer to their correct branches when they had been assigned incorrectly. Sykes' motives were morale and money. He knew machine-gun volunteers would maintain a loyalty to their former units, just as RFC airmen remained close to their Army past. In addition, different Army branches had different pay rates. Hence keeping soldiers aligned, regardless of their function, would keep payments consistent.[12] To accommodate this system of recruitment and assignment Sykes needed to reorganize.

Sykes and Lieutenant-Colonel P. E. Lewis worked for Brigadier-General FRC Carleton, the Director of Organization. Together they reorganized the Machine-Gun Corps into four sections: Infantry, Cavalry, Light Motors and Heavy Motors, the last of which developed later into the Tank Corps.[13] Although Sykes was not formally attached to tank work, there was an informal link between all the mechanized forces, and he participated in some of the testing of tank technology. In particular, he attended Churchill's secret 'landship committee' experiments at Thetford Park in Norfolk, where 'Big Willie' was developed, and he helped to select the site at Wool in Dorset where the Tank Training Centre was established.[14]

The Machine-Gun Corps organization was significant for the BEF in that it established the framework for a number of mechanized divisions in the future, including some in the Dominions.[15] Sykes and Lewis agreed that the reorganization was effective, but they had a difference of opinion regarding recruitment. When Grantham opened, the Machine-Gun Corps had received 3,000 men a week. At the height of the Battle of the Somme, however, Sykes noted that the number of recruits had fallen to 496 per week, even though the Army called for 996 men each week as casualty replacements. In addition, Grantham was supposed to supply another 8,000 machine-gunners for the Heavy Branch that was just being formed. Furthermore, Sykes noted on 5 October 1916 that GHQ wanted the BEF's machine-gun companies in France to increase in size by 33 men per company.[16] Although the Machine-Gun Corps had started to enlist the Territorial NCOs who had worked at Grantham as instructors, required manning levels could not be met. On 20 October 1916 Sykes argued that the number of men entering training had to be increased immediately or the Machine-Gun Corps would cease to function effectively in the future due to the poor training that was certain to result from haste.[17]

Lewis maintained that the battle then in progress would not last much longer and that the drain on Grantham would diminish accordingly. Hence, according to Lewis, they needed more men, but not at the precise recruiting interval that Sykes wanted in order to ensure the best possible training. Lewis promoted a short-term, reactionary approach and voiced his frustration with Sykes' grand plans: 'This discussion seems to be getting rather academic.'[18] Lewis simply wanted more men for the Machine-Gun Corps and did not care when they arrived.

Sykes was looking beyond the Somme to a technological war in which Britain would depend on an effective and elite Machine-Gun Corps for victory. That long-term solution required anticipation – it required an integrated training and recruitment program that could accommodate the Army regardless of its offensive or defensive situation. Sykes' vision required manning levels at Grantham at the proper time, not just to fulfill immediate demands.

The Battle of the Somme did end, but the manpower problem within the Machine-Gun Corps did not. In May 1917 GHQ notified the Corps that they had to reduce recruitment from the infantry because it was more important to keep infantry levels adequate.[19] Yet within ten days GHQ stated precisely the opposite in a letter to Grantham:

> The experience of recent fighting is that the employment of machine guns in adequate numbers both in attack and defense, operates in reducing casualties amongst the Infantry so directly as to make the provision of fourth Companies a measure of economy of man-power.[20]

By the end of 1916 the shortage of personnel in nearly all areas became the dominant concern of politicians and military commanders. French army commanders, in particular General Henri Petain, argued that GHQ was extravagant and top-heavy with officers and that the BEF had to take responsibility for more of the Western Front, an argument not well received by Haig, who had just lost more than twice as many soldiers as the French during the costly Battle of the Somme. The War Office reassigned Sykes to be Deputy Director of Organization in charge of manpower and promoted him to temporary Brigadier-General on 8 February 1917.[21]

The Organization Directorate was responsible for overseeing all BEF recruitment, as well as employing a labor force of 325,000 conscientious objectors and foreign nationals to assist with the war effort. Sykes helped organize two census returns to try to assess the availability of British personnel for uniformed service or in war industries. His studies proved that the 1915 Derby Scheme and the subsequent National Service Act of 1916 had failed, and that there were many able-bodied men who simply disregarded any responsibility to serve, something that infuriated Sykes. He wanted a comprehensive plan – an effective national registry and enforced national conscription.[22]

Sykes objected to the British tradition that abhorred conscription and relied on a professional navy for insular security. He argued that German air power had demonstrated that the Royal Navy could no longer provide such protection, and that the war had evolved from a war of armies to a war of nations. British citizens had to do their part – whatever that might be – to save the Empire. In March, one month after assuming his position in the Directorate, Sykes helped to initiate the Women's Army Auxiliary Corps (WAAC) and organized it into a viable institution.[23] Women of the WAAC were assigned a variety of tasks, but the original focus was to alleviate the duties men performed in control and communications links. Although logical, the move to create the WAAC was criticized by both men and women. Soldiers were upset that they were being released to fight at the front, and the widows of those killed as a result blamed WAAC members for destroying families.[24]

Despite long hours at the Directorate trying to match decreasing personnel rosters against increasing demands from GHQ, Sykes was unable to solve the manpower dilemma. Thousands of replacements arrived in France each day; yet overall the BEF was being reduced by approximately 20,000 soldiers per month. Public and political reluctance to mobilize the nation increased when the government and the press started to speculate that Haig and GHQ were out of control. Sykes himself began to suspect the same when he visited the front in Flanders in autumn 1917. He wrote:

> I went up to the line and was dismayed by what I saw. The Germans occupied the high ground, while we floundered in the morass below. The country had been churned up by the shells into a vast sea of liquid mud, broken here and there by a forlorn ruined cottage or tree stump. Advance was only possible over duck-boards which ran over vast swamps, on either side of which were shell-craters filled with water, coloured by high explosives. To slip off the duck-boards might mean a horrible death, and many wounded men perished in this way.[25]

Sykes doubted that many GHQ officers had visited the front line, stating that Haig would have ended the Passchendaele attack in September rather than in November had he known the gravity of the situation. Sykes had gone to the front to witness tank performance. What he saw left an indelible impression of how not to employ technology.

He recalled that the solution to his manpower problem came not from any action on his part nor that of the Directorate; rather it came from Germany's resumption of unrestricted submarine warfare on 1 February 1917. On 6 April, the United States declared war on Germany. Sykes finally had manpower, but his duties had increased tenfold. He had to incorporate American supplies and soldiers into the Allied war effort.

The Directorate orchestrated the arrival of 1,250,000 American soldiers, providing them with necessary supplies and accommodation. The Americans had no equipment, no weapons, no ammunition, no aircraft. Hence their initial arrival hindered Britain's fight against the enemy. Sykes knew United States help could lead to victory, but only if the Allies were united. Sir Henry Wilson had recognized this issue and had urged Lloyd George to establish a Supreme War Council (SWC) to co-ordinate Allied efforts.[26] Dissatisfied with high BEF losses, Lloyd George, over Haig's and Robertson's objections, announced the formation of a Supreme Council of the Allied Forces at Rapallo on 12 November 1917. The SWC was to be a political body, meeting once a month at Versailles, and advisory only. Its link to the military forces was through Military Representatives, the position which Wilson held for Britain.[27]

When Wilson organized his staff at Versailles, one of the primary problems on the SWC agenda was the shortage of manpower. Wilson needed a capable staff officer who had worked on personnel issues, and he selected the person who had impressed him before the war. Sykes was to direct 'M' Branch (Man-Power and Material), which was in charge of all Allied manpower problems, as well as supplies of aircraft, munitions and transport equipment. Rather than establish a traditional staff with operations and intelligence, Wilson divided his staff into allied and enemy sides. Sykes' branch worked closely with Brigadier-General Hereward Wake's 'E' (Enemy) Branch, to assess Germany's manpower levels and quantities of war-fighting material.[28] The other branch under Wilson was 'A' (Allied) Branch, headed by Brigadier-General H. W. Studd. In addition, the SWC had a Political Branch under the War Secretary Milner and Leo Amery.

The SWC and Wilson's military branches faced numerous organizational obstacles. French and British commanders questioned the Military Representatives' legitimacy, and the Treasury was slow to fund Wilson's enterprise.[29] When Wilson went to Haig with requests for staff personnel, Haig objected. Reluctantly, Haig had acquiesced to the SWC idea but was not about to reduce his staff any further to support it. He sent word to the War Cabinet that Wilson had a larger staff than authorized, which aroused Lord Derby's concern that Wilson was trying to create his own empire at Versailles.[30] Confusion ensued between Derby and Wilson regarding the size of the military staff, and Derby finally wrote to Wilson that they needed to come to an understanding and common agreement so that the SWC could proceed as planned.[31] Sykes did not balk at the lack of pay and support and was the first to establish his branch, setting a model for the others to follow.[32]

Sykes served as Wilson's emissary to the War Cabinet, traveling to London to lobby in support of the Versailles staff. Sykes convinced

Lord Milner, a War Cabinet member, that Wilson needed more support if the SWC were going to function effectively, and Milner wrote to Wilson that after meeting with Sykes he understood the situation. Milner promised that the Prime Minister was behind Wilson's effort 100 per cent and that personnel and supplies would be forthcoming. Yet, due to the politically sensitive nature of the situation in France, Milner urged Wilson not to rush.[33] In particular, Lloyd George told Wilson to concentrate on the Western Front rather than Palestine and Mesopotamia, because the French were against the Middle East option.[34] Wilson had encouraged Sykes' and Studd's 'Easterner' determination that the Allies' best opportunities lay in holding the Western Front and moving against the enemy in the Ottoman Empire.

While Wilson, Haig and the Cabinet were embroiled in the formation of the military staff, Sykes immersed himself in the two pressing manpower issues facing the SWC: ownership of the Front Line and the formation of a General Reserve separate from the authority of the French and British Armies.[35] The manpower studies performed by Sykes' 'M' Branch were pivotal in answering French arguments that Haig should assume responsibility for more of the Line. In addition, Wilson used Sykes' figures to prove that France and Great Britain could not withstand the expected German spring offensive in 1918.[36] Without having to face a General Reserve under SWC authority, Wilson argued that Germany would successfully sever the line between French and British forces, capture vital communication links around Amiens and threaten to win the war in 1918.[37]

Wilson's argument for a strategic General Reserve was demonstrated at two successive war games at Versailles on 10 and 29 January 1918.[38] Sykes was a key participant when Wilson's staff played Allied and German roles to show representatives from GHQ and the War Cabinet that Germany would attack near the end of March and that a reserve was necessary to ensure Allied survival in 1918. The war game predicted that Germany's attack in March would be followed by two more attacks in May and July, all designed to consume Haig's and Pétain's reserves.[39] Sykes contributed to the war game by explaining why German capabilities appeared to be enhanced. His comparison of German and Allied forces showed that, while German combat arms were balanced, Allied armies were heavy in infantry.[40] According to Amery, Lloyd George was 'profoundly thrilled and convinced' by the war game, but Haig 'quite ostentatiously showed his boredom and contempt during the proceedings'.[41] Sykes recalled that Haig sat across the room reading a newspaper.[42] Haig had argued earlier that manpower shortages were as problematic for Germany as they were for the Allies and hence that

Germany would be unable to launch an all-out offensive but would be forced to make limited attacks.[43]

Battle ensued between the Haig and the Wilson camp. As usual, rumors circulated quickly within the RFC, and Haig's strong supporter, Trenchard, who had left France to be the CAS in London, wrote to John Salmond about Wilson and the General Reserve: 'I quite see they are trying to get control which could be fatal if they did.'[44] Robertson, the CIGS, also had objected to an Inter-Allied reserve because it would come under General Ferdinand Foch's authority. Robertson's argument was that he should command any reserve and hence that he should be made a member of the Versailles staff.[45] Wilson would not agree to this, because Haig would gain control. According to Amery, Lloyd George also disagreed with Robertson and replaced him as CIGS by Wilson.[46] Lloyd George decided to remove Haig as well, but Wilson intervened, arguing that a change of command would be dangerous at such a critical time.[47]

The contention over the strategic reserve involved strategy and doctrine as well as control. By forming such a reserve the Military Representatives were advocating a 'definite defence' that violated the offensive doctrine behind French and British operations since the start of the war. In addition, it took control away from British and French Army commanders-in-chief, who were strident in wanting to maintain control of their own reserves at critical times. Wilson's men suggested that after a defense-in-depth had been established on the Western Front with the aid of a general reserve of 36 divisions (11 British, 18 French and seven Italian), another 'Easterner' operation would attack Palestine. This was the option contested by Georges Clemenceau, which had Lloyd George politically concerned enough to urge for Wilson's patience.[48] Hence Wilson was seen as a revolutionary. Resolutions signed by Wilson, General Weygand (Foch's Chief of Staff) and General Luigi Cadorna of Italy called for radical ideas: a co-ordinated defense from the North Sea to the Adriatic, the use of mechanical means to free manpower for a reserve, co-ordinated Allied production of armaments and an Inter-Allied air force. An Inter-Allied Aerial Committee was to determine the minimum requirements for each nation's air service so that a strategic long-range bombing force could be formed scientifically and systematically to obliterate the enemy's vital rear areas of production.[49] Wilson was convinced aerial bombing would be effective against enemy morale. He had written to General Launcelot Kiggell in October that public reaction in London to two or three bombs 'is really mortifying'.[50]

Wilson's staff was encouraged to think strategically, and they formed an Inter-Allied Tank Committee as well as a Naval Liaison Committee to work with the Inter-Allied Naval Council in London.

The strategic ideas about air power and the formation of a bombing force by establishing minimum Army requirements had far-reaching effects when Sykes left Versailles for London in April 1918. They were precisely the ideas Sykes championed as CAS.[51]

Sykes continued to study manpower and *matériel* figures, and he devised numerous schemes to reduce manpower requirements. He worked with GHQ to enhance the transportation of reinforcement by rail, and his plans became critically important once the German spring offensive hit.[52] Sykes reorganized food supplies, depots and receiving points for personnel and equipment in an attempt to increase logistical efficiency.

Largely due to Wilson's war game, the SWC passed a contentious resolution to form the General Reserve. Signed during the fifth meeting of the SWC's third session, on 2 February 1918, the resolution stipulated that the Reserve was to be commanded by an Executive Committee of the Permanent Military Representatives, with Foch as president.[53] The General Reserve decision had been reached, but its implementation stalled, as became evident during the next SWC session on 3 March 1918 in London. Foch argued that Haig and Pétain were acting independently and not following his directives. By January 1918 Haig and Pétain had finally come to a compromise agreement over the issue of British ownership of the line, and they now had a common foe.[54] They claimed that they were supporting the intended Reserve and that Foch was at fault. When Clemenceau supported Haig and Pétain rather than Foch, Lloyd George became irritated with Clemençeau and turmoil erupted in the French leadership.[55] At the same time, commanders in the Allied armies were arguing that the SWC and its system of military representatives needed to be dissolved now that the General Reserve had been established under an Executive Committee. This argument did not sit well with political representatives such as Amery, who wanted to maintain some influence in the conduct of Allied military operations.[56]

The SWC organization remained. Wilson had predicted the German attack correctly in time and place – 21 March, adjacent to Amiens. When Pétain misread the attack as a feint and failed to order adequate French defenses, he lost his credibility, which allowed Foch to step back into the French military leadership and bolstered the status of the SWC.

While the Allied governments and Army commanders were embroiled in the great debate over military strategy, doctrine and control, Sykes remained busy with the government's top priority – to save manpower. The War Cabinet had formed a 'Man-Power' Committee which reported in December 1917 that Haig's methodology was inefficient.[57] The Army Council and Haig agreed that the manpower shortage had become the critical issue of the war, but Haig disagreed with the proposed solutions. He reported to the War Cabinet that the Man-Power Committee's suggestions were 'quite inadequate' and that they involved 'a steady diminution of the British forces in France during the coming year'.[58] Haig was convinced that the manpower issue was the key to victory because it involved morale. With reduced numbers, the BEF became demoralized and fought with less enthusiasm and hence less effectiveness. Haig stated there were only two ways to win a war: 'by destroying the moral of the enemy's Army', or 'by destroying the moral of the enemy people'.[59] Therefore, according to Haig, his only option was to have large resources of manpower to win. Trenchard supported this concept in the air service and matched Haig's tactics with his own offensive aerial tactics.

Haig had lost credibility within the War Cabinet, however, and, as part of their effort to change the way Haig was sacrificing infantry manpower ordered Wilson on 15 January 1918 to investigate the expanded use of 'mechanical devices' to reduce Army losses.[60] This was the conceptual turning point in the First World War, for it broke with a military tradition where morale and technology were antagonistic in war-winning.[61] Ironically, the order came during the same meeting in which Trenchard argued against the SWC's resolution to form an Inter-Allied strategic air force.[62] The document Sykes produced as a result of the War Cabinet's request would change his career. Trenchard and Sykes were on an air force see-saw, and as Trenchard began to sink, Sykes began to rise.

Each of Wilson's branches produced mechanical/manpower documents in February and March 1918, and each advocated technologies and mechanical means to reduce casualties. Yet the approaches were different, particularly in regard to air power. 'Mechanical Weapons and Devices to Save Man-Power' was 'E' Branch's report, and it effectively avoided the air power issue, stating that nothing more could be done.[63] Studd's 'A' Branch memorandum, 'Methods of Saving Man-Power', was a tactical study, arguing that tanks and aircraft could reduce infantry losses with increased fighting in the zone of the Army.[64] Studd predicted that long-range bombing would be haphazard at best and that air supremacy over the battlefield would be infinitely more helpful to the Army. Sykes' focus, in 'Notes on Economy of Man-Power by Mechanical Means', was strategic.[65] He wanted to reduce Army casualties by winning the war.[66] Air power was not to be a bandage to stop the flow of infantry blood, it was to be a spear to strike at the heart of the enemy.

Sykes' approach was scientific and contrary to Army tradition. He argued that the Allies had to *reduce* their infantry strengths – the reverse of anything proposed by Haig.[67] Sykes maintained that the war would be won by the Army, but not without the co-ordinated efforts of naval and air components as well. The combined use of Army, Navy and Air Force machines would claim victory, and without such technologies the infantry would continue to be slaughtered. In particular, Sykes wanted to employ effectively the Machine-Gun Corps he had organized the previous year. With elite mechanized corps, the Allies would combine efficiency and morale. Sykes' ideas about integrating technologies on and over the battlefield were leading-edge theories foreshadowing modern warfare. Having witnessed the failure of traditional methods of handling manpower and appreciating the capabilities of machines, he comprehended a new reality about victory in the Great War. Rather than outlast Germany through the mutual sacrifice of lives, the Allies could out-produce and outwit the enemy by employing effective technologies.

Wilson reviewed the manpower studies and endorsed Sykes', sending it to the other Allied Military Representatives of the SWC.[68] 'Notes on Economy of Man-Power by Mechanical Means' went to the War Office, GHQ and the War Cabinet, where Lloyd George read it the same day Trenchard tendered his resignation as CAS.[69] The Cabinet was favorably inclined toward the document and asked Robertson to review it. Robertson replied that he had read the memorandum already and that GHQ was implementing it – which was pure fabrication. At Versailles, General Tasker H. Bliss, United States Chief of Staff and SWC Military Representative, generally concurred with the document, although he was hesitant about promising American aircraft production sufficient to supply the intended strategic bombing, and he was not about to place such strategic operations on a higher priority than Army support.[70] Lloyd George recognized that implementation of mechanical means would be difficult, and on the same day that he read Sykes' memorandum in the War Cabinet the Prime Minister wrote to Wilson for his opinion of the document.[71] There is no record of Wilson's response, but he undoubtedly supported the report and its author. Wilson did not circulate the other branches' submissions, and he would not have sent Sykes' out had he disagreed with its contents. Within two weeks, Sykes was asked to be CAS.

THE AIR WAR AND MORALE

Sykes had been uninvolved with air power for two years, and much had changed within the RFC, in Britain and on the Western Front, since his departure for Gallipoli. Trenchard had fought two primary battles: to supply the air service and to maintain morale. Trenchard's solutions to these two problems remained contradictory. He forced the RFC to fly offensive operations on the German side of the line to maintain morale; this cost the RFC aircraft and airmen, which hurt morale. Trenchard's tactics were predictable, susceptible to unfavorable winds, and thus placed his airmen at such great risk that their life expectancy at times was less than a month. Trenchard demanded that squadron size be maintained to foster morale; but an accelerated replacement process to keep rosters filled resulted in poorly trained pilots who did not survive aerial combat.[72]

Trenchard's morale fight involved two concepts. He tried to obtain 'positive morale' by flying in the zone of the Army. Soldiers' spirits were boosted when they looked up to see friendly airmen and realized that they were not alone on the front line. Within the squadrons positive morale was maintained by attacking the enemy. Trenchard also attempted to force 'negative morale' on the enemy. When German airmen were unable to fly owing to RFC superiority, then German soldiers would see only enemy aircraft overhead. In addition, a negative spirit would infiltrate enemy squadrons when they were forced to fly continually on the defensive. Even Trenchard's concept of long-distance bombing in 1917 was focused primarily on morale – negative morale in Germany and positive morale in Britain.[73] The home populace suffered from negative morale and wanted reprisals.

Trenchard formed his offensive-morale doctrine in late 1915 and early 1916 when he blamed the 'Fokker scourge' on German offensiveness as much as on any technological advantage. Trenchard cemented his dogma in 1916 when Haig applauded the RFC's assistance during the Battle of the Somme and did not condemn RFC losses.[74] Whether intentional or not, the German air force provided Trenchard and Army Intelligence with ample evidence that German flyers were upset that they had to fly defensively, and that German soldiers condemned their air service for its lack of aggression.[75] Such intelligence information was contrary to numerous personal accounts by German airmen who stated that they were quite content to have the RFC 'come into the store' and that flying over their own territory was, in fact, a positive morale booster.[76] Regardless of Trenchard's motives or justification, while Sykes was away from flying, the RFC pursued an offensive doctrine for the sake of morale, despite the cost.[77]

The cost was considerable, particularly when Germany developed effective technologies and tactics. The Fokker *Eindecker* in late 1915, and the *Halberstadt* and *Albatros* aircraft in early 1917, incorporated leading-edge technologies.[78] The German air service commander Ernst Von Hoeppner's reorganization into 'flying circuses' produced tactical advantages in spring 1917. RFC losses also escalated when British labor strikes and poor Allied workmanship produced aircraft that fell apart in the air.[79] Trenchard and Brancker struggled together, and occasionally fought each other, in attempts to improve the supply of engines and aircraft.[80] Yet, through all the obstacles, Trenchard maintained his standard offensive policy, formally published as a pamphlet in October 1917: 'Offence versus Defence in the Air'.[81] This memorandum summarized RFC history to date and claimed that offensive aerial doctrine was the key to victory.

Although Trenchard raised his concept of morale to the extreme, stating that morale was to *matériel* as 20 was to one, he was not alone in his offensive pursuit of morale. In 1917 Henderson condemned press articles that attacked the air service for its high casualties. Henderson said that such articles served simply to help the enemy and to hurt RFC morale.[82]

Since May 1917 Haig had fought to keep Trenchard in France to support the Army with offensive tactics. Haig argued that aerial losses had been acceptable, and that the Air Board and Smuts' committee were ignorant because they had no input from any experienced airmen in the field.[83] The Air Board and the War Cabinet overcame Haig's objections to losing Trenchard, however, precisely under the same rationale: they needed the most experienced airman in the field to step into the air bureaucracy in London. They recalled Trenchard to London to be the CAS in a new Air Ministry. Upon his departure from France on 7 January 1918, Trenchard's farewell address focused primarily on one issue – morale – and the address was designed to build that morale. Trenchard noted that the RFC had suffered severe casualties against difficult odds, but that their greatest testimony was steadfast courage and honor.[84]

Sykes had been stamped with the same staff college impression that morale and offensive action were the key to victory. Yet, as this chapter has shown, in the middle of the war Sykes recognized the imperative for using offense at the right time and in the correct way. Blind offense was ineffective and hurt morale. Hence Sykes had to reject many traditional military attitudes in becoming a progressive technologist and rational strategist. He argued for an offensive defensive, with large raids, limited objectives and a deep defensive system, where increased mechanical fighting on the ground and in the air would be employed scientifically to reduce human casualties. The tank was to be employed defensively for counterattack; the machine-gun was to be used much more extensively on offense and defense; and aircraft were to achieve 'absolute air superiority' and deliver unremitting attacks on enemy industries and communications.[85] Sykes was convinced the war had proven that large set-piece battles designed to break through the enemy line were a failure. He would have the opportunity to pursue some of his progressive ideas as the new CAS.

From 1916–18 Sykes survived Henderson's and the air service's rejection; he instituted several useful Army organizations and matured as a staff officer under Wilson. Most importantly for the new RAF, Sykes grew to appreciate that effective use of technology, incorporated into efficient and co-ordinated operations, was just as essential as morale in modern warfare. The air service Sykes was about to inherit had endured substantial losses, poor leadership, unfavorable press reports and Parliamentary inquiries. Furthermore, despite Trenchard's, Henderson's and Haig's dogmatic doctrine to boost morale, the Royal Air Force suffered from low morale at many organizational levels. The CAS appointment renewed Sykes' air career, but his old RFC reputation had not died. Furthermore, Sykes had just emerged as one of Wilson's righthand men, and Wilson, too, was viewed with skepticism by most within the military system.[86] Once again, Sykes faced difficulties as an underdog – this time as CAS of the service Trenchard had left in the heat of crisis.

NOTES

1. Brancker to Trenchard, 13 March 1916, Trenchard Papers, MFC 76/1/5, RAFM.
2. Trenchard to Brancker, 14 March 1916, Trenchard Papers, MFC 76/1/5.
3. Brancker to Trenchard, 16 March 1916, Trenchard Papers, MFC 76/1/5.
4. Sykes, *From Many Angles*, 190. Sykes wrote: 'This did not take long, and the appointment seemed rather a backwater.'
5. Memorandum on Machine-Gun Corps History, WO 32/5453, PRO.
6. WO 32/5453/28A.
7. WO 32/5453.
8. Haig to War Office, 3 March 1916, WO 32/11392/20A.
9. Sykes, *From Many Angles*, 191.
10. Sykes to Regimental Paymaster (G. Gollins) 7 August 1916, WO 32/5453.
11. Sykes, *From Many Angles*, 192.
12. Ibid.
13. Ibid., 191.
14. Ibid., 193.
15. As Inspector of Motor Vehicles in India, Montagu telegraphed from Army HQ, India, Military Works Branch, on 17 January 1917, that he proposed forming a school of instruction in armored car and motor machine-gun duties along the lines of the Machine-Gun Corps in Britain. Montagu Papers, VII/27, Liddell Hart Centre for Military Archives.
16. Sykes Minute, 5 October 1916, WO 32/11392/70B.
17. Sykes Memorandum, 20 October 1916, WO 32/11392/72.
18. Correspondence between Sykes and Lewis, WO 32/11392/72.
19. GHQ to Machine-Gun Corps, 31 May 1917, WO 32/11392/98A.
20. GHQ to Machine-Gun Corps, 11 June 1917, WO 32/11392/101A.
21. War Office Records, WO 158.
22. Sykes, *From Many Angles*, 198. Sykes' argument mirrored Douhet's in *Command of the Air*, 10: 'There will be no distinction any longer between soldiers and civilians.' Liddell Hart, 80, wrote that there was a 'dawn of another new form of

war which helped drive home the new reality that the war of armies had become the war of people.'

23. James, 202; and Sykes, *From Many Angles*, 197. Sykes proudly wrote, 'We blazed the trail for the employment of women in all sorts of capacities.' James incorrectly wrote that Sykes invented the WAAC. Sykes simply implemented the idea that had been considered before Sykes' arrival at the Directorate.

24. Beryl E. Escott, *Women in Air Force Blue, The Story of Women in the Royal Air Force from 1918 to the Present* (London: Patrick Stephens, 1989), 34.

25. Sykes, *From Many Angles*, 201–2.

26. Leo Amery to Sykes, 13 October 1941, Sykes Private Papers.

27. PRO, CAB 25/121. From November 1917 to November 1918, the SWC met monthly during eight sessions, each one comprising numerous meetings, mostly at the Trianon Palace, Versailles. Participants were the Prime Ministers and designated members of each government, as well as their permanent Military Representatives, who were to comprise Inter-Allied military committees to advise the SWC. Sykes worked with each of the following SWC participants in some capacity:

> M. Clemenceau, President of France
> Signor Orlando, President of Italy
> Colonel House, Head of the United States section
> Mr David Lloyd George, Prime Minister of Great Britain
> Lord Milner, Minister without Portfolio
> General Sir William Robertson, Chief of the Imperial General Staff
> General Sir Henry Wilson, British Military Advisor
> Major General Sir G. Macdonogh, British Military Intelligence
> Brigadier-General C. J. Sackville-West, Chief of Staff to Wilson
> Secretaries:
>> Lieutenant-Colonel Sir Maurice Hankey, War Cabinet Secretary
>> Lieutenant-Colonel L. Storr
>> Captain L. E. O. Amery
>> Lieutenant-Colonel E. L. Spires, Interpreter.

28. 'The Man-Power of the Central Powers', 26 November 1917, CAB 25/96. 'E' Branch personnel reportedly wore their caps backwards, so as to portray their role as the enemy.

29. Derby to Wilson, 7 February 1918, Wilson Papers, File 3A/VIII, IWM. Derby apologized to Wilson that his staff was still unfunded.

30. Wilson to Derby, 7 December 1917, Wilson Papers, File 3A/IV. At the time, Derby was Secretary of State for War. Wilson complained to Derby that the information he had received was incorrect. Derby had been told that the French had only two staff officers, but Wilson claimed the French had 14. Wilson stated he had only three – Generals Sackville-West, Studd and Sykes – and that those three were inundated with work and needed help.

31. Derby to Wilson, 11 December 1917, Wilson Papers, File 3A/V.

32. Wilson to Derby, 24 December 1917, Wilson Papers, File 3A/VII.

33. Milner to Wilson, 12 December 1917, Wilson Papers, File 2/11/2.

34. Minutes of Second Session of Supreme War Council, 1 December 1917, CAB 25/121. Wilson and his staff simply had followed orders – the SWC told them to concentrate first on crushing Germany's allies, and that once American forces were in place, the Military Representatives could focus on Germany. Also, Callwell, 51–2. Perhaps Sykes could be labelled an 'Easterner', along with the rest of Wilson's staff, who appeared to favor another option rather than continuing the Western Front stalemate.

35. SWC documents, WO 158/58.
36. Index no. 13, Comparison of Strengths of Belligerents, 30 January 1918; Index no. 15, Wastage in Man-Power of the Allies on the Western Front, 28 January 1918; Index no. 16, Note on British Effectiveness in France, 1 February 1918; Index no. 18, Reserves Available for 1918, British, German, and Austrian, 31 January 1918; and Index no. 20, Strengths (British and Enemy) on Western Front, January 1918; in WO 158/58.
37. 'Joint Note of the Executive War Board to the Commanders-in-Chief on the Western Front', 6 February 1918, WO 158/58.
38. Wilson had been working on the war game for over a month. On 28 December 1917 he wrote to Kiggell that he was playing the game as if Germany were facing one nationality from the Adriatic to Belgium, and he predicted Germany would achieve an offensive climax in March. Wilson to Kiggell, Kiggell Papers, 28 December 1917, III/6, Liddell Hart Centre.
39. Callwell, 50–1.
40. 'Proportion of Other Arms and Services per 1000 Infantry', 21 January 1918, Sykes Private Papers. This document is also in CAB 25/93. Sykes' study showed that Germany had 936 other arms for every 1,000 infantry, while all the Allied armies were much heavier in infantry compared with other arms. As a result, since the modern war had become dependent on mechanization and firepower, Sykes determined that German fighting effectiveness was greater than that of the Allies. Hence to match Germany on the battlefield, the Allies had to arrive with a larger army.
41. Amery to Sykes, 13 October 1941, Sykes Private Papers.
42. Sykes, *From Many Angles*, 209.
43. War Cabinet Minutes, 7 January 1918, War Cabinet 316A, WO 158/45.
44. Trenchard to Salmond, 11 February 1918, Trenchard Papers, MFC 76/1/92.
45. Robertson to Haig, 1 February 1918, WO 158/58.
46. Amery to Sykes, 13 October 1941, Sykes Private Papers.
47. Sykes, *From Many Angles*, 209; and Amery to Sykes, 13 October 1941, Sykes Private Papers.
48. Ibid.
49. SWC 15, Joint Note 1, 13 December 1917, Index no. 1, WO 158/57; and SWC 44, 'Resolution Passed by Military Representatives', 8 January 1918, Index no. 7, 10 January 1918, WO 158/57.
50. Wilson to Kiggell, 25 October 1917, Kiggell Papers, III/5.
51. There is little evidence of Sykes' precise responsibility for the SWC's concepts of strategic air power. He was simply a member of the team. Later as CAS, however, he had great responsiblity in promoting those concepts.
52. Stanwith to Sykes, 15 August 1942, Sykes Private Papers. Stanwith reminded Sykes that GHQ had been less than co-operative in Sykes' efforts, but that they had been eager to use his work once they needed it at the end of March 1918. On 1 December 1917 Wilson and Lloyd George had assigned Sir Eric Geddes as the primary project officer of the Allied transport assessment. See Minute of Second Session, SWC, 1 December 1917, CAB 25/121.
53. SWC Minutes of Third Session, 30 January 1918 to 2 February 1918, CAB 25/121.
54. Untitled document, WO 158/45.
55. Amery to Sykes, 13 October 1941, Sykes Private Papers.
56. 'The Future of the Supreme War Council', 3 April 1918, CAB 25/121.
57. Man-Power Committee Report, WO 158/45.
58. BEF 4/26, 8 January 1918, Haig to War Cabinet, WO 158/45.
59. War Cabinet Minutes, 7 January 1918, War Cabinet 316A, WO 158/45.

60. War Cabinet Minute 16, 15 January 1918, War Cabinet 322, CAB 23; and telegram to SWC, 15 January 1918, CAB 25/93. The order read: 'In order to secure the advantage of the experience of other Allied armies, the Military Representatives at Versailles are requested to report as soon as possible on the economising of man-power, casualties and tonnage, which might be effected by the fullest and most scientific employment of machine-guns, automatic rifles, tanks, and other mechanical devices.' The Inner War Cabinet at this time consisted of the following members:

> Prime Minister David Lloyd George
> Right Honorable Earl Curzon of Kedleston
> Right Honorable Viscount Milner
> Right Honorable G. N. Barnes, Member of Parliament
> Right Honorable Andrew Bonar Law, Member of Parliament
> Lieutenant-General J. C. Smuts
> Right Honorable Sir Edward Carson
> Lieutenant-Colonel Sir M. P. A. Hankey, Secretary

61. Howard, 'Men against Fire, The Doctrine of the Offensive', 519, in *Makers of Modern Strategy*, ed. Paret, 510–26. Although military history is full of examples where technological advances were used effectively with offensives and to bolster morale, Howard correctly noted that there was a trend in the British Army to chastise intellectual and technological achievements as less than heroic.
62. Trenchard stated that it was impracticable to plan such operations and that the SWC simply was not informed on air matters. Hence he recommended sending an air representative to the SWC, to which the War Cabinet agreed.
63. 'Mechanical Weapons and Devices to Save Man-Power', 3 February 1918, CAB 25/93.
64. 'Methods of Saving Man-Power', CAB 25/93.
65. 'Notes on Economy of Man-Power by Mechanical Means', Sykes Papers, MFC 77/13/50.
66. 'Notes on Economy of Man-Power by Mechanical Means' (G. T. 3947), 28 February 1918, CAB 25/93. To save manpower, Sykes addressed three primary areas: machines, prepared defensive positions and regulated shipping. His discussion of air power was in Recommendation no. 4.
67. Sykes' concepts, which countermanded army practice, supported an up-and-coming trend from a few visionary theorists at the time. Lord Montagu, for example, had argued to the Air Board in January 1917 that it was better to use men in industry (constructing aircraft) than to waste them in the trenches, and he maintained that continuous long-range bombing was the 'most promising method of smashing the enemy at a comparatively early date, say November 1917'. See 'Memorandum on the independent use of Aircraft', January 1917, Montagu Papers, IV/C/1; and 'Memorandum for Air Board', 31 May 1916, Montagu Papers, V/R/2, Liddell Hart Centre.
68. Sykes' memorandum was not precisely the same document that circulated as Wilson's response to the War Cabinet tasking (from War Cabinet 322). Yet Sykes clearly had done the work, and it was his title that remained on the document.
69. War Cabinet Minutes, 19 March 1918, War Cabinet 367, CAB 23.
70. Bliss to SWC, 6 March 1918, CAB 25/93.
71. Prime Minister to Wilson, 19 March 1918, Lloyd George Papers, Series F/Box 47/Folder 7, House of Lords Record Office.
72. Higham, *Air Power*, 28, noted that Trenchard was so consumed with maintaining the offensive *à l'outrance* that in 1917 he launched pilots into aerial combat who had no more than 20 hours of flying time.

73. Trenchard memorandum on long-distance bombing [no date], Trenchard Papers, MFC 76/1/67.
74. For a synopsis of Trenchard's aerial plan for the Somme, see Collier, 57–9, and Cooper, *The Birth of Independent Air Power*, 71–2. There is a strong argument that Trenchard could hardly have adopted a limited strategy for the RFC when the BEF was engaged in an all-out offensive and suffering grievous losses. As the RFC was tied organizationally to the Army, he had little choice but to mirror Haig's approach.
75. German Documents, Trenchard Papers, MFC 76/1/73. Examples of what Trenchard read during the Somme Battle: a German soldier of 8th Company, 28th Infantry Regiment, wrote in his diary 13 August 1916, 'I have got stomach pains and diarrhea. We suffer much from thirst. It is torture . . . Everybody is wishing for rain or at least bad weather so that one may have some degree of safety from the English aviators.' A letter found on a dead German soldier of the 179th Regiment, 24th Saxon Division, 11 August 1916, stated: 'A word about our own aeroplanes, really one must be almost too ashamed to write about them, it is simply scandalous. They fly up to this village but no further, whereas the English are always flying over our lines, directing artillery shoots thereby getting all their shells even those of heavy calibre right into our trenches. Our artillery can only shoot by the map as they have no observation. I wonder if they have any idea where the enemy line is, or even ever hit it. It was just the same at Lille, there they were, sitting in the theatre covered with medals, but never to be seen in the air.'
76. Kennett, *The First Air War*, 77; and Stark, 18. Also Groves, 'This Air Business', 25–6, Groves Papers, box 3, Liddell Hart Centre, noted that at Arras in 1917, the RFC had a three-to-one advantage in aircraft as well as superior machines. Yet the British offensive policy led to their decimation at the hands of German aviators. There was an obvious dilemma, for a strong argument could be made that it was impossible to achieve 'command of the air' or 'absolute air superiority' without an offensive aerial strategy. Offensive doctrine, pursued constantly, rather than applied logically at the best times, however, forced untrained pilots into combat as wastage rates exceeded the supply of flyers. Groves argued that German morale did not suffer from a defensive doctrine at all, because their doctrine was offensive-defensive – designed to achieve air superiority at decisive points. The German doctrine, however, was driven by economy of force, something the RFC failed to acknowledge.
77. 'A Review of the Principles Adapted by the Royal Flying Corps since the Battle of the Somme', August 1917, Brooke-Popham Papers, IX/5/2, Liddell Hart Centre; and Trenchard memorandum, 18 January 1917, Trenchard Papers, MFC 76/1/73. Trenchard noted from captured documents that the German air service had discovered the key to success was offensive air. Trenchard's greatest fear was that the German Air Force would be able to go on the offensive because of their new technologies and that the RFC would have to go on the defensive in order to protect ground units. Evidence suggests that Trenchard was successful in ensuring that his offensive-morale policy was maintained throughout the RFC. Major F. J. Powell, Commander of 40th Squadron, noted that his top priority was to keep up morale. Major F. J. Powell, sound recording, Reel No. 6, IWM sound recordings. According to Divine, 83–5, it was for the sake of morale that Brancker initiated the formation tactics that Trenchard then pursued to counter the 'Fokker scourge' in 1916.
78. 'Memorandum for the Judicial Committee', 26 May 1916, Montagu Papers, II/C/12.
79. G. Arthur Whigfield to Montagu, 2 August 1916, Montagu Papers, III/C/32. An

observer stated: 'A lot of "foreign stuff" has arrived, "dud stuff", I have refused to go in one of them.' Also Guy Dent to Montagu, 25 May 1916, Montagu Papers, III/C/29. Montagu reported in the House of Commons on 24 May 1915 that only 3 of 18 aircraft made it from Gosport to France without having to land with engine trouble. Dent stated, 'No one can imagine here, why the Government continue to order thousands of pounds worth of this sort of rubbish – the hours of labour spent in repairing minor defects in their by no means cheap engines, would make a business man weep.'

80. Trenchard–Brancker correspondence, Trenchard Papers, MFC 76/1/16.
81. 'Offence versus Defence in the Air', October 1917, Trenchard Papers, MFC 76/1/73. Trenchard had written an earlier document dated 22 September 1916, which supported the offensive-morale link just as strongly. It was entitled 'Future Policy in the Air'. See Trenchard Papers, MFC 76/1/42.
82. Henderson memorandum, 1917, Henderson Papers, AC 71/4/4. Henderson stated bluntly, 'The casualties must be faced.'
83. Haig to Derby, 4 June 1917, Kiggell Papers, V/109; Derby to Haig, 30 May 1917, Kiggell Papers, V/108; and Haig to Robertson, 21 October 1917, Kiggell Papers, V/126.
84. Baring, 264.
85. 'Notes on Economy of Man-Power by Mechanical Means', Sykes Private Papers; Cab 255/93.
86. In addition to Sykes, Wilson had a few other supporters. Arguing against the prevalent army attitude toward Wilson, Gen. Sir Lancelot Kiggell praised his ability to keep a sense of humor and meet politicians on equal terms. Wilson was 'I think the only VIP I ever felt completely at ease with.' Kiggell Papers, box 3.

6

Chief of the Air Staff: Administrative Turbulence, April–August 1918

In spring 1918 the friction in the Air Ministry had ignited, and Sykes was recalled to be the fireman. He played a successful role in the bureaucratic wars of RAF reorganization – in establishing an effective staff system and the necessary support organizations to salvage the fledgling air service. Until Sykes arrived as CAS, the RAF and the Air Ministry had failed the test of independence. Now at the Hotel Cecil, Sykes was able to use the staff abilities he had learned at Quetta, in the War Office and at Versailles. Sykes was the right man for the critical job of directing the new air administration.

His metamorphosis from an Army staff officer in the obscurity of the War Office and the Supreme War Council (SWC) to CAS of the RAF in April 1918 initiated the greatest year of conflict in his life. While British aviators fought the enemy, Sykes struggled against political, economic, technological and ideological forces. From the outset of his appointment as CAS he faced the fires caused by Trenchard's departure, interservice rivalry resulting from the amalgamation of the RNAS and the RFC into the RAF, and intraservice inefficiency in the new and inexperienced Air Ministry. Against these obstacles Sykes maintained control and resuscitated the stillborn RAF. He brought new thinking into aerial strategy, helped to create strategic bombing and commanded the RAF staff that contributed to Allied victory. His efforts in long-range bombing will be considered later.

Many of the problems Sykes inherited in 1918 had existed when he left the RFC three years earlier, but they had grown in the interim. Germany had bombed England, and the British public demanded a response. The RFC and the RNAS had continued to compete for resources in watertight compartments, and neither service would take responsibility for aerial home defense. After the third Air Board failed to direct aviation policy in 1917, the Cabinet decided to establish a separate air service to satisfy public desires as well as settle ideological differences in air strategy and interservice competition.[1] Henderson and Smuts drove this seminal decision without any influence from Sykes. The decision, however, was easy compared with its implementation, and when Trenchard gave up that effort Sykes was saddled with the responsibility. In addition, the war had just reached its most critical phase – the Germans had launched their spring offensive and seemed near to victory. To understand the gravity of the situation Sykes inherited it is necessary to review the incidents that led to his assumption of command: the formation of the RAF and Trenchard's resignation.

Historians have argued recently that the decision to form the RAF was a serious mistake. Claiming that it was an ill-conceived political reaction to quell public fears incited by insignificant German bombing, they contend that the RAF was formed not to satisfy organizational problems but to enable the retaliatory bombing of Germany, which, according to some, proved to be ineffective.[2] Hence a current interpretation: that the RAF was an inconvenient administrative change designed primarily to permit the formation of the Independent Force (or Independent Air Force, IAF) and the undertaking of long-range bombing, and that the decision was based on inaccurate production estimates which led to the IAF's failure to live up to expectations.[3] This argument is invalid for several reasons. First, no one can say whether or not the IAF would have been significant in 1919; it was never expected to be decisive in 1918. Secondly, British production estimates were established with the awareness of forthcoming American industrial help. The facts that the United States failed to supply engines as anticipated and that British labor struck in 1918 should not be used to condemn prior estimates. Thirdly, three successive Air Boards had considered a separate air service already – not as a step toward retaliatory bombing but to solve the inefficiency of interservice competition. Finally, that Sykes and Weir were able to produce the IAF despite all the production obstacles shows that the estimates were not unrealistic.[4]

Sykes was not involved in the decision to form the RAF, but as the implementor he had to contend with many issues that did not subside simply because the War Cabinet had decided to form a new ministry and to bomb Germany. It is many of these issues which historians have overlooked in their efforts to criticize the decision to form a separate air service.

The second Smuts Report had not given priority to the two major objectives: bombing Germany and quelling parochial friction. The public demanded retribution for German bombing, but they also demanded an efficient air service. Competition for aviation resources had undermined efficiency for six years. In addition, reciprocity was only half of the strategic bombing issue. The other half was how to win the war. Sykes did not want to use aircraft to punish the enemy; he wanted to crush the German desire and ability to fight.

The Prime Minister and Lord Weir, Director General of Aircraft Production (DGAP), had the same strategic concepts in mind when they pushed for a separate air service, but their rationale has been missed by historians because it did not surface in the Smuts Report.[5] One of their paramount war-winning objectives in creating the RAF and the IAF was to employ American air power – specifically, American production.[6] Weir's role in the RAF decision undoubtedly led to his selection as Air Minister when Rothermere resigned in April 1918.[7] Weir understood that the decision to form a separate service was a strategic one. The old air services had been driven by limited tactical decisions made by a commander in the field – Trenchard. The new RAF was part of a war-winning strategy to maximize air developments and use air power to its fullest possibilities. Part of this process was to incorporate American assets, and it required Sykes and the Air General Staff to make the system work. Weir told the Prime Minister that, although Trenchard had been a good tactical commander, he did not have the abilities that Sykes had to command strategically.[8]

Before Smuts and Henderson had analyzed the possibilities of a separate service, Cowdray's Air Board was discussing with the American Aircraft Production Board contracts for supplies. Lord Weir was communicating with the American liaison officer in London, Major Raynal C. Bolling. At the same time, the British newspaper magnate Lord Northcliffe was in the United States visiting industrial centers and discussing aircraft production.[9] A major British concern was that the United States' involvement in Italian aerial activity would come at the expense of support to British flying, and the Air Board knew that a sustained British bombing campaign would be impossible without American help.[10] A separate air service would not only amalgamate the British air services, it would also combine British and American production of resources.

The link to American production was an important step in the birth of the RAF and the IAF, but it created problems for Sykes once he assumed command. In the first place, the Americans failed to live up to their part of the contract to supply 'Liberty' engines. This caused a shortage in IAF supplies and severely hampered the bombing effort in 1918. Secondly, American airmen demanded greater representation in decision-making and forced Sykes' council to spend considerable time and effort trying to placate American interests. Eventually, Sykes was forced to resist the Americans' M-5 Branch reorganization.[11] Thirdly, in exchange for the American supplies that never materialized, the Air

Ministry had agreed to organize, train and equip the American air service. Sykes had to contend with this drain on British resources and manpower. Finally, American aviators never fully embraced the bombing effort. When France objected to supporting the IAF in 1918, American military representatives at the SWC and at the Inter-Allied Aviation Committee sided with the French against Sykes. In fact, the Commander of the American Expeditionary Force General John J. Pershing warned the new Chief of the American Air Service General Mason M. Patrick that American air service officers had better not consider any ideas of independence. In Patrick's final report after the Armistice, he stated that observation (not bombing or fighting) was still the most vital role for air power.[12] Overall, the decision to incorporate American interests into RAF operations created as much turmoil for Sykes as some of the other issues involved in the RAF decision.

While the Smuts Report was first being implemented, the Admiralty was in chaos. Sir Eric Geddes had replaced Sir Edward Carson as First Sea Lord and, with a promise of unconditional support from Lloyd George, Geddes fired the Secretary of the Admiralty Sir W. Graham Green and Admiral John Jellicoe.[13] Many Naval officers had learned the lesson from Jutland that air power was crucial, but Admiral David Beatty was one of the few supporters of an amalgamation of the air services.[14] Admiralty frustration over losing control of the RNAS was due half to parochial interests and half to a matter of protocol. As members of the senior service, Navy personnel simply did not want to have to stoop to deal administratively with junior air force officers.[15] Naval hostility plagued Sykes' administration throughout 1918.

In addition, he inherited a situation where the traditional military system of personalized command, gossip and sponsorship hampered RAF functions. Many of Sykes' fellow airmen were discontented at the formation of the RAF because their careers had been adversely affected. Cowdray, Brancker and Henderson had expected high positions within the new air service, but the Prime Minister bypassed all three when he asked Northcliffe and then his younger brother Rothermere to be Air Minister.[16] When Brancker found out Col. John Capper had been selected as DGMA, the post Brancker had wanted, he could not contain his bitterness.[17] He wrote to Trenchard that he had been passed over because the authorities did not think Trenchard would 'take orders' from him, and he suggested that Sykes had been behind the decision.[18] Such speculation was absurd, considering that Sykes was far removed from air service matters at the time. Trenchard knew that and was unwilling to promote Brancker's gossip. Nevertheless, Trenchard did agree with Brancker that Capper was a poor choice: 'Your private letter about Capper. This is a bit thick and I am going to fight and see what I can do. Either you must be DGMA or I quite agree we shall all have to go back to our units.'[19] Brancker and Trenchard were clearly not above intrigue themselves, and this was the atmosphere Sykes inherited as CAS.

But the discontent was even greater than this. Trenchard suspected that the RAF decision was partly a matter of power politics. The government was dissatisfied with the way Haig and his Chief of Staff Robertson had handled the war. In addition, Lloyd George may have suspected that Asquith was attempting to take over the government with the help of a conspiracy of military men including Haig, Robertson, Jellicoe and Trenchard. Trenchard speculated that the Prime Minister was out to gain political hegemony and to regain control of part of the war by taking air resources away from Haig.[20] Amery, the British emissary at Versailles, recalled that when Haig had refused to listen to Wilson's predictions about a German spring offensive, 'Both Lord M. [War Secretary Milner] and Lloyd George were agreed that Haig ought to go.'[21] Haig adamantly objected to a separate air service and fought to maintain Army control as well as to keep the air commander in the field – Trenchard.[22]

Henderson had fought against Haig's obstruction and had been a major influence in the decision to separate from the Army.[23] Yet Henderson was also upset. The Air Ministry and the RAF had been formed too quickly and had moved in a different direction from the one he had envisioned.[24] Most importantly, it had refused to give him the top military post.[25] Henderson remained loyal to the RAF until the Trenchard–Rothermere relationship erupted into dual resignations and Sykes and Weir assumed command.[26] Henderson notified Andrew Bonar Law that he believed it to be necessary to resign so as to not be 'a focus of discontent and opposition'.[27] Bonar Law reported in the House of Commons that Henderson had resigned owing to his inability to work with Sykes. Henderson may have resigned to create trouble for the new CAS, but Weir would not allow it. As former head of aircraft production, Weir had been plagued by problems with Henderson for too long and recommended to Lloyd George a Parliamentary response to Henderson's resignation: 'A new minister must not be handicapped by past difficulties and troubles. Any ordinary explanation should suffice.'[28]

Regardless of his motives in April 1918, Henderson knew that he was leaving Sykes in troubled waters and was quite content to do so. Upon his departure from the RAF he expressed to his son Ian his exasperation that the War Cabinet had appointed Sykes, and he suspected as a result many Army and Navy officers would refuse to transfer to the Air Force.[29] Ian Henderson was a flight instructor in

England, and his reply to his father reveals much of the atmosphere Sykes inherited:

> Thank you for your letter. Sykes of all people, I [*sic*] hardly seems believable at all. . . .. You can't imagine the things people up here are saying. I think Rothermere will end by being damned unpopular. I've heard more stories about Sykes lately, all of which go to show what a [deleted] he is. As far as I can see they [*sic*] RAF will be run but [*sic*] a mixture of journalists and [deleted].[30]

Such scathing remarks may not necessarily have been representative of widespread feelings in the RAF, but they show how Henderson had at least some loyal following that began within his own family. Unfortunately, these were among Ian Henderson's last words. He was killed shortly after he sent this letter to his father, and Sykes was the only senior airman not to send a letter of condolence to the Hendersons.

The person most concerned by the new air service was Trenchard. Wanting to remain in France to support Haig, Trenchard had accepted the position of CAS reluctantly from an Air Minister he did not respect and with whom he soon found it impossible to work.[31] Lord Haldane had anticipated the problem on 21 November 1917 when he objected to Clause 8 of the Air Bill, which established the Air Council. He noted that the Council was administrative, but that 'between administration and command there are infinite gradations'.[32] Haldane argued that the establishment was too flexible and that composition of the Air Council had to be better specified. Rothermere and Trenchard had a personality conflict, but they also disagreed on air strategy. Rothermere wanted Trenchard to fight parochial games to build a larger air force, and Trenchard simply wanted to support Haig's Army.[33] Haig noted in his diary: 'Trenchard stated that the Air Board are really off their heads as to the future possibilities of aeronautics for ending the war.'[34]

Trenchard was convinced that his Air Minister knew nothing about air power and refused to take orders from his civilian superior. He resented Rothermere's going through any other departments than the CAS, and Trenchard complained to John Salmond about his lack of power compared with Rothermere's: 'It is impossible for me to impress myself on [the Air Council] as a dictator. I hope to do this in six or eight months time, but at present it is far from it.'[35]

Under Trenchard and Rothermere, the new air service was slipping into chaos. In February 1918 Trenchard and Salmond complained of an atmosphere of 'gossip flying about' and rumors of the administration's 'hopeless inefficiency and general muddle'.[36] Rothermere was grieving over the loss of his two sons in the war, and Trenchard was too exhausted to show sympathy. Their fight, however, was creating great confusion within the new air service.[37] By the end of February neither wanted to communicate with the other, and Trenchard continued to complain about Rothermere's motives and methods.[38] In return, Rothermere replied he was tired of Trenchard's 'pontifical' responses to enquiries and he objected to Trenchard's habit of intriguing and surrounding himself with yes-men.[39] In a fit of rage, Trenchard submitted his resignation on 19 March, two days before the expected German offensive – Operation Michael.[40]

Rothermere would not accept Trenchard's request at such a critical moment. Trenchard later remarked that he tried to withdraw his resignation when he realized that the RAF was in a crisis, but his correspondence with Rothermere suggests otherwise.[41] Trenchard demanded repeatedly that Rothermere accept the resignation even though Rothermere told Trenchard that he, himself, was going to resign as Air Minister. Rothermere finally gave in to Trenchard's pressure on 13 April 1918:

> I now accept your resignation tendered to me on the 19th March. I cannot say I do so with any particular reluctance. Every man is the best judge of what he does but I believe your act in resigning your post of Chief of the Air Staff twelve days before myself [sic] and the large staff here were going into action to accomplish the gigantic task of the fusion of the Royal Naval Air Service and the Royal Flying Corps is an unparalleled incident in the public life of this country.[42]

Unfortunately for Sykes, however, the Rothermere–Trenchard affair did not end with the resignation.

During the next two months, while Sykes attempted to salvage the air service, the War Cabinet and Parliament were preoccupied with two Trenchard issues: the legitimacy of the resignation and how to employ Trenchard in the future.[43] The new Air Minister, Lord Weir, who replaced Rothermere on 1 May, offered Trenchard a number of positions, all of which Trenchard refused. Weir would not release Trenchard to Haig, who had offered his old friend a brigade, and at the same time Weir was adamant that he should not have to create a position for Trenchard or yield to Trenchard's desire to be a controller-general of the RAF with more authority than the CAS.[44] Trenchard tried to influence the situation by soliciting friends in Parliament and the government, including the new Secretary of State for War Lord Milner.[45] Trenchard even went to the King to voice his complaints.[46] During War Cabinet and Parliamentary discussions, however, Weir objected to considerations of moving Trenchard back into the position of CAS, stating firmly that Sykes was the better man for the job.[47]

In both Houses of Parliament members were concerned about Trenchard's status.[48] Parliamentary debate soon exposed a strong faction of Trenchard support that linked him to a popular triad of displaced commanders and threatened the Lloyd George government.[49] The House of Lords met for a special debate on 29 April 1918 to discuss the issue of Trenchard's resignation, as the House of Commons tackled the same subject.[50] Discussion in both Houses continued for weeks and evolved into a more complicated issue concerning the constitutional liberties and privileges of Members of Parliament. This was because some of Trenchard's support in Parliament was coming from military members who had worked for Trenchard.[51] Adding more fuel to the fire, Sir Henry Norman resigned as a member of the Air Council and the Parliamentary Air Committee passed a resolution that praised Trenchard and welcomed the Prime Minister's promise that he would retain him for work in the air service.[52]

The Trenchard affair also aroused concern from the King. Not only was he upset that he had been improperly notified of the resignation and of Sykes' subsequent appointment, but his secretary Lord Stamfordham wrote that the King was apprehensive about the loss of Trenchard's personality in the RAF.[53]

The turmoil created by Trenchard eventually subsided. The King acknowledged that Trenchard had been insubordinate and an investigation by another committee under Smuts concluded that Rothermere had been justified and had acted according to the proper procedures in releasing Trenchard.[54] It also affirmed that Sykes was the best man for the CAS post.[55] The principal supporters of Sykes at this point were Weir and Rothermere, and although it is possible that Sykes had political connections which influenced his selection, the two Air Ministers were most impressed with Sykes' abilities, not his politics. In Rothermere's letter of resignation he wrote to the Prime Minister:

> The recommendations set out in my secret memorandum which received the sanction of the War Cabinet are being carried out. The Strategic Council has been formed and has already held meetings. In a few days Major-General Sykes has impressed his personality on all with whom he has come in contact. In my opinion this brilliant officer with his singularly luminous mind, great knowledge of staff work, and grasp of service organization, is an ideal Chief of Staff of the Royal Air Force. He has the sovereign gifts, particularly necessary now, of elasticity of outlook and receptivity of mind combined with youth and energy. Aided by the able coadjutors he has found on the Air Council and at the Air Ministry the future of the Air Force can safely be left in his hands.[56]

Had Rothermere been more popular, his departure at the end of a brief ministry would have provided Sykes with more support. Rothermere, however, had joined the anti-Trenchard ranks and consequently was destined to receive chastisement and historical abandonment.[57]

Trenchard had attacked Rothermere's intransigence as the principal cause for their inability to work together.[58] The press, Members of Parliament and officers in the RAF criticized the War Cabinet for permitting Rothermere to accept Trenchard's resignation before obtaining his view of the situation.[59] Tormented by poor health, Rothermere refused to justify his actions and exonerate himself in Parliament. He did agree, however, to the Prime Minister's request to submit a revised resignation letter that omitted Trenchard's insubordination as a contributory factor.[60] Rothermere was content to slip away from the turmoil, pleased that he had taken Trenchard down with him:

> In getting rid of Trenchard I flatter myself I did a great thing for the Air Force. With his dull unimaginative mind and his attitude of 'Je sais tout' he would within twelve months have brought death and damnation to the Air Force. As it was he was insisting on the ordering of large numbers of machines for out-of-date purposes.[61]

The King refused to raise Rothermere to a peerage, and Parliament voted not to provide Rothermere with the customary departure salary.[62] All in all, Sykes assumed command under difficult conditions.

THE GREAT OFFENSIVE

On 21 March 1918 the Germans launched their greatest offensive of the war, which was designed to crush the BEF, whereupon France would fall.[63] In practice, the attack tried to sever the line between the French and the British forces, creating an Allied crisis before the Americans could enter the battle. The German gamble nearly succeeded.[64] The story of the air battle in spring 1918 is important to a study of Sykes because it shows that the air service had progressed to a level of organizational maturity where it was able to continue the fight even though its top leadership had temporarily evaporated.[65] While Trenchard was consumed by interpersonal and administrative issues and Sykes was in transition from the War Office to the Air Ministry, the work by Salmond's squadrons in France never faltered.[66]

Wilson's staff at Versailles had anticipated the German attack; however, British forces were thrown back until they nearly lost the crucial location of Amiens (see Appendices).[67] On 25 March British and French representatives met at Versailles and agreed to a unified command under General Foch, but by 27 March the Germans were within 25 km of Amiens, and General Hubert Gough's 5th Army was shattered.[68] The War Cabinet was so consumed with ensuring Allied survival at the end of March and in early April that on 1 April there were no RAF birthday cakes – not even a word mentioned about the new force.[69]

The nascent RAF, however, was fighting for its life according to the offensive tactics that Trenchard had developed during the preceding two years. Flying low-level over enemy troops in the zone of the Army, British aviators sacrificed themselves in helping to thwart the German thrust.[70] A primary difficulty British flyers encountered was the immobility the air service had acquired during the years of static trench warfare. In March 1918 the air force was once again on the move as it had been in 1914. In addition, the weather was as crucial as ever. British aviators had learned to fly in poor weather and at night, but such conditions hampered their effectiveness.[71] That the flying service was significant during the offensive is suggested by the direct correlation between the weather conditions and the German advance.[72]

The German air war had changed.[73] German pilots had new tactics and positive morale now that reinforcements were arriving from the Eastern Front.[74] Before the great offensive, German flyers had refrained from flying in order to maintain secrecy.[75] Yet once the attack had commenced, German airmen fought offensively on the enemy's side of the line to support the new combined-arms, nearly blitzkrieg-type tactics of their pioneer forces.[76] These were successful but costly, and the German aircraft industry was not prepared to pay such a price if it did not guarantee victory. In this sense the RAF bled German air resources dry, and the infant air service did live up to expectations.[77] The subtle question of semantics is whether the RAF achieved aerial victory, or whether the German air force simply defeated itself by going on the offensive. The answer leans more toward the victorious RAF.

Apart from the air war, there is evidence that British aviators disrupted the German ground effort and helped to frustrate and fatigue enemy troops, who were already near exhaustion.[78] In particular, captured documents and statements from prisoners verified that the German failure to capture Amiens was directly attributable to British air power.[79] Owing to the RAF's bombing of enemy aerodromes, the German attack flights were forced to move back out of the zone of the Army and hence were unable to sustain their part in the combined-arms attack.[80] In addition, the RAF prevented German flyers from exploiting the British retreat. As B. E. Smythies recorded, the miles of road, packed four abreast with retreating troops, horses and vehicles provided German aviators with a lucrative target. Yet there were few enemy attacks from the air because of the RAF's protection.[81]

As the head of the SWC's manpower branch, Sykes was in England, concerned that the British Army had lost 10,000 men a day to the offensive. The War Cabinet ordered the Minister of National Service to increase the procurement of manpower, and Sykes was asked to help.[82] He had anticipated the offensive in his seminal memorandum 'Notes on Economy of Man-Power by Mechanical Means' and had already formed contingency manpower plans that GHQ now was able to use.[83]

When Sykes had submitted his visionary memorandum on 13 March 1918, he had called for a technological solution to the man-power problem. Sykes believed that the war was too costly when fought with unprotected infantry and the cavalry's 'extravagant animals', and he urged a reduction in the numbers of soldiers and of the animals employed by the Army in the field. Hence his strategic emphasis was that inefficient and costly manpower was to be replaced by machine-power and that the Allies could defeat Germany by fighting a war of production and technology rather than one of human wastage. No single technology could win alone, but the proper use of combined arms, including aircraft, machine-guns, tanks and gas would enable the Allies to break the stalemate and achieve victory.[84] Tactically, Sykes advocated a two-line defensive system, with a thin outpost line and a strong and deep defense to the rear. His offensive idea was to wear down the enemy by striking at a 'series of points in succession, with a limited objective in depth'.[85] The ground gained was not to be held. Sykes also recognized that earlier failures had resulted as much from poor co-ordination as from short-sighted strategies and tactics. Therefore a key to victory would be the improvement of communications, command and control, and the successful interruption of the enemy's co-ordination. In particular, deception with the use of 'dummy batteries' and air attacks on German communication centres, supply lines and 'root' industries would help to cripple their effort.[86] Wilson endorsed Sykes' arguments as a step in the right direction and sent them to the War Cabinet.

Sykes' most recent technological studies had been in machine-gun and tank tactics, but when Trenchard left the RAF without an Air Chief, Sykes' memorandum happened to be on the Prime Minister's desk. Sykes recalled that he was surprised when Milner notified him that he was to assume the CAS position as a Major-General.[87] Sykes had left the RFC in 1915 with nine squadrons; now the RAF was to have 292.

THE HOUSE OF BOLO

Sykes assumed command of the Air Staff at the Hotel Cecil, the notorious 'House of Bolo', during a crisis on the Western Front.[88] The RAF was new, Rothermere was resigning, Sykes was unpopular with Henderson and Trenchard, Parliament was debating the Trenchard affair, and Sykes had to complete his duties with the SWC.[89] The Air Ministry was full of people trying to compete for new positions and, even though Trenchard had resigned, he continued to address the War Cabinet and correspond with the Allies as if it were business as usual.[90] Furthermore, Trenchard attempted to ensure that his plans and air ideology would be followed even though he was leaving.[91] The press covered the transition by giving the outgoing CAS much more attention than the incoming one, and the War Cabinet avoided the issue.[92] The exchange of the baton between Trenchard and Sykes was a rerun of 1914. Neither man said much in the thick atmosphere of resentment.[93] Trenchard was exhausted and immediately requested two to three weeks of leave.[94] Sykes had work to do.

His most immediate task was to salvage an administration so that the Air Staff could be effective and regain the confidence of the public and the air service. He had little political support in April 1918. Parliament was divided on the issue of Sykes' assumption of command, and many members believed that the House of Bolo was 'crammed with utterly useless officers doing utterly useless work!'[95] While some Members suggested that Trenchard should be reinstated, others supported Sykes.[96] Some suggested that the very idea of a separate air service had been a mistake, and Opposition members attacked the Prime Minister and his 'amateur strategists' in the War Cabinet for creating such a mess. When Lloyd George defended his government, Lord Hugh Cecil responded: 'The Right Honorable Gentleman really seems to care about nothing except his own retention in office – himself, personally.'[97] Owing to such government chaos, on 11 April, the day before Sykes assumed command, the Admiralty expressed concern that RNAS and RFC co-operation in the mandated amalgamation would be problematic if the Admiralty was uncertain who was to lead the new service.[98] Undoubtedly, from all the debate and corresponding press coverage, the new CAS felt that he was a second-choice substitute with an uncertain future.

Fortunately for Sykes, the German offensive attracted political attention away from air service problems, and Salmond's effectiveness in France also provided a small reprieve.[99] By the time Sykes had moved into the Hotel Cecil the Germans had forced a salient into the British line between La Bassée and Hollebeke, and German troops were within three miles of Béthune, four-and-a-half miles from

Hazebrouck, and six miles from the main road from Cassel to Ypres. The SWC's 'E' Branch reported that the British were short of reserves, and that the Germans had reorganized since their first attack: 'The situation N. of the La Bassée Canal is plainly one of extreme danger.'[100] If the enemy were able to cut the road, there was nothing between them and Calais.[101]

The weather during April was so poor that British flyers had to face two enemies in the air. At the height of crisis on 12 April, however, the weather cleared, and the RAF was able to fly a record day, dropping 45 tons of bombs, shooting down 49 enemy aircraft, and forcing down another 25.[102] RAF communiqués reported that air-to-ground and air-to-air activity was concentrated north of the La Bassée Canal, which was precisely where the British Army needed the most help.

Flying against rain, fog, wind and hail, the RAF downed 333 enemy aircraft in April and helped to stop the German ground advance. Most significantly, the German air service received a mortal blow to morale exactly one month after the Supreme Army Command had launched the spring offensive. The RAF communiqué of 21 April stated:

> Capt A. R. Brown, 209 Sqn, dived on a red triplane which was attacking one of our machines. He fired a long burst into the E. A. [enemy air-craft] which went down vertically and was seen to crash on our side of the line by two other pilots of 209 Sqn.[103]

Captain Manfred von Richthofen had been killed, and the entire German Air Force reeled in emotional shock.[104] The Under-Secretary for Air, Major John L. Baird, reported to Parliament that the RAF was surviving the offensive and that they were turning the air war in their favor.[105] Hence Sykes was able to concentrate on administrative and organizational issues at home.

Sykes' first Air Council meeting was on 4 April, when, curiously, no Council Member commented on the fact that the senior post had changed. As Sykes assessed his command, he identified several *objectives* and *responsibilities*. His objectives included, first, the need to enhance the amalgamation of Army and Navy air services and improve the co-ordination between them. Secondly, he had to reduce the casualty rate British flyers had endured for the past two years, particularly during the spring offensive. Thirdly, he felt driven to form an independent, long-range bombing force. Sykes also had a final goal to develop the long-term future of the Empire's air power, but that endeavor was contingent upon first winning the war.

He knew that the solution to his first objective lay in reducing traditional interservice rivalry and competitive friction. The second goal involved the improving of training and the instilling of new thinking into aerial tactics.[106] The third objective would be his most difficult because it depended on supply and Allied co-operation. He laid his final goal aside for a few months until the RAF had survived the German offensive and was on a more solid footing. He was only partially able to achieve the other objectives by turning to his immediate responsibilities.

Sykes' position called for three primary RAF responsibilities: (1) operations and policy, (2) administration and management and (3) home defense. To help with the first Sykes called P. R. C. Groves away from his staff position with Middle East Brigade in Egypt and assigned him to be Director of Flying Operations. Sykes established air policy, but Groves was an invaluable director, co-ordinating operations in Britain, where RAF training was divided into six District Areas, with Areas further subdivided into Training and Equipment Groups.[107] The RAF Commander in France, John Salmond, directed flying operations there, but Groves was Salmond's link to the Air Staff and responsible for general supervision and support of Salmond's squadrons.

Sykes' second role – RAF management – was a task that mirrored the one he had endured in 1912 with the new RFC. He had to organize, train and equip a new and separate service. The Air Council had acknowledged that all eyes would be on the RAF and that it needed discipline, bearing, *esprit de corps*, efficiency and effectiveness.[108] Sykes faced an administrative nightmare. RAF resources were to be under Air Ministry administration, but proper procedures were not yet in place. The air service was still an Army service – using Army forms, log books, regulations and procedures – 'by Army Commands under arrangements now in force'.[109] RAF supplies were a constant source of concern, since the service had no contracts department. All orders had to go through either the War Office or the Ministry of Munitions.[110] One of the greatest administrative concerns was pay. Personnel were reluctant to transfer to the new service when they had no guaranteed income.[111] The changeover and the new Military Service Bill had created oversights and interrupted payments to military and civilian staff, in particular to members of the new Women's Royal Air Force (WRAF).[112]

The WRAF proved to be a valuable asset to the RAF, but with its laborious birth and turbulent formative months, it created a constant source of concern for Sykes and the Air Staff. Sykes had come from work that made him acutely aware of manning problems and he took a progressive stand in supporting the formation of the WRAF to assist with administrative, technical and non-technical duties.[113] However, the position of WRAF Chief Superintendent was problematic, and Sykes also had to contend with inadequate WRAF housing, lack of a uniform, organizational confusion, poor discipline and a lack of legality in terms of Treasury funding.[114] Sykes and the rest of the Air Council were concerned as well that WRAF members should not simply be auxiliary to the RAF but comprise an autonomous organization. This objective, however, was plagued by the infighting and lack of discipline in the WRAF 'system', which mirrored unprofessional traits that had existed in the military system for years. In all, the WRAF was a substantial obstacle in Sykes' administrative battle, but its establishment was an important step in the formation of the modern air force. Sykes' other organizational and administrative battles were no less difficult.

Competition between the War Office and the Admiralty had been partly responsible for the decision to create the RAF, but this inter-service rivalry did not subside just because there was a new Air Ministry, particularly since the Admiralty had fought against the decision and because the RNAS had to make the most adjustments during the amalgamation.[115] The Navy resented the irreparable loss of its most experienced airmen to the new service. Furthermore, naval officers were upset that Haig had taken the Navy's Dunkirk bombers at the end of February to help the Army to initiate strategic bomb-ing.[116] From all indications, the Army side of the new Air Ministry was going to receive most of the benefits from the creation of the RAF.

Within the Air Ministry numerous administrative and organiza-tional details had to be worked equitably between the services: discipline, pay, staffs, control over aircraft, terminologies, missions and roles, promotions, transfer details and ranks.[117] Confusion was rampant.[118]

The amalgamation plan had called for 'Air Force contingents' to serve with the Navy and to be under the operational control of the Admiralty. Yet, administratively, all flying units were to be under the Air Council, and the Air Ministry had assumed the War Office model of administration – something the Admiralty resented.[119] This incoherent system was disastrous for naval officers trying to train and discipline troops.[120] Furthermore, the Navy soon complained that the air resources they had been promised were not arriving, and it was not long before naval officers argued that naval flying should return to its former status as a separate RNAS.[121] Further contributing to the turmoil, Auckland Geddes wanted the unemployed Trenchard to be assigned as an Army–Navy liaison officer to work out the organiza-tional difficulties. When Weir did not consider Trenchard for such a position and, instead, assigned him to France to head the IAF, Geddes was insulted – it was another slap in the face for the Admiralty.[122]

Hence the new Air Ministry was a *Sonderweg*, and it needed a Bismarck. Sykes' asset was that he had worked with both the Army and the Navy, and he had witnessed the competition for resources from both sides. Yet, more importantly, Sykes knew how infighting had hurt the aerial effort, and he had departed from the Dardanelles resenting the Admiralty's failure to support his air operations. Sykes' broad perspective led him to squash rivalry wherever and whenever possible, focusing totally on RAF efficiency.[123] To help to balance interests, two members of the Air Council were from the Navy and under Sykes the Air Council created several organizations to try to quell interservice tensions by smoothing transitional difficulties.[124] However, Sykes led a pro-Army Air Staff that relegated naval flying to a secondary role and supported it more to appease the powerful Admiralty than to incorporate naval air power into Allied strategy.[125]

In creating the RAF the Air Board had agreed that the new air service would cater for both Army and Navy needs, but the RAF and its CAS basically dictated naval air power once the Air Ministry was formed.[126] The major issue that the Air Ministry failed to appreciate in its irreverent attitude toward naval flying was that the RNAS was not an insignificant force. By 1 April 1918 it had the personnel to man 2,949 aircraft and seaplanes, a force not simply to be dismissed.[127] The war, however, placed the least demand on naval air, and Sykes' focus away from the Navy matched this.[128] Some Air Council actions were completely in favor of the RAF. For example, when the Admiralty asked whether the Navy could use RAF personnel stationed aboard ships to do ship-duty, the Air Staff said no, but that sailors aboard ships should be required to assist with RAF duties such as handling aircraft.[129] In October, when the Admiralty asked the RAF for help in providing storage, the Air Staff responded that the RAF could not possibly relinquish anything.[130] The most obvious indication that the Air Staff slighted naval flying was the marginal support the Royal Navy received.

The interservice rivalry had been due partly to bureaucratic pettiness; but the two primary issues of contention were lack of supplies and poor training.[131] From May 1918 to the Armistice – when British and Allied aircraft production climbed geometrically – the Royal Navy received only 216 seaplanes, 190 land aircraft, 85 flying boats and 75 dirigibles.[132] Responding to Admiralty accusations that the RAF was not supporting naval flying, the Air Ministry said that delays were unavoidable and that the Navy was at fault for losing correspondence sent to keep the Admiralty up to date.[133] Just as readily, the Air Staff dismissed the Navy's complaints that their pilots and observers were receiving poor training, and the Air Staff countered the complaints by noting many areas where the Navy failed to support the RAF.[134] In general, Sykes was uninterested in creating more Navy-specific training schemes when the system in progress was adequate to meet the demands of naval aviation. In addition, he refused to redefine roles and change terminology simply because the RNAS had joined the RAF air war.[135]

Home defense was Sykes' third responsibility and another issue of Army–Navy contention that had existed since pre-war years (defense against German bombing had been a paramount issue behind the creation of the RAF). The night before Sykes became CAS, four Zeppelins attacked the Midlands.[136] The airships did little damage, but the 27 aircraft launched to intercept and attack the Germans were unsuccessful. In addition to the enemy, home defense faced other threats. During Sykes' first Air Council meeting, members considered Sir John French's proposal to rely primarily on RAF aircraft to quell domestic unrest in Ireland. But RAF Home Defence still lacked organization as well as effectiveness. In fact, records of the 12 April German raid showed that 'RFC' and 'RNAS' aircraft had flown the intercepts even though those two organizations no longer formally existed.

Aerial home defense was complicated as it involved day and night attack squadrons, anti-aircraft guns, searchlights, balloon barrages, the hardening of targets, a civil program to reduce lighting and camouflage. RAF Home Defence was organized into geographic areas, one of which was the London Air Defence Area (LADA), commanded by Major-General E. B. Ashmore.[137] Ashmore organized LADA with a control and reporting center and nine Home Defence Squadrons.[138] With the use of wireless telegraphy and radio telephony, and 80 night fighters, home defensive capability improved quickly but unevenly, as LADA adequately handled the daylight bombing threat but was unreliable in darkness.[139] Hence offensive night bombers still held an edge over defensive aircraft, and organizational problems mounted for Sykes. As late as August, Groves wrote to Geoffry Salmond about the difficulties:

> The Area System is only just beginning to shake down. The still recent amalgamation, the lack of efficient staffs, the pinching of new shoes everywhere, the very limited number of revs. given out by the ponderous house of Bolo combine to make this a time of extraordinary difficulty and stress.[140]

Groves said that they were trying to eliminate the overlapping of duties and increase efficiency, but that the main obstacle to efficiency was the 'RNAS v RFC Factor'. He noted that each senior Naval officer still saw aircraft as his own property, and hence areas were not working together in a common defense.[141]

The Michael Offensive had threatened British survival more than German Gothas or Zeppelins, and the Western Front battle had also shifted the German air effort away from strategic bombing.

Consequently home defense had a reprieve from German attack during Sykes' first month as CAS. On the night of 19/20 May, however, the Germans launched their most aggressive long-range bombing mission of the war, claiming 214 deaths and injuring 700 people in northern France.[142] Although the Germans planned later missions and attempted more long-range bombing, the May raids caused the last significant harm to Allied civilians from bombing.[143]

The German authorities may have determined that strategic bombing was not cost-effective and, therefore, elected to end that strategy. Yet Ashmore, Sykes and the Air Staff did not have the advantage of such hindsight. RAF Intelligence suspected that German long-range bombing would fall during the summer, because of the shorter nights, but could still threaten London up to the date of the Armistice. The British government in August 1918 agreed to increase RAF Home Defence to 20 squadrons, and it was not until October – when the Allied offensive forced Germany to relocate its bomber aerodromes further east – that the Air Council predicted that there would be no more attacks on Britain.[144]

Although the threat from German bombing was declining, organizational battles within RAF Home Defence continued unabated. Ashmore fought strongly for air defense, more specifically, for aircraft and equipment. He objected when the Air Council voted to stop work on a defensive balloon barrage designed to force enemy aircraft to fly up to a predictable altitude when making raids.[145] When the Air Council further depleted RAF Home Defence by taking three squadrons over to France, Ashmore was indignant that the LADA would be reduced by 40 machines.[146] In October 1918 he bypassed the Air Council and appealed to the War Cabinet that, without the balloon barrage and fewer defensive aircraft to fight, the Germans would attack London regardless of how far back their aerodromes had been pushed.[147]

Like the RFC–RNAS rivalry, Sykes' primary struggle with home defense involved competition for aerial resources. This competition had begun before Sykes was CAS over an ideological and strategic debate involving the desire to 'maintain the moral of the capital of the Empire' versus 'the great importance of superiority in the air on the Western Front'.[148] Ashmore felt threatened by the loss of squadrons, but it was an RAF Home Defence commander, Higgins, who suggested moving the defensive night-fighter squadrons forward behind the British Front to attack German bombers coming and going and to exploit the German retreat.[149] Sykes was troubled by the competition, but he was most hampered by the administrative system: the Air Council could not move squadrons without Army Council consent and War Cabinet approval. Furthermore, Wilson, the CIGS, stood as a middle-man between those two organizations and usually added his input.[150] Hence, as the air war grew more complex, the competition for aerial resources correspondingly encouraged a distribution system that was increasingly cumbrous.

In this system Sykes, however, was most concerned about strategic bombing, not home defense, and any aircraft going to Ashmore or the Navy meant fewer going to the Independent Force. Sykes wrote that home defense used excessive resources and hence that the supporting of home defense simply worked to the advantage of the enemy.[151]

In addition to the problems of Trenchard's resignation, the amalgamation, the WRAF and home defense, the infant RAF organization required daily work with numerous other issues involving administration, experimentation, production, training, the weather service and intelligence, to name a few. Air staff work was endless and often intractable, but the War Cabinet and the Air Minister had hired the person they thought could keep the Air Force functioning effectively, despite the pressures of politics and the demands of war.

Although air service administration had changed with the amalgamation, Army and Navy flying operations remained as they had been.[152] The weather in May was better for flying than it had been for months and RAF activity on the Western Front increased accordingly. Encounters with the enemy, however, started to decline – particularly from 20 to 28 May – when few German flyers appeared.[153] The Navy continued to bomb facilities at Bruges, Ostend and Zeebrugge, as it had previously, and in War Cabinet meetings the First Sea Lord reported these activities, even though the CAS was present and probably should have represented all British air operations.[154] In essence, although the name had changed, RFC and RNAS procedures remained.

Sykes and Weir had an uphill battle to institute RAF procedures as well as an independent administration. Weir had recognized that the RAF existed only on paper, and on 14 May he presented the War Cabinet with a proposal to take control of the air service as the Smuts Report had intended.[155] In his memorandum Weir argued that the Air Ministry had to be responsible for all aerial activities and assets. It had to be independent from the Army and the Navy or there was no sense in having an Air Ministry. If the Army or the Navy objected to Air Ministry allocations, then the War Cabinet would make the final ruling. Weir also told the War Cabinet that he would keep them apprised of the state of the RAF in weekly reports.[156] In addition, Weir was aware that communication between the United States and the British air service was ineffective and hampered a major facet of the decision to create the RAF to link British and American air assets. Hence he advocated having an authoritative American Air Staff in London.

The War Cabinet agreed to the establishment of such an Air Staff but rebuffed Weir's attempt to gain overall control of British flying. They notified Weir that the War Cabinet would send a delegation to Washington, but that the War Cabinet Air Policy Committee had ultimate authority over air assets and that any questions of policy had to go through that committee first. Hence the War Cabinet ruled that the initial item of business for the War Cabinet Air Policy Committee was to adjudicate on the issues raised by Weir's memorandum.[157]

Meanwhile, Sykes was having difficulty working with the Army because every time he needed aerial machine-guns he had to go through the War Office. If the RAF was to be an independent fighting force it needed its own allocation.[158] The Army Council disagreed and stated that any other system would create dual control; however by 4 June the Air and the Army Council were able to reach agreement that the Air Ministry would be able to work directly with the Ministry of Munitions. Sykes had already notified Churchill that in the future the RAF wanted to be represented on the Ordnance Committee.[159]

Within the RAF itself Sykes and Weir began to create the institution they desired. The Air Staff recognized that because flying was uniquely tied to weather conditions, the RAF required a separate meteorological office.[160] In addition, flyers needed their own medical service with trained specialists.[161] The RAF would no longer accept pilot applications from civilian training firms, only the Air Ministry would select its pilots and, in addition, would begin appointing women to serve as RAF staff officers.[162] Furthermore, Sykes was dissatisfied with the existing system of aerodrome construction that appeared to cater to political and economic criteria more than military suitability. The Air Board had suspected that aerodromes in poor locations had been responsible for numerous training deaths. Sykes announced that he would replace Brancker as chairman of the Aerodrome Committee and would inspect aerodromes and proposed sites for future airfields to determine their potential.[163] The Air Staff objected to a Canadian request for their own air service on the basis that it would interfere with efficiency. They decided, instead, to promote Canadians publicly so that Canadian flyers would be recognized and appropriately rewarded for their service within the RAF.[164] Finally, the Air Staff decided on a new blue uniform to help to promote RAF *esprit de corps*.[165]

By the end of May Weir was fully engaged in his fight for more Air Ministry autonomy and authority within the British political-military system, and in June he brought his proposals before Parliament.[166] He attacked past procedures as inefficient, having led to the major problem of poor co-ordination between the supply of squadrons, pilots and aircraft. He promised that during his term in office the RAF

would be a new institution with new training schemes, better production standards and improved discipline and morale. He intended to
close the gap between the Air and the Munitions Ministry by linking
the GCE to the Director General of Aircraft Production (DGAP) via a
joint department. Critical to Weir's plan was the position of the CAS.
He was determined that the confusion and infighting that had
occurred between the previous CAS and Air Minister would not
happen again, and he reinforced his position that Sykes was the person
responsible to determine air strategy and all programs with strategic
purposes.[167]

Sykes eagerly accepted his responsibility and formally established
his air-power policy and strategic ideas in a memorandum sent to the
Imperial War Cabinet.[168] This was not a short-term reaction to the
war, but a visionary approach to air power that encompassed the next
decade of Imperial existence. Sykes discussed the next war as much as
he did the one then in progress, and he predicted a world where air
power would be the dominant power factor. Britain was no longer an
island, and seapower would no longer guarantee peace and security.
He saw the war not as a predicament but as an opportunity for Britain
to develop its aerial technology in a way that it could never do in
time of peace. He did not advocate a military-industrial complex, but
wanted a civil air fleet that could be converted readily into a war-
making power in time of emergency – not just for Britain but for the
entire Empire.

In the light of the RAF's position in June 1918, Sykes was both
ahead of and behind his time. He predicted a decisive aerial offensive
in June 1919 leading to victory later that year; his vision called for the
Empire to embrace air power and the long-range offensive and to
discard the ideas of auxiliary air, 'national attrition', and 'battering-
ram tactics.'[169] According to Sykes, this was the only way to counter
the enemy's advantage of interior lines. He did not claim that air power
would win the war, but he assumed that it would play a key part when
combined with a land campaign of wide attack, limited objectives and
not aiming to hold the ground gained. Sykes' technological ideas were
more moderate than those of a British tank officer Lieutenant-Colonel
J. F. C. Fuller, who in May prepared 'Plan 1919', which envisioned
the use of 5,000 tanks to break through the Western Front.[170] While
Fuller concentrated principally on the use of the tank, Sykes advocated
combined arms – in particular, the use of aircraft to assist the tank.

June was a month of relatively good weather on the Western Front,
and the RAF continued to make progress against the German air
service, but not without corresponding losses.[171] The Air Ministry was
busy trying to maintain reinforcements as well as to build a larger
force. Sykes spent most of his time publishing orders and attending

Air Staff, Air Council and War Cabinet meetings. Aircraft, personnel and squadrons had to be allocated, buildings and aerodromes built, and politicians placated. Many decisions were critical to the war effort and affected thousands of lives; others were simply mundane and ranged from selecting furniture to purchasing band instruments. Sykes' staff were efficient but not particularly expeditious. The average turn-around for staffing action on various projects was seven days, which was good during peacetime but not in war. Some of the most difficult decisions were technological: which aircraft to produce for which duties? What types of armament to develop? How to procure the most war-making capability for the least cost?

Sykes' enthusiasm for technology did not wane as CAS, but it matured to conform to reality. He could no longer promote technology to the extreme as he had in 1917 as a staff advisor; as CAS his decisions translated into expenses and had political repercussions. The Experimental Branch was familiar with German parachute technology and had approved several British types, but surprisingly, Sykes and the Air Staff ruled against the use of parachutes in aeroplanes.[172] Ten days after RAF flyers first reported seeing Germans successfully parachute out of burning aircraft, Sykes notified the War Cabinet that British parachute tests were not satisfactory.[173] Sykes never made any statements nor issued any orders that would confirm the general understanding among British airmen that the Air Ministry was trying to enforce courage by eliminating an escape from aerial combat. It is more likely that Sykes believed parachutes would hamper piloting and presented as much of a risk as trying to recover an aircraft.[174] He did not think that they would appreciably help the problem of pilot shortages.

Sykes did appreciate technologies that could make an impact on the war. He wrote to the War Cabinet in June:

> Technical progress must be achieved if the performances of our squadrons in the field are to be maintained in the present high level of success, and technical advisors are continuously studying, with what is believed to be considerable success, the design and production of machines with better performance than the existing types and ones more suited to the work for which they are to be used . . . In the design of machines, every effort is made to achieve the advantage of standardization, but the policy is to regard this as a secondary object, the primary object being to secure the very best design.[175]

In one instance Sykes recommended that the Air Council should not only send a letter of appreciation to the two airmen who had designed the standard 'course and distance calculator' used by RAF flyers but should also determine an appropriate gratuity.[176] On the other hand,

Sykes at times allowed fiscal realities to dictate tactics, such as in tactical bombing. Even though there was a consensus among airmen and experts that it was more effective to bomb with greater numbers of 20lb bombs than fewer 50lb ones, the Air Staff voted to continue using the larger bombs simply because they were available.[177]

Sykes fought for technology when he thought that it was critical to the mission, such as providing wireless-capable bombers for the IAF over the objections of the Admiralty.[178] The Admiralty believed that all sensitive British technology should be kept at home to ensure security, and flying long-range over German territory presented a clear risk. Sykes was sensitive to the need for security and he issued orders for airmen and contractors to stop providing the press with classified information.[179] Yet Sykes knew strategic bombing required formation flying, and that required effective interplane communication by wireless. Sykes endorsed the Wireless Conference decision on 7 August to equip 18 squadrons with wireless sets and to start phase training in which 800 officers at a time would be sent back to Biggin Hill, England, for wireless training.[180]

July was a busy month for the RAF, with air-to-air fighting continuing and low-level attacks on enemy aerodromes increasing. The United States Air Service scored its first victory, and the RAF shot down 318 enemy aircraft at a cost of 156 of its own aircraft missing.[181] One of the RAF's most successful missions of the war was on 16 July, when bombers hit an ammunition train at Thionville, stopping all German traffic in that sector for 48 hours. The Germans introduced their Fokker DVII aircraft, and the RAF initiated work with specialized night-fighter squadrons armed with Sopwith Camels to attack German bombers. In the same month the RAF started a new tactic of air-dropping supplies to advanced infantry formations.

Despite the RAF's achievements, flying in July created a delicate situation for Sykes. Labor difficulties had made the press and the government very concerned about the continuing British manpower shortage, and the new RAF was under as much scrutiny as the Army.[182] Balfour, who had become Foreign Secretary, questioned Sykes' report to the War Cabinet that recent increases in aerial losses were due to the RAF's now having to fly farther to reach the enemy. In addition, Lord Curzon, former head of the failed Air Board, stated that King Albert of Belgium had noticed that 'there was some recklessness in our use of our flying man-power, and that our losses in the air were proportionately heavier than those of the French'. Curzon also commented that the Belgian King's 'impartial observations' had been sent to Sykes, according to the Prime Minister's request, and inquired whether Sykes had any response. Typically, Weir was not at the meeting to support Sykes.[183] Sykes quickly retracted his comment about air losses and stated that earlier he had conveyed the wrong impression. He now claimed that air losses were actually decreasing and that such losses were not due to recklessness but to unfavorable southwesterly winds. Sykes further promised a full report, and the War Cabinet adjourned, emphasizing their desire to see it.[184]

Sykes jumped from his uncomfortable spotlight into a tornado in August. The air war had accelerated from a synergistic growth of new morale, tactics and technology. German airmen had rebounded from the blow of von Richthofen's death with new moral intensity; the RAF was flying new tactics to support Haig's final offensive; and new fighter aircraft had emerged on both sides. The Germans introduced the Fokker D VIII monoplane, regarded by some experts as the best fighter of the war. But new air-to-ground tactics at Amiens helped the Allies to turn the war in their favor. Groves wrote to Geoffrey Salmond: 'All Intelligence Reports tend to show that the low flying offensive in the recent show has had a terrific effect upon the Boche morale.'[185] He continued: 'Clouds of low-flying scouts maneuvered in front of hundreds of tanks and indicated the whereabouts of bunches of Boches by diving at them and firing machine-guns, and by dropping smoke bombs.'[186] A report from 22nd Wing noted success in attacking enemy anti-tank guns to protect the British Whippet tanks. 'The success of low flying attacks on ground targets has never proved itself better.'[187] The report continued that such tactics should be pursued until the enemy could organize a defense, at which point RAF operations would have to return to the previous air-superiority role. The new tactics to support the combined-arms offensive had given the RAF a new mission and helped to boost morale.

Despite RAF tactical success, 8 August was a black day in terms of losses. Sykes flew to France to observe RAF operations and upon returning to London reported the losses to the War Cabinet as ordered. He admitted that the wastage was heavy and noted that ground fire had accounted for three-quarters of the 45 British aircraft destroyed on 8 August.[188] He then informed the Cabinet that such losses affirmed his earlier arguments for specially armored aircraft for the ground-attack role. From 5 to 11 August, the RAF fought favorably, losing 93 aircraft while shooting down 177 of the enemy.[189] Yet RAF communiqués show that, by the end of August, the British and the Germans were trading aircraft nearly one for one – the worst ratio the RAF had experienced since the Michael Offensive.[190] The RAF tried to bomb the Somme bridges but was much less successful in that role than in escorting tanks. The bridge-bombing Campaign began on 8 August and the RAF lost 17 aircraft in the bombing role alone. Although no aircraft were lost that evening, night operations were fairly ineffective against difficult targets such as bridges. Between

8 and 12 August only four bridges were destroyed and another six damaged by bombing.[191] Part of the reason the bridge bombing failed was the RAF's focus on other areas. After the initial attacks on 8 August the objectives shifted more toward attacking aerodromes, fuel depots and railway lines.

RAF supply and manpower shortages continued, and the Air Council voted to recruit foreigners to serve in the RAF – specifically from Greece, India and the United States. Weir notified the staff, however, not to release this information. He did not want the public to discover that the RAF needed Americans as well as their engines.[192] Sykes also got into trouble with the India Office when he issued a request to the War Cabinet regarding a proposed Indian Army contingent without first going through the proper India Office channels.[193]

The manpower issue reached a climax in August as the SWC continued to study manpower problems and Lloyd George tried to help the situation by requesting French assistance. The French Lieutenant-Colonel Roure visited London to assess British manpower and to provide suggestions.[194] His report, however, backfired on the government when he noted that Britain had substantial manpower reserves compared with France's.[195] The War Cabinet Secretary Maurice Hankey advised the SWC to deliver the report to Clemenceau by hand so that any attempts by the French to argue for more British war support could be pre-empted. The tactic was unsuccessful, and when France used Roure's report to demand that Britain maintain 50 Divisions on the Western Front, in addition to ten Dominion Divisions, Lloyd George complained to Clemenceau: 'I have read Colonel Roure's report with great care. It appears to me to be an unscientific, misleading and fallacious document.'[196] The War Secretary Lord Milner noted that the report was based 'on a purely arbitrary assumption as to the number of men required for our maritime and industrial effort', and 'on certain false analogies and misleading comparisons'.[197]

The irony was that the government then turned around and used the same report to question the RAF's manpower. Roure had reported that the RAF's use of manpower was inefficient – that the air service had 214,000 but only 100,000 of them on the Western Front (where people were needed in combat). Sykes was forced to justify his institution against Roure's statistics. He argued that Roure's inaccuracy applied to the RAF as well as to the BEF, and that the best assessment was to compare British and French aerial accomplishments. The French had shot down a third fewer German aircraft and they were not bombing Germany. He noted that, unlike the French air service which had the French Army Staff, the RAF was independent, which meant that it had to do all its own staff work. In addition, the RAF was much more dispersed and hence had to have many more auxiliary units. Finally, Sykes admitted that the RAF had administrative problems, but noted that it was a young service learning how to become more efficient.[198] Sykes knew that his administration was cumbrous at times, but his Air Staff was much better co-ordinated than Weir's Air Council. Groves wrote to Salmond, 'The [Air] Council system of settling great questions of this description by debate and correspondence between co-equal members appears to me – I say it with due diffidence and deference – to be a very ponderous and extraordinarily slow method of procedure.'[199]

The Germans at this time also experienced manpower shortages, as confirmed by the fact that two Austro-Hungarian divisions were transferred to the Western Front.[200] Wilson reported to the War Cabinet that the loss of integrity in the German Army had resulted in much looting in Germany and poor confidence with the high command. Captured German orders indicated 'no doubt that the enemy's discipline is becoming very shaky.'[201]

Weir was excited to report a potential boost to RAF manning and supply. He had heard not only of the availability of American cadets but, unofficially, that the America Program had been reduced to 202 squadrons. With the United States forming fewer squadrons, this would free some American engines for another air service and Weir wanted to ensure that they went to the IAF. The SWC had established two new committees – an Inter-Allied Air Policy Committee and an Inter-Allied Air Munitions Committee. Hence the Air Council decided to send a representative to the latter to lobby for the engines.[202] This was good news for Sykes, who had become frustrated with the difficulties of keeping Trenchard supplied.

By the end of August the RAF had survived its greatest test and was growing rapidly. New aerodromes were needed to provide more training, and the Hotel Cecil could no longer accommodate the Air Staff. Sykes chaired a committee on 24 August to discuss a new location and a new administration. He decided to eliminate the drawing rooms in the hotel and to acquire the bedrooms of the Constitutional Club. With room to expand, Sykes was ready to recreate the air administration: an increased Air Staff, an expanded Meteorology Department taken completely away from the Admiralty, an Inspector General's Branch, a new Air Intelligence Directorate, a Directorate of Training, a new Civil Aerial Transport Department, an expanded Medical Department and an Air Ministry Library for technical research.[203] By the end of August the RAF had become a legitimate service under effective management and leadership. Sykes' bureaucracy was far from perfect, but it was united against the enemy rather than itself. The 'system' had changed since the chaos of 1 April. Sykes had killed the 'House of Bolo'.

He had taken command of a crisis in the air service. He had quenched the fires of discontent and intrigue that plagued the Air Ministry, he had stabilized the upper tiers of the Air Staff to support the RAF's struggle for survival against the Michael Offensive, and he had established an effective working relationship with Weir to develop several RAF organizations and support agencies. The air service had survived due to Sykes' successful implementation of the revolutionary idea that independence from Army and Navy control would permit a more efficient and effective use of aerial technologies. As the BEF finally implemented new tank tactics successfully, Sykes kept his word regarding ground support and aided the battle with new combined-arms aerial tactics. Sykes introduced new training schemes to reduce combat wastage, but the effect was offset by the dangers of low-level flying to protect infantry and tanks. Hence RAF losses did not decline from what they had been previously under Trenchard. However, the RAF proved to be a decisive obstacle to German war-fighting and contributed to the failure of the final German gamble – the spring offensives – and Germany's defeat. In addition, Sykes provided the organizational stability vital to Salmond's continued tactical air battle during the most critical time of the entire war. Sykes' administrative battles were nothing revolutionary in themselves, but the fight for strategic bombing was, and it was Sykes' most difficult endeavor as CAS. It involved not only tremendous organizational and supply problems, but competition with the Allies – particularly France. While the Air Council debated how to allocate supplies to different home areas, it also published an emotional outburst that if General Foch were to demand French possession of long-range bombing, then the Air Council would 'recommend and . . . carry into effect the transfer of the whole of the Independent Force, lock stock and barrel, to England'.[204] Such a pyrrhic victory would not realize Sykes' dream of an Inter-Allied bombing force to strike at the German heartland.

NOTES

1. War Cabinet Committee on Air Organization and Home Defence Against Air Raids, 2nd Report, 9 August 1917, Public Record Office (PRO), Air 9/5. On 11 July 1917 the War Cabinet had decided that Prime Minister Lloyd George and General Smuts should consider two issues – home defense and the Air organization. Smuts' second report on 9 August recommended: (1) forming an Air Ministry; (2) forming an Air General Staff to plan and direct all air strategy, operations, training and intelligence; (3) amalgamating the RNAS and the RFC into one air force; (4) allowing RNAS and RFC officers to choose service in either the new air force or in their old service; and (5) placing all air resources under Air Staff control, even though air units could attach to Army or Navy units for assistance. The Cabinet concurred with Smuts' recommendations and

the Air Force Bill was passed in the House of Commons on 13 November 1917. The Air Council was established on 3 January 1918 and the Air Staff (known as Air Members) met at the Hotel Cecil on the Strand in London to assume the duties of Cowdray's failed Air Board. The Air Council established the orders to transfer personnel from the RNAS and the RFC to the RAF on 9 March, and King's Regulations establishing the duties and responsibilities for posts within the Air Staff were published on 26 March. By the time Sykes arrived on 12 April the organization was in place. See 'Order of the Air Council for the Transferring and Attaching Officers and Men to the Air Force', Air 6/16, Precis No. 84; and 'King's Regulations and Orders for the Royal Air Force, 1918', Air Pub. 141, Royal Air Force Museum (RAFM), Accession No. 001282.

2. Cooper, 'A House Diyided', 190; and *The Birth of Independent Air Power*, 14 and 105–7. Also Higham, *Air Power*, 48–52. Higham noted that the first two institutional changes in the air service were the formation of the War Production Committee and the Air Ministry. He said that the RAF was simply a logical afterthought that 'would cause endless trouble in the years to come'.

3. Cooper, 'A House Divided', 190, and Higham, *Air Power*, 48–52. The RAF and the IAF were founded on a prediction. Aircraft and engine production estimates in 1917 showed a surplus by the middle of 1918 that would allow the air service to build a long-range bombing force. Hence forming the RAF was a dangerous gamble in time of war. One may appreciate the gamble when comparing its birth to that of the US Air Force in 1947, when reports of aerial results (not predictions) following the Second World War recommended a separate air force. See Gordon Daniels, *Guide to Reports of Strategic Bombing Survey*, Vol. 25. The 'Summary Report, Pacific War of the United States Strategic Bombing Survey' stated that bombing 'had turned the tide'.

4. Because the war had not ended quickly, as hoped for, production had now become perhaps the most critical aspect of a war-winning strategy. Yet the complex interaction of forces involved in production made it a difficult factor to predict.

5. Lord Weir had been the Scottish Director of Munitions in 1915 and an Air Board Member as Controller of Aeronautical Supplies in 1917. He moved from his DGAP position to became the Secretary of State for Air on 1 May 1918 after Rothermere resigned. Sir Arthur Duckham replaced Weir as DGAP on 16 May and Weir immediately made Duckham a member of the Air Council.

6. Weir realized that to win the war meant out-producing the enemy. Hence Weir wanted to amalgamate all production – including British and American. He did not want government interference in aircraft design, which was to remain in private industry, but he wanted one centralized authority for all supply in all its phases. American parts needed to be standardized to fit British. Under the then Air Board this would not happen because the Technical Department did not have a representative on the Air Board. Flyers' needs were not being heard by the Aircraft Production Department, and modifications to equipment and aircraft were arriving in the field without any explanation regarding why or how to use them. Overall, Weir advocated an efficient system where design and supply were co-ordinated. He argued: 'The chief anomaly that arises under [the present] system is the technical guidance and instruction of draughtsmen under one Department by Officers of another Department.' Weir to Colonel Alexander, 16 December 1917 and CAS Memorandum, 11 October 1917, Weir Papers 1/2, Churchill College, Cambridge. Henderson also recognized the need for a better system than the one he had implemented and promoted the previous three years, and he argued for a 'Controller of Equipment' to work out technical details. See Henderson Papers, AC 71/4/4, RAFM.

7. Ironically, Henry Wilson had suggested to Lloyd George that Arthur Lee should replace Rothermere. Yet, fortunately for Sykes, Weir got the position and supported Sykes as Rothermere's choice for CAS. Wilson to Lloyd George, 25 April 1918, Lloyd George Papers, Series F/Box 47/Folder 3/Item 23, House of Lords Record Office.

8. Weir to Lloyd George, 27 April 1918, Weir Papers, 1/6.

9. Weir to Bolling, 4 August 1917, Air 1/26/15/1/124; Minutes of 123rd Meeting of Air Board, 8 August 1917, Air 1/26/15/1/124; and Northcliffe to War Cabinet, Derby, Cowdray and Trenchard, 31 October 1917, Air 1/26/15/1/124. The American link was always paramount in the formation of the RAF. One of the CAS's duties specifically delineated in Parliamentary debates was to work with the Allies. See House of Commons Debates, Vol. 103, Col. 956, 21 February 1918. Major Bolling was head of the American Aeronautical Commission and worked at the American Embassy in London. On 4 August the Air Board notified Bolling that Britain wanted a total of 3,000 engines suitable for fighting or bombing, supplied at a rate of 500 a month. Northcliffe complained that the liaison between Cowdray's Air Board and the American Aircraft Production Board was ineffective in notifying the Americans that Britain wanted their equipment. Northcliffe stated some American factories were able to produce 3,000 automobiles a day and that the British government had better make it clear to the President that they wanted the Americans to standardize parts to fit British machines and to begin supplying long-range bombers. The Prime Minister's secretary, however, was concerned that Northcliffe might be 'talking a bit too much for American taste'. See Hankey to Prime Minister, 20 Oct. 1917, Lloyd George Papers, Series F/Box 23/File 1.

10. Northcliffe to Cowdray, 10 August 1917, Air 1/26/15/1/124. Northcliffe complained that the British military representative in Washington had told the Americans that the Italian Caproni bomber was better than the British Handley Page! During summer 1917, the American Bolling Commission had studied strategic bombing. In the process, Bolling had corresponded with Douhet, and by November Bolling told the American Aircraft Production Board to give bomber production higher priority than fighter production. See Futrell, 24.

11. Precis No. 219 and No. 235, Air 6/18; and Meeting No. 46, 30 August 1918, Air 6/13. Sykes created the M-5 Branch as the single point of contact for all American issues. The Americans, however, objected to their having to go through that procedure and demanded the ability to go direct to branches within the Air Ministry. This created friction between Sykes and Brancker when on 24 August Brancker tried to appease the Americans by moving M-5 under the Directorate of Training and Manning (Master-General of Personnel MGP), arguing that most of the branch's activities dealt not with policy but with training issues. Sykes, however, resisted, and on 30 August kept M-5 under the CAS.

12. Futrell, 24–5.

13. Roskill, xiv.

14. Ibid. 'Additional Reports of Gunnery Committee', 24 June 1916, *Beatty Papers*, ed. B. M. Ranft (London: Naval Records Society, 1989), No. 173, 1:359; and Brancker to Trenchard [no date], Trenchard Papers, MFC 76/1/16, RAFM. Brancker wrote regarding the amalgamation: 'Carson and Eric Geddes are against it, the rest are for it so far as I can say.' He was talking about the War Cabinet, however, and not the Admiralty. Brancker also mentioned that Godfrey Paine was strongly in favor of amalgamation. According to Cooper, *The Birth of Independent Air Power*, 101, the only other pro-independent air force Navy man besides Beatty was the former Director of Naval Aviation Services Murray F. Sueter.

15. Admiralty letters M. 0319 and M. 81376, January 1918, PRO, Adm 1/8504 and 1/8512.
16. Brancker to Trenchard, 21 August 1917, Trenchard Papers, MFC 76/1/16. Brancker was excited that Henderson was 'going to be Cowdray's Chief advisor'. Lloyd George did not select Cowdray as Air Minister, however, apparently because Cowdray had sponsored an article that had implicated the Prime Minister in a cowardly act (leaving London during an air raid). See Boyle, 247.
17. Brancker to Trenchard, 29 August 1917, Trenchard Papers, MFC 76/1/16. Brancker exclaimed to Trenchard that the only reason he had been so disgraced in front of his friends and the entire Army was because 'I haven't a sufficiently bald head or pot belly for the Army Council.'
18. Brancker to Trenchard, 30 August 1917, Trenchard Papers, MFC 76/1/16. Brancker stated, 'I am not at all sure that Sykes isn't at the bottom of this, in the hopes that he would kill two birds with one stone – become GOC Tanks – and do me in – do you think it possible?' Brancker's 'abandonment' was a position with the Palestine Brigade in Egypt, but instead he traveled to the United States to help co-ordinate American supplies.
19. Trenchard to Brancker, 30 August 1917, Trenchard Papers, MFC 76/1/16.
20. Boyle, 241. According to Boyle, Robertson also suspected such power politics and therefore took revenge on Henderson and Brancker for their part in helping Smuts form a separate air service.
21. Amery to Sykes, 13 October 1941, Sykes Private Papers.
22. Trenchard to Haig, 31 December 1917, Trenchard Papers, MFC 76/1/18; Haig to Trenchard, 31 December 1917, Trenchard Papers, MFC 76/1/18; and Haig to Derby, 10 January 1918, Trenchard Papers, MFC 76/1/18. Haig wrote to Derby that it was important not to lose Trenchard due to the critical nature of the war during the coming four months. Also, Raleigh and Jones, Appendix III, 17. According to intelligence reports, the air service had been effective during summer 1917 in demoralizing the enemy by flying low-level attacks. Haig stated that the air service had to support the Army, and, hence, had to be owned and run by the Army.
23. 'Remarks on Sir Douglas Haig's Despatch', 20 September 1917, Henderson Papers, AC 71/4/4, RAFM. Henderson fought against 'divided responsibility' by advocating an air service that controlled all aspects of the air war, including ground air defense (anti-aircraft guns). Henderson also wanted a separate air medical service.
24. Ibid. Henderson was much less concerned about reprisals and attacking the enemy's morale than he was about interdicting German supplies. His strongest argument was that the air force could help to cut German supply lines.
25. Henderson had argued that a separate air service could not be formed too rapidly or it would disrupt the war effort. In order to keep the new service legitimate, Henderson had proposed a new nomenclature and ranks, with the most senior post of the 'Air Fleet' to be an Air Marshal. Henderson Papers, AC 71/4/4.
26. Henderson to Rothermere (no date), Henderson Papers AC 71/12/75. Henderson wrote: 'After our conversation on Friday last, when I expressed to you and to General Smuts a very unfavourable opinion of Major-General Sykes, and considering my previous relations with that officer, his appointment as Chief of the Air Staff makes it most undesirable, in the interests of the Service, that I should remain in the Air Force.'
27. Henderson to Bonar Law, 26 April 1918, Henderson Papers, AC 71/12/75.
28. Weir acknowledged Henderson's 'alleged inability to work with the new Chief of the Air Staff'. Weir to Lloyd George, 27 April 1918, Weir Papers 1/6.
29. David Henderson to Ian Henderson, 13 April 1918, Henderson Papers, AC

71/12/449. Considering the message his departure conveyed, it is tempting to criticize Henderson for leaving. On the other hand, given his opinion of Sykes at this point, his staying on might have caused worse turmoil for the RAF.

30. Ian Henderson to David Henderson, 17 April 1918, Henderson Papers, AC 71/12/450.

31. Autobiographical recollections, Trenchard Papers, MFC 76/1/61. The first Secretary of State for Air was Harold Sidney Harmsworth, Lord Rothermere. According to Trenchard, Rothermere and his brother, Lord Northcliffe, black-mailed Trenchard with the CAS position as part of a plot to oust Haig. See Boyle, 250–2.

32. Parliamentary Debates, House of Lords, 21 November 1917, 1111, Air 9/5.

33. Trenchard to John Salmond, 25 March 1918, Trenchard Papers, MFC 76/1/92. Trenchard told Salmond he was against the Secretary of State for Air, who was trying to increase numbers of squadrons. Trenchard was convinced that the most important aspect of air power was to maintain squadron strength, and he would not jeopardize that to increase numbers of squadrons. Also, autobiographical recollections, Trenchard Papers, MFC 76/1/61; and Boyle, 263.

34. Boyle, 252.

35. Trenchard to John Salmond, 13 February 1918, Trenchard Papers, MFC 76/1/92.

36. John Salmond to Trenchard, 2 February 1918, Trenchard Papers, MFC 76/1/92; and Trenchard to Salmond, 4 February 1918, Trenchard Papers, MFC 76/1/92.

37. Geddes to Rothermere, 19 March 1918, Trenchard Papers, MFC 76/1/19. Geddes complained to Rothermere that Trenchard was giving the Navy completely different figures from the ones the Air Minister had submitted to them.

38. Trenchard to Rothermere, 18 March 1918, Trenchard Papers, MFC 76/1/19; and Rothermere to Trenchard, 28 March 1918, Trenchard Papers, MFC 76/1/19. Rothermere was eager to cut home defense and training and send more squadrons to France. Trenchard believed that adding more squadrons of older-type aircraft would not help the Western Front, and he was adamant that Salmond's squadrons should not be overly taxed.

39. Rothermere to Trenchard, 19 March 1918, Trenchard Papers, MFC 76/1/19.

40. Trenchard to Rothermere, 19 March 1918, Trenchard Papers, MFC 76/1/19. Trenchard submitted his resignation letter in an emotional state; most of it is too grammatically flawed to make any sense – Trenchard's famous idiosyncrasy.

41. Rothermere to Trenchard, 13 April 1918, Trenchard Papers, MFC 76/1/19. In response to Trenchard's memorandum to the War Cabinet, in which he stated that he would never have resigned in time of crisis, Rothermere brings up the point that Trenchard, two days earlier (11 April), had complained about Rothermere stalling on the acceptance of Trenchard's resignation. The main weakness in Trenchard's defense is simply that the German offensive was widely expected by the British military and government. Certainly he knew it was imminent on 19 March when he submitted the resignation, and clearly there was a state of crisis on 11 April when he accused Rothermere of stalling.

42. Ibid.

43. Minutes of Meeting, 24 April 1918, War Cabinet 398, PRO, CAB 23.

44. Trenchard to Weir, 1 May 1918; Trenchard to Weir 4 May 1918; Trenchard to Weir 5 May 1918; Weir to Trenchard 6 May 1918; and Trenchard to Weir 6 May 1918; all in Trenchard Papers, MFC 76/1/20. Trenchard rejected many offers: Inspector General Overseas; Commander-in-Chief, Middle East; Inspector General in England; Commander of 8th Brigade; Commander of the RAF in the Field; and Commander of the IAF. Trenchard demanded that he should not

be given responsibility without authority, and he did not want to supplant people such as Newall, John Salmond and Geoffrey Salmond, who were performing well in their positions. Trenchard asked Weir to make him GOC of the Air Force, with a seat on the Air Council, and 'the power to put forth my views of policy'. Weir rejected the request, and Trenchard finally acquiesced to taking charge of the IAF.

45. Trenchard to Milner, 25 April 1918, and Milner to Trenchard, 25 April 1918, Lloyd George Papers, Series F/Box 47/File3/Item 2.

46. Boyle, 277–8.

47. Weir to Lloyd George, 27 April 1918, Weir Papers 1/6. Weir was simply reaffirming that Rothermere's decision to give the command to Sykes was the right one.

48. *The Times* (London), 8 May 1918, 10. In the House of Commons Asquith asked Bonar Law whether Trenchard had been offered a position. Law replied that he had, but that he had not accepted anything.

49. Collier, 76 and Beaverbrook, 225. Speculation arose and was reported in the London *Daily News*, 16 April 1918, that Trenchard, Jellicoe (removed as First Sea Lord) and Robertson (removed as Chief of the Imperial General Staff) had been fired as part of a political move to remove those people who were against Lloyd George's 'wild schemes'. Members of Parliament were concerned that Trenchard should not be dismissed as readily as Lord Jellicoe. The phrase in use at the time was the 'Jellicoe mould'. See *The Times*, 3 May 1918, 10.

50. Minute 17, 25 April 1918, War Cabinet 399, CAB 23.

51. Rothermere to Lloyd George, 23 April 1918, Beaverbrook, Appendix IV, 380–2. Major the Right Honorable Sir John Simon had been Trenchard's assistant secretary, and Lieutenant the Right Honorable Lord Hugh Cecil was a junior staff officer at the Hotel Cecil. Rothermere complained to Lloyd George that military Members should not be allowed to divulge privileged information in Parliament, that such action flouted disciplinary codes.

52. *The Times* (London), 1 May 1918, 7.

53. Beaverbrook, 224–5. The King had learned of Trenchard's replacement from the newspapers on 13 April and sent a letter of criticism to Lloyd George on 16 April.

54. Weir to Lloyd George, 27 April 1918, Weir Papers 1/6.

55. Beaverbrook, 225; and Higham, *Military Intellectuals*, 155.

56. Rothermere to Lloyd George, 23 April 1918, Beaverbrook, 380–2.

57. Boyle, 263. Rothermere may have been inflexible and impersonal – a better manager of numbers than leader of men. Yet, he was faced with a formidable task in trying to amalgamate the RFC and the RNAS while suffering from poor health and the loss of his sons.

58. Hankey to Trenchard, 15 April 1918, Trenchard Papers, MFC 76/1/19; and Trenchard to Rothermere, 14 April 1918, Trenchard Papers, MFC 76/1/19.

59. Weir to Lloyd George, 27 April 1918, Weir Papers 1/6.

60. Beaverbrook, 230–5. According to Beaverbrook, he and Churchill drafted Rothermere's second resignation letter, which was published on 25 April 1918.

61. Private letter from Rothermere to Bonar Law, 3 May 1918, Beaverbrook, 236.

62. Lord Stamfordham to Prime Minister, 25 April 1918, Lloyd George Papers, Series F/Box 29/File 2. Less than a month earlier the King had congratulated Rothermere as the 'General-in-Chief' of the new Royal Air Force. By May 1918 Rothermere was an outcast. The vote in the House of Commons on 29 April was 127 to 37 against paying Rothermere £900, which was £100 less than the customary figure.

63. Ludendorff had pronounced before 21 March: 'If the enemy does not want

peace, he shall have battle. The battle will naturally be the most tremendous of the entire war, but our splendid soldiers, and the same spirit of resolution and self-sacrifice at home, will, with God's help, win us an honorable peace – a German peace, not a soft peace.' From *The Times* (London), 27 October 1918.

64. War Cabinet Minutes, 21 March 1918, War Cabinet 369, CAB 23; and War Cabinet Minutes, 23 March 1918, War Cabinet 371, CAB 23. According to Martin Middlebrook, *The Kaiser's Battle, 21 March 1918: The First Day of the Spring Offensive* (London: Allen Lane, 1978), 63, the RFC sent a sortie on 19 March to drop leaflets over the German lines with the message: 'Best of luck for your attack on March 21.' The Germans initiated their attack on a front 80 km wide. They struck with 191 divisions against an Allied total of 165 French, British, Portuguese and Belgian divisions. The War Cabinet noted, 'This front of attack was in general accord with the one anticipated by the British Staff at Versailles.' Along with those divisions, the Germans attacked with 730 aircraft (against 579 British aircraft available). Kennett, *The First Air War*, 208, called the German action a tactical revolution. Also see Chamier, 176.

65. In particular, John Salmond was a capable field commander who maintained effective control during the offensive. Weir later commented that Salmond was superior to Trenchard in that capacity.

66. Air Council Minutes, 22 March 1918, Air 6/12. The minutes prove that air service work during the German offensive had no guidance from London. In Council, there was not one word mentioned of the German attack. Instead, Trenchard, Brancker and Weir were debating issues regarding the raising of future squadrons and how to supply them with engines.

67. Supreme War Council Joint Note No. 24, Annex C, 18 April 1918, CAB 25/121. The Inter-Allied Transportation Council identified Amiens as a key strategic location on the Western Front owing to the confluence of Allied railway lines. Its loss would mean the loss of American supplies.

68. War Cabinet Minutes, 27 March 1918, War Cabinet 374, CAB 23; and War Cabinet Minutes, 23 April 1918, War Cabinet 379, CAB 23. The CIGS reported: 'Fifth Army can no longer be regarded as a fighting unit.' Also Amery to Sykes, 13 October 1941, Sykes Private Papers. The press reported that Fifth Army failed to hold the line because the French had forced Haig to extend his line beyond British capabilities.

69. War Cabinet Minutes, 1 April 1918, War Cabinet 379, CAB 23. On 15 April Haig issued his famous order: 'With our backs to the wall . . . each one of us must fight to the end.' See Beaverbrook, 224.

70. War Cabinet Minutes, 4 April 1918, War Cabinet 382, CAB 23; and Air 1/6A/4/54. From 19 March to 1 April British flyers dropped 319 tons of bombs, fired 1,000,000 rounds of ammunition at ground targets, and downed 366 enemy aircraft at a cost of 550 British aircraft and 315 aviators (killed, wounded or missing). Trenchard praised the effort, claiming that they had 'attained definite supremacy in the air on the battle-front'. During the offensive, all British air resources on the Western Front, including the newly formed long-range bombing Eighth Brigade under Colonel Newall, were focused against the German advance. Baring's poem, 'Per Ardua', described the scene:

> And in the dark hour when the foe broke through,
> The message was 'Tails up' from those that flew.

See Trenchard Papers, MFC 76/1/114. On 27 March George V sent a message of appreciation to John Salmond and the RAF in France for their work against the German attack. The historiography of the spring offensive air war is mixed. Kennedy, in 'Britain in the First World War', 50, noted that the RAF was effective in bombing and strafing German targets to interdict their supply lines. See also Liddell Hart, 316. Higham, *Air Power*, 29, noted that most of the British losses in aircraft were upon landing and that the air service's greatest difficulty was its poorly trained pilots. Boyle, 273, predictably credited Trenchard as the commander who guided Salmond to victory and reinforced the air service with emergency supplies so that it was able to survive.

71. Lt J. C. F. Hopkins sound recording, Reel No. 4, IWM sound recordings. Hopkins recalled that they averaged two sorties per night and that such flying and poor weather created considerable pilot fatigue during the March offensive. Yet he maintained that air power was effective: 'But of course we did a great deal of damage; we stopped these columns from going along the [Bapaume–Albert] road.'

72. Aaron Norman, *The Great Air War* (New York: Macmillan, 1968), 439–51. The Germans attacked during poor weather for a reason. The weather did not clear until 24 March, at which point British flyers were able to mount a substantial attack. Within a few days, German operations slowed, and within two weeks Ludendorff had recalled his squadrons from the front to sit at Cappy. Norris, 235, stated that 26 March was the real birthday of the RAF since it was the pivotal day when British flyers helped to stop the Germans.

73. 'Handbook of German Military and Naval Aviation', Air Pub 71, RAFM, Accession No. 005113, 71. In 1918 German Air Force tactics changed from a defensive offense to an offensive offense. Accordingly the *Schutzstaffeln* were renamed the *Schlachtstaffeln*. The German 'Manual of Position Warfare for All Arms', Part 12, stated: 'The greatest effect is obtained if at battle flights cross the front line at the same moment that the infantry advances to the attack.' According to Norman, 447, the German Air Force reverted to defensive aerial tactics at the end of March due to high loss rates against British pilots.

74. 'Precis of Mr W. G. Max Muller's Report for February 1918', CAB 25/91.

75. Stark, 28.

76. 'The Attack in Position Warfare', Part VI, translated German documents, Trenchard Papers, MFC 76/1/73. The document was dated 1 January 1918 and was marked 'Secret, Not to be taken into the Front Line, Distribution Down to Battalions'. Haig reported in his dispatch that German aircraft had helped to overwhelm British defenses: 'large numbers of low-flying aeroplanes attacked our troops and batteries'. In 'Despatch from Field-Marshal Sir Douglas Haig', *London Gazette*, 21 October 1918, 7.

77. Amery to Sykes, 13 October 1941, Sykes Private Papers. Amery told Sykes that the Amiens failure was not the turning point for the Germans. It was the attrition expended in April which led to failures in July. The 8 August defeat simply cemented the situation. For an assessment of German aircraft attrition and their loss of the war of production, see Morrow, *German Air Power*, 140 and Cooper, *The Birth of Independent Air Power*, 144.

78. German Documents, Trenchard Papers, MFC 76/1/73. German prisoners of war repeatedly mentioned that British aviators had control of the air and interfered with operations so extensively that they were forced to advance only at night or in poor weather when the enemy could not fly.

79. Ibid. Translation of a captured German letter reads, 'The British aviators bothered us most – they always came over in squadrons, while of our own, it was seldom that more than one or two could be seen.' The diary of an infantry soldier with the German 478th Infantry Regiment, 243rd Infantry Division, mentioned the devastating attacks from British aircraft machine-guns on 2 April 1918. The soldier recorded that the aviators flew within 10 m of the ground while attacking. Another German recorded in his diary that his position south of Amiens was

precarious because of RAF bombing: 'One doesn't know where to bury oneself.'
80. Ibid. Captured German diaries mention that the German attack flights had to move back to Epiny owing to the continuous aerial bombing.
81. 'Experiences during the War 1914–1918', Air Pub 956, RAFM, Accession No. 001525, 82.
82. War Cabinet Minutes, 23 March 1918, War Cabinet 371; and War Cabinet Minutes, 12 April 1918, War Cabinet 390, CAB 23. Also Sykes, *From Many Angles*, 214. To help to provide more soldiers, the War Cabinet considered various measures: reducing the 'calling-up' notice time from 14 days to seven, streamlining the medical review process, withdrawing men from the Admiralty, recruiting Russian labor and lowering the age limit to 17 years. Sykes determined that 170,000 men were still available in Britain for service, and he worked the emergency plans to ship supplies and 30,000 men a day across the English Channel. Between 21 March and 12 April the British Army lost more than 130,000 men.
83. Drafts of 'Notes on Economy of Man-Power by Mechanical Means', Sykes Private Papers.
84. Kennett, *The First Air War*, 212, noted that the British copied the German *Schlachtstaffeln* concept when they co-ordinated ground attack with tanks. Yet Sykes published similar tactics before the spring offensive when the Germans foreshadowed the blitzkrieg with quick combined-arms attack.
85. Drafts of 'Notes on Economy of Man-Power by Mechanical Means', Sykes Private Papers.
86. Ibid.
87. Sykes, *From Many Angles*, 215. Unbelievable as it might appear, Sykes stated that he was actually reluctant to take the job because he did not want 'to be dragged into the vortex' at the Hotel Cecil.
88. Named after Bolo Pasha, a notorious French spy.
89. James, 66, implied that Sykes actually had to take the CAS position as a part-time job because of his work at Versailles.
90. Trenchard to Brigadier-Gen. Benjamin D. Foulois, 11 April 1918, Trenchard Papers, MFC 76/1/72. General John J. Pershing appointed Mason M. Patrick as Chief of the Air Service, American Expeditionary Force and Benjamin D. Foulois as Chief of the Air Service, First Army, and assistant to Patrick.
91. Trenchard to Weir, 1 May 1918, Trenchard Papers, MFC 76/1/20. Trenchard told Weir that he had specific ideas regarding offensive air superiority in relation to bombing, and that Sykes had Trenchard's plans. His intention was to ensure that the new Air Minister made the new CAS follow the outgoing CAS's methodology.
92. War Cabinet Minute Four, 24 April 1918, War Cabinet 398, CAB 23. This was the first meeting in which the War Cabinet ever raised the issue of Trenchard's replacement by Sykes.
93. Autobiographical notes, Trenchard Papers, MFC 76/1/61. Trenchard recalled Sykes' saying: 'Lord Rothermere has sent me, I didn't ask to come.' Then apparently Trenchard replied, 'I am not interested in your explanations, is there anything you want to know about the work?' Sykes said nothing. See Divine, 131 and Boyle, 277.
94. Trenchard to War Office, 14 April 1918, Trenchard Papers, MFC 76/1/19. Trenchard spent the next three weeks in London, much of the time in civilian clothes sitting on a bench in Green Park. See Boyle, 282.
95. Nole Pemberton Billings, House of Commons Debates, 29 April 1918, col. 1363, Trenchard Papers, MFC 76/1/19.
96. Ibid. Sir Eric Carson noted that the airmen considered Trenchard 'Father of the

Air Service', and Sir John Simon argued that Trenchard's departure had struck a mortal blow to a service that depended on the psychological factor of leadership. Mr Joynson-Hicks responded, 'If General Trenchard is not to be the Chief of the Air Staff, I know no man better able to succeed him than General Sykes.' He called Sykes a man 'of great determination and devotion to duty'. Lloyd George stated that the Air Board had considered carefully the duties of the CAS. In his words, the CAS needed to be a person able to

> think out carefully, slowly, laboriously, plans not merely for tomorrow, not for the day after tomorrow, but for next year . . . There is a vast difference between the qualities required for that and the qualities you require for great leadership and inspiration of the Air Force. Having been faced with the accomplished fact of the resignation of General Trenchard, having to consider as between General Trenchard and General Sykes for the position of Chief of the Air Staff, there is absolutely no doubt in the minds of those who investigated the matter on behalf of the Cabinet that for that particular post General Syke's [*sic*] qualities and mind were better adapted than those of General Trenchard.

97. Ibid.
98. Geddes to Rothermere, 11 April 1918, Adm 116/1807.
99. Salmond to Trenchard, 31 March 1918, Trenchard Papers, MFC 76/1/92. Salmond thanked Trenchard for his support and stated that the line was more stable and that the Army had credited the RFC for pulling them 'out of a tight place'. Unknown to Salmond, however, the crisis was not over.
100. 'E' Branch, 'Notes on Situation on the British Front, 13 April, 1918, From the German Point of View', CAB 25/121.
101. Liddell Hart, *The Real War*, 408, recorded the situation on 13 April 1918: 'This was the crisis'.
102. Christopher Cole, ed., *Royal Air Force Communiqués 1918* (London: Tom Donovan, 1990), 27–39.
103. Ibid., 39–45. The story of von Richthofen's death remains under debate. Some historians have claimed that an Australian gun crew shooting at him may have been just as responsible for hitting the triplane.
104. Stark, 47. Stark recalled that von Richthofen's death marked the end of the spring offensive's air war: 'Richthofen dead! We whisper the dread tidings softly to one another . . . a gloomy silence broods over all.'
105. House of Commons Debates, 29 April 1918, col. 1368, Trenchard Papers, MFC 76/1/92.
106. Major F. J. Powell, sound recording, Reel No. 5, IWM sound recordings; C. V. Lacey's Flying Log Book, 1918, NMM, Log/N/34/1–2; and Montagu to Prime Minister, 10 July 1917, Lloyd George Papers, Series F/Box 39/File 3. Powell described the dangerous offensive patrols that by 1916 guaranteed RFC pilots a fight every time they crossed the line. He noted that pilots flew on average two patrols a day, or four hours a day under fire from the enemy. It is understandable, under such conditions, that the survival rate was so low. Sykes, *From Many Angles*, 220, wrote that the high wastage rate had been due to Trenchard's strong support of Haig's 'battering ram tactics'. Sykes also knew that too many poorly trained pilots were arriving at the front. To gain control of training and promote better tactics, Sykes took the Training Department from the Personnel Branch and placed it under himself on 8 June 1918. He promoted a new Training Expansion Committee designed to oversee facility production, established a School of Aerial Photographic Training, eliminated all civilian training schools for the RAF and established a six-week aerial tactics course that studied German

tactics and appropriate countermeasures. See 'Notes on Aerial Fighting', July 1918, Air Pub 156, RAFM, Accession No. 001169; 'Syllabus for a Six Week's Course at Schools of Aeronautics', 1 October 1918, Air Pub 156, RAFM, Accession No. 001301; Air Staff Minutes, 28 May 1918, Meeting No. 56, Air 8/15; and 'Reasons for Suggested Transfer of Training from Personnel to the Air Staff Department', Air Council Minutes, 8 June 1918, Air 6/12.

107. Precis Number 86, Air 6/16. The six Areas had the following headquarters: No. 1 at London, No. 2 at Bristol, No. 3 at Birmingham, No. 4 at York, No. 5 at Edinburgh and No. 6 at Dublin.

108. 'Air Force Memorandum No. 3', 18 March 1918, RAFM, Accession No. 001280.

109. 'Provisional Instructions Regarding Non-Technical Supplies and Services', April 1918, Air Pub 7, RAFM, Accession No. 001110.

110. October Air Council Minutes prove that this problem was never solved. On 3 October 1918 the Air Council was trying to work a solution because uncoordinated RAF orders had created confusion in the Ministry of Munitions.

111. Air Pubs 1–4, RAFM, Accession No. 001107. The first four official RAF publications concerned finance.

112. Air Council Minutes, 18 April 1918, Meeting Number 24, Air 6/12; and 'Instructions for Payment of Women's Royal Air Force, Civil Subordinates, & at Home Stations', Air Pub 16, 23 March 1918, RAFM, Accession No. 001115. The regulation noted that the payment system was not consistent, and that the RAF had a pressing need: 'The essential point being that there shall be no discontinuity of payment during the transitional period.' There was, however, discontinuity.

113. Air Council Minutes, 28 March 1918, Meeting Number 22, Air 6/12; Precis No. 304, Air 6/19; and 'Standing Orders for WRAF', 8 October 1918, Precis No. 250, Air 6/18. Members of three organizations – the Women's Royal Naval Service (WRNS), the Women's Army Auxiliary Corps (WAAC) and the Women's Legion Motor Drivers (WLMD) – were invited to join the new WRAF. The initial transfer was 2,867 from the WRNS, 6,805 from the WAAC, and 496 from the WLMD. See Beryl E. Escott, *Women in Air Force Blue, The Story of Women in the Royal Air Force from 1918 to the Present* (London: Patrick Stephens, 1989), 19. Also *The Times* (London), 24 January 1919, 9. On 8 October 1918 the Air Council agreed to honor the WRAF Commandant's request to change the name from 'Women's Royal Air Force' to 'Women of the Royal Air Force' and to refer to the women not as 'members' but as 'air women'. See also Peter Liddle, *The Airman's War 1914–1918* (Poole: Blandford Press, 1987), 92.

114. Godfrey Paine, the Master-General of Personnel (MGP), determined that the highest-ranking woman, Lady Gertrude Crawford, lacked 'the qualities necessary for organizing a large body of women'. Miss Violet Douglas-Pennant replaced Crawford as Lady Commandant, but met with organizational disaster when she tried to instill discipline. She was replaced by Mrs Gwynne-Vaughan, who was not officially appointed head of the WRAF until after the Armistice. See also, Weir's Speech to House of Commons, June 1918, Air 1/8/15/1. Weir stated that the greatest problem in creating the WRAF was the housing shortage. While WRAF 'immobiles' lived at home and commuted to work each day (costing the RAF 14 shillings a week each for transport), 'mobiles' had to have government housing. Escott, 24–34, noted that by May 1918 there were WRAF mobiles living at over 500 camps in Great Britain.

115. 'Order of the Air Council for Transferring and attaching Officers and Men to the Air Force,' Admiralty Weekly Order 886a, 14 March 1918, Adm 1/8512;

Admiralty Letter C. W. 10698, 2 April 1918, Adm 116/1822; and Cole, 11. The fact that the Navy had to adjust to Army flying caused resentment. For example, RNAS squadrons were renumbered (No. 1 becoming No. 201, etc.) to fit into the RFC numbering scheme. The orders read that RNAS officers would be transferred to the RAF with or without their consent, but that after three months they could return to the Navy without prejudice, if they desired. Initial anti-RAF hostility was revealed in an earlier Weekly Order No. 695, 28 February 1918, Adm 116/1822, which stated: 'In any case it is probable that the number of Officers who can be spared for transfer will be very limited.'

116. Admiralty Letter No. 1651, 1 May 1918, Roskill, 611. Vice-Admiral Sir Roger Keyes, Commander of the Dover Patrol, protested that this move prevented a critical mission – bombing the U-boats at Bruges – from being completed.

117. Brancker to Robinson (Air Council Secretary), 25 October 1918, in Precis No. 280, Air 6/18. Also, Sykes, *From Many Angles*, 219. By the end of the war the Air Council was still trying to make RAF ranks equivalent to those of the Army and the Navy.

118. Admiralty to Beatty, 30 March 1918, Air 1/274, and Admiralty Weekly Order No. 1391, 19 March 1918, Adm 1/8504.

119. Roskill, 609.

120. Admiralty Weekly Order No. 1391, 19 March 1918, Adm 1/8504.

121. Memorandum by Captain F. R. Scarlett, July 1918; Admiralty Memorandum, 8 July 1918; and Beatty to Admiralty, 30 July 1918, all in Roskill, 681–5. Also Sir Stanley Colville to Admiralty, 14 August 1918, Adm 1/8534. Colville argued for a return to the RNAS: 'I am of opinion that the present arrangement of dual control whereby one authority controls operations and another is in charge of administration and discipline cannot prove successful.'

122. Geddes to Weir, 22 May 1918, Roskill, 668–71. Actually, it was not Weir, but Trenchard who was responsible for this decision. Weir knew Trenchard had no desire to be a liaison officer, but wanted his own command.

123. Sykes, *From Many Angles*, 218.

124. Precis No. 215, Air 6/18. The Air Policy Committee was designed to co-ordinate policy between the RAF, the Army and the Navy, and the 'Training Expansion Committee' organized a 'Programme of Development for Naval Co-operation Units'. The two Naval representatives were Rear-Admiral Mark Kerr (Deputy Chief of the Air Staff) and Commodore Godfrey Paine, MGP.

125. Air Council Minutes, 24 July 1918, Meeting No. 80, Air 8/5. Sykes tried to placate the Navy, responding to requests and answering complaints. Overall, however, the Air Staff let the Admiralty know that the Air Ministry was in charge, regardless of what the Admiralty thought. For example, during the Air Council's eightieth meeting, the Council addressed an Admiralty complaint that personnel were being moved around simply to make up for shortages. The Air Council's answer was that RAF personnel belonged to the Air Ministry and could be moved whenever and wherever needed.

126. Air Board Letter 6206, 30 March 1918 and Admiralty Letter M. 03369, 23 April 1918, Air 1/652. The influence of Army flying was seen when the Air Board suggested that the Admiralty should order aeroplanes rather than seaplanes. The Admiralty's negative response was predictable, but their prejudice had backing. Admiralty figures for May and June showed that seaplanes were the most effective aircraft for anti-submarine patrol, the major naval air role to develop in 1918. By May 1918 seaplanes and airships flew 1,000 hours per week each and aircraft flew 650 hours per week. During May and June RAF naval flyers had attacked 46 German submarines. See Air 1/17/15/1/89. The document that dictated naval flying duties was in the appendix of 'Review of the Air Situation',

Sykes' memorandum that went before the Imperial War Cabinet, 27 June 1918. Drafts of this document are in the Sykes Private Papers.

127. Roskill, Appendix I.
128. Naval flying had three primary objectives: fleet protection, reconnaissance and anti-submarine bombing. The RNAS had bombed the Zeebrugge, Ostend and other submarine bases since late 1914, but Geddes and Beatty were in agreement that such long-range bombing was ineffective until the Navy had more aircraft carriers. See 'Record of Discussion at the Admiralty on the Occasion of a Visit by Admiral Sir David Beatty, 2–3 January 1918', Adm 116/1806. By 1918 anti-submarine work had joined more with fleet protection and reconnaissance so that anti-submarine patrols were a primary mission. Captain W. W. Fisher was Director of the Anti-Submarine Division and was developing the use of hydrophones to detect submarines, but when the Air Ministry failed to deliver anti-submarine bombers, the Admiralty became very concerned. See Memorandum by Captain F. R. Scarlett and Minute by Captain W. W. Fisher (no dates), Air 1/274. Also, 'Memorandum by Scarlett, 4 May 1918', Roskill, 668. Scarlett promoted many technological innovations for anti-submarine work and tried to form an anti-submarine school.
129. Air Staff Minutes, 12 August 1918, Meeting No. 87, Air 8/5.
130. Air Staff Minutes, 21 October 1918, Meeting No. 113, Air 8/5.
131. Geddes Memorandum, 'Programme of the Royal Air Force to 30th September 1919. Allocation of Aircraft to the Navy', 31 August 1918, Roskill, 611; and Admiralty to Air Ministry, 19 April 1918, Air 1/274.
132. Kennett, *The First Air War*, 198.
133. Admiralty to Air Ministry, 8 August 1918 and Air Ministry to Admiralty, 16 September 1918, Air 1/643. The Admiralty complained: 'The production of aircraft and training of personnel for Naval purposes has been most unsatisfactory and is now proving a serious handicap in carrying out Naval Operations.'
134. Air Staff Minutes, 10 June 1918, Meeting No. 61; and Air Staff Minutes, 26 June 1918, Meeting No. 68, Air 8/5.
135. 'Minutes by Captain F. R. Scarlett, 4 May 1918', Roskill, 668. Also, Raleigh and Jones, 1:210–11. The official historian mentioned that language difficulties presented problems and that the Air Ministry did make some concessions.
136. E. S. Montagu to Prime Minister, 10 July 1917, Lloyd George Papers, Series F/Box 39/File 3. Montagu was one of Britain's strongest proponents of air power in 1916 and 1917 and, while a member of the Reconstruction Committee, he conceded in July 1917 that there were no aircraft available to defend London. Also Christopher Cole and E. F. Cheesman, *The Air Defense of Britain 1914–1918* (London: Putnam, 1984), 410. Zeppelins L60, L61, L62 and L64 killed seven people, injured 20 and did £11,000 worth of damage.
137. Air Pub 956, RAFM, Accession No. 001525, 70. The LADA was authorized on 8 August 1917 and the Northern Air Defences were organized on 21 May 1918. Also Gollin, 228. Ashmore replaced the man first in charge of Home Defence, Major T. C. R. Higgins, who was ordered to establish a unit of night-fighting aircraft which was eventually mission-ready as 6th Brigade in late October 1918. In assuming command, Ashmore stated that he had left the relatively safe environment of machine-gun bullets, gas and shelling north of Ypres, to work in the dangerous atmosphere of London, where he might be lynched.
138. Cole and Cheesman, 415 and 456. The control and reporting center was at Spring Gardens, Admiralty Arch, and the nine squadrons were based at North Weald, Hainault, Suttons Farm, Biggin Hill, Goldhanger, Stow Maries, Rochford, Throwley, Bekesbourne and Detling (one squadron was split).
139. John Ferris, 'Airbandit: C3I and Strategic Air Defence during the First Battle of

Britain, 1915–1918', in M. L. Dockrill and David French, eds, *Intelligence and Strategy During the First World War* (London: Hamdon Press, 1995).

140. Groves to Salmond, 27 August 1918, Groves Papers, 69/34/1, IWM.

141. Ibid.

142. Liddle, 39; and Cole and Cheesman, 457–62. The night raids by the German *Brieftauben-Abteilung-Ostend* had begun in September 1917, and when they ended in May 1918 a total of 26 missions had been flown against Great Britain. In addition to Zeppelins, the Germans bombed with two heavier-than-air forces: Gothas and Giant aeroplanes. Giant crews had completed 93 per cent of their missions; the Gothas 76 per cent. No German bombers were intercepted by British aircraft.

143. Cole and Cheesman, 416.

144. 'Appreciation of the Probability of Raids by Hostile Aircraft on London', 27 October 1918, Folio No. 7, Air 9/69. Also, Cole and Cheesman, 459–60.

145. 'Anti-Aircraft Defence of the United Kingdom', 15 October 1918, Folio No. 7, Air 9/69. Wilson concurred with the Air Ministry's request to reduce the ten balloon aprons to one, which would release 2,500 personnel for work in other areas.

146. Sykes first initiated the strategy of moving Home Defence units from England to France on 10 June 1918 when he sent one night-fighting squadron to help to defend the Abbeville area against German night bombing. War Cabinet Minutes, 10 June 1918, War Cabinet 429, CAB 23.

147. War Cabinet Minute 9, 18 October 1918, War Cabinet 489, Air 8/3. When Smuts concurred with Ashmore, the Cabinet agreed to keep the balloon apron already in place. As a result of Haig's success with night fighters against night German bombing, the Air Ministry had proposed to the War Cabinet on 24 August 1918 to release five Home Defence squadrons to France. Later this number was reduced to three.

148. 'Memorandum on Air Requirements for Defence of London', 22 February 1918, Folio No. 6, Air 9/69.

149. T. C. R. Higgins to Air Ministry (no date, but October sometime), Folio No. 7, Air 9/69.

150. 'Memorandum on Air Requirements for the Defence of London', 22 February 1918, Folio No. 6, Air 9/69. Wilson's memorandum referred to an earlier one by Field Marshal Sir John French, who had taken over Home Defence after being removed from France. The system within which Sykes had to work was one that French had designed. RAF Home Defence forces came under French's authority.

151. 'Review of the Air Situation and Strategy for the Information of the Imperial War Cabinet', 27 June 1918, Sykes Private Papers.

152. This was known as the Brigade System, where Air Brigades were attached to Armies.

153. Cole, 97–9.

154. War Cabinet Minutes of May 1918, War Cabinet 408, 410, 411 and 413, CAB 23. On seven occasions in May the Admiralty reported aerial operations to the War Cabinet. Not once did Sykes object or report any activity himself. From May until November, Sykes rather than Weir represented the Air Ministry at the majority of War Cabinet meetings. Occasionally both attended (see Note 167).

155. 'Memorandum for the War Cabinet on Certain Lines of Main Policy Involving the Activities of the Air Ministry', 14 May 1918, Weir Papers, 1/2. Also published in Raleigh and Jones, Appendix VII, VI:26–8, as 'Memorandum by Sir William Weir, Secretary of State for the Royal Air Force, on the

Responsibility and Conduct of the Air Ministry, May 1918' (G. T.-4622).

156. War Cabinet Minute 22, 14 May 1918, War Cabinet 411, CAB 23.

157. War Cabinet Minute 13, 24 May 1918, War Cabinet 417, CAB 23.

158. Air Ministry to War Office, 28 May 1918, Air 6/17.

159. Air Staff Minutes, 27 May 1918, Meeting No. 55, Air 8/5.

160. Precis No. 45739/1918, Air 6/17. The Air Council had first discussed creating an air force weather service on 15 January 1918, but the issue had been dropped after the Boards of Trade, Agriculture and Fisheries complained to the Treasury. The idea surfaced again in June, when Sykes agreed to send a proposal to the Treasury.

161. The formal move for Treasury funding for the medical service was not until 13 June 1918. Air Council Minutes, 13 June 1918, Meeting No. 33, Air 6/12. The creation of RAF medicine was severely shaken in July when the Medical Administrator, Gen Munday, appointed five staff members without consulting the Medical Administrative Committee. The Air Council promptly cancelled the appointments and fired Munday, replacing him by Colonel Fell. Air Council' Minutes, 11 July 1918, Meeting No. 38, Air 6/13. In August, Col. Fell also got into trouble when he approved the construction of an expensive hospital without consulting the Director of Works and Buildings, but three of Munday's appointees were reinstated. Air Council Minutes, 23 August 1918, Meeting No. 45, Air 6/13.

162. Air Staff Minutes, 31 May 1918, Meeting No. 57, Air 8/5.

163. 'Aerodrome Committee Memorandum', May 1918, Air 6/17. Rothermere had established the first Aerodrome Committee with Sir Henry Norman as chairman. Subsequently, when Norman left the Air Staff, Brancker proposed a new committee to be headed by himself as Controller General of Equipment (CGE).

164. Air Council Minutes, 23 May 1918, Meeting No. 30 (?), Air 6/12. The RAF deliberately boosted the fame of Canadian flyers, and Sykes even considered going beyond publicity measures and violating established regulations to elevate the rank of the Canadian Billy Bishop. Sykes' proposal was rejected, however, by Canadian authorities. Air Member Minutes, 2 August 1918, Meeting No. 84, Air 8/5.

165. The King approved the new uniform on 21 June 1918.

166. 'Progress of the Royal Air Force', speech by Sir William (later Lord) Weir to the House of Commons, 20 June 1918, Air 1/8/15/1.

167. Ibid. Weir simply confirmed the King's Orders that had defined the duties and responsibilities of the CAS: all air policy, operations, orders, intelligence and training. In addition, the CAS was to be the public relations officer as well as the liaison with sister services and Allied air services. In King's Regulations for the RAF, 26 March 1918, Air Pub 141, RAFM, Accession No. 001282.

168. 'Review of the Air Situation and Strategy for the Information of the Imperial War Cabinet', 27 June 1918, Sykes Private Papers; and Sykes, *From Many Angles*, Appendix V, 544–54.

169. Ibid.

170. Martin Gilbert, *First World War* (London: Weidenfeld & Nicolson, 1994), 420.

171. Cole, 100–24. The RAF shot down 262 enemy aircraft while losing 79.

172. 'Handbook of German Military and Naval Aviation', Air Pub 71, RAFM, Accession No. 005113, 107. By 1918 the Air Ministry knew in precise detail how the German parachute was constructed and worked.

173. War Cabinet Minute 8, 20 August 1918, War Cabinet 461, CAB 23. RAF communiqués first mentioned German parachutes on 11 August 1918, but according to Peter Kilduff, *Germany's First Air Force 1914–1918* (London: Arms & Armour Press, 1991), 13 and 109, the Germans first flew with the

Henecke parachute in 1917. He records that Manfred and Lothar von Richthofen promoted the technology after witnessing a demonstration earlier that year. The British parachute was called the 'Guardian Angel' and was under experiment at the Armament Experimental Stations at Martlesham Heath and Orfordness. Bremner, sound recording, Reel No. 8, IWM sound recordings.

174. Even after the war Sykes suspected parachutes to be dangerous and was reluctant to allow even one member of the RAF to serve as a volunteer to test them. Air Staff Minutes, 1 January 1919, Meeting No. 142, Air 8/5.

175. 'Review of the Air Situation and Strategy for the Information of the Imperial War Cabinet', 27 June 1918, Sykes Private Papers.

176. Precis No. 246, Air 6/18.

177. Air Staff Minutes, 12 July 1918, Meeting No. 75, Air 8/5.

178. Trenchard to Air Ministry, 11 July 1918, Air 1/18/15/1/94/56; and Air Ministry to Trenchard [no date], Air 1/18/15/1/94/54A.

179. Precis No. 234, 16 September 1918, Air 6/18. Sykes stated,

> Technical information of any kind may not be communicated to unauthorized persons without the consent of the Director-General of Aircraft Production. Information on other subjects may not be communicated except through the Department of the Chief of the Air Staff, whose consent will in every case be necessary. All ranks are responsible for bringing to the notice of the Chief of the Air Staff, through proper channels, all cases of indiscreet communications or conversations which may come to their knowledge.

180. 1918 Wireless Conference Reports, Air 1/32/15/1/169. This specialized training was not to take place at the normal Wireless Telephony School, which was first located at Chattis Hill and then moved to Bournemouth.

181. Cole, 125–49.

182. War Cabinet Minutes, 16 July 1918, War Cabinet 446; and War Cabinet Minutes, 19 July 1918, War Cabinet 449, CAB 23.

183. Weir to Lloyd George, 14 June 1918, Lloyd George Papers, Series F/Box 47/Folder 3. Sykes attended the majority of War Cabinet meetings without Weir, who was often away inspecting aerodromes.

184. Minute 5, War Cabinet Meeting, 26 July 1918, War Cabinet 452, CAB 23.

185. Groves to Salmond, 27 August 1918, Groves Papers, IWM 69/34/1.

186. Ibid.

187. 'Report from 22nd Wing, RAF, 19 August 1918', RAF Staff College 2nd Course, RAFM, Accession No. C/5/1/1.

188. War Cabinet Minute 7, 20 August 1918, War Cabinet 461, CAB 23.

189. Cole, 151–8.

190. Ibid., 175–9.

191. 'Bombing of the Somme Bridges, 8 August to 1 September 1918', Air 9/6.

192. Air Council Minutes, 1 August 1918, Meeting No. 42, Air 6/13; and Air Council Minutes, 22 August 1918, Meeting No. 44, Air 6/13.

193. Air Council Minutes, 17 August 1918, Precis No. 206, Air 6/18.

194. Roure was a French officer from the 1st Bureau, French War Office.

195. Lt-Col. Roure's Report, 4 August 1918, CAB 25/94.

196. Lloyd George to Clemenceau, 30 August 1918, CAB 25/94.

197. Ibid.

198. 'Notes bt [*sic*] the Chief of the Air Staff on References to the Royal Air Force' (no date), CAB 25/94.

199. Groves to Geoffrey Salmond, 27 August 1918, Groves Papers, IWM 69/34/1. Groves wrote that his enormous labor in working out a plan of aircraft production through 1919 had turned his remaining hair white: 'This momentous

document, or rather pamphlet, is now in the bear-pit and the roars of the great ones come daily to my ears.'

200. 'MaCready's [Macready] Report, 3 August 1918', CAB 25/96. British and SWC intelligence on German manpower was uncertain. This report stated that the best way to determine German strength was to assess British manpower reserves and assume similar numbers for Germany.
201. War Cabinet Minute 1, 21 August 1918, War Cabinet 462, CAB 23.
202. Air Council Minutes, 22 August 1918, Meeting No. 44, Air 6/13.
203. Precis No. 222, Air 6/18.
204. Air Council to War Cabinet (no date), Air 1 460/15/312/101.

7

The Air War Finale: Supply, Bombing and Tactics, August–December 1918

Sykes' supreme effort of 1918 was to create the Independent Air Force to bomb Germany. In addition, he oversaw the culmination of the air war with his leadership in organizing, training and equipping the RAF during its final fight for victory in the First World War. By June 1918 Sykes had regained credibility as the most senior RAF staff officer; the air service had not collapsed under his leadership as Henderson had predicted. Yet Sykes was still handicapped in some respects. Many British and Allied commanders considered his long-range bombing ideas unrealistic and dangerous to the war effort, and Trenchard, among others, resisted their implementation. At the risk of reducing home defense and tactical air support to the Army, Sykes wanted to create an independent, strategic strike force, which would encompass the air element of an Allied reserve. He desired the continuous long-range bombing of German industries. These ideas were indeed revolutionary but not overly optimistic, and as the German war effort began to show signs of decay in autumn 1918, Sykes focused aerial support on a combined-arms, technical knock-out on the front. By the time of the Armistice the IAF had started to bomb the German heartland: the RAF had won the air war, and the Air Ministry had proved its validity as a separate service. Sykes deserved much of the credit for these accomplishments, but such recognition soon vanished.

As indicated earlier, Sykes' paramount goal as CAS was to establish the long-range bombing force. The bombing problem was multifarious and full of dilemmas: moral versus material targeting, safe flying versus accurate bombing, and ideology and logic versus pragmatic politics. Sykes was attempting to expand the role of air power in war, and he faced an uphill battle against technological limits as well as organizational and fiscal constraints. He had not initiated the move toward strategic bombing, but he was a major player in the movement to implement it with the formation of the Independent Air Force.

Like the initial, conceptual and organizational phases of many revolutions, the process involved in creating this new type of warfare was complex, confusing, inefficient and even humorous at times. Sykes reported on 20 August 1918 that the strategic bombers had been partially successful in setting the Black Forest on fire.[1] The effectiveness of such endeavors was marginal in terms of a war-winning impact. Yet it was the organization and new thinking that made long-range bombing a seminal feature in the war, not its direct or indirect moral and material effects.

Historians have noted correctly that bombing by the IAF was an insignificant side-show in terms of bombs delivered and damage caused.[2] Sykes and the rest of the Air Staff never intended it to be anything more than that in 1918. Before the formation of the RAF, the Air Board recognized that British technological and production limitations prohibited the carrying out of an effective bombing campaign and that an appropriately large force would not be ready until autumn 1919. Hence on 25 March 1918 Rothermere and Weir discussed the necessity for a Strategic Council to co-ordinate the program of aircraft production so that output would be based on strategy. Aircraft design was to match the range and ability needed to bomb targets that fitted the objectives of the campaign to attack Germany.[3]

The Strategic Council first met on 22 April when it decided to submit a bombing policy to the War Cabinet. After that, however, the Council failed to meet regularly, owing to changes in membership and functions. Hence it failed to formulate any definitive policy.[4] Weir had moved from Aircraft Production to Air Minister, so theoretically the production program maintained its strategic awareness. Weir made Sykes chairman of the Strategic Committee and responsible for its membership.[5] Yet Weir and Sykes had to contend with politicians who were more concerned with copying German bombing than formulating a British strategy.[6] Compounded by increasing public pressure for reprisals rather than military strategies, the situation jeopardized not only the effective production of machines but also led to the formation of a bombing force that lacked a specific doctrine.

The desire to create a capable bombing force caused an organizational nightmare. On 13 May the Air Council sanctioned the proposal to form an IAF as part of the RAF but administratively separate – hence its 'independent' name.[7] Sykes wanted the IAF to receive its orders direct from the Air Ministry in London so that it would not be required to respond to GHQ in France. The IAF's purpose was to bomb Germany. At the same time the Allies were planning to form an Inter-Allied IAF with the same strategic objective. Sykes intended that the British IAF would be both a model for and the nucleus of the Inter-Allied IF, since the British government was the only one supporting such a force and because the RAF was the only Allied air service to have any long-range bombing capability at all. The Inter-Allied Aviation Committee met at Versailles from May to July, with Sykes one of the committee members. Yet the committee was slow to reach agreement on any aspects of strategic bombing and eventually decided that only the military representatives of the SWC had the authority to make morally questionable decisions.[8]

The strategic bombing problem became even more peculiar and complex when Sykes concurred with Weir's selection of IAF commander: Trenchard. Sykes was too intent on creating the bombing force to be concerned with personality conflicts, especially when he knew Trenchard had excellent leadership skills and experience. In his words, 'An officer of General Trenchard's standing' was his proof to the Allies that the Air Ministry was serious about strategic bombing.[9] Sykes was more concerned about the creation of the IAF than its long-term effectiveness under an adversarial personality; hence Trenchard was a short-term solution. But Sykes' ambition blinded him to the potential problems Trenchard's assignment might bring – that, regardless of Trenchard's abilities, his desires might compromise the strategic endeavor. Trenchard did not want the job, had resisted the decision to bomb strategically, and still believed that the best use of air power was to pursue offensive tactics in the zone of the Army.[10] In 1917 Trenchard and Haig had submitted a report which stated that strategic bombing was 'repugnant to British ideas' and impossible without suitable aircraft.[11] Furthermore, Trenchard resented that Sykes was now CAS, and he was no more willing to work under Sykes than he had been in 1914. Throughout his IAF command Trenchard bypassed Sykes and corresponded direct with Weir.

Trenchard's IAF was formed out of the Nancy Bombing Wing, which was Newall's Eighth Brigade. Trenchard arrived in France on 16 May and visited RAF squadrons until meeting Sykes in Paris at the end of the month to discuss bombing policy and attend the Inter-Allied Aviation Committee. With the IAF stationed in France, the Air Ministry needed French concurrence, but Foch, the supreme commander of the Allied force, in France, objected. Hence Trenchard was in a tenuous situation when he took command on 6 June. He was not recognized by the French as the commander and his IAF was not supported as a legitimate force.[12] He wrote in his diary: 'General Sykes informed me that Mr Lloyd George had talked to M. Clemenceau on the subject of the Independent Force, and asked him to help. This is no good.'[13]

Although Trenchard reluctantly agreed to command the long-range bombing force, he believed that strategic bombing was a luxury and a 'terrible waste of manpower' that could not be afforded until they had defeated German aviation and their armies in France. Furthermore, he was convinced that everyone at RAF HQ in France held the same beliefs and that they blamed him for the IAF's creation, and hence for dislocating British air power.[14] Trenchard did not object particularly to the concept of strategic bombing; he objected to its timing and methodology.[15] Specifically, he resented the IAF's independence because it forced him to do his own administration. On 20 June he told American visitors that irresponsible newspapers had 'forced our government into adopting an unsound organization,' and that with American help he might be successful, even though such success would be a needless expense of energy.[16]

As bombing operations commenced, however, Trenchard reversed course and wanted more independence. He had complained about having to handle administrative duties, but when the Air Ministry sent more staff he argued that they were a waste of manpower and did not help to add a single mission to his bombing effort. He objected to Air Ministry interference and complained that publicity for the IAF should not only be promoted to enhance the moral effect of the bombing but that it should not be linked to Air Ministry operations at all.[17] Trenchard was never satisfied. He had argued repeatedly that his force was insufficient to do little more than pin-prick bombing and most of his correspondence with Weir consisted of complaints about lack of support. By the end of July, however, Trenchard told Weir that he could not possibly handle Sykes' proposed 104 squadrons, at which point Weir reduced the number to 54.[18]

Trenchard was correct that the IAF organization was premature – Britain did not have a capable bomber force, either in terms of carrying and delivery capacity or in numbers of aircraft. Yet Sykes accurately assessed that the costly air strategy Trenchard had pursued for two years would never allow such a bomber force to come into existence.[19] It was time for new thinking.[20] Home defense was not the solution; the best defense was a counteroffense.[21] Sykes had to start somewhere, and based on the premise that the war would last until autumn 1919, the initiating of an independent force in summer 1918 was logical.

The historian Malcolm Cooper has written that in May 1918 Sykes further alienated his fellow airmen by pushing for independent bombing.[22] He was a traitor to traditional war-fighting. Sykes was a revolutionary and he let others know it. He wrote to the Prime Minister, 'you are fully aware of my views'.[23] Sykes had witnessed the disastrous results of using technology inappropriately – the tank on the Somme and at Passchendaele. He did not want to abuse bombers similarly and imagined an 'allied aerial navy' to bring air power against the enemy.[24] Air technology had become specialized and had to be incorporated by commanders who understood both its limits and its capabilities. It had to be independent. Sykes' key move was to convince the War Cabinet in June that the air requirements of the Army and the Navy had been met and hence that the formation of an IAF was feasible. He argued that the preceding four years had shown that demands would always exceed supplies, but now that there were air experts in charge of distribution, those experts could best utilize air power by meeting the Army's and the Navy's needs rather than their desires. Sykes ensured that the official IAF dispatch to the Army on 11 June 1918 stated, specifically, that Haig was to have 'no control'.[25]

Sykes' struggle to create the IAF continued. In May he had notified the Air Council of his plan to divide responsibility between Britain and the United States. British aircraft production would supply machines for tactical work in the zone of the Army, and the United States would supply anti-submarine machines and long-range bombers.[26] Yet, once Sykes realized that he could not count on American production, he quickly abandoned this plan.[27] American aircraft production was capable of building what the IAF needed, but the American supply system was stalled by lack of co-ordination between American Army and Navy aviation – a problem familiar to Sykes and Weir.

As CAS, Sykes was responsible for allocating all aircraft. Hence he had to supply the IAF from British production against the claims of the Army, the Navy and even members of his own Air Staff. Specifically, Sykes wanted to take 14 squadrons intended for the Army and divert them to the IAF. Paine objected to Sykes' new plan, partly because it reduced the number of flying boats going to the Navy (and Paine was a Navy man). Paine wanted the old development program Trenchard had formulated. Major-General E. L. Ellington, then Comptroller-General of Equipment, noted that Sykes' proposal obviously viewed victory as being achieved through an air offensive conducted by the IAF and warned of the danger of taking resources away from the Army. Ellington predicted 'a weakening of the offensive power of the Army' and argued that Sykes should have to justify his distribution.[28]

When the first Inter-Allied Aviation Committee stalled in early May, owing to French fears of vulnerability to German reprisal bombing of Paris, Weir and Sykes were convinced that Britain would have to carry the weight of strategic bombing and that the Air Ministry would have to initiate the effort. Weir's memorandum on long-range bombing went before the War Cabinet on 24 May 1918.[29] He argued that Germany would continue to bomb from the air regardless of what the IAF did, and that the only way to defeat the enemy in this regard was to out-bomb them. Hence, according to Weir, the Air Ministry needed to pre-empt Germany in establishing an effective strategic bombing force. Weir agreed with Sykes that this would not happen if the IAF were placed under Foch, as the French demanded, because Foch did not believe in strategic air power and would simply revert to using the force to support the ground forces.[30] Sykes had been part of the SWC effort to gain control of a strategic reserve, and he now translated that concept to the IF and the IAF, seeking to place strategic bombing under SWC authority and under a single British commander.[31] Sykes had assured French representatives that IAF resources would be lent to their Army if needed, but Foch wanted guarantees not assurances. The French were still convinced that Britain was not carrying its fair share in the war effort. Sykes wrote to the Prime Minister that Britain needed to maintain command and that Trenchard was the best man for the job:

> Logic may be on the side of the French rather than on ours; but success in such operations as these depends on practical considerations rather than on those of logic, and it is after a close study of these that my conviction has been reached. I have dealt with the question of the single command and in my opinion General Trenchard should receive the appointment.[32]

The War Secretary Milner doubted whether Britain could do anything about French resistance. The War Cabinet decided that they could only support the formation of the IAF and give it a few months under Trenchard to get established. The Foreign Office officially notified France of Trenchard's situation and requested co-operation.

Since the Inter-Allied Aviation Committee had passed strategic bombing decisions on to the SWC, Sykes determined that the time was critical to force French co-operation. During a SWC meeting at Versailles on 3 June 1910, Sykes waited in the halls for a break in the meeting, and at 1830 hours intercepted both Lloyd George and Clemenceau as they were leaving the conference room. The French Brigadier-General Maurice Duval, the officer who had notified the Air Ministry of Foch's determination to control the IAF and the Inter-Allied IF, was with Clemenceau.[33] Lloyd George told Clemenceau that Trenchard needed French help and Clemenceau agreed heartily, ordering Duval to make sure that the French co-operated. Clemenceau then told Sykes to approach him personally if there were any future problems.[34] Relieved, Sykes dined in Paris that evening with Weir and Trenchard.

Sykes' return to England, however, foreshadowed the foreboding reality that strategic air power was not in the clear. After 'hugging the deck' through fog in a DH4 aircraft across the English Channel and then climbing to miss the Dover cliffs, Sykes attempted to find a landing field. Small pockets of clear air in cloud banks are known among flyers as 'sucker holes' for a reason. After descending through such a gap, Sykes found himself on a collision course with the dome of St Paul's Cathedral, which he narrowly missed after breaking into a hard left turn.[35]

Clemenceau's encouraging remarks did not translate into French support. The Tiger represented the French government at that point, but he could not speak for the SWC. In addition, Clemenceau had agreed to provide French help, but, as Sykes and Weir later discovered, he apparently had not agreed that Trenchard should command the IAF on French territory.[36] On 10 June, a visiting American colonel told Trenchard that General Pershing would have difficulty placing squadrons under Trenchard since they were to be under Foch.[37] The IAF remained on unstable ground.

Trenchard was concerned about his predicament, but the Air Ministry was not. In fact, Weir relished such a situation: he wanted the issue to be resolved locally and unofficially in France and ordered Trenchard to stop complaining. Weir also instructed Sykes to 'disagree' at the next Inter-Allied Conference so that the issue would be tabled for a decision in the future.[38] Weir advocated such bureaucratic confusion and stalling because he realized that Britain was out-voted in the SWC and would lose both the IF and the IAF if it came to a hard decision.

Sykes understood Weir's motive but preferred more direct methods. At the same time, Sykes did not trust Trenchard to have the diplomatic skills to arbitrate any kind of agreement with the French. In a letter to Trenchard, Sykes advised him to lie low and let the Inter-Allied Aviation Committee work out a settlement: 'You should act entirely as though the independent force had been recognized and let [the] French raise the question if they wish.'[39] By the middle of July, Sykes was prepared to work out a compromise with the French if it would establish the strategic force.[40] Sykes proposed that, since Britain was committing the majority of its resources to strategic bombing, the IAF should remain under Trenchard's command. Because the IAF was flying out of French territory, it would come under General Foch's authority and could be used in emergency situations. Sykes knew that under French control the IAF would continually support such emergency situations – resulting in technology being used incorrectly. Yet Sykes hoped that a compromise over authority and control would result in orders coming from Trenchard, but policy from the SWC – since Generalissimo Foch still had to answer to that organization.[41] With German forces retiring, Foch would have difficulty in calling for emergency help. This compromise had the potential to resolve Anglo-French disagreements over strategic bombing, but it became much more complicated when it concerned not just the IAF but the Inter-Allied IF as well.

Compromise was not reached until the Allies had debated the issue for three and a half more months.[42] The third session of the Inter-Allied Aviation Committee on 21 July was particularly frustrating for Sykes. He arrived at Versailles well prepared to defend his views about creating the IF. The other members of the Committee had no facts or figures, only traditional opinions, and they again stalled making a decision.[43] The harder Sykes fought to stick to the agenda, the more the other members pushed decisions on to the SWC. Wilson reported to the War Cabinet on 24 July that he had talked to Foch, who was of the opinion that the IF and the IAF either came under him or they moved out of France.[44]

In August the SWC began to repeat the same decision-making process about an Inter-Allied strategic bombing force that the British War Cabinet had made with the IAF. At a meeting on 3 August of the SWC, the Military Representatives agreed that as soon as the supply of Allied resources permitted, an Inter-Allied Bombing Air Force should be formed under the authority of Foch.[45] The SWC also talked of a dual-track strategy whereby announced reprisals would deter enemy aggression and enhance negotiations, while at the same time long-range bombing would undermine the enemy's war effort. Sykes had agreed to such a strategy at Versailles but, 'coming from a soldier's perspective', as he stated, Sykes maintained that threats without action were useless.

On 12 August Weir and Sykes were dismayed to discover that their efforts with the French had been jeopardized by the British War Cabinet. Weir complained to the Prime Minister about the problematic British bureaucracy that had allowed a document to go before the SWC that was contrary to the Air Ministry's bombing policy:

> A perusal of the document will shew you that it is of a most dangerous nature and totally neglects the great development work and elaborate preparations made by this country to bomb Germany properly, not as a reprisal, but as a definite war campaign.[46]

This was not the first time that there had been confusion about British air policy, and Trenchard had added to the turmoil because he had not kept quiet as ordered and had alienated Clemenceau, who questioned Weir about removing him as commander of the IAF.[47] Weir continued to back Trenchard, but Sykes was upset and told Weir that this was precisely the type of situation he had been trying to prevent by having established an Air Attaché in Paris.[48]

Sykes and Weir continued to develop proposals supporting the policy for an Allied strategic offensive force, several of which they sent to Clemenceau after receiving approval from Lord Derby and Lloyd George.[49] A draft of one of these memoranda strongly stated that it was the 'feeling of the British people that deep resentment would be aroused against any government which did not take every step to further this policy'.[50] But the issue had become more politically complicated than Sykes had imagined: Smuts notified Weir that the Prime Minister intended to use the IAF argument as a bargaining counter to settle other disagreements between the French and the British.[51] Sykes and Weir simply wanted their strategic force, but they had no recourse but to modify their fight to accommodate domestic politics.

By September they were becoming exasperated by this situation and French recalcitrance. Weir was worried about Foch. Foch had been promoted to marshal, and not only had he gained more political power since his first objection to the IAF but he was still against the strategic air concept, both organizationally and theoretically.[52] Foch would agree to long-range bombing only during quiet intervals on the front, and thus giving him control could lead to disaster now that the front had become unstable.[53] Sykes further attacked Foch's stand, noting that one of the long-range IAF bases was not to be in France but in England.[54] Yet the majority of Sykes' arguments had to do with function not geography. He continued to argue for new thinking – the vision of a combined Allied strategic air offensive that would become not only the dominant factor in air power but the dominant factor in war.[55] Foch thought otherwise: 'The British were overdoing the Air and the Tanks', and British use of technology was inefficient.[56] Weir objected to Foch's anti-technological attitude and reminded the Prime Minister of strategic air power's effect: 'Is the low morale of the Rhine towns entirely due to the purely [army] situation?'[57] Weir and Derby compromised to the point that they did not require the French to supply any part of the strategic force, but needed them simply to agree to its principle. Yet Clemenceau still expressed concern. Perhaps to ensure that France would share in the possible success, Clemenceau did not want an entirely British strategic strike force.[58] Formal agreement with the French was reached finally in October, less than a month from the Armistice. Sykes' and Weir's battle had been concerned as much with keeping the IAF out of French hands as it had been in trying to dislocate the German war effort.

SUPPLY BATTLES

In addition to the contentious organizational debate with the Allies, supplies and equipment were some of strategic bombing's principal handicaps. While Sykes fought to supply the IAF, British workers struck and the American air service decided to keep their engines for themselves. This left Trenchard with a serious shortage, and most of his correspondence with the Air Ministry concerned supply issues.[59] Some historians have argued that combined Anglo-American aircraft production never had the capability the Smuts Committee used to justify bombing Germany and have depicted the shortage of engines as the result of a conspiracy designed simply to gain control of air power.

Speculation aside, by August 1918 the IAF was short of supplies, and one way to maintain a viable strategic force was to reduce wastage. Weir constantly urged Trenchard to fly more night missions, which were safer.[60] Trenchard, however, liked flying during the day for two reasons: it created a greater moral effect and it was easier for his inexperienced pilots. Higham has noted that there was a traditional resistance to night flying from Army commanders who believed that it was ungentlemanly and 'downright dangerous to their reputations'.[61] Trenchard wrote to Sykes that he needed more fighters to fly escort and that in the interim perhaps the best solution was to fly in formation at 19,000 feet. Accuracy at that altitude would have been minimal, even in daylight.[62]

Strategic bomber technology was very new and to cut losses in long-range flying was a hard task. The bombers were difficult to fly and one of the greatest dangers was landing. Inexperienced pilots faced their first major challenge in flying to France, when Trenchard's force sustained a 16 per cent loss rate. Hence Sykes agreed to reduce the number of legs in the route from England to Nancy.[63] Yet this route was complicated further by a changing front and French demands, as the French wanted the IAF to fly in specific corridors and at specific times so that French ground troops would have a free hand attacking any other aircraft in the sky.[64] When the front changed in June due to the German salient at Château Thierry, the IAF route to Nancy had to change as well.[65] The implementation system continued to plague IAF progress as well, and Sykes became irritated in August when he found out that No. 97 Squadron had taken over a month to mobilize. He demanded to know why the supply system had not kept him informed.[66] Weather also accounted for many deaths, regardless of the presence of the enemy. Overall, the IAF was an expensive program in terms of engines, aircraft and personnel, and it was difficult to match supplies and equipment with demands. The IAF failed to materialize into the size of organization Sykes had wanted; however, small as it was, it did establish itself as an operational force. Sykes' impact on creating strategic bombing, however, went beyond organization.

THE TARGETING DEBATE

When the War Cabinet and the Air Ministry established the IAF in late May and early June, they may have believed that they had established policy.[67] They had not. There was still a great debate over whether to attack German morale or German *matériel*. Were the bombers to target industries or towns? Was bombing to be scattered to create popular unrest, or concentrated to interdict key supply lines? Experts, including Sykes, had agreed on only one issue – that for any type of bombing campaign to be effective, it had to be continuous.[68]

Since summer 1917, when the government first considered the bombing of Germany, policy makers had examined this aspect of the bombing problem, and from April through to the end of June Sykes received numerous memoranda from British and Allied civilian scientists, military commanders, politicians and members of the Air Ministry regarding the type of strategic bombing the IAF should pursue.[69] Sykes had to match means with aim – capability with objective – and there were many factors to consider. The two major objectives were interdependent: physical and psychological damage.[70] Yet they involved different targets and different tactics. German airmen had shown that the strategic bombing of cities could create public panic, disrupt government, dislocate fighting forces and obstruct production. The German objective, according to General Ludendorff, in his *Kriegführung und Politik*, had been 'to make war on the morale of the enemy peoples and armies'.[71] The British demand for reprisals, however, had shown that sporadic bombing simply aroused popular clamors for revenge. Hence, German long-range bombing was one of the most counterproductive endeavors of the war. It created interservice friction within the German military and led to the creation of the RAF and the IAF, which, in turn, helped to incorporate American air assets into Allied air power. Sykes knew that British bombing could be disastrous if done incorrectly.

The consensus among air strategists was that strategic bombing would not be a decisive factor toward victory if designed merely to strike enemy morale. As early as 21 October 1917, the Munitions Minister Winston Churchill wrote, 'It is improbable that any terrorization of the civil population which could be achieved by air attack would compel the Government of a great nation to surrender'.[72] Yet Churchill knew, as did Weir and Sykes, that Britain did not have the air power to destroy German industry, even though that industry's vulnerability to bombing was much greater than Britain's due to its concentration in specific valleys and its greater sophistication.[73] The Air Board recognized the meager physical results German bombing had caused in London, one of the most densely populated cities in Europe.[74]

The moral and *matériel* dialectic presented a difficult dilemma. Military planners wanted to hit military targets, but British politicians needed to meet public demands for reprisals against population centers. Perhaps reprisal bombing could be justified on moral grounds, but an actual strategic campaign against civilians raised questions. Used in such a manner, air power was as reprehensible as unrestricted submarine warfare, for there was little difference between bombing a population center and torpedoing a liner. Already Belgium had remonstrated that civilians in German-occupied territory had been killed by RFC bombing, and these complaints continued while Sykes was CAS.[75] On 18 March the War Cabinet had upheld a SWC resolution calling for reprisals to be limited to 'objectives of military importance'.[76]

Hence the moral issue translated into a targeting problem. Because industry was more difficult to target, bombers were more effective during daylight raids when visibility enhanced their accuracy. Daylight raids also incited more fear because people were away from their homes and able to see the bombers and the destruction. In addition, since most industrial activity occurred during the day, such raids could hurt German industry whenever warning sirens sounded, regardless of whether the bombers hit their targets. But daylight raids were significantly more dangerous for British airmen, particularly if flown at low altitude to ensure bombing accuracy. Also, if the objective was a moral one to hit industry and avoid killing civilians, then factories should not be attacked when they were filled with workers.

Most members of the Air Ministry and the government resolved the moral dilemma by accepting the immoral implications of bombing German towns.[77] IAF technological limits necessitated bombing whatever was possible with the least loss of British airmen. If British bombers, whatever their capabilities to inflict damage, could dislocate some of the German war effort by forcing the country to redirect its resources to air defense, then IAF air power could be a key to victory.[78] Under public and political pressure, Weir told Trenchard that he did not care if bombers missed their industrial targets and hoped that the bombers would set off large fires in German villages.[79]

Nevertheless, Sykes was not keen on bombing civilians, and the main IAF objective remained the damaging of German industry not morale. Sykes, personally, would not sanction reprisal bombing but tabled the issue as a War Office responsibility when it arose.[80] British

Intelligence had determined that German industry was vulnerable and that by July 1918 it could collapse. Hence bombing could deal a crippling blow.[81] Physical destruction would lead to public loss of confidence in the country's leaders, and public terror would cause work stoppages and impair the war-making capability. The policy which gradually emerged from the War Cabinet was to attack German factories and specifically those concerned with chemicals and metals.

However, from a policy standpoint, the IAF's plans were vague and gave Trenchard indefinite guidance. Organizationally, Trenchard had a free hand to use his bombers as he desired. Although Sykes had established the IAF and was in charge of committing resources to it, he influenced its command very little. Trenchard corresponded with Weir, not Sykes, and Sykes visited the IAF only once between April and November.[82] Rather than target specific locations until they were destroyed in order to stop a particular industry, Trenchard chose to attack a wide spectrum of targets to create general panic.[83] At the same time, Trenchard maintained that strategic bombing was impossible without air supremacy, so he diverted a third of his resources to attacking German aerodromes.[84] Many people, including Weir, Sykes and Groves, criticized him for this, claiming that Trenchard was simply returning to his former methodology of supporting the Army.[85] That may have been Trenchard's motive, but he was not singularly guilty. Sykes and Groves reminded Newall in April not to forget about hitting aerodromes, and Sykes authorized two IAF squadrons to be diverted to RAF forces supporting the BEF on 28 June 1918.[86] Salmond was to give the squadrons back as soon as possible. In addition, the French continually pressed for more Army help – specifically aerodrome attacks, which Petain had stressed in 1917.[87]

In addition to bombing aerodromes, Trenchard's IAF concentrated its attack on railways to interdict German supply lines.[88] The reason for this was obvious – rail sidings were the easiest target to hit, and the most congested railway centers were in the middle of industrial towns. Hence, the targeting of railways provided the greatest measure of success, regardless of where the bombs landed.[89]

In effect there was a general derailment between the Air Ministry and the IAF. As a planner, Weir was consumed with politics, and he harassed Trenchard to bomb in whatever way might appease influential strategists, the press and the government.[90] As the organizer, Sykes was thinking strategically – how to reduce losses with technology, how to win with air power. As the implementor, Trenchard's perspective was tactical. He had inexperienced pilots, thus he chose to attack close aerodromes, so that his pilots would not have to fly far into enemy territory, while at the same time knocking out enemy air power. When decision-makers decided to place *matériel* damage ahead of moral damage in documents such as 'Operations for 1918 for a strategic bombing of Germany', they established the bombing priority: first, chemical industries; second, iron and steel works; and third, railways.[91] Yet, a post-war official RAF publication recorded that the following priority was followed: first, railways; second, aerodromes; and third, factories.[92]

By September 1918, the Air Ministry was under attack from strategists who argued that the IAF was not performing as intended, and that it needed to concentrate bombing on specific industrial targets to 'de-munitionise' Germany.[93] Widespread bombing of aerodromes and railways and to harm morale was not attacking the German Achilles' heel.[94] Trenchard was convinced that his tactics were killing three birds with one stone, but he and Sykes were unable to establish a co-operative effort that would satisfy all the critics. Trenchard wrote to Weir, 'I have had a long talk with Sykes on the subject, and I think the correct solution is for me to come home at once and explain to the critics and I am perfectly certain I can fix up the whole thing.'[95]

Trenchard did not fix a thing. By October, the IAF was under ever-increasing pressure for a large psychological impact to help create a German implosion. In the War Cabinet, the Foreign Secretary Sir Arthur Balfour urged an end to widespread IAF operations against military targets in favor of a campaign to bomb only five critical cities to create panic and destroy property. Weir responded that already the IAF was 100 per cent devoted to bombing Rhineland towns, a statement that was far from true.[96] Wilson recorded in his diary that he told Sykes to take training squadrons from England to reinforce the RAF, but also to bomb Berlin immediately.[97] Weir urged Trenchard to pursue the Berlin mission, and Trenchard reluctantly agreed.[98] The IAF planned to use the Vimy bomber with Eagle VIII engines to bomb Berlin with two 230-lb bombs on 12 November 1918. The day before, the head of strategic bombing, Marshal Foch, notified Trenchard that hostilities were to cease and that his troops were not to cross the line or communicate with the enemy.[99] Trenchard concluded that never in the entire war had there been such inefficient use of man-power as the IAF, and he telegraphed Foch requesting that the IAF be placed under Haig.[100] As demonstrated by this final act, he had fought Sykes to the end.

The war ended prematurely for the IAF, and the Inter-Allied IF never flew. It will never be known whether strategic bombing would have fulfilled Sykes' dream for 1919. Sykes and Weir fought a long, political, logistical, and moral battle to achieve strategic bombing, but during the last weeks of the war activities at the front became paramount. Sykes had shifted his focus away from the IAF to aerial help in the tactical arena.

The IAF's long-range bombing effort, however, had contributed to the tactical opportunities at the front. On 10 September the British minister at the Hague reported to Balfour: 'According to various sources the despondency in Germany is at the present moment intense, and that this would be greatly increased by air raids on German towns and that the moment would appear to demand the exercise of this method of warfare to its utmost extent.'[101] Wilson notified the War Cabinet that German morale was very low and that German soldiers were spreading an atmosphere of 'despondency and alarm' throughout Germany. A captured Army High Command order mentioned that for any soldier inciting despair, leave was to be cancelled and replaced by an immediate posting to the front. In one Prussian regiment over a hundred soldiers had simply walked across the line to surrender.[102]

The London *Times* reported daily on deteriorating conditions in Germany, but the German Air Force continued to fight well. Sykes reported to the War Cabinet that the air war on the Western Front and in Germany was as active as it had been at any previous time – particularly in air-to-ground fighting.[103] The night-fighting squadron at Abbeville was succeeding against German bombers and hence providing the effective home defense he had anticipated. Sykes had long understood the advantages of damaging enemy morale with strategic bombing, but now he recognized the *Schwerpunkt* on the Western Front. Sykes was ruled not by ideological or traditional principles, but by the desire to win a war. Hence he shifted focus from the IAF to the breakthrough and sent an additional 30 squadrons into the zone of the Army.[104]

The weather in September deteriorated to the point that the air forces had difficulty in flying and were grounded a third of the time. Yet aerial fighting did not subside. The RAF shot down 420 enemy aircraft and lost 181, 83 of those losses occurring in one week.[105] Yet, low-level bombing tactics in support of the infantry and tanks were proving to be effective. For months the enemy had been forced to move only at night, supplies had been cut off, and troops were exhausted and demoralized. Before the British air presence developed over the trenches, German soldiers had fought only when attacking or defending ground armies. Now they had to fight continuously, because of aerial harassment, and lost hundreds of men a day to air strikes.[106]

Although Sykes was primarily concerned with the IAF and the Western Front, where the fighting was reaching a climax, it should be mentioned that the September air war was not limited to Western Europe. RAF activities in the Middle East were also part of Sykes' job as CAS, and despite the fact that they had little to do with the IAF, were important in the strategic air war. British aerial operations in

Palestine against German and Turkish forces were some of the RAF's most successful of the war and served to illustrate that the RAF was 'a new factor of war'.[107]

Sykes had instituted an increasingly effective administrative and organizational system in the RAF, but by late September he feared losing control. The RAF was expanding rapidly beyond comfortable boundaries and threatened to surpass Sykes' vision of an Empire air service. Daily, the Air Council was considering proposals for RAF activities with other countries and colonies: Russia, India, Rhodesia, Italy, Brazil, Japan, Greece, Canada, the United States, Ireland and Australia. Sykes promoted the concept of an Empire Air Force but said that he was against the principle of employing foreigners in the RAF, particularly as pilots.[108] Sykes had a reason: foreign personnel and governments complicated his command. Americans continually complained about poor British hospitality and demanded their own autonomous units on British soil.[109] The American staff was still dissatisfied with the M-5 Branch administrative system, leading Sykes to make another change in October – this time creating a department head within each Air Ministry branch to be the sole point of contact with the Americans.[110] Not only did Sykes have difficulty in working with the Americans, but the Liberty engine failure had created turmoil for the IAF. Churchill complained that he could never get the Americans to make a decision because they were always changing personnel.[111] Ellington was upset by the Americans as well. He refused to supply them with more aircraft; they bypassed him and acquired machines direct from the DGAP.[112] This improper procedure was repeated several times in October and created friction within the Air Council. Other problems stemmed from poor Allied equipment that had cost British airmen their lives.[113] The Air Staff understood that Russian pilots were trying to avoid having to serve as army privates in Archangel, but the staff voted that Russians could fly for France, not Britain.

Sykes tried to maintain control with a British RAF policy and adherence to established procedures to enhance communications within the Air Ministry. He ruled that the RAF would grant no commissions to non-British personnel and directed that from 1 October all units would issue daily routine orders to keep the Air Staff apprised of all activities and changes.[114] Tired of American demands and the risk they posed in coming from a country not a member of the Empire, Sykes ordered that the RAF would not allow the American Air Service in France to use wireless communication.[115] He ruled that all visits by RAF personnel to the Army had to be approved by him first and that he would cut weekly orders authorizing such visits.[116] The Air Staff demanded that accident reports be kept away from the press and that all accident information should go to the Air Ministry first. The Air Ministry then would decide what details to release to the several RAF agencies.[117] The attempt to control rumors also applied to court-martial proceedings, which were not to be published. Sykes wanted continuity within all branches, and thus the Air Staff turned down repeated WRAF requests for specialized insignia. In addition, Sykes rejected numerous proposals for individuals to receive honorary promotions and titles or to be authorized to wear honorary badges and uniforms.[118] He disapproved of promotional schemes from entrepreneurs wanting to use aircraft for fund raising. The RAF was not only to remain British, it was to remain legitimate and professional. Although Trenchard and other airmen have accused Sykes of maneuvering unprofessionally to obtain greater rank before the war ended, there is no evidence that Sykes attempted to promote himself. In fact, at the end of October, when the Air Staff decided to discuss higher ranks, including a 'general-in-chief', Sykes was absent from the meeting.[119]

Sykes was particularly concerned about the RAF's status after the war, which appeared to be ending much sooner than anyone had anticipated. He published another visionary document, 'Memorandum by the Chief of the Air Staff on Air Power Requirements of the Empire', on 12 September, recording his highly optimistic concept of a post-war air service of approximately 194 squadrons to promote the British Empire.[120] He noted that, although the war would end at some point, the economic conflict would continue, and the air service would be an important part of the process. Just as the RAF had helped to defeat the enemy militarily, a large commercial air fleet would enhance Britain's future economic and political position in the world. Sykes spelled out in specific detail how the Empire's military and civil air service would be organized functionally and geographically. His memorandum was not just a concept, it was a plan of action; not just a dream, but his reality. Far too extreme for politicians, however, it became his own downfall.

The RAF had a little over a month of fighting left before Sykes would start to feel the pain of demobilization. Intelligence from the SWC indicated that the enemy was in a critical situation, having lost possession of the Hindenburg Line. North of Lys 10,000 German prisoners were taken on 14 October. Yet the Allied armies were exhausted as well, and the prospect of ending the war in 1918 was 'not anticipated with certainty'.[121] A report of 4 October by Sykes' former 'M' Branch of the SWC still assumed that the war would culminate in spring 1919 and called for heavy pressure throughout the winter so that new German reserves would have difficulty in mobilizing.[122] The weather had cleared a little since September, and the air war remained hot. The RAF reported that the Germans had lost 352 aircraft in October and early November, compared with its own loss of 183.[123] The tightest margin of success was during the last week of October when the ratio was 41 to 45 in favor of the RAF. Nevertheless, Sykes and the Air Staff knew that German airmen could not sustain the fight if the Army collapsed, and Sykes continued to implement his decision to reinforce aerial aid to BEF operations.

The staff at RAF HQ published a memorandum specifying how the RAF could help the Army, and more training squadrons from the CFS were ordered to France.[124] Flyers at the front had detected German reluctance to engage in combat except when the odds were in their favor. Specifically, the enemy flew only in large formations and preferred to attack British bombers or single scouts. Salmond was convinced that the best way to help the BEF was to deny airspace to German flyers so that they would be unable to attack the Army. Hence he ordered the RAF to increase the targeting of German aerodromes and force a battle for air superiority.[125] Sykes concurred, and the tactic worked to some extent. On 31 October Sykes reported to the Air Council that the RAF had brought down a record 96 enemy aircraft the previous day.[126]

The decision to concentrate on Army help in October and early November led to the final arbitration of IAF/IF status in France. On 3 October Weir stated that France had finally accepted the policy of long-range bombing, but that the force still had to come under Marshal Foch.[127] The French decision was ironic considering that Sykes had now shifted focus to the Army. Sykes did not care anymore whether Foch gained control.[128] The danger from Foch had been his desire to use the IAF to support Army operations and that was now the RAF's main objective. Weir notified Clemenceau that Foch could assume ultimate authority, but that Trenchard should have 'wide latitude . . . in regard to tactics and complete latitude as to selection of bomb targets.'[129] The Air Council officially notified Trenchard of the agreement on 23 October 1918, and the Inter-Allied IF came into existence 26 October.[130]

Although the Air Staff had agreed to concentrate on Army help, Sykes and Weir were not about to relinquish control of aerial resources nor revert to pre-RAF organizations. Weir was adamant that assistance to tanks was to be tactical only; the RAF would not reduce its requirements to give the Army more tanks.[131] As the air war slowly began to wind down in October, Sykes became more concerned that the RAF would correspondingly vanish as a separate service. Hence he initiated measures to ensure the survival of a post-war RAF, including trying to reacquire airships from the Navy – a battle he had fought and lost before the war.[132]

At the same time, Sykes was practical and not simply trying to pro-tect his institution. He fought against wartime procurement that would be wasted once hostilities had ended and directed the Air Staff to consider all purchases and programs in terms of a future Air Force rather than in terms of the immediate war.

Because Sykes was one of few members of the Air Ministry looking beyond the war, Weir relied on him to establish the future RAF. Weir told the Air Council to 'take the paper prepared by the CAS point by point as a means of arriving at specific decisions'.[133] Unfortunately for Sykes, Weir did not remain Air Minister.

As the German Army retreated in November, sabotage destroyed as many aerodromes as RAF bombing had in weeks.[134] Italy was fighting well in the air and against ground targets along the Piave, and Austria sued for peace.[135] This provided the IF with locations from which to bomb German industries up the Elbe valley, and German leaders feared that the IF's Handley Page and six-engine Tarant Tabor bombers were about to arrive over Berlin.[136] German and Allied leaders anticipated the end of the war, but RAF commanders realized that the immediate battle would rage until it was ended officially.

The Air Council continually offered the Army Council more help in the zone of the Army.[137] During the last week of fighting, 60 British aircraft were lost while destroying 68 enemy craft. Since 1 April the RAF had brought down 2,463 enemy aircraft.[138] The last IAF sortie was flown by Handley Page bombers from No. 214 Squadron against the railroad at Louvain, and, typically, damage was unconfirmed.

Peace returned to Europe on 11 November 1918. The German Army and Air Force did not die of exhaustion. As Bidwell and Graham have noted, victory came from a 'technical knockout', and air power played a key role in that process.[139] On 11 November Sykes terminated all flying activities and canceled all building programs. Personnel with employment already established were to be released; demobilization had begun.[140]

The War Cabinet now initiated work on the official history of the war, and Sykes complied by ordering his staff to begin writing the history of the air war.[141] In addition, the Air Staff established a demobilization committee for the RAF to start the enormous and unpleasant task of bringing the force home. Most Air Ministry leaders were prepared to initiate a predictable draw-down; Sykes, on the other hand, saw demobilization as a temporary lag in the progression of British aviation. He was willing to accommodate the necessary demobilization but more eager to establish a remobilization committee to rebuild the Royal Air Force once demobilization was complete.[142]

Sykes' air power battles did not subside once the war ended. He joined Weir at Buckingham Palace for a reception with the King, who had written a final message to the RAF: 'The birth of the Royal Air Force, with its wonderful expansion and development, will ever remain one of the most remarkable achievements of the Great War.'[143] The war had become 'great', but amid the jubilation and sighs of relief was an undertone that the RAF had now lost its *raison d'être*. Haig's final dispatch made no reference to strategic air power and implied that the RAF still belonged to the Army: 'During the past year the work of our airmen in close co-operation with all fighting branches of the Army has continued to show the same brilliant qualities which have come to be commonly associated with that service . . .'.[144]

Britain was no more prepared for peace in 1918 than it had been for war in 1914, and the political and military atmosphere was as chaotic as the one Sykes had faced in August 1914. Terms of peace were critical to the Lloyd George government that had feared an Asquith assault and had fought for a non-German peace to ensure the Prime Minister's survival in office.[145] Now that the war had ended, Lloyd George needed a party, not just a following. He survived the 'Coupon Election', but the armed forces were in turmoil over demobilization.

Both the Admiralty and the War Office had immediate concerns, part of which involved campaigns to maintain their RAF contingents and to acquire new air assets.[146] The WRAF Commandant Mrs Gwynne-Vaughan wanted to ensure that the WRAF remained a service. Dissatisfied with past WRAF ranks, duties, pay and training, she proposed new procedures two days after the Armistice.[147]

Sykes had to move in three different directions at once. He was responsible in France for the air terms of the peace negotiations and flew to Versailles to present Britain's proposals for German aerial disarmament and world-wide air navigation. Sykes believed that Germany should forfeit all air activity for a period and he was not unaware of the relative economic advantage Britain would receive from such a move. Great Britain had earned it. Sykes' work contributed to the Versailles diktat that prohibited German aviation, and he helped to write and institute the International Air Code ratified by the Treaty of Versailles. When Sykes returned to Britain, he placed Groves in charge in Paris.

Sykes had to direct details of RAF demobilization abroad and at home and had to organize an immediate air force to continue service to the Empire as needed. Furthermore, he needed to establish the long-term prospects for service and civil aviation, a task he had already begun with his two earlier memoranda: 'Review of Air Situation and Strategy for the Information of the Imperial War Cabinet' in June and 'Memorandum by the Chief of the Air Staff on Air-Power Requirements of the Empire' in September.

Sykes recognized the need for a subsidy program for civil aviation,

1. Sykes mounted as a trooper in the Boer War. [Courtesy of Bonar Sykes]

2. Sykes as a prisoner of the Boers. [Courtesy of Bonar Sykes]

3. Sykes in the dress uniform of the 15th Hussars.
[Courtesy of Bonar Sykes]

4. Aerial photographs from Sykes' personal album, probably of the airfield [top] and harbor [bottom] at Imbros. [Courtesy of Bonar Sykes]

5. Wing camp [top] and aerodrome [bottom] during the
Gallipoli campaign, 1915.

6. Sykes as Chief of the Air Staff, 1918. [Courtesy of Bonar Sykes]

7. Sykes and colleagues from the British Air Section at the Paris Peace Conference, February 1919. Seated, from left to right: Col. P. R. C. Groves (Air Adviser to the British Ambassador), Sykes, Mr H. White-Smith (representing civil aviation); standing: Capt. Crosbie, Capt. Tindal-Atkinson, an unidentified major, Col. Blandy, Capt. Lyall.
[Courtesy of Bonar Sykes]

8. Sykes and Bonar Law in 1920 at the Air Conference, Croydon.
[Courtesy of Bonar Sykes]

9. Sykes as Governor of Bombay, at his desk in Government House, 1932. [Courtesy of Bonar Sykes]

10. Sykes in later life, *c*. 1940. [Courtesy of Bonar Sykes]

11. Lord Trenchard, Marshal of the Royal Air Force. Relations between Trenchard and Sykes were always difficult, and Trenchard's long tenure as Chief of the Air Staff saw a diminution of Sykes' reputation.
[Courtesy of Air Historical Branch (RAF)]

12. Henri Farman biplane. [Courtesy of RAF Museum, Hendon]

13. Sopwith Camel, with 110hp Le Rhone engine. The aircraft was well armed and highly manoeuvrable. This example has suffered damage to its mainplanes from enemy fire. [Courtesy of RAF Museum, Hendon]

14. Fokker D VII, with 160hp Mercedes engine. Very fast, maneuverable and well armed, this machine was considered by many flyers the best fighter aircraft of the First World War. [Courtesy of RAF Museum, Hendon]

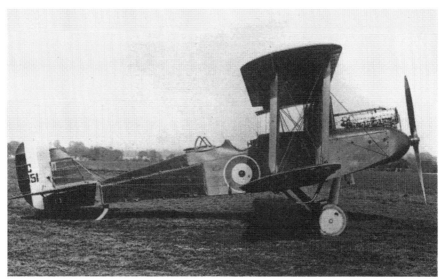

15. DH9 bomber aircraft, of which Trenchard wrote: 'I do not know who is responsible for deciding upon the DH9, but I would have thought that no one would imagine we should be able to carry out long-distance bombing raids . . . with machines inferior in performance to those we use . . . at present.' [Courtesy of RAF Museum, Hendon]

16. The ubiquitous BE2c, which served the Royal Flying Corps so well in the early phase of the war. Its chief virtue was its inherent aerodynamic stability, but this asset proved a liability against more agile enemy machines once serious air-to-air fighting began. [Courtesy of RAF Museum, Hendon]

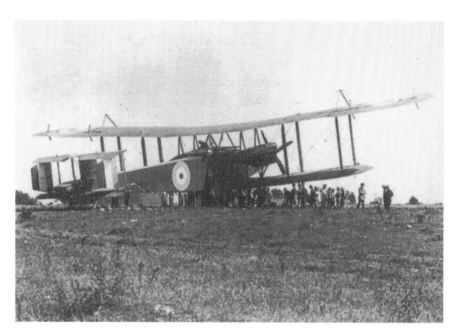

17. Handley Page [top] and Vickers Vimy [bottom], the RAF's first heavy bombers. Sykes anticipated that strategic bombing utilizing such aircraft would prove decisive. [Courtesy of RAF Museum, Hendon and Air Historical Branch (RAF) respectively]

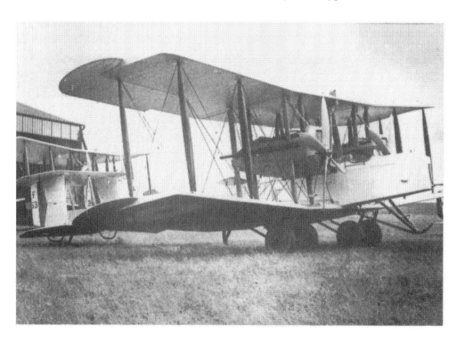

anticipating that the RAF's survival depended on a civil reserve air fleet. He agreed with the recommendations of Weir's Civil Air Transport (CAT) Committee in 1917, that once wartime contracts ended the British aviation industry would crumble without government assistance.

On a larger scale, Sykes predicted that British civil aviation could not exist without its international aspect. Unlike other, larger nations, Britain was too small for civil aviation to be profitable. Hence Sykes investigated the future of international flying. He clarified the Air Staff's position regarding two future options: complete freedom of the skies with certain prohibited areas within each nation, or a divided airspace with each nation having sovereignty and permitting international flights through specified channels of passage.[148] Sykes wanted to promote free trade, but the CAT had recommended complete British sovereignty, which ran contrary to the Allied nations' desire for peace. Sykes knew some type of compromise would be necessary for Britain to be able to take advantage of the position she had gained in world air supremacy. His memorandum passed the Air Council and went before the War Cabinet for incorporation into Britain's 'War Aims Index' at future peace negotiations.

Sykes tried to satisfy the demands of the War Office and the Admiralty, and now that Weir had resigned he submitted a new proposal for a peacetime civil and service air force to Lloyd George's newly appointed Secretary of State for both Army and Air Winston Churchill. Churchill was a gifted man, but the decision to combine the positions of Air and War Minister was ill-conceived. As Minister of Munitions, Churchill had been embroiled in post-war negotiations with British, French and American aircraft contractors who expected immediate bankruptcy.[149] As a former soldier in Africa and previous First Lord of the Admiralty, Churchill held loyalties to the Navy and the Army, but he had been a strong advocate of air power as well. The Prime Minister had offered Churchill either the Admiralty or the War Office but said that either way he would take the Air Ministry as well. Churchill wanted the Navy, but Army unrest led Lloyd George to press him in that direction. Perhaps suspicious of the two-hatted job the Prime Minister proposed, Churchill resisted Lloyd George's request until the Prime Minister reassured him that the Air Ministry was not to be dissolved.

Once in office on 15 January 1919, Churchill was inundated with the tasks of Army demobilization, which ran counter to concurrent requirements to man the occupation Army of the Rhine. At the same time, the Treasury demanded severe budget cuts, approximating to 20 per cent less service spending than the real 1914 expenditure, and Parliament established a committee headed by Eric Geddes to determine where such cuts could be levied. In the Army and the Navy, displaced servicemen were on strike and threatened to riot. Churchill was preoccupied with such anarchical tremors when he read Sykes' unrealistic proposals for a future air force nearly 30 times larger than the 1914 RFC.

Sykes was too far ahead of his time. He had great ability to think in grand strategic terms, but had a poor grasp of post-war economic and political realities, which led to his demise as the head of British air power. Grand strategy had won a war, and for Sykes' part in it he was made a Knight Commander of the Order of the Bath on 1 January 1919. Yet the war was history, and the emerging post-war era was eventually to be dominated by ten-year rules and fiscal constraint. Sykes had written his detailed and carefully developed memorandum for Weir, and although Weir had agreed generally with its concept of civil and military aviation, he had recommended that the Air Council should reduce Sykes' figures to meet fiscal demand. Once Weir resigned as Air Minister, Sykes' reworked proposal went to Churchill, who in September had suspected inefficiency on the part of the air service and had written: 'There is no doubt that the demands of the Air Force on men and material are thought to be much in excess of the fighting results produced.'[150] Churchill was under extreme pressure from the Treasury to cut Army and Air Force spending, while Sykes was asking for a cost-prohibitive program of 154 service squadrons, world-wide aerial routes and subsidies for the aircraft manufacturing industry. Sykes knew that he had to make his program less ambitious and reluctantly began revising his estimates.[151]

Meanwhile, the already popular Trenchard, who had resigned immediately after the Armistice, regained more notoriety by quelling a dockyard mutiny. When Churchill asked Trenchard for a proposal for a peacetime air force, he let him know clearly that he did not want any of the problems Trenchard had given Rothermere, and that Trenchard's proposal had to be minimal to accommodate low funding. Trenchard's quickly prepared, two-page response for 82 squadrons was precisely the more realistic one that Churchill wanted:

> Dear Mr Churchill,
> I send you a very short and badly written memorandum of what my policy is. I can explain the diagram better when I see you. I agree with you that unless the First Lord (of Air), or whatever he is called, sees eye to eye with his Minister or nearly so, he is no good to him. If you think the enclosed is sufficiently close to your policy then I am very willing to accept the appointment, and would thank you for offering it to me.[152]

While Churchill and Trenchard negotiated their agreement, which relegated Sykes to direct civil aviation, Sykes was busy negotiating peace at Versailles, setting peacetime rules for civilian aviation in Great Britain, and framing the Air Navigation Convention that would establish the future of international aviation. That Trenchard's first proposals put forward in February and March 1919 were not much different from Sykes' final proposals indicates that Churchill wanted Trenchard for other reasons in addition to the issue of Sykes' non-conformance with fiscal restraint. Like so many British soldiers who had lost their occupations and risked their lives on the battlefield to be abandoned during demobilization, Sykes, too, was discarded.

His accomplishments as CAS were integral to the survival and effectiveness of the British air service and constituted new thinking in terms of aerial warfare. He fought against fellow airmen, the Army, the Navy and foreign military leaders to create the IAF, and he provided the top-tier stability that the RAF needed to compete against a formidable aerial adversary. Just as the strategic air war was unfolding, Sykes recognized that a critical opportunity had presented itself in the tactical arena, and he provided increased air support to the BEF as the German Army began to retire from the front. A year earlier, Sykes had condemned Trenchard's costly offensive-pursuit tactics, but in autumn 1918 he supported the tactical air war as a means to victory in that year. As a result, British low-level bombing in the zone of the Army was decisive in destroying enemy morale and jeopardizing German operations. It is clear that Sykes' strategic ideas were new, but his primary goal as CAS was to win the war, not promote his own ideas simply because they were his – and different from Trenchard's, Haig's or Foch's. Hence what finally provided the most decisive aerial impact on the war were the costly tactics that had been pursued for years. The RAF loss rate was as severe during the last three months of the war as it had ever been, and Sykes had failed to improve upon Trenchard's loss of manpower, which he had so readily condemned. Yet, as shown by German diaries, the effectiveness of tactical air power in supporting the Army had increased. While German accounts of the Somme had complained about artillery, diaries from Amiens demonstrated conclusively that aerial attack harassed, interrupted operations, denied sleep and broke the will to continue the fight. The most graphic example of aerial effectiveness occurred in Palestine in September. Where Sykes was important was in his ability to establish the administrative and organizational infrastructure necessary to support the air war in 1918. His behind-the-scenes management of resources ensured that air power arrived when and where it was most needed, which probably would have been against German industry in 1919, had the war lasted that long. The war ended, however, as Sykes was in mid-stride to create the world's greatest military and civil air service for the Empire. His countrymen were uninterested in such ambitions in 1919, and Sykes ended by jeopardizing his Air Force career in trying to support his vision of the future. This, in turn, was deleterious to Sykes' place in the history of air power. If measuring the revolutionary aspects of air power in terms of RAF and IAF success in battle against the enemy, as most historians have done, then the conclusion is that the revolution was cut short by the Armistice and, therefore, did not exist in effect. However, when assessing Sykes' role and air power development in its organizational and conceptual aspects, one may conclude that a revolution was successful. Due to such behind-the-scenes organization of the air service, tactical air power was able to prove its decisive influence on the battlefield, where combined-arms tactics in support of the Army were carried out by an independent RAF. Less important to the war effort but a much more revolutionary development in concept, was the creation of the IAF. By 11 November 1918, the IAF had the technology, the organization, the resources, the ability and the moral conviction (and orders) to bomb the capital of Germany. With such a development in air power, warfare had evolved from a war of fronts to area warfare involving not just armies but industrial areas and civil society.

NOTES

1. War Cabinet Minute 8, 20 August 1918, War Cabinet 461, Public Record Office (PRO), CAB 23.
2. IAF bombing totals wane in comparison with the rest of the air service, much less Army shelling. From July 1916–November 1918, the air service dropped 6,402 tons of bombs on the Western Front; the IAF only 540 tons. In 'Results of Operations in the Air', Air Ministry History, PRO, Air 8/13. Also Kennett, *The First Air War*, 217, noted that Edmonds's official history of the Army recorded air service bombing as 'without important results'. Corum, 17, wrote that British air service effectiveness was such that British airmen were traded for German civilians, one for one. For a complete list of IAF bombing and losses sustained see Newall Papers, Card Index of Bombing by 8th Brigade, RAFM, B391. More IAF statistics are in Air 1 460/115/312/101 and Trenchard's historical account of IAF activity is in Precis No. 327, Air 6/19. In all, the IAF sent 504 missions against 107 different towns.
3. Henry Norman to Rothermere, 25 March 1918, Weir Papers 1/2, Churchill College, Cambridge. Norman was a member of Rothermere's Air Council and an early advocate of strategic bombing, but his influence did not last. Smuts and Lloyd George found Norman to be 'an irresponsible politician with no definite duties on the Air Council', and partly responsible for Air Council friction that may have contributed to the trouble between Rothermere and Trenchard. See Lloyd George to Bonar Law, 18 April 1918, Bonar Law Papers, 83/2/19, House of Lords Records Office.
4. Lord Tiverton to Sykes, 22 May 1918, Air 1 460/15/312/101. Tiverton argued that British inability to establish a coherent bombing policy with specific targets and dates led to France's reluctance to support strategic bombing.

5. Air Council Minutes, 2 May 1918, Meeting No. 25, Air 6/12.
6. 'Notes on Sir Henry Norman's Memorandum', Weir Papers 1/2. Norman was concerned that British bombing would not be successful and that it did not follow German technologies. Ever since the 'Fokker scourge', there was a British tendency to assume that the Germans were more advanced in aviation.
7. W. A. Robinson (Air Ministry Secretary) to War Cabinet, 13 May 1918, Churchill Papers 15/59/1, Churchill College, Cambridge; and Sykes, *From Many Angles*, 228. An indication of the IAF's confusing administration was that, after the Armistice, it came under the command of Haig, not the RAF. See Baring, 301.
8. Minutes of first three meetings of the Inter-Allied Aviation Committee, 9 May, 31 May and 21 July 1918, Air 1/26/15/1/121/34A. By the third meeting, the Committee still could not decide whether to create an Inter-Allied IF. They could not even decide whether to warn Germany that they were going to bomb – if indeed they bombed. Cooper, *The Birth of Independent Air Power*, 137, stated that the Committee was a total failure.
9. 'Independent Bombing Command', Sykes, *From Many Angles*, 542.
10. Collier, 75 noted that Trenchard's acquiescence in the new air service was based on a belief that the independent air force would not survive and would eventually return to the Army.
11. Kennett, *The First Air War*, 60; and Boyle, 223. Trenchard may well have been correct in his belief that the German aim in attacking London was to draw British fighters away from the Western Front.
12. Baring, 274, stated that had it not been for the benevolent hospitality of the French General de Castelnau, who was in favor of an offensive air policy, Trenchard's IAF could not have operated. Also, Boyle, 291.
13. Independent Air Force Diary, 3 June 1918, Trenchard Papers, MFC 76/1/30, RAFM.
14. Ibid., 18 June 1918.
15. 'Memorandum by Major-General H. M. Trenchard to the Prime Minister, Mr Lloyd George, 13 January 1918', Raleigh and Jones, Appendix V, 22–4. Trenchard had helped to create the first bombing force and reported to the Prime Minister that it would bomb industrial centers in Germany as well as aerodromes and submarine docks. This force, however, was not expected to play a major part in the air war, and Trenchard intended to keep RAF priority centered on Army operations. Trenchard's bombers were to placate politicians who were trying to respond to public demands for revenge. Trenchard clearly entertained no ideas of 'independence'.
16. Independent Air Force Diary, 20 June 1918, Trenchard Papers, MFC 76/1/30.
17. Independent Air Force Diary, 29 June to 3 July 1918, Trenchard Papers, MFC 76/1/30. Trenchard complained that the Air Ministry would not let him run his own show, and that by publishing IAF communiqués as Air Ministry ones, it would appear that the IAF was under the Air Ministry (which it was). Trenchard wrote, 'Chaos seems to reign at the Air Ministry.'
18. Boyle, 297.
19. Weir also thought this, arguing that rather than try to achieve total air dominance, as Trenchard had, the air service should simply try to maintain air parity with the Germans on the Western Front and then take the remaining air resources to create the IAF. In Weir to Trenchard, 29 June 1918, Trenchard Papers, MFC 76/1/94.
20. Hans Delbrück, *Geschichte der Kriegkunst*, wrote that there are two kinds of strategy: *Niederwerfungsstrategie* (annihilation), and *Ermattungsstrategie* (attrition). The costly Haig/Trenchard offensive was a war of attrition against

Germany and, owing to Germany's smaller production potential, it would eventually succeed. Yet the expense made it unacceptable, and hence Sykes and the SWC had started working toward the new technological approach in 1917.

21. Sykes, *From Many Angles*, 223.
22. Cooper, *The Birth of Independent Air Power*, 130.
23. Sykes to Prime Minister, 1 June 1918, Sykes Private Papers.
24. Sykes, 'Notes by the Chief of the Air Staff on the Independent Royal Air Force, and the Proposed Inter-Allied Strategic Bombing Force', *From Many Angles*, 558.
25. Air Ministry Dispatch AO/094, 11 June 1918, Air 1/18/15/1/94. Also, Trenchard to Air Ministry, 8 July 1918, Air 1 30/15/1/155/28A. Trenchard wrote that he had notified RAF HQ that he was taking over all administration of the IAF: 'From this date Independent Force will deal direct with you on all matters.'
26. Air Council Minutes, 2 May 1918, Meeting No. 25, Air 6/12.
27. US guarantees of machines and engines did not materialize, and by August Churchill was livid about the 'flagrant breakdown'. He complained that after all the work that had gone into forming strategic bombing, the key link (American engines) was going to stall the effort. Churchill urged British leaders to get the United States government to act in the matter, stating it was not a 'profound military debate' but a 'perfectly simple business arrangement which, after the main fact and figures have been assembled, should be settled by Ministers in a couple of hours of friendly talk across the table'. See memoranda and letters to Lord Reading, the British Ambassador to Washington, Churchill Papers, 15/59/34 and 15/59/26.
28. Air Council Minutes, 15 July 1918, Meeting No. 39, Air 6/13. The Air Council fought Sykes, as noted in the minutes: 'There was ground for the view that the allocation of strength to the Independent Air Force was on the liberal side.'
29. 'Memorandum on Independent Force Command for Long Range Bombing of Germany', 23 May 1918, Weir Papers 1/2; and War Cabinet Minutes, 24 May 1918, War Cabinet 417, CAB 23. Also in Raleigh and Jones, Appendix VII.
30. Weir's memorandum was similar to Sykes' memorandum, 'Independent Bombing Command'. See Sykes, *From Many Angles*, 543; and Sykes Private Papers. Sykes was so adamant that the IAF not be under the French that he stated that it would be better to make strategic bombing purely an Anglo-American effort than to have French help at the cost of having French control.
31. 'Independent Bombing Command', Sykes memorandum to Prime Minister, 1 June 1918, Sykes Private Papers.
32. Sykes minute to Prime Minister, 1 June 1918, Sykes Private Papers.
33. Clemenceau was an advocate of strategic bombing. He had led the French Air League in 1916 that had called for reprisal bombing against Germany. See Kennett, *The First Air War*, 56. Gen. Duval, who was Marie-Victor-Charles-Maurice Duval, the Directeur de l'Aéronautique Militaire, represented France at the Inter-Allied Aviation Committee meetings at Versailles.
34. 'Record of meeting between M. Clemenceau, David Lloyd George, and Sykes at Versailles, 3 June 1918', Trenchard Papers, MFC 76/1/68.
35. Interview with Bonar Sykes, 17 July 1994, Conock Manor, Devizes; and Sykes, *From Many Angles*, 241.
36. Derby to Weir, 6 September 1918, Lloyd George Papers, Series F/Box 47/Folder 3/Item 9, House of Lords Record Office.
37. Diary of the IAF, 10 June 1918, Trenchard Papers, MFC 76/1/30. The US colonel was Van Horn.

38. Weir to Trenchard, 29 June 1918, and Weir to Trenchard, 16 July 1918, Trenchard Papers, MFC 76/1/94.
39. Sykes to Trenchard, 8 July 1918, Air 1/30/15/1/155/26A.
40. 'Note on the Inter-Allied Bombing Force Problem', 13 July 1918, Sykes Private Papers. Sykes submitted the note to the SWC: 'It would seem advisable that in order to avoid endless discussions which are delaying the achievement of the very desirable ends we have in view, we should suggest the following compromise – taken collectively.'
41. Sykes' memorandum to SWC, 13 July 1918, Sykes Private Papers.
42. Weir would not agree to this compromise until 28 September 1918. Weir to Prime Minister, 28 September 1918, Lloyd George Papers, Series F/Box 47/Folder 3.
43. Draft Procés Verbal of the Third Session of the Versailles Inter-Allied Aviation Committee, 21 July 1918, Air 1/26/15/1/121. The Committee consisted of Sykes and Generals Bongiovanni of Italy, Foulois of the United States and Duval of France.
44. War Cabinet Minutes, 24 July 1918, War Cabinet 451, CAB 23.
45. Supreme War Council Resolution, 3 August 1918, Meeting No. 42 of the SWC at Versailles, Air 1/26/15/1/121/34B. See also, Joint Note No. 35, Raleigh and Jones, Appendix IX, 30–1.
46. Weir to Prime Minister, 12 August 1918, Lloyd George Papers, Series F/Box 47/Folder 3/Item 7.
47. Air Council Minutes, 22 August 1918, Meeting No. 44, Air 6/13.
48. Ibid. Sykes sent Lieutenant-Colonel Malone to Paris to be the Air Attaché.
49. Weir to Prime Minister, 27 August 1918, Lloyd George Papers, Series F/Box 47/Folder 3; Memorandum to Clemenceau, 31 August 1918, Trenchard Papers, MFC 76/1/94; and Sykes, *From Many Angles*, 234.
50. 'Draft Note for M. Clemenceau', Lloyd George Papers, Series F/Box 47/Folder 3/Item 8.
51. Weir to Lloyd George, 27 August 1918, Lloyd George Papers, Series F/Box 47/Folder 3/Item 8.
52. 'Memorandum on the Subject of an Independent Air Force', by Marshal Foch, 14 September 1918, Raleigh and Jones, Appendix VIII, 29–30; and Air 1/30/15/155/33B. Foch was a true army man, unwilling to allow any new strategy or technology to jeopardize land operations. Foch argued that land could be separated from sea, but it was impossible to separate air from air. Hence, air power belonged to the army.
53. Weir to Trenchard, 17 September 1918, Trenchard Papers, MFC 76/1/94. Weir wrote that, because of recent ground success, he was receiving political pressure that too much effort was going toward the air war.
54. Sykes, *From Many Angles*, 235. Specifically, the IAF was to fly out of Norwich.
55. 'Notes by the Chief of the Air Staff on the Independent Royal Air Force, and the Proposed Inter-Allied Strategic Bombing Force', 28 June 1918, Air 1/26/15/1/121. This was sent to the Imperial War Cabinet, 7 August 1918.
56. Weir to Prime Minister, 17 September 1918, Lloyd George Papers, Series F/Box 47/Folder 3/Item 10.
57. Weir to Prime Minister, 28 September 1918, Lloyd George Papers, Series F/Box 47/Folder 3/Item 11.
58. Derby to Weir, 6 September 1918, Lloyd George Papers, Series F/Box 47/Folder 3/Item 9.
59. Weir to Trenchard 9 August 1918, Trenchard Papers, MFC 76/1/94. Brancker had been in Washington to work the issue of Liberty Engines, but he had returned with disappointing news. Also, correspondence, Trenchard to Air

Ministry, Air 1/18/15/1/94/125.

60. Weir to Trenchard, 10 September 1918, Trenchard Papers, MFC 76/1/94; and Lieutenant J. C. F. Hopkins, sound recording, Reel No. 9, IWM sound recordings. Hopkins noted that night flying was much safer. Also Morrow, *The Great War in the Air*, 321. Morrow recorded that day bombing had a 70 per cent monthly wastage rate.

61. Higham, *Air Power*, 27.

62. The IAF trained with a camera obscura and bombed with the Batchelor bomb-dropping apparatus and the CFS 4B bomb sight. The technology was rudimentary, and W. E. D. Wardrop recalled that the safest place for observers during bombing training was the center of the target. In W. E. D. Wardrop, sound recording, Reel No. 2, IWM sound recordings.

63. Groves to Air Ministry, 26 June 1918, Air 2/76/B55; and IAF Standing Orders: 'Arrangements for the Control of Machines Flying from England to the Independent Force', 11 August 1918, Air 2/76/B55. Sykes complied with the request of Major-General Mark Kerr.

64. Trenchard to Director of Air Organization, 14 August 1918, Air 2/76/B55.

65. The original route had been north of Paris and direct to Nancy, but it changed to one south of Paris and then up to Nancy. This route had to accommodate another change, as well, when the headquarters moved from Ochy to Autreville on 12 August 1918. Evelyn B. Gordon (for Trenchard) to Director of Air Organization, 10 August 1918, Air 2/76/B55.

66. Air 1/18/15/1/94/91.

67. Cooper, *Birth of Independent Air Power*, 132, stated that the first really coherent bombing policy came 18 April 1918 when the Strategic Committee was established. The policy at that point, however, had much to be resolved.

68. Ibid; and Sykes, *From Many Angles*, 233.

69. Newall, 'The Scientific and Methodical Attack of Vital Industries', John Salmond to Sykes, 27 May 1918, Air 1 460/15/312/101; and Memoranda from S. Caproni, M. Theunissen and Lt Beauti, Air 1 460/15/312/101. Also 'Extract from a paper by Mr Winston Churchill, Minister of Munitions, 21 October 1917', Raleigh and Jones, Appendix IV, 19. Churchill stated air power could not win alone and advocated bombing combined with ground attack. Trenchard wrote in September 1917 that the best operation would be to attack at night for material damage and during the day for moral effect. Trenchard to Air Board, September 1917, Air 1 921/204/5/889.

70. Paret, 'Clausewitz', in *Makers of Modern Strategy*, ed. Paret, 206. Clausewitz wrote that victory required occupation of the battlefield as well as destruction of the enemy's physical and psychic forces.

71. Freiherr von Bülow, 'The Air Raids on Great Britain by Bogoal 3', Folio No. 8, Air 9/69. 'The main object was the moral intimidation of the British nation, the crippling of the will to fight, thus preparing the ground for peace.'

72. 'Extract from a paper by Mr Winston S. Churchill, Minister of Munitions, 21 October 1917', Raleigh and Jones, Appendix IV, 19.

73. Weir to Trenchard, 29 June 1918, Trenchard Papers, 76/1/94; and Air 1/17/15/1/88. Mr Titcomb, an American expert on the German mining industry, advised the Air Ministry that there were four main mining districts that produced 83 per cent of the output: Lorraine, Saar, Coblenz and Westphalia. All were within 200 miles of Nancy. F. W. Lanchester also submitted a report on the vulnerability of German industry to aerial bombing. German industry was organized into 45 principal *Bauaufsichten* or Construction Inspectorates. Nine were in the Rhine Valley. See Morrow, *German Air Power*, 211.

74. 'Operations for 1918 Strategic Bombing', Air 1 460/15/312/101. On 31 May

1915 Zeppelin LZ38 dropped 600 pounds of explosives on London, yet this killed only seven people. The extensive list of damage caused to Britain by German raids is in Folio No. 8, Air 9/69.

75. In response to a Belgian complaint in 1917, Haig ordered that only military targets were to be bombed. Haig to Petain, 20 September 1917, Air 1 921/204/5/889. Sykes had to respond to the Belgian Monarchy in June 1918 for apparent bombing inaccuracies that killed Belgian civilians. J. T. Davies (Prime Minister's private secretary) to Sykes, 19 June 1918, Lloyd George Papers, Series F/Box 46/Folder 4.

76. War Cabinet Minutes, 18 March 1918, War Cabinet 366, CAB 23.

77. Rothermere to Trenchard, 24 November 1917, Air 1 921/204/5/889. In late 1917 the Admiralty Intelligence Department received a report from a reliable Danish businessman who said that public morale in German towns had been dangerously low until Germany learned that the Air Ministry had decided to attack only targets of military importance. Hence the Air Ministry was readily aware of the military advantage that could be gained by attacking civilians. Of the numerous Air Ministry documents on strategic bombing in Air 1 460/15/312/101, there are few that refer to the immorality of bombing civilians in towns.

78. Boyle, 315. Weir wrote, 'It is not the destructive effect but the effect of what we cause the Germans to do.'

79. Weir to Trenchard, 10 September 1918, Trenchard Papers 76/1/94; and Boyle, 312. Weir wrote to Trenchard, 'The German is susceptible to bloodiness, and I would not mind a few accidents due to inaccuracy.'

80. Air Staff Minutes, 12 June 1918, Meeting No. 62, Air 8/5. Parliament had asked whether the RAF was going to carry out reprisals for German attacks on French hospitals. Even if such reprisals were to come from the RAF rather than the IAF, Sykes' action in this instance was peculiar. The RAF was a new service, supporting the War Office, but no longer under its authority. If anything, he should have referred morally difficult decisions not to the War Office but to the War Cabinet.

81. Kennett, *The First Air War*, 215.

82. Eighth Brigade Visitors' Book, Newall Papers, B394. Sykes and Groves visited on 17 September 1918. In his diary, Newall never mentioned any praise or guidance coming from Sykes. Sykes did meet Trenchard occasionally away from Nancy – 14 June at RAF HQ and 5 July in Paris, where they again had dinner together. See IAF Diary, Trenchard Papers, MFC 76/1/30.

83. This was in accordance with Air Council policy established in Air Staff Minutes, Air Council to War Cabinet (no date), Air 1 460/15/312/101. The Air Council knew that even though the IAF would target industry, it would not have the initial capability to cause much destruction. Hence, until the IAF had such a capability, it was to bomb as wide an area as possible to produce a moral effect and to cause the enemy to distribute aerial defenses widely.

84. War Diary, Newall Papers B392. For example, on the last day of the war, every IAF mission except one targeted aerodromes. Also, *London Gazette*, 10th Supplement, 31 December 1918, 134–5.

85. Groves to Sykes, September (no day) 1918, Air 1 460/15/312/101.

86. Sykes was responsible for allotting all squadrons to the RAF and IAF, Air 1/18/15/1/94/42. In addition, the Air Council determined that the only way to respond to inevitable retaliation was to hit German aerodromes, and such bombing was to be left up to the discretion of 'the Commander of the Force'. See Air Staff Minutes, Air Council to War Cabinet (no date), Air 1 460/15/312/101.

87. Haig to Pétain, 15 October, 1918, Air 1 921/204/5/889.

88. 'Experience of Bombing with the Independent Force in 1918', Air Pub. 956, RAFM, Accession No. 001525.

89. Trenchard to Weir, 20 September 1918, Trenchard Papers 76/1/94.
90. Weir to Trenchard, 12 September 1918, Trenchard Papers 76/1/94. Weir notified Trenchard that Cabinet members were unhappy with the IAF's performance and asked Trenchard to rephrase his reports to satisfy 'old friend Impatience'.
91. Air 1 460/15/312/101.
92. 'Experience of Bombing with the Independent Force in 1918', Air Pub. 956, RAFM, Accession No. 001525.
93. 'The Possibilities of Long Distance Bombing From the Present Date Until September 1919', Air 1 460/15/312/101.
94. In Trenchard's defense, the SWC's 'E' Branch published a paper on 13 October entitled 'German Retirement on the Western Front'. This cited German dependence on railway communications during a retirement, PRO, CAB 45/168.
95. Trenchard to Weir, 20 September 1918, Trenchard Papers 76/1/94.
96. War Cabinet Minutes, 15 October 1918, War Cabinet 486, CAB 23.
97. Major-General Sir C. E. Callwell, *Field Marshal Sir Henry Wilson* (London: Cassell, 1927), Vol. 2: 135. The major obstacle to the Berlin mission was range. As early as October 1917, Major P. Babington of 13th Wing had proposed to use the Handley Page V 1500, fitted with extra fuel tanks, to bomb Berlin and then fly on to Russia for landing.
98. Trenchard to Weir, 17 October 1918, Trenchard Papers 76/1/94.
99. War Diary, 11 November 1918, Newall Papers, B392, RAFM.
100. IAF Diary, Trenchard Papers, MFC 76/1/31. Most likely Trenchard's request was motivated by two desires: he wanted to be immediately released from his tiring responsibilities, and he wanted Haig to reacquire the force Trenchard had wanted Haig to own all along. It was a curious unilateral move by Trenchard, considering that Trenchard had no such authority to act on behalf of the Air Ministry.
101. Foreign Office No. 153287, 10 September 1918, Brooke-Popham Papers, IX/5/6, Liddell Hart Centre for Military Archives, King's College.
102. War Cabinet Minutes, 27 September 1918, War Cabinet 479, CAB 23.
103. War Cabinet Minutes, 4 September 1918, War Cabinet 469, CAB 23.
104. Sykes still supported strategic bombing as well. He visited Trenchard in France on 20 and 21 September to discuss technical details and then met Trenchard, Weir and the King on 27 and 28 September to consider bringing in more strategic squadrons. IAF Diary, Trenchard Papers, MFC 76/1/31; and Sykes, *From Many Angles*, 241.
105. Cole, 181–205. Some records indicate that as many as 582 German aircraft were shot down in September.
106. Tagebuch v. Hutier, W-10/50640, Bundesarchiv-Militärarchiv, Kriegsgeschichtliche Forschungsanstalt des Heeres, Freiburg. Numerous German war diaries attest to the impact of British tactical bombing on German soldiers.
107. Geoffrey Salmond to Groves (no date), Groves Papers, 129/2(a), Liddell Hart Centre; and J. E. Borton to Groves, 25 October 1918, Groves Papers, 129/2(a), Liddell Hart Centre. Borton wrote, 'we have seen enough for ourselves to realize what an appalling effect systematic bombing can have provided you have winged the enemy.'
108. Air Council Minutes, 26 September 1918, Meeting No. 51, Air 6/13.
109. Air Council Minutes, 5 September 1918, Meeting No. 47, Air 6/13. The American General Biddle had sent a letter complaining about accommodation. Earlier in June the American Naval Air Service had demanded control of two coastal air stations in exchange for the 50 America flying boats being delivered to the RAF.

110. Air Council Minutes, 3 October 1918, Meeting No. 52, Air 6/13.
111. War Cabinet Minute 4, 4 September 1918, War Cabinet 469, CAB 23.
112. Air Council Minutes, 10 October 1918, Meeting No. 53, Air 6/13.
113. In particular, spiral spruce had led to many accidents.
114. 'Instructions for the Preparation and Issue of Daily Routine Orders', September 1918, Air Pub. 69, RAFM, Accession No. 005112.
115. Sykes did not implement this order until 23 October 1918. Air Staff Minutes, 23 October 1918, Meeting No. 114, Air 8/5.
116. Air Staff Minutes, 16 October 1918, Meeting No. 111, Air 8/5.
117. Air Staff Minutes, 7 October 1918, Meeting No. 107, Air 8/5.
118. Air Staff Minutes, 9 September 1918, Meeting No. 98, Air 8/5.
119. Air Staff Minutes, 25 October 1918, Meeting No. 115, Air 8/5.
120. Sykes, *From Many Angles*, Appendix VII, 558–74.
121. 'Appreciation of Enemy Situation', 9 October 1918, 'E' Branch Report at Versailles, CAB 25/79.
122. 'M' Branch Statistics and MaCready Report, 4 October 1918, CAB 25/96.
123. Cole, 207–34.
124. 'Notes on Recent Operations', RAF Staff College 2nd Course, Appendix 4, RAFM, Accession No. C/5/1/1. The report listed six roles:

  1. Close co-operation with cavalry, artillery, infantry and tanks.
  2. Reconnaissance and photography.
  3. Destruction of enemy communication links.
  4. Attacking enemy troops and transport with bombs and machine-guns.
  5. Forming smoke screens using smoke bombs.
  6. Dropping supplies, such as ammunition and food.

125. Ibid.
126. Air Council Minutes, 31 October 1918, Meeting No. 56, Air 6/13.
127. Air Council Minutes, 3 October 1918, Meeting No. 52, Air 6/13.
128. Sykes, *From Many Angles*, 236.
129. Ibid.
130. Air 1/30/15/1/155/33B; and Boyle, 313.
131. Air Council Minutes, 10 October 1918, Meeting No. 53, Air 6/13.
132. Air Council Minutes, 31 October 1918, Meeting No. 56, Air 6/13.
133. Air Council Minutes, 23 October 1918, Meeting No. 55, Air 6/13. Specific items included:

  1. Ownership of balloons – Sykes stated the RAF should own them.
  2. Coastal patrol – Sykes stated the RAF should have the mission.
  3. Commercial Air – Sykes stated it should be part of the Air Ministry.
  4. Pilot training – Sykes stated the RAF should train all service or civilian pilots doing any government work.
  5. Size of the peacetime RAF – Sykes stated it would need to be larger than 100 squadrons.
  6. Research and development – Sykes promoted it as critical.

134. Stark, 213.
135. John Gooch, 'Italy during the First World War', in *Military Effectiveness, Vol. 1, The First World War*, ed. Allan Millett and Williamson Murray (Boston: Unwin Hyman, 1988), 173.
136. Liddell Hart, 386, stated that this knowledge contributed to Germany's surrender. The IAF was poised to attack Germany from two directions – from Bircham Newton, England as well as from Nancy in France. See Waterhouse, 162.

137. Major Swinton (Air Staff) minute to Groves, 4 November 1918, Air 1 460/115/312/101.
138. Cole, 235–40.
139. Bidwell and Graham, 129 and 143–4. 'The memory of the invaluable contribution of the RAF and wireless to the ground victory was a casualty of a post-war political struggle between the services.'
140. Air Council Minutes, 11 November 1918, Meeting No. 59, Air 6/13.
141. Sykes' orders, 2 November 1918, Air 1 460/15/312/101. Sykes gave the Air Staff a 17 November deadline, which was met with the product entitled 'War Effort of the Air Services'.
142. Air Staff Minutes, 8 November 1918, Meeting No. 121, Air 8/5. The first RAF Demobilization Branch was established 2 October 1918.
143. The King's address, Sykes Private Papers; and Sykes, *From Many Angles*, 245.
144. Sykes, *From Many Angles*, 243.
145. Lord Esher to Henry Wilson, 1 May 1918, Lloyd George Papers, Series F/Box 47/Folder 3.
146. Admiralty to Air Ministry letters, Roskill, 693 and 715–34. Sykes met Admiralty personnel on 4 December to discuss future Naval aviation.
147. 'Post War Employment of Women in the RAF', 13 November 1918, Precis No. 296, Air 6/18.
148. Air Council Minutes, 10 October 1918, Meeting No. 53, Air 6/13.
149. Post-Armistice papers, Churchill Papers, 15/59/141.
150. Churchill to Lloyd George, September 1918, Groves, 90.
151. 'Memoranda on Air Power Requirements of the Empire', initially 9 December 1918, Sykes Private Papers; and 'Memorandum of the post-war functions of the Air Ministry and the Royal Air Force', Air 6/19/305. It is difficult to determine precisely what Sykes finally proposed. He initially advocated a program of nearly 350 squadrons, but Air Council records of 13 November 1918 show a proposal of 154 squadrons. Sykes revised his original proposal numerous times to try to satisfy Churchill, the Air Council, the War Office, the Admiralty and the Treasury.
152. Trenchard to Churchill, 5 February 1919, Trenchard Papers, 76/1/164; Divine, 155; and Boyle, 331. Trenchard's final plan for 82 squadrons amounted to a difference of only £6 million from the cost of Sykes' final plan (or less than half the price of one 1918 battleship).

8

To Reconnoiter the Enigma:
Sykes and his Environment

Why then, after such accomplishments before and during the First World War, did Sykes become a mystery and his influence in the first air war become scarcely discernible? Something caused him to have such antagonistic relationships with Trenchard and Henderson, and something about his personality made him unable to fit harmoniously into the air service environment. Furthermore, for some reason many historians have overlooked his role in contributing to the beginning of a revolution in air power. A study of Sykes is not complete without addressing these issues. It is particularly important to assess Sykes' principal antagonists as well as the air service in which he served.

TRENCHARD

The most obvious antagonist in Sykes' life was the person whose fame has outweighed Sykes' anonymity. Historians have given Trenchard a mixed review, but unlike Sykes, a bright spotlight. The primary error of the Trenchard story is historicism – Trenchard has been credited with visions to which he shut his eyes. Early on, he was less visionary and more pragmatic – he simply wanted to help to win the war with air power in the way he thought it could be used most effectively. Writers have attributed to Trenchard ideas and actions during the First World War that, for the most part, he did not exhibit until years later. Although he did, indeed, express ideas on the strategic and independent use of aircraft during the war, he did not pursue them but, rather, pursued the opposite. Therefore it is going too far to claim, as one historian has, for example, that Trenchard 'was to exercise a virtual monopoly on strategic thought within the service.'[1] That was true after the war, but from 1917 to 1918 Trenchard fought adamantly against strategic air and its independence.[2] Some historians conclude that Trenchard did an about-face in strategic thinking after the war because of lessons he had learned.[3] More likely, he simply determined that the timing was not good during the desperate war situation to change aerial roles and organizations.[4] Nevertheless, the trend to attribute Trenchard's post-war activities to the First World War period continues, with authors describing Trenchard as the staunch fighter for air force independence from the beginning.[5]

Although Sykes and Trenchard had opposing personalities, their military careers were remarkably similar. Marshal of the Royal Air Force Viscount Trenchard was born in 1873, which made him Sykes' senior by four years. This may have been an important issue between them. Trenchard was commissioned in the Royal Scots Fusiliers in 1893, and, like Sykes, served in India and in South Africa before arriving in England to join the RFC as a 39-year-old major. Trenchard was seriously wounded in the Boer War – shot through the chest just as Sykes was during the same war. In his first aviation post Trenchard served as Deputy to Captain Godfrey Paine, RN, the first Commandant of the Central Flying School (CFS). He was in this post when Sykes threatened the organization of the CFS. A year later, when the RFC's Military Wing left for France in 1914, Trenchard reluctantly inherited Sykes' position as Commander of the Military Wing in England. Trenchard tried to get to France in any capacity and eventually arrived four months later as the Commander of No. 1 Wing. By August 1915 he had become General Officer Commanding (GOC), RFC in the field.

During the battles of 1916 and 1917, Trenchard established his reputation as an air commander who supported the Army at all costs, even if it meant matching devastating ground losses with air wastage. His offensive doctrine was designed to achieve and maintain control of the air, an objective the Army required in order to carry out its operations without enemy aerial interference. Trenchard's offensive stand endeared him to the new GOC of the British Expeditionary Force (BEF), General Sir Douglas Haig, who had taken command following the demise of Sir John French. Haig and Trenchard became friends and supported each other against increasing criticism that offensive tactics were excessively costly.

Historians have portrayed Trenchard both positively and negatively. To some he was a 'whiskered prima donna' who suffered from paranoia and pique.[6] To others, he was a greater figure than either Churchill or de Gaulle. One airman's recollection was a popular one – that Trenchard was simply 'the greatest man I ever met'.[7] The official air historians maintained this great-man image of Trenchard, and he corresponded regularly with Jones and the official War Office historian Sir James Edmonds to applaud the achievements of his friend Haig.[8]

It appears that there was little middle ground with Trenchard's popularity. Even though most associates and subordinates loved him like a father, a few despised him as a contemptuous megalomaniac. Carrying the standard for the latter was one of Sykes' strongest advocates – Groves. He attacked Trenchard personally for short-sighted policies and a post-war plan that was 'a narrow parochial scheme drawn up with a circumscribed military horizon and modelled on the scale of a small regular army'.[9] Groves noted that it took four costly years and the genius of Sykes finally to have the 'air view' of air power dominate the 'military view', and that after Churchill replaced Sykes with Trenchard as CAS in 1919, the RAF slipped from first to fifth place in world power. According to Groves, Sykes' splendid concept had vanished: 'Thus one of the greatest blunders of the war, for which the nation paid dearly, was repeated in peace.'[10] Another slanted opinion provided by Divine is that Trenchard suddenly became a convert to the idea of air independence, helping air power to become 'the predominating factor in all types of warfare', which was what Trenchard stated in the last sentence of his famous White Paper.[11] Hence, while Trenchard advocates have exonerated him, claiming that situations were contrary to his desires and beyond his control due to war-time dilemmas and fiscal constraints, anti-Trenchard writers have condemned him simply because those situations occurred under his watch and were, therefore, his responsiblility.

Trenchard's own opinion of the post-war RAF episode was that he was left with 'heaps of rubble' and had to 'create something out of nothing', a claim that sounds remarkably similar to an earlier one he had made when he was left behind in England in 1914, but a claim that was partially correct.[12] Because he agreed to drastic reductions (on paper), Trenchard, in a way, produced some of his own 'rubble'.[13] Yet 'Geddes axe' budget reductions clearly did force Trenchard to accept such political realities, although he then was able to turn a poor situation in his favor. He had learned valuable bureaucratic skills, which he used to convey the negative effects on to civil aviation, the Army and the Navy so that the RAF side of the Air Ministry was able to prosper during the next decade.[14] Where Trenchard's pronouncement fell short, however, was in lack of recognition that he was assisted greatly in his rebuilding effort by the administrative and organizational work Sykes had already done.

In addition to the post-war denouement, Trenchard's air power ideology during the war is critical to the story of Sykes. Trenchard considered long-range bombing a 'luxury fleet' that could not be afforded during the First World War.[15] He had noted before the war that air power could transform the battlefield, but he resisted putting the idea into practice, believing that the timing was wrong.[16] Trenchard's objections to long-range bombing supported his ally

Haig, who was steeped in Army tradition and the opinion that air power needed to be auxiliary to the Army in order to win the war.[17] Groves suggested that Trenchard was too preoccupied with the local battle and tactics to consider air power in its operational or strategic context – that in order to support the land war, Trenchard discarded the vision of the future to pursue the blindness of the past.[18]

Consequently, even though he was the IAF's first commander, Trenchard believed that he had to resist the intention to bomb Germany. He wrote, '11 Nov. 1918: The Armistice was signed this morning. Thus the Independent Force comes to an end. A more gigantic waste of effort and personnel there has never been in any war.'[19] Major-General Patrick of the American air service said that Trenchard had told him that he had fought against the IAF idea for several years, but that it had been forced upon him.[20] Webster and Frankland have suggested that Trenchard's objection to strategic bombing was the critical issue between Lord Rothermere and Trenchard that resulted in Trenchard's resignation as CAS in March 1918. Trenchard simply would not support the independent bombing force at the expense of the tactical forces in France.[21]

As already mentioned, Trenchard also fought against forming a separate air force – the RAF.[22] Wing-Commander H. R. Allen, a Trenchard antagonist, remembered his statement that the establishment of the RAF was 'the successful culmination of a German plot aimed at dislocating the RFC in the field'.[23] Boyle noted Trenchard's belief that the timing for the RAF was premature, and that Trenchard disagreed with both of Smuts' reports which advocated a separate air ministry. Thus Trenchard sided with many Admiralty and War Office decision-makers who tried to keep their own air power.[24]

This is not to suggest that Sykes influenced the decision to form the RAF. Henderson, the DGMA, was the real key to the amalgamation process. He had experienced three and a half years of infighting between the War Office and the Admiralty over aircraft production, and he had seen three Air Boards fail to rectify the situation. As Smuts' advisor on the Air Committee, Henderson led the charge for a separate service, a move which Trenchard later applauded when he realized that the end of 1917 was perhaps the *only* timing for such a change.[25] Once Trenchard had accepted the independence idea, he fought more tenaciously than anyone for the RAF's survival – to the extent, according to Higham, that it was fundamental to his doctrinal perspectives. While Sykes had seen strategic bombing as a way to win the First World War, Trenchard recognized it as a method of preserving the post-war RAF.[26]

The most intriguing issue of Trenchard's career was his resignation as CAS in 1918. Trenchard had told John Salmond on 18 December

1917, 'You cannot resign in war.'[27] Yet exactly three months later Trenchard became the only CAS in the RAF's history to do just that.[28] Trenchard's action jeopardized the British war effort during one of the most critical phases of the war – the German spring offensive in March 1918. Although he quickly rationalized that he would never have resigned had he known there was such an immediate danger, on the very day he forced his resignation, Trenchard reported to the War Cabinet that the RFC's air superiority may have been a factor in delaying 'the expected German offensive'.[29] Hence he weakened his own excuse, and the entire resignation episode has cast a shadow on the image of Trenchard as the steadfast, wartime leader many authors have portrayed.[30]

At the time of his resignation, rumors of a court-martial circulated within political and military circles; however, it is questionable as to what charges could have been brought against such a powerful personality. Trenchard commanded respect and convinced his peers and subordinates that he was concerned about their welfare. His personality matched his demeanor; his towering figure was surpassed only by his booming voice. Officers cowered in fear, and subordinates followed behind him at the requisite 20 paces.[31] Trenchard treated them as his boys, and to them he *was* the father figure.[32] When he left France in 1917 to be CAS, he wrote, 'This will undoubtedly interfere with my close personal touch with the Flying Corps in France . . . I hope you will still look upon me as a personal friend who will do his utmost to help you.'[33] Ironically, Trenchard was partly responsible, through his offensive policy and abrogated training plans, for the tremendous wastage rates the RFC experienced under his command.[34] Nevertheless, most members of the RFC and the American air service revered 'The Big Noise'.[35]

Many historians have criticized Trenchard's inability to articulate – further linking him with Haig, who was equally inept at communicating.[36] Yet, despite his limitations, Trenchard was able to make soldiers follow orders and, in this respect, was a great military commander. He established supportive friendships and used an exceptionally capable right-hand man, Maurice Baring. No doubt Baring was a critical factor in Trenchard's success as a commander.

Hence, in the difficult circumstances of the first air war, Trenchard was able to overcome seemingly insurmountable obstacles and rise above other commanders to lead the air service during most of the war. Yet, despite his charisma and remarkable leadership qualities, Trenchard clearly did not impress Sykes.

SYKES VERSUS TRENCHARD

In a note to Weir, Sir Sefton Brancker (the former Deputy DGMA under Henderson, who took over civil aviation from Sykes in 1922) included a copy of a cartoon he had taken from a 1920 newspaper. This showed two doctors disagreeing about a patient's diagnosis. Brancker had labeled the patient 'aviation', one of the doctors 'Gen S', and the other doctor 'Air Marshal T':

Air Marshal T: 'Dear me, while we've been talking the patient has expired.'

Gen S: 'How very extraordinary! So he has!'

Brancker then mentioned his fears that the Air Ministry was in for the same future.[37] This piece of evidence is one of very few that blatantly discloses the animosity between Sykes and Trenchard. Yet their quarrel dominates the history of Sykes.

In the wartime environment where tempers were short, friction such as that between Sykes and Trenchard was not unusual. Their hostility grew out of differences in personality, leadership style and concepts of how to apply air power. They were professional soldiers, however, and generally set aside their personal feelings and worked well together to accomplish their mission. In myriad documents an unsuspecting researcher can find little indication that Sykes and Trenchard fought. Most sources indicate unidirectional enmity during the war: some hostility toward Sykes, but little in return. After the war, however, mutual animosity grew, when Trenchard may have fueled most of the fire. As Lord Beaverbrook stated, Trenchard 'enjoyed bitter hatreds'.[38]

Trenchard wrote about Sykes: 'I fear none of the RFC thought much of this officer as he was too secretive and narrow-minded to the last degree.'[39] Ten years later, after reading Sykes' autobiography, Trenchard mentioned his 'colossal conceit' and described him as the 'very curious staff officer who never tried to help anybody but himself and never would discuss anything'.[40] As Trenchard criticized *From Many Angles*, he stated that Sykes had always been 'underground'. 'I have never read a book so egotistical and so "smug" as this. My recollection is exactly the opposite of everything that is written in this book.' Trenchard continued, 'Sykes was always trying to work against anybody having any authority in the Air Force which would deprive him of getting command . . . He was always so secret. He openly said he thought it was dangerous to discuss things and he never initiated a free discussion with anybody in the Flying Corps that we could ever find.'[41] Trenchard habitually passed along his personal opinions as representative of the entire air force, and many historians have obliged him by continuing the practice. They have treated Trenchard's

20-year-old opinion as truth and have written his post-war, anti-Sykes antagonism into the war years.

There were many potential reasons for competition between the two. Trenchard was superior to Sykes in years; but for a time Sykes was Trenchard's superior in rank and position. Writing years after the war, Trenchard mentioned that it was 'most difficult' to work under Sykes in France in 1914.[42] At a time when the 'first hundred' pilots were held in high esteem, Trenchard's Royal Aero Club Aviator's Certificate was number 270; number 95 belonged to Sykes.[43] Sykes was also Trenchard's intellectual superior, a natural organizer who was at home in staff work.[44] As W. J. Reader noted, Sykes was a 'cleverer man than Trenchard'.[45]

Yet Reader and others agreed that Sykes did not have the drive to carry through his ideas, nor the warmth to win affection from his peers and subordinates – he was too calculating to be an inspirational leader.[46] Airman Kenneth Reid van der Spuy said that Sykes was 'secretive and over-cautious', traits that do not enhance the appeal of a leader.[47] Hence Sykes may have resented Trenchard's leadership abilities.[48]

During the First World War Sykes and Trenchard had different ideas regarding organization and the application of air power. Trenchard's focus was on morale – defeating the enemy's morale with one's own. Hence the key to victory lay in maintaining a positive, offensive spirit at all costs, and he loudly encouraged his troops with his dominating voice and daunting presence. Sykes, on the other hand, saw victory in terms of efficiency. The side that could fight more effectively would defeat the less efficient side. Rather than sacrifice enthusiastic soldiers inefficiently, he promoted technological advancements and strategies as the means to victory.[49] Thus, while Sykes promoted innovation by organizing new experimental branches, Trenchard fought experimental organizations if they threatened squadron integrity.[50]

Another Sykes–Trenchard difference was their view of air power. As Morrow mentions, Sykes and Henderson pushed for an autonomous flying organization to promote efficiency. Trenchard, on the other hand, sided with Kitchener and Haig for a flying service tied strictly to the BEF.[51] This difference of opinion in organization may have resulted from Trenchard's concept of air power more in terms of tactics and from Sykes' seeing it more strategically.[52]

Overall, Trenchard's influence played a large part in Sykes' role as an air power thinker and air service leader. Yet, as has been argued, that influence had an even greater impact on the stature of Sykes in history. Trenchard's antagonistic influence overshadowed Sykes and created a skewed historical record. Trenchard, alone, was a formidable opponent, but Sykes also had trouble with a second power-ful antagonist – Brigadier-General Sir David Henderson.

HENDERSON

Part of the mystery of Sykes is that the Trenchard–Sykes controversy has eclipsed the relationship between Sykes and Henderson. Henderson's animosity toward Sykes, which started before the war, had a greater impact on Sykes' career and the air war than any influence from Trenchard. In fact, Henderson's wrath was partially responsible for Trenchard's attitude and, subsequently, for Sykes' estrangement from the air service. As mentioned already, there is little evidence of Trenchard's supposed intrigue to convince Henderson or Kitchener that Sykes needed to leave the RFC in 1915.[53] On the other hand, Henderson resented Sykes' youthful enthusiasm and higher commitment to the air war than to individuals – particularly to Henderson. One might suspect, therefore, that Trenchard attacked Sykes simply to appease Henderson, who was the highest ranking RFC officer. Not only could Trenchard align himself with power, but he could jeopardize the career of a potential rival at the same time.[54] The Henderson–Sykes friction never cooled even though it was eventually overshadowed by the discord between Trenchard and Sykes. Even then, however, one of Trenchard's major complaints was that Sykes tried to take credit for Henderson's achievements.

There were several apparent reasons for Henderson's attitude toward Sykes. As war loomed in 1914, Sykes' publicity eclipsed that of his superior at a time when Henderson and Sykes were at odds over the reorganization of the RFC. Then Henderson knowingly created resentment in Sykes when he usurped his command of the RFC in France. Next, Henderson's repeated departure from the RFC in late 1914 and early 1915 was painful in that it afforded Sykes the opportunity to demonstrate his potential. Finally, Sykes determined that Henderson's failure to accomplish his duties jeopardized the British war effort. Sykes was guilty of over-criticizing a superior officer, and he definitely wanted to reclaim his command of the RFC. However, he was not devious, and perhaps Henderson should have been more willing to acknowledge his own limitations. Not only was Sykes' observation of Henderson properly expressed in a memorandum, but it was in accordance with the opinions of other air-men, particularly Brancker and John Salmond, who had noticed the command predicament created by Henderson's illness and over-extended responsibilities. Just as Sykes had recommended, Henderson did, indeed, leave France in 1915.

Historians have portrayed Henderson as the grand old general of aviation – the reputed 'Father of the RFC'. Henderson deserves credit for the decision to form the RAF, but Cooper was correct that Henderson was a career-minded commander who placed personal opportunities for advancement higher in priority than other consideration involving the good of the new air service.[55] This was the side of Henderson that many have overlooked, but Sykes was too intelligent a person not to have discerned it. Historians have maligned Sykes, however, not Henderson, and any oversights or failings on Henderson's part have been dismissed as the natural result of a man suffering from illness and the loss of his son.

Not only was Henderson career-minded, he maintained strong control over the RFC and created within it a social system that blocked suggestions that might infringe upon his authority – it was well known in the RFC not to cross Henderson as Sykes had. To illustrate: Henderson's network of control ensured that he maintained the decision-making authority for selecting machines and engines for use by the service.[56] By 1916, however, aircraft production problems led to a Parliamentary investigation of the RFC and the Royal Aircraft Factory by Judge Bailhache's Judicial Committee.[57] Not one witness was available to testify against Henderson, and had it not been for the heroic efforts of Lord Montagu, who was relatively immune from Henderson's wrath, the Committee might have ceased to function.[58] Montagu wrote to Mr D. Cotes-Preedy, secretary of the Committee:

> Whether rightly or wrongly, all those connected with aviation have a rooted distrust of Sir David Henderson, although they desire to help the Committee. . . . If Sir David Henderson was to know, for instance, the names of officers, there is no doubt they would be marked men, and for this reason they cannot come before you or allow their names to be known.[59]

Montagu had written earlier that Henderson's reputation was such that the aircraft industry was unwilling to trust any assurances from military authorities. In the inquiry proceedings, Henderson replied that it was insulting to infer that he would take action against officers for testifying. However, he then added, 'Although I gave the assurance that the officers will not be victimized, of course, I cannot answer for the view that their brother officers will take of them.'[60] In other words, Henderson's system was in place.

His selfish character and bitterness toward Sykes were demonstrated by two other incidents. He would not employ Sykes in 1916, when the RFC could have used Sykes' experience and abilities, and Henderson resigned in 1918 as Sykes became the CAS. At the time, Henderson wrote that he 'earnestly desired to escape from the atmosphere of falsehood and intrigue which had enveloped the Air Ministry'.[61] The statement certainly implied that Henderson refused to work with Sykes, but, as Henderson later clarified, Sykes' appointment was not the real issue of his resignation. Henderson was upset with the entire Air Ministry situation and the fact that he had been bypassed as chief. In fact, the date of Henderson's letter shows that the falsehood and intrigue to which he was referring had developed *before* Sykes' appointment – when Trenchard was the CAS and Sykes was still at Versailles. Nevertheless, Henderson knew that his resignation at such a critical time would hurt Sykes' image and the RAF's effort. Ironically, Sykes had finally inherited Henderson's command – this time, his hard-earned, separate air service – and he felt the wrath that came with it.

THE RFC/RAF SYSTEM

Another cause of Sykes' relegation in history was his inability to fit into air service circles and the established social system. The command system which had developed from the Army was an integral part of the British flying establishment. It was a system plagued with infighting and dominated by command sponsorship. Its characteristics included respect for tradition, emphasis on morale, reverence for valor, suspicion of intellect and superstition. The RFC was a social club and its successor, the RAF, was hardly any more professional during its early days.

Within this system, sponsorship was the key to command.[62] To attain a desirable position, one had to have high-ranking friends in influential places – military and political. The system hurt Sykes more than it helped him because, compared with Trenchard, Sykes simply had the wrong sponsors. As one historian noted, Sykes 'was a Wilson man', who may have suffered setbacks due to friction at GHQ between Henry Wilson and the other generals. When Wilson left to become the Military Representative of the BEF at the French General Staff 'Sykes thus found himself isolated.'[63]

Lieutenant-General Sir Henry Hughes Wilson was Sykes' principal sponsor during the war. Hearing of Sykes' superior performance at the staff college, Wilson hired him as an Intelligence Staff Officer in 1911 and again in 1916 when Sykes returned from Gallipoli. When Wilson became the British Military Representative to the Supreme War Council in 1917 and replaced General Sir William Robertson as Chief of the Imperial General Staff (CIGS) in February 1918, Sykes was close at hand to work on manpower issues. As Beaverbrook noted, however, 'Wilson had bitter enemies . . . . Most of his colleagues in the

Army were opposed to him.'[64] Wilson recognized Sykes' abilities
and provided the staff positions where Sykes could demonstrate his
potential. Yet Wilson's reputation may have stained Sykes' as well.
Wilson was assassinated in 1922, the same year that Sykes left aviation
permanently.

Sykes' other military sponsor, Major-General Sir Thomas Capper,
had influence until he was killed in 1915. Capper was the Staff College
Commandant at Quetta, where Sykes attended. Ironically, Wilson had
been the Camberley Staff College Commandant when Sykes had failed
to qualify earlier. At Quetta Capper quickly recognized Sykes'
intellectual abilities and hard-driving work ethic and helped Sykes to
become established in the military system. Although Capper's
brother, Brigadier-General John Capper, was involved in early air
activities as first Commandant of the Balloon School, Thomas Capper
was the one who supported Sykes. As the war broke out, Thomas
Capper moved from Inspector of Infantry to GOC of 7th Division and
in that capacity was killed while leading an assault.

Sykes may have had other political help, in particular from the
future Prime Minister Andrew Bonar Law. Yet this had nothing to do
with Sykes' marriage to Isabel Law, the Prime Minister's daughter.
Not only did 'Bel' or 'Tiz' (to her close friends) not play power-
politics for her future husband, but the couple did not even meet until
after the war. Bonar Law appreciated Sykes' abilities and simply
helped Sykes for what he believed was the good of Britain. Thus, near
the end of the war, Sykes' link with Bonar Law was a sponsorship, but
one that did not prove to be influential within military circles. Bonar
Law's correspondence indicates that his assistance came without any
requests from Sykes.[65] In August 1918 Bonar Law wrote to the King,
praising Sykes and pushing for a promotion for him:

> I am very much perturbed about the present state of affairs in the Air
> Ministry in regard to which I think I have probably as good means of
> obtaining information as anyone else. I am coming steadily to the con-
> clusion that in a short time the whole machine will break down unless
> some step is taken to put the relations between the Chief of the Air Staff
> and the Secretary of State on a constitutional basis and of making the
> Air Council, various members of which hold divergent views of policy,
> pull together as a team. At the present moment Sykes, who I know has
> impressed the Imperial War Cabinet with his great grip, imagination
> and ability equal to either the First Sea Lord or the CIGS, is a junior
> Major-General on the Council and although it may be said that he holds
> the senior post nevertheless there can be no question that the position of
> the CIGS at the War Office would be quite impossible if he were equal
> in rank and lower in seniority to the other members of the Air Council.
> There are members of the Air Council who can best be described as of
> the 'Trenchard School' who are opposed, as Trenchard was, to the

principles of the Independent Air Force and, one of them quite openly expresses the hope that Sykes will be downed'. This must prove disastrous not because it may mean the fall of a particular individual but because it is completely contrary to the policy of the Government. Personally, and this I think is the universal opinion of those who know him intimately, I believe that Sykes is the only man who can carry the load which is and will remain prodigious . . . I need not labour the point but I hold most strongly that the appointment of Chief of the Air Staff should carry with it the temporary rank of Lieutenant General . . . . If Sykes had the slightest shadow of suspicion that I was writing he would slay me![66]

Sykes was too intelligent, however, not to have suspected such help. He understood the sponsorship system and appreciated opportunities when they arrived, but in this case, he remained a major-general.

As Bonar Law implied, 'Trenchard School' sponsorship led to warring factions in the Air Ministry at the Hotel Cecil and elsewhere within the air service. By 1917 Trenchard had created a powerful following. His reputation was such that he could survive scandals; but he had not obtained that status on his own. While Sykes worked alone, Trenchard had the wisdom to recognize his limitations and surround himself with capable people. According to Morrow, Trenchard was supported by the Secretary of War Kitchener, whose personality was similar to Trenchard's. Kitchener's support ended abruptly with the sinking of the *Hampshire* in 1916, but he had already cast the die in 1914 and 1915 by gaining for Trenchard key leadership positions.[67]

As has been noted, Trenchard's most significant help, however, came from General Sir Douglas Haig, General Officer Commanding of the BEF. Not only were Trenchard and Haig friends, but they both disagreed with Sykes' theories of air power. While Sykes promoted mechanized warfare and envisioned aerial armor, Trenchard and Haig stuck to a traditional pattern of warfare, employing air power for the infantry. Haig had influence and his friendship with Trenchard not only boosted the latter's image, but their similar approaches to offensive warfare synthesized the fighting tactics of ground and air armies. Similarly, the corresponding wastage rates were mutually supportive, and Haig continually defended Trenchard as the proper air architect for victory:

The Air Service under [Trenchard] has done and is doing invaluable work, and has secured practically complete mastery over the Germans. This could not have been attained, and cannot be maintained, without casualties, which, in my opinion, have been extraordinarily small in proportion to work done and results achieved.[68]

In the RFC's Orders of the Day Trenchard constantly ensured that

Haig's messages which congratulated RFC flyers and their leader Trenchard were published.[69]

However, although a powerful ally, Haig was not bullet-proof. When Trenchard needed Haig's support the most in late 1917 Haig was having his own difficulties in trying to save a waning image caused by attacks from the press and politicians who were tiring of the tremendous wastage rates and becoming increasingly frustrated at his inability to control the situation. Haig failed to sway opinion against the formation of the RAF and was unable to keep Trenchard as the commander of the flying forces in the field. Even upon Trenchard's resignation as CAS in 1918, when Haig quickly offered him a job in the Army, the War Cabinet was unwilling to release their Air Ministry man to the War Office. The Haig–Trenchard link did regain prominence, however, as their mutual support and praise reflected each other's achievements in the official histories.

The air force practice of sponsorship was part of a larger system that has been called 'personalized command'.[70] This system played a major part in influencing promotion and command assignments and indirectly affected critical decisions regarding doctrine, strategy and tactics. Thus personality conflicts and quests for power led to the needless sacrifice of front-line soldiers and airmen. As a famous German operations' planner on the Eastern Front stated, 'The race for power and personal position seems to destroy all men's characters.'[71] Liddell Hart remarked, 'Too often in this war did the leaders fight each other while the troops fought the foe.'[72] As Cooper expressed it, 'simply stated, Britain's senior air officers could not get on with each other.'[73] Perhaps Sykes' achievements therefore appear more significant when it is considered that they occurred in the RAF HQ's environment of infighting and intrigue in 'the dark recesses of "Bolo House"'.[74]

Sykes' personality and background did not fit well into the system of personalized command. His focus was on organizational efficiency to promote the air force's mission, and he did not recognize interpersonal relationships as part of that. Yet the social-club atmosphere rewarded those who could carry on a good conversation at the club, and a positive 'squadron feeling' was more important than the need for discipline and a professional military attitude. In fact, the RFC strove to establish that atmosphere because flyers were intimidated by their low social status when compared with that of the older services. The social network abounded with unofficial talk and superstitions about aircraft, missions and certain flyers. Unlike the other military arms, the air service was undisciplined, sloppy and full of pranks and jokes.[75] And within the RNAS, officers were idiosyncratic and lacked conventional discipline, thus arousing the Admiralty's 'jaundiced view' of them.[76]

Against this tide, Sykes was a strong disciplinarian who had little time for socializing. Trenchard, on the other hand, promoted morale above all else. Hence it is easy to understand how, in various inner circles and cliques, flyers could love Trenchard and suspect Sykes.

Ironically, Sykes would have been better suited to the German air force, which was more professional than its British counterpart. Compared with the Germans, British flyers were younger, less educated and less experienced in war.[77] While a prisoner of war, Major F. J. Powell noted that he and his comrades considered the BEF to be a civilian army compared with the German flyers, who were more proper in saluting officers and maintaining military discipline.[78] The air war was closer to sport for the British; to the Germans it was duty.

Positive squadron morale certainly helped British flyers to cope with the stress and danger of aerial combat; but lack of discipline hampered effectiveness and efficiency – the two hallmarks of Sykes' ambition. Personalized command was simply unprofessional, allowing personality conflicts, friendships and rumors to influence decision-making. Just as the personalized command structure created inter-personal friction, so the parochial service structure led to interservice rivalries. Petty jealousies have always existed between the services, and the new air service naturally received criticism from the senior services. But the consequences in war were significant when they involved competition for scarce resources. Sykes mentioned this after the war, noting that 'an exceptional personality as head of the Admiralty, War Office or Air Ministry, would manage to get his department strengthened at the expense of one, or both of the others.'[79]

Tradition was also a key part of the air force system. Because the RFC had sprung from the Royal Engineers (commonly known as 'Sappers') and remained a War Office resource for most of the war, there remained strong Army sentiment among many of the commanders. In fact, Henderson, Trenchard and Sykes all attempted to return to the Army at one point or another during the war. Gradually, the flying service developed its own traditions, however, and then held on to those with great tenacity against the influences of change. Most of the traditions were simply social customs that developed within the squadrons: mess procedures, protocol among flyers and customary attitudes toward the war and the enemy. Yet some traditions extended into critical areas such as tactics, missions and the types of aircraft to employ, and the commander played an important part in the promotion or obstruction of these traditions.

One was the glorification of valor and morale. If new technologies or techniques threatened old heroic methodologies and weapon systems, it might not matter that the new methods could save lives. Lewis Mumford once condemned such military systems, stating that armies were the strongholds of inferior minds.[80] Fuller, as well, proclaimed that the Age of Valour in Western warfare established a system where 'valour looked with disdain upon inventiveness'.[81] Most military historians have followed the same tradition of rewarding heroes and overlooking intellectuals, and this may account partially for their omission of Sykes. Sykes' private secretary, Colonel Sir Ronald Waterhouse noted that, even though Sykes was heroic and inspiring to some, he was a dour and defiant intellectual to those who misunderstood him.[82]

Against the traditional suspicion of intellect within the military, the fledgling air service was by nature technological, which simply necessitated thinking on a higher plane rather than blind courage. The official air historian stated, 'A machine is the embodiment of human thought . . . the men of science, who worked for humanity, must have an honour only less than the honour paid to the men of action, who died for their country.'[83] Airmen had to be men of action and science. They ensured that the air war was offensive like the ground war, but with a different type of offensiveness – one based on the scientific capabilities of a machine rather than on the traditional spirit of the Victorian Army, in which morale eclipsed thinking. Sykes recognized and promoted the difference.

He also perceived a transformation in leadership. While the Army required charismatic and courageous leaders, airmen depended on good machines and technologically educated commanders who knew the capabilities and limits of air power. Flight-Lieutenant N. W. Wadham noted that modern air warfare had taken away the role of the commander as leader – the leader was removed too far from the battlefield to command attention.[84] Air commanders did not fly combat missions and, as Higham noted, airmen were simply not trained to command.[85] The prime example of this removal of the leadership role occurred in 1918 when Trenchard resigned as CAS. Throughout the air service there were rumors that without Trenchard at the helm the new RAF would collapse. In fact, the British air effort hardly skipped a beat.

SYKES WITHIN THE SYSTEM

Sykes' personality did not accommodate the social, unprofessional and anti-intellectual aspects of the air service environment. He was not one for small talk or idle chatter and, perhaps as a result, he had few close friends during the war. He encouraged abstinence from alcohol at a time when it was part of the military tradition. He joined clubs out of a sense of obligation rather than desire.[86] As for intrigue, besides the fact that he did not have any close associates with whom to conspire, it was against his character. He was integrity-bound, and the few Machiavellian ideas he did entertain were focused strictly on the Germans.[87]

Nevertheless, his true character did not reveal itself to those who suspected a devious nature. A short, thin man who stood erect but exhibited the effects of battle on his small frame and the strain of command on his face, Sykes was not physically impressive compared with Goliaths such as Trenchard. A (London) *Times* article once mentioned that Sykes' face did not reveal his thoughts: 'he would make an excellent poker player'. One fellow airman mentioned that Sykes had a first-class brain, but a personality which strangely engendered mistrust in those with whom he served.[88] Sykes was clever, but not witty; to him most military humor was of too low an intellectual level – not funny, just vulgar. Any man who kept to himself, would not laugh at jokes, and had such a serious attitude toward his work could leave the erroneous impression of a scheming introvert.

Sykes' tragic flaw was his intellectual gift, not his ambition. He was perceptive enough to recognize the hostility he aroused, but was unwilling or unable to do anything about it. Unlike Trenchard, he did not appreciate the importance of working within the system. Working around it, he was content to appear as an intellectual superior, which was not the type of personality the military generally respected.[89]

Because Sykes corresponded with family or friends as little as he gossiped, it is difficult to assess his wartime personality. Recollections of his service enemies, such as Henderson and Trenchard, are merely unsubstantiated opinions that historians have used to the point of exhaustion. Equally difficult to evaluate are laudatory letters from Sykes' friends, written years after the First World War. One friend mentioned Sykes' 'brilliance of mind' and his 'unfailing kindness to me and a sense of friendship which I deeply valued.'[90] Another wrote that Sykes was a kind and wise counselor who gave him a sense of security: 'Sir Frederick taught me it was possible to mount three stairs at a time.'[91] A comrade from Gallipoli days said he had admired Sykes' abilities there and had watched 'with awe the intense will power and application which he brought to bear on all his great endeavors.'[92] These assessments were 30-year-old recollections sent to a grieving widow.[93]

Despite his abilities, Sykes was somewhat self-contained and reserved, which helps to explain the animosity and suspicion felt toward him.[94] He avoided crowds because they often became chaotic and crude.[95] As a commander, his lack of desire to socialize led to his concentration on results rather than on personalities. Since he was devoted more to service than to people, he lacked patience and, at times, understanding. Sykes enjoyed work itself; it was the means by which he tested himself.[96] One subordinate wrote, 'If one had a criticism of him it was that he had, in those days, a certain incomprehensibility of those who had not the high idea of service and work which he conspicuously possessed.'[97] He was a self-demonstrating taskmaster rather than a perfectionist; as long as subordinates gave their total effort, he was content.

Despite his impatience with laziness and his personal compulsion to complete a task, other aspects of his personality showed flexibility and adaptability. He experienced many failures: unprosperous tea-planting as a youth in Ceylon, getting knocked out of action in South Africa, failing the 'Q' for the Staff College, crashing during his first flight check for a pilot's certificate, losing the command of the RFC in 1914 and again in 1915, joining the other Dardanelles participants in the Gallipoli disaster, losing the RAF to Trenchard in 1919, and then losing support for civil aviation. In each of these setbacks, however, Sykes did not break down nor give up. He simply pressed forward in whatever direction appeared most favorable. He never rejected an assignment, and he never resigned from military office.[98] While many of his contemporaries were unwilling to accept demotions or positions that they felt were demeaning, Sykes simply chose to serve.

As a result of his intelligence and experience, he had unusual abilities. He was perhaps the only senior British airman fluent in four languages as well as an expert on foreign aircraft and flying. Such knowledge helped him to organize Britain's first squadrons and choose the first military aircraft. He was the only high-level air commander to have had experience in India, Africa, England, France and the Mediterranean, and to have served in both military and naval capacities. Furthermore, he was more knowledgeable than most when it came to technological innovations.[99]

Sykes' character may have changed following the war, especially during his years in retirement. He appears to have become more patient and more mellow in his attitudes.[100] A colleague mentioned that Sykes was invariably correct in his judgements, but that he would never say 'I told you so.'[101] If accurate, such an opinion reflects a change in him. Throughout the Second World War his habitual practice was to exclaim that he had told leaders repeatedly that the Empire needed strong air power and a unified defensive effort![102] Sykes remained steadfast in his commitment to ideals such as Empire air power or the task at hand, but he did allow his formerly fanatic approach, which had made many associates uncomfortable, to mellow.

His life was marked by antagonism. He was self-reliant, a trait he had acquired from an early age, as he went without much support from his family. His independence, coupled with intellectual gifts and a narrow focus on the task at hand, made him suspicious to colleagues. Sykes' abilities to organize units and direct staffs were practically unmatched, but he lacked the tact and social graces necessary to encourage friendship and comradeship from associates. Despite antagonisms and setbacks, he was rarely bitter, enjoyed life and was content to remain somewhat misunderstood. In some respects Sykes was a strange mixture of character and ideology – strongly conservative personally and innovative technically at the same time. He lived a paradoxical life, as his outstanding knowledge of languages, cultures, technologies and politics was matched by periods of social immaturity. He had brilliant insight and intuition, but was occasionally ignorant of the obvious. He had a sincere concern for others, but often failed to show it. He was rather selfless, but appeared selfish. Overall Sykes was perplexing, even though his organization of the air service and his visionary approaches to the use of aircraft were significant contributions to the rise of air power that has revolutionized warfare.

THE AIR WAR

In addition to Sykes' confusing personality, the air war itself has been part of the enigma of Sykes in history. Specifically, recent histories are clouded with historicism. Military institutions and air historians have condemned air power in the past to promote its more recent effectiveness, and, left unabated, the trend will have historians lambasting the 'Desert Storm' air war of the recent Gulf War as an insignificant puff of smoke compared with the next air war. Air power has progressed continually from mere reconnaissance in 1914 to multifaceted roles and unimaginable fire power today, but contemporary capabilities had to start somewhere: the First World War. The prevailing historical trends have been either to exaggerate the aerial role and air power's significance in the war or to denigrate it as ineffective and the air war as insignificant. Yet the air war was an important revolution in its own right, independent of how the other services were fighting, and Sykes played a principal role in that rise of air power.

The chronology of the air war most familiar to readers is of the sharp edge of the sword – the fighting on the Western Front.[103] Less attention has been given to the administrative infighting within the RFC and the RAF, within the Air Ministry and the War Cabinet, and between the British government and the governments of the Allied nations.[104] Yet these were Sykes' battlefields, and it was in these arenas that the aerial revolution began. Sykes was clearly in a dogfight, where he remained ever the challenger.

Historians have argued that airmen simply adopted trial-and-error

methods of fighting which did not live up to expectations.[105] According
to David MacIsaac and Lee Kennett, the First World War shaped air
power more than air power shaped the war.[106] Sir John Slessor wrote
that before the Second World War, air power was just ancillary.[107]
Admittedly, early air power was employed inefficiently as new
technologies led to adaptation and learning. Yet, from 1914–18, intellectuals such as Sykes anticipated new uses of aircraft and designed
new tactics and strategies. Hence in the First World War airmen flew
most of the missions seen in modern warfare: dive bombing, ground
strafing, strategic and tactical bombing (air interdiction), air-to-air
combat, air transport, aerial mapping, reconnaissance, photography,
communication, escort, artillery spotting, forward air control and
torpedo dropping. The RFC even flew espionage missions starting in
1915, by flying secret Intelligence Service agents behind enemy
lines.[108] This change in warfare did not begin over the front, but back
at headquarters, in the Air Staff, and in the experimental sections that
Sykes promoted.

Two of the air war's greatest difficulties were organization and
supply, which led to the formation of a separate service under a new
Ministry.[109] This revolutionary move was not a perfect cure, but,
contrary to some opinions, an improvement that also established a
world precedent. Although some authors have considered the birth of
the RAF a knee-jerk reaction to the German bombing of London, as
already mentioned, it was more an issue of supply – an attempt to
obtain American resources and ease the interservice friction that
plagued British aircraft production.[110]

The creation of the IAF was another revolutionary step, implemented by Sykes, to solve supply and organizational problems by using
air resources effectively against German war-making. In their focus on
results rather than on the significance of the creation, historians have
seen the IAF as an impossible dream. Infighting for control delayed the
IAF's formation to the point that it was not officially sanctioned under
Foch's authority (with Trenchard as GOC), until a month before the
end of the war. This, however, was not a failure, as historians have
implied, but, rather, the successful creation of a revolutionary strategic
force that, had the war continued through 1919, would most likely have
played a significant role. Consequently, although much of the actual
revolution was pre-empted by the Armistice, the revolution began as
Sykes realized his vision and achieved his goal.

Historians, however, have preferred to applaud heroes and legends,
a practice that began within the squadrons. John Salmond wrote to
Weir in June 1918, 'If we had a dozen Bishops there would not be
much Hun aviation left in a fortnight.'[111] Bomber crews lay obscured in
shadows, and observers felt like 'RFC doormats'.[112] Such thinking

eclipsed the team concept, and histories of air force maintenance, for example, are rare. Few readers know that Baron Manfred von Richthofen's administrative and leadership abilities were more important to the German war effort than his aerial achievements.[113] There was nothing revolutionary about heroic flyers – armies and navies had required the courageous for centuries. The revolution in air power was in the new uses of technology and in new organizations, where Sykes was hard at work. His concepts of strategic interdiction and combined-arms attack were as revolutionary as the idealistic visions of the Italian Giulio Douhet, the 'Prophet of Air Power'.[114]

Sykes advocated 'air mindedness', the idea that independent air power could transform the battlefield if applied correctly. He developed this concept over the course of the war, which placed him at odds with Army and Navy traditionalists, who wanted auxiliary air forces. Theorists have described two air power schools of thought: the air school and the military school. The militarists, including Trenchard and Haig, maintained that air power was auxiliary to ground and seapower and was, therefore, to be employed to help those forces break the front and defeat the enemy. On the other hand, air-school advocates such as Weir, Montagu, Sykes and Groves envisioned a new war that extended beyond the front to 'areas'. Air-school disciples determined that German industry was vulnerable in this new area war, and that the effective exploitation of the situation could save British manpower.[115] The main issue of contention was priority. Military-school advocates were unwilling to contribute significant resources to enable the concept of area warfare to work, which often caused air power to fail to meet expectations. As Higham has stated, people had transformed air enthusiasts' prognostications into 'imminent realities'.[116]

Sykes' battle for air mindedness has escaped historical attention, eclipsed by inter-war air power theories that promoted the aircraft as an invulnerable war-winning weapon that had changed the principles of war and made surface warfare more or less obsolete. While staunch military-school champions fought against radical air thinking to regain Army and Navy control of the air arm in support of the new mechanized surface battle, Sykes argued for a synthesis of the extremes, recognizing that air power had not negated the principles of warfare, that the Army and the Navy did need air support and that integration and co-operation between the services ensured the most efficient fighting force. He maintained, however, that only by the administrative independence of the specialized aerial arm would Britain properly allocate air resources and maintain an integrated fighting force.[117] With Trenchard back in control of the RAF in 1919, however, the military school of thought ruled the staff college curriculum until, following the war, Trenchard became a convert to the air-mindedness revolution in thinking that Sykes had promoted during it.[118]

In addition to theory, the technological history of the first air war also has problems which involved Sykes. Historians have rationalized the limits of airmen and the air service by pointing to the faults in early equipment. Just as the Austrians in 1866 were quick to blame their defeat on the Prussians' needle gun, so too did British flyers identify the 'Fokker scourge' when they were losing air battles.[119] The mystique of German technological superiority continually loomed within the minds of British flyers, and, even though analysis has shown that British and German aircraft were generally competitive in the air, many historians have continued to promote the British excuse that they were out-gunned by superior machines.[120]

Sykes recognized the erroneous interpretation and argued that Britain's major technological disadvantage was quantity – the air service was not adequately supported by the government and society. Near the end of the war, as the Air Ministry struggled to field a long-range bombing force, labor problems occupied half of the War Cabinet's time and led to poorly constructed aircraft.[121] The IAF's effort stalled because Britain was dependent on American supplies of Liberty engines, which failed to materialize.

Historians have further overlooked Sykes' achievements by concentrating on physical damage statistics to show that air power was ineffective and insignificant.[122] Many of air power's roles and impacts, as on morale, cannot be assessed scientifically, because numbers tell only part of the story. For example, the RFC at the Somme constituted approximately 3 per cent of the BEF, and on 1 July 1916 five airmen died, compared with 57,000 British soldiers killed or wounded.[123] Yet captured German documents show that the air services had more than a 3 per cent impact on the battle.[124] Military-school advocates, who were convinced that the air service was jeopardizing the British war effort by taking valuable resources from the Army and the Navy, argued that physical damage from air attack was too small to matter. Yet four years of statistically huge armies were unable to produce an end to the war.

Sykes agreed with the official air historians' correct contention that, although the air service did not have the size, range or accuracy needed to deliver decisive physical damage, it hurt enemy morale and dislocated his resources by forcing Germany to transfer materials from offensive war-fighting action to defensive protection.[125] The concepts of morale effect and indirect damage were not fabricated after the war to justify air power; they were part of Sykes' fundamental argument behind the formation of the IAF and part of the reason that the government decided to form a separate RAF. Historians should not forget that the IAF was not even intended to be of formidable size until the latter half of 1919.[126] How could air power have failed to live up to expectations, when such expectations were to be fulfilled by a force that never existed?

Why did the revolution in air power begin, and why have many historians failed to appreciate it? It began with a change in thinking – in rejecting past military traditions that morale and the offensive were more important than development of new technologies and effective use of them. Sykes' part in the revolution revolved primarily around new concepts of long-range reconnaissance and long-range bombing – the strategic arena – however, all aspects of aviation were new and revolutionary. The revolution required new organizations, new strategies and new tactics.[127] In helping to orchestrate the revolutionary preamble, Sykes made some enemies. Yet, by concentrating on Sykes' interpersonal battles, historians have missed his achievements as well as his shortcomings. By thinking of First World War aviation in terms of the daylight precision bombing of World War II, writers have inappropriately assessed the early efforts.

In the complex interaction of social and political forces at work during Sykes' time, three primary factors account for the Sykes enigma and his disappearance from air power history: (1) his distant and misunderstood personality, which did not mix well with the social-club and personalized command structure of the air service; (2) the influence of several high-ranking officers, whose personalities clashed with Sykes' as they took different approaches to the use of air power and had different commitments to the air service and its role in the war; and (3) the air war itself, which has remained a topic of dispute among historians. Hence the final evaluation of Sykes necessitates the redressing of the traditional implications that he was at fault somehow, guilty of intrigue and unimportant in the air war. Most important, the analysis must clarify how intelligent thinkers such as Sykes began to revolutionize warfare as they started to develop the concept of war in the air.

NOTES

1. Cooper, 'A House Divided', 181.
2. Malcolm Smith, *British Air Strategy Between the Wars* (Oxford: Clarendon Press, 1984), 21.
3. Charles Webster and Noble Frankland, *The Strategic Air Offensive against Germany, 1939–1945*, vol. 1 (London: HMSO, 1961), 42.
4. Tony Mason, *Air Power: A Centennial Appraisal* (London: Brassey's, 1994), 34 and 42, implies this, noting that Sykes' approach to strategic bombing was 'a

launch into strategic unreality' and that his vision was 'flawed by his failure to acknowledge the limitations of contemporary air power.'

5. Probert, 1–2. Later in his book Probert acknowledged that Trenchard attempted to block the formation of the RAF and IAF in 1917 because Haig opposed it, and because Trenchard did not wish to leave his command in France to return to England.
6. Robert Pitman, 'Was this Man a Hero or a Prima Donna?', *Sunday Express*, (London), 25 March, 1962.
7. Maj. (Wing Commander) Archibald James, sound recording, Reel No. 4, IWM sound recordings.
8. Correspondence between Trenchard and Jones, MFC 76/1/503, Trenchard Papers; and correspondence between Trenchard and Edmonds, MFC 76/1/474, Trenchard Papers.
9. 'This Air Business', box 3, pp. 24 and 92, Groves Papers, Liddell Hart Centre. Groves stated that it was impossible to challenge policy without challenging the man responsible.
10. Ibid., 31, 43.
11. Divine, 156. Cmd 467 is in the Brooke-Popham Papers, IX/5/9, Liddell Hart Centre.
12. Chaz Bowyer, *RAF Operations 1918–1938* (London: Kimber, 1988), 17–18; Raleigh and Jones, 1:420; and John W. R. Taylor, *C.F.S.: Birthplace of Air Power* (London: Jane's Publishing, 1987), 60. Bowyer stated that 'Trenchard's task, to rebuild an air force from the ashes of its former giant strength, was daunting.' As for Trenchard's 1914 episode, Taylor said that 'a man of vision and tremendous energy' was needed to create a new air force in England.
13. Donne and Fowler, 46. Some historians have suggested that Trenchard tried to destroy an established fighting force just to rebuild it his own way. Perhaps he simply desired to eliminate any vestige of Sykes' work.
14. Until 1925 the Treasury bark was worse than its bite. Nevertheless, by 3 January 1920 the RAF had lost 26,087 officers, 21,259 cadets and 227,229 other ranks. Of the 99 squadrons that had existed on the Western Front at the Armistice only one remained. The only well-researched, authoritative source on the effects of the budget on the post-war RAF in relation to the other services is John Robert Ferris, *Men, Money, and Diplomacy: The Evolution of British Strategic Policy 1919–26* (Ithaca, NY: Cornell Universitiy Press, Macmillan, 1989). Ferris, 27, shows that RAF estimates rose dramatically from 1922 to 1925 due to Treasury inability to control Trenchard, and on pp. 7 and 72, that Trenchard succeeded by superior infighting against the other services.
15. Mason, 32 and 37. According to Trenchard, 'Germany and German troops is [*sic*] the only enemy that counts.' Everything else was a luxury until sufficient numbers of aircraft would arrive – which was not expected to be achieved until 1919.
16. Boyle, 110 and 225.
17. Ibid., 233.
18. Groves, 137.
19. IAF Private Papers, MCF 76/1/32, Trenchard Papers.
20. Mason M. Patrick, *The United States in the Air* (Garden City, NY: Doubleday, Doran, 1928), 20–2. Patrick was correct in his recollection of Trenchard, but it is interesting to note his omission of Sykes. In fact, Patrick recalled incorrectly that in summer 1918 the chief British air officer under Weir was General Guy Livingston.
21. Webster and Frankland, 38.
22. Sir Maurice Dean, *The Royal Air Force and Two World Wars* (London: Cassell,

1979), 29.
23. Wing Commander H. R. Allen, 'Lord Trenchard: Long Range Bomber Off Target', *The Times* (London), 3 February 1973.
24. Boyle, 230.
25. Ibid., 233.
26. Higham, *Air Power*, 70.
27. Trenchard to Salmond, 18 December 1917, MFC 76/1/91, Trenchard Papers.
28. Probert, xxi.
29. War Cabinet Minutes, 19 March 1918, War Cabinet 367, PRO, CAB 23.
30. Trenchard to Churchill, 3 March 1919, Martin Gilbert, *Winston S. Churchill, January 1917–June 1919* (London: Heinemann, 1977), 4, companion volume 1:562. It is interesting that Trenchard attempted to resign again – one year later – less than a month after reassuming his position as CAS. Trenchard stated that the RAF situation was very difficult and that he simply did not 'have the guts to pull it through now.' Churchill dismissed the resignation as a plea for convalescent time, which he wisely ordered Trenchard to take, for Trenchard was indeed ill. The question which arises, however, is why he agreed to take the mantle of CAS if he was worn out, and why he would resign rather than request leave of absence (as Henderson had repeatedly done in 1914–1915), in the light of the fact that Trenchard had created such turmoil the previous time he resigned.
31. Sgt. Cecil Reginald King sound recording, Reel No. 3, IWM sound recordings.
32. Air Marshal Sir Victor Goddard sound recording, Reel No. 10, IWM sound recordings.
33. Trenchard Papers, MFC 76/1/65.
34. Under Trenchard's command in 1917 aviators received an average of 17.5 hours of instruction before being sent to the front. Sir Philip Gibbs, quoted in Groves, *Behind the Smoke Screen*, 125, condemned the sacrifice: 'Our aviators had been trained in the school of General Trenchard, who sent them out over the German lines to learn how to fight.' To correct the situation, Sykes established the training policy in 1918 that minimal instruction would increase to 50 hours per student before combat flying.
35. Futrell, 22. Trenchard welcomed the Americans, meeting Brigadier-General Billy Mitchell in France to discuss the air organization and mission.
36. Boyle, 249. Major Desmond Morton, aide to Haig, observed Trenchard and Haig together: 'They seemed to read one another's thoughts by some form of instinctive telepathy, expressing themselves aloud with gestures and agricultural grunts rather than with words.'
37. Brancker to Weir, 24 February 1920, Weir Papers, 3/11.
38. Beaverbrook, xxv.
39. Autobiographical notes, 66, Trenchard Papers, MFC 76/1/61.
40. Sykes, *From Many Angles*, 146. Passages in the autobiography such as the following no doubt aroused Trenchard's wrath: 'Trenchard was a man with a forceful personality and great drive, but, looking at the matter from my point of view, I thought his conception of the higher issues involved to be fundamentally wrong. If persisted in, the danger was that the strength of the RFC would be dissipated in auxiliary routine work on behalf of units of the Army, without any wider co-operation, and his subsequent handling of the Independent Air Force confirmed my opinion. The problem is one on which there are even today [1942] two schools of thought, though the experience of both the last and the present war tends, I think, to show that I was right.'
41. Note by Lord Trenchard, Trenchard Papers, MFC 76/1/542, p. 4.
42. Autobiographical notes, Trenchard Papers, MFC 76/1/61.
43. *Royal Aero Club Year Book, 1915–1916* (London: Royal Aero Club of the

United Kingdom, 1916). The yearbook lists other certificates of interest: Henderson no. 118, Brooke-Popham no. 108, Samson no. 71, and Moore-Brabazon no. 1.

44. H. Montgomery Hyde, *British Air Policy between the Wars* (London: Heinemann, 1976), 37.
45. W. J. Reader, *Architect of Air Power: The Life of the First Viscount Weir of Eastwood* (London: Collins, 1968), 68.
46. De la Ferté, 28.
47. Kenneth Reid van der Spuy, *Chasing the Wind* (Capetown: Books of Africa, 1966), 64.
48. Norris, 144.
49. Robert R. Blake and Jane S. Mouton, *The Managerial Grid* (Houston: Gulf Publishing, 1964), 10. The Blake-Mouton Managerial Grid is useful in assessing leadership styles based on organizational levels of maturity.

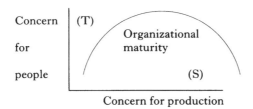

Concern for production

The RFC in 1914 was a relatively immature organization – new and without war experience. The RAF in 1918 had matured to the point that it maintained mission integrity regardless of who was in command. As depicted, Trenchard was mission-oriented via concentration on people, while Sykes was mission-oriented via concentration on technology and efficiency.

50. Brancker to Trenchard, 16 August (no year) and Trenchard to Brancker 17 August, Trenchard Papers, MFC 76/1/16.
51. Morrow, *The Great War in the Air*, 80.
52. James, 75–6.
53. Henderson and Trenchard correspondence, Trenchard Papers, MFC 76/1/76. In five fiches of correspondence between Trenchard and Henderson, Sykes is not mentioned. In addition, there is no mention of Sykes in correspondence between Henderson and Kitchener, Kitchener Papers, PRO 30/57/78/WU/57 and 30/57/50/WA/86.
54. Ferris, 7, described the post-war Trenchard as a 'cunning and ruthless bureaucratic infighter' as a result of his experiences in 1918. Yet Trenchard appears to have acquired such skills several years earlier when he used them to establish his predominance in the British air effort on the Western Front. His 1918 resignation debacle simply demonstrated that he failed to understand the limits of political intrigue and power-politics.
55. Cooper, *The Birth of Independent Air Power*, 22. For example, according to his adjutant, Baring, Henderson eagerly left the RFC to command 1st Division on 22 November 1914 because of personal desires.
56. RFC production study, Brancker Papers, 73/183/1.
57. Judicial Committee papers, Montagu Papers, III/C/35, Liddell Hart Centre.
58. John Walter Edward Douglas-Scott-Montagu, Lord Montagu of Beaulieu, had worked as Inspector of Mechanical Transport in India in 1915, where he studied aviation problems of the North-West Frontier. A staunch proponent of air

power, Montagu was a member of Derby's Joint War Air Committee in February 1916 until resigning over issues of authority.

59. Montagu to Cotes-Preedy, 3 July 1916, Montagu Papers, II/C/24; and Montagu to Cotes-Preedy, 5 June 1916, Montagu Papers, II/C/20.

60. Extract from the sixth day's Proceedings of the Royal Flying Corps Inquiry, 22 June 1916, Montagu Papers, II/C/23.

61. Morrow, *The Great War in the Air*, 319.

62. This type of system is prevalent in many, if not most, military organizations.

63. James, 54–5.

64. Beaverbrook, xxvi. His opinion of Wilson's intellectual ability mirrors what many thought of Sykes. Beaverbrook said that, while Asquith hated Wilson, Bonar Law was a friend. Apparently another political friend was Amery, who also worked at Versailles at the end of the war, Amery to Sykes, 13 October 1941, Sykes Private Papers.

65. Law to Gordon, 3 August 1918, Bonar Law Papers, 84/7/56, House of Lords Record Office. Bonar Law tried to help Sykes to obtain a foreign medal, stating 'the Chief of the Air Staff does not carry enough guns . . . I know him well enough to realise that he would never ask for one himself.'

66. Law to Lord Stamfordham, 27 August 1918, Bonar Law Papers, 84/7/73.

67. Morrow, *The Great War in the Air*, 80.

68. Haig to Henderson, 10 September 1916, Kiggell Papers, V/41, Liddell Hart Centre. Trenchard unofficially used Haig to achieve his objectives. In this letter to Henderson, Haig pressed Henderson to send the reinforcements that had been promised for Trenchard, and he objected to Henderson's earlier comments that wastage in the air was 'unpleasant' or 'useless'. He reminded Henderson that Trenchard had his full support and that the air enterprises had been under his (Haig's) complete control (in other words, he was taking responsibility for the wastage rates).

69. O.A.D. 151/3, 17 September, Trenchard Papers, MFC 76/1/65. The orders read:

> The splendid achievements of the Royal Flying Corps during the last few days have if possible surpassed all that they have already done. They have played a great part in the battle. My warmest congratulations to you [Trenchard] and them.
>
> D. Haig, Gen.
> Commander-in-Chief
> British Armies in France

70. Tim Travers, *The Killing Ground* (London: Unwin Hyman, 1990), 3–6, has brought to light this trait of the Victorian Army.

71. B. H. Liddell Hart, *The Real War* (Boston, MA: Little, Brown, 1930), 140.

72. Ibid.

73. Cooper, 'A House Divided', 198.

74. Dean, 30–2.

75. Kennett, *The First Air War*, 142.

76. Roskill, xii.

77. Schroder, 173.

78. Maj. F. J. Powell, sound recording, Reel No. 8, IWM sound recordings. Unlike the German air force, British social-club pilots were mostly officers.

79. Sykes, 'Reduction of Armaments, Economy, and Imperial Defense', in *The Army Quarterly*, Vol. 12, No. 1, April 1926, 23. This described Trenchard well.

80. Lewis Mumford, *Techniques and Civilization* (New York: Harcourt Brace, 1935), 95, said that such inferior minds are unwilling to accept new technologies

into traditional military systems.

81. Fuller, 24, 27. According to him, leaders were the brave men, not the crafty ones.

82. Nourah Waterhouse, *Private and Official* (London: Cape, 1942), 158.

83. Raleigh and Jones, 1:12.

84. 'An Essay on Morale', 162, Air Publication 956, RAFM, Accession No. 001525.

85. Higham, *Air Power*, 30.

86. Interview with Bonar Sykes, 21 April 1994, Conock.

87. Sykes recognized the value of psychological warfare and, besides Weir, was the principal actor in Air Council schemes to undermine German morale.

88. Maj. Archibald James sound recording, Reel No. 4, IWM sound recordings.

89. In terms of Berne's transactional analysis paradigm, Sykes probably crossed transactions, taking a parent-to-child approach with associates. See Susan Sinclair, 'Transactional Analysis', in *Communicating with Subordinates* (New York: Amacom, 1974), 85–90.

90. Vivian Bulkeley-Johnson to Isabel, 16 October 1954, Sykes Private Papers.

91. (?) Moore to Lady Sykes, 1 October 1954, Sykes Private Papers.

92. Sir Patrick Duff to Lady Sykes, 2 October 1954, Sykes Private Papers.

93. The Sykes Private Papers contain many letters that mention Sykes' friendliness, his valuable advice and his fatherly image within organizations. He was kind and helpful and had an 'aura' of calm and a statesmanlike quality about him which inspired others. A friend from New York wrote that every time he met Sykes he learned something. Another wrote that his life was 'the very pattern of a true and gentle knight . . . It is not often that such great gifts are so united to a real humility of spirit. Perhaps that has brought less than the recognition deserved.' Such evidence used alone would paint a saintly picture indeed.

94. Max (Beaverbrook?) to Lady Sykes, 2 October 1954, Sykes Private Papers. 'But we know he was a bashful type, never advertising himself or his deeds of courage.'

95. Sykes to Ethel, 10 August 1916, Sykes Private Papers. Sykes liked proper procedures and control. Writing about his trip to GHQ in France, he complained about the crowded boat full of 'cantancerous' people. He wondered how they did not sink to the bottom and how he managed to serve with 'such a motley bunch'. He liked the French, apart from their vulgarity and simplicity.

96. Interview with Bonar Sykes, 21 April 1994, Conock; and (?) Hall to Lady Sykes, 13 October 1954, Sykes Private Papers.

97. (Vivian) Johnson to Isabel, 16 October 1954, Sykes Private Papers.

98. Technically Sykes did resign as Director-General of Civil Aviation, but his resignation came after the appropriate term in the position and was, therefore, not an untimely one.

99. Sykes' interest in technology was later reflected in his chairmanship of the committee which established the British Broadcasting Company.

100. Reginald Maxwell to Lady Sykes, 3 October 1954, Sykes Private Papers. Maxwell noted Sykes' 'calm and steady outlook, his unruffled temper, and, above all, his personal gentleman [*sic*] and unassuming ways, and his unbound capacity for seeing the point of view of others.'

101. Lawrence (?) to Lady Sykes, 5 April 1954, Sykes Private Papers. The date proves this was not simply a letter of condolence.

102. Sykes, *From Many Angles*, 232. Sykes argued that the country could have avoided its current problems if leaders had listened to him.

103. Historians write little about the air war in other theatres – in Palestine with the Middle East Brigade, in Rahad and Darfur, in the Sudan, and actions out of Ismailia. The RAF fought in Mesopotamia, Italy and Russia, and it was instrumental in raising air forces in Greece, Belgium, Japan, Brazil and Rumania. See

Groves Papers, 69/34/1, IWM; and Sykes, *From Many Angles*, 238–9.

104. David MacIsaac, 'Voices from the Central Blue: The Air Power Theorists', in *Makers of Modern Strategy*, ed. Peter Paret, 626, stated that aviation was a young man's game, one that attracted physically strong and mentally adventurous people.

105. David Divine, *The Broken Wing* (London: Hutchinson, 1966), 134; Kennett, *The First Air War*, 218; and Dennis Winter, *The First of the Few* (London: Allen Lane, 1982), 13–14.

106. MacIsaac, 629; and Kennett, *The First Air War*, 226.

107. Slessor cited in Norris, 10.

108. Nigel West, *MI6: British Secret Intelligence Service Operations 1909–1945* (London: Weidenfeld & Nicolson, 1983), 10, 16.

109. War Cabinet Minute 8, 24 August 1917, War Cabinet 223, Air 8/3. The War Cabinet accepted the Second Report of the Prime Minister's Committee on Air Organization (the Smuts Committee) on 24 August 1917, and appointed another committee to investigate how to amalgamate the RFC and the RNAS. Smuts had been requested to look into two issues: home defense and air organization. His first report dealt with the former, the second with the latter. The second Smuts Report is document G.T.-1658, in Appendix II of War Cabinet 223.

110. The reason why the Smuts Committee determined that a separate service would best provide home defense was that, as Henderson argued, it would be the most efficient type of air service, Jones, Appendix I, 6–8, and Appendix II, 8–14.

111. Salmond to Weir, 19 June 1918, Weir Papers, 1/4, Churchill College, Cambridge.

112. Kennett, *The First Air War*, 160.

113. John H. Morrow, *German Air Power in World War I*, 115.

114. Although the first edition of Douhet's *Command of the Air* was published in 1921, he started expressing ideas on air power a decade earlier.

115. 'This Air Business', 16–18, Groves Papers, box 3, Liddell Hart Centre.

116. Higham, *Air Power*, 2.

117. Sykes, *From Many Angles*, 3–4; and *Aviation in Peace and War*, 131–4. Sykes stated that aviation had helped to win the war, was here to stay, and was an essential ingredient in Britain's future, both in terms of defense and of economy.

118. RAF Staff College 2nd Course, Appendix 3, RAFM, Accession No. C/5/1/1.

119. Kennett, *The First Air War*, 69, and Paul Kennedy, 'Britain in the First World War', in *Military Effectiveness*, ed. Allan R. Millett and Williamson Murray (Boston: Unwin Hyman, 1988), 1:60. Kennedy claimed that the British air war was successful, but that the major handicap was better German aircraft. Yet Corum, 13–18 has effectively argued that, although the Germans did have superior technical innovations, they were simply better flyers – they had better training programs (with a 25 per cent wastage rate compared with 50 per cent for the British program) and more common sense, when it came to tactics and strategies. Groves, *Behind the Smoke Screen*, 130, argued similarly – that the constant complaint of superior German aircraft was simply an excuse. He called Trenchard's offensive policy a 'school-boy policy' that was defeated by a defensive doctrine and better trained flyers. The 'Fokker Scourge' began with the first Fokker Eindecker victory in July 1915 and really took hold in late 1915 and early 1916.

120. Morrow, *The Great War in the Air*, 375, noted that, while the Germans had slight airframe superiority with metal aircraft and cantilever wings, the Allies were superior in engines.

121. Sykes, 'Notes by Chief of the Air Staff on the Independent Force, Royal Air Force, and the Proposed Inter-Allied Strategic Bombing Force', Air 1/26/15/

1/121.
122. See George Kent Williams, 'Statistics and Strategic Bombardment', unpublished dissertation, Oxford University, 1987.
123. Richard P. Hallion, *The Rise of Fighter Aircraft, 1914–1918* (Annapolis: The Nautical & Aviation Publishing Company of America, 1984), 66.
124. German Documents, Trenchard Papers, MFC 76/1/73. A captured regimental order of 18 June 1918 of the German 111th Division stated, 'The Field Kitchen leaves here at 0100 hours. Earlier start is impracticable owing to bombing by enemy planes up to midnight. It must then go a roundabout way through the trench system.' In Raleigh and Jones, 1:352, the official history mentioned that two captured airmen, Fribenius and Hahan, had stated that the RFC was doing such great damage that orders went out for them to attack the British flyers whenever possible.
125. Raleigh and Jones, 2:117; and Hew Strachan, *European Armies and the Conduct of War* (London: Allen & Unwin, 1983), 152–3.
126. Air 1 460/15/312/101. The entire long-range bombing plan was geared for 1919, with 1918 operations a preamble to take advantage of low German morale. The decision-maker whose signature authorized the bombing was not Weir, but Sykes.
127. Kennett, *The First Air War*, 73, mentioned a 'tactical revolution' involving a quantum leap in methodologies when air fighting went from chance single-machine encounters to planned missions of formations seeking air engagements.

9

The Forgotten Theorist and Air Power Leader

Air power historians have, for the most part, painted the wrong picture of Sir Frederick H. Sykes, the first Military Wing Commander of the Royal Flying Corps and Chief of the Air Staff of the Royal Air Force during the First World War. Scholars have obliged Trenchard and the RAF by relegating Sykes to the shadows. Hence a significant chapter in the story of air power in the First World War has been missing. This study of Sykes shows that he was a visionary theorist, an important organizer and leader of the British air service and the revolution in air power that began during the First World War, and that he has been deliberately neglected in RAF history.

Sykes was not the selfish intriguer his RAF enemies contended; there is simply no evidence of any intrigue on his part – including that referred to by Trenchard in his letter to Brancker in March 1916 – any more than the supposed intrigue on Trenchard's part mentioned by Rothermere in March 1918. The air service was ripe with the suspicion of intrigue, and no person in any position of command or authority was immune from it. Sykes was particularly vulnerable, as his distant manner and failure to demonstrate compassion were misperceived by fellow airmen. He was not insensitive, but simply too consumed by his work under the stress of war to show much sympathy or to consider the enhancing of his career by socializing and otherwise conforming to the atmosphere of the personalized command system.

Much more importantly, in respect to the first air war, the history of air power has failed to record that Sykes helped to orchestrate the development of this power and its fundamental effect on modern warfare. He fought military traditions in implementing the world's first independent air service to ensure its effective employment in support of the BEF and the Royal Navy and to establish strategic bombing. Sykes should have received a proper historical portrait, and it has been the intention of this study to bring him from obscurity to light.

Malcolm Cooper exemplifies the historiographical trend when he writes: 'In 1918 Sykes emerged temporarily as the head of the new air force. For most of the war, however, he exercised neither authority nor influence.'[1] Cooper went on to claim that even as CAS he failed to overcome the 'military' domination of air power.

This history has shown, however, that Sykes did not 'emerge' into his CAS position; he took command of a dying infant. He did not hold a temporary command; he was in charge of the Air Staff for a year during some of the most critical months of the war. The King and the Air Minister gave Sykes, in writing and in practice, the responsibility and authority to decide air policy and allocate resources to the Navy and the Army, as well as to the strategic strike force. Air Council and Air Staff Minutes demonstrate that Sykes was the driving spirit behind many developments: the meteorological service, flight medicine, more effective training, long-range bombing, improved air-to-air and air-to-ground communication, aerial photography, the creation of the WRAF, accident investigation procedures, mission planning and post-mission reporting and Air Intelligence. Sykes, not the Army, determined where air resources were to be deployed – tactically in low-level support to infantry, tanks and guns, and strategically in the long-range bombing of German industry. Sykes did overcome the military domination of air power. Had he not, the RAF would have vanished during or soon after the war. Instead, under him it became the world's largest air force – until Trenchard and Churchill were forced to allow it to slip to fifth place after the war. In October 1918 Sykes did not succumb to Army pressure in his decision to send more squadrons to the zone of the Army. His was a decision to help to win the war, which was the mission of the RAF. Unlike many other British commanders who stubbornly enforced their principles and doctrines without regard to effect, Sykes made sure that his conformed to reality and kept air power flexible.

SYKES' VISION

Air power did not determine the outcome of the First World War, but it did have a substantial influence and constituted the preamble to the revolutionary change in warfare that has continued to today. Sykes had captured the vision of air power before 1914, and his theories, strategies and application during and after the war were ahead of their time. His ideas were visionary and contributed to a new aerial awareness – an air power intellectualism that has existed world-wide since 1918.[2] His tactical and strategic concepts, employed in an air policy of independence and specialization, were cornerstones in the revolutionary growth and development of air power.

The term 'air power' is misleading, and, when misunderstood, can contribute to an incorrect analysis of the first air war. When considered simply as aerial firepower, early air power was insignificant compared with the land battle. Since the mid-nineteenth century, however, when soldiers first started using balloons to see the enemy, air power has involved more than firepower. The preliminary air transport role during the recent Gulf War, for example, was just as critical in defeating Iraq as the attacks by bombers and interceptors. Aerial reconnaissance can be as powerful a weapon as shooting or bombing from the air, and this was demonstrated in 1914 by the RFC, when its only air-power role was reconnaissance. During the subsequent four years air forces developed many more roles, and technologies expanded to accommodate numerous demands, which produced a quantum leap in air power that cannot be dismissed simply because technological capabilities then were embryonic when compared with modern standards, or because the RAF's and the IAF's firepower was small compared with that of the BEF. Sykes' vision of aviation expanded and matured over the course of the war as he witnessed aerial capabilities jump from reconnaissance and communication to multiple forms of firepower delivery. He concluded that the growth in air power between 1914 and 1918 was as revolutionary in warfare as the development of gunpowder.[3]

Sykes correctly promoted air power as a broad concept that was not focused exclusively on bombing or fighting, even though historians have directed attention to those areas. As General of the Air Force H. H. (Hap) Arnold stated, air power is 'the total aerial activity, civilian and military, commercial and private, potential as well as existing'.[4] Major-General Giulio Douhet considered air power to be 'the practical use of the air arm'.[5] It is in this dimension of total air power, used practically in its tactical and its strategic realm, that Sykes contemplated the use of the air service.

His primary vision was the efficient and effective employment of air power to help to win the war, but the key to his strategy was the machine. He recognized that the fighting methods then practiced wasted manpower, and he condemned the 'national attrition' strategy current in June 1918.[6] Hence Sykes fought against traditionalists such as Haig and Robertson, who saw victory through the increased use of men in cavalry and infantry roles, rather than the employment of machines such as aircraft and tanks. Aligned with what Travers has labeled the 'mechanical school', Sykes predicted that only by saving manpower through machines could the Allies achieve a decisive victory.[7] This was the fundamental argument he made in March 1918 with his memorandum 'Notes on Economy of Man-Power by Mechanical Means'. Sykes had recognized what the military theorist MacGregor Knox has noted about warfare since the Industrial Revolution – that there has been an increased emphasis on strategy due to the fact that invention gives its possessor a decisive edge, provided such invention is accompanied by the means of production.[8] Hence in the linking of strategy to machines Sykes envisioned a victory that would involve mechanical battle and the need to thwart enemy attempts to produce war-fighting machines.

Sykes did not contend that machines could change the nature of war or alter the fundamental principles of strategy.[9] Quite the opposite, he maintained that properly employed machines reinforced the principles of war.[10] Thus Sykes argued for proper tank and machine-gun usage, and he recognized the aeroplane as an even more capable and versatile machine that was easier to use effectively. It was quick, long-range, provided intelligence and delivered firepower at the decisive point. In addition, with command of the air, aircraft promoted surprise and security.[11] With the air machine and a *coup d'œil*, commanders could achieve victory.

From Sykes' perspective, victory through air power meant fighting offensively with air machines. Sykes had seen the offensive fail repeatedly during the war, and he had condemned it and lamented its toll on the air service when used ineffectively. Yet he never doubted the necessity for the offense, provided that it was carried out in the correct circumstances; in 1918 he still repeated the prevalent dictum: 'by offensive action alone can decisive results in war be obtained'.[12] The war had reinforced Sykes' staff college lessons regarding Clausewitzian analysis of offense and defense. When offense was impracticable, then defense had to be pursued. Likewise, the offensive had to be at the appropriate time and place, and it had to be carried out in the proper manner. Sykes did not attack Trenchard's past tactics because they were offensive; he condemned them because they were defensive. Sykes determined that the RFC's offensive doctrine had been forced inappropriately – that by supporting the Army and the Navy in their zones of operations, the air services had, in reality, been fighting a costly and ineffective defensive air war.[13] Hence Sykes tried to reverse that trend by carrying out a true aerial offensive against the German heartland.[14]

According to Sykes, German industry was the *Schwerpunkt* for offensive aerial attack, and the 'culminating time' was in 1918 following the failed German offensives, when momentum and morale would be suffering. Sykes was well aware that strategic bombing had marginal capability, but he, alone, was convinced that, due to that limitation, long-range bombers would avoid the 'big battle' that had stalemated the Western Front and would provide a crippling blow to Germany in the process.[15] In June 1918 he stated that strategy was driven by three new factors: the national aspect, air combat and submarines.[16] All three related well to strategic bombing directed against enemy industry and morale, but he was emphatic that his air force should take the initiative and beat Germany to the punch. He claimed that a timely strategic air offensive would cripple German industry, submarine power and the country's political and moral force.[17] In their official air history of World War II, Sir Charles Webster and Noble Frankland acknowledged that this strategic idea was a 'revolutionary conception', and they noted the 'astonishing speed with which that [strategic air power] kind of warfare had been evolved'.[18]

Sykes' strategic and tactical concept were harmonious. He did not want to jeopardize Army and Navy tactical air support, but he believed that strategic air operations would provide the best support possible to those services. The key to strategic success, however, lay in the air service's continued independence. According to Sykes, both tactical and strategic air operations were too complicated for management by the Army or the Navy, and only commanders educated in the specialized aspects of air warfare could successfully direct the air force. He argued to the Prime Minister Lloyd George that 'independence of action must be secured' and fought American, French and Italian generals at the Inter-Allied Aviation Committee to keep the air forces out of other hands.[19]

Perhaps Sykes' most significant insight was his delineation of air power into different categories – strategic, tactical, specialized and non-specialized – so that it could be employed most appropriately by adequately trained personnel using the equipment best suited for each mission. He first tried to keep tactical and strategic reconnaissance apart in 1914, with strategic orders coming only from GHQ, and in 1918 he again maintained a separation between tactical and strategic missions – both reconnaissance and bombing. Within bombing itself, Sykes' two categories – specialized and non-specialized – were part of the rationale for air force independence. He noted that non-specialized activity was carried out by auxiliary squadrons to help the Army and the Navy, but it could involve both tactical and strategic operations. The primary targets were railways and aerodromes. Specialized bombing was only strategic, against German industry, and it should not be intermittent or indefinite.[20] Such strategic operations necessitate specialized equipment and training involving improved technical designs and a reorganized system of training.[21] Sykes argued that strategic bombing had to be scientific or it would fail. He was convinced that only a specialized and independent force could successfully implement the all-important strategic air offensive. His contemporaries at Versailles, as well as follow air staff members, simply combined tactical and strategic air concepts, believing that all tactical and strategic roles could be performed by non-specialized air forces attached to armies or naval forces.[22]

As part of Sykes' tactical and strategic plan, he also wanted a 'strategic reserve' within the air force, a concept clearly taken from his work at Versailles in late 1917 and early 1918. He was convinced that the only way to have such a reserve was to create the independent, specialized, Inter-Allied IAF, which would serve as such a reserve. He refused to see the aircraft as an auxiliary weapon system. It was to be the main thrust; it was to be strategic. Sykes recognized that air power was a broad concept that involved many different roles, but he also realized that the differences between tactical and strategic missions necessitated specialization. By 1918 his primary focus was on the strategic potential, and he wrote in August that 'the development of Air Power affords the best and most rapid return for the expenditure of national resources of man-power, material, and money . . . the Strategic Air Offensive is the dominant factor in air power'. He continued, 'Air Power of the Allies . . . could be accepted even now as the most prominent determining factor for peace.'[23] In sum, Sykes' battle against the traditionalists was to change the way war was fought, using air power as the 'right hand of strategy'.[24]

Sykes predicted that, as war progressed, the cavalry role would disappear completely owing to air capabilities. The infantry would remain, but their existence would depend on effective air reconnaissance, air-to-ground attack, air-assisted artillery and tank co-operation, and air interdiction of enemy supply lines and communication links. Hence air and ground tactics had to develop together.[25] He acknowledged the valuable role aircraft had to play with the navy as well – in coastal defense, reconnaissance, anti-submarine warfare, escort and the bombing of enemy bases. He anticipated that air-delivered torpedoes would threaten the future of battleships and fleets, but admitted that the future of naval air was more difficult to assess, because so few naval battles had been fought during the war.[26]

Although Sykes' primary focus in 1918 was on the immediate war, his strategic concepts involved post-war considerations as well. After four years of fighting, he abhorred the thought of another war. He reminded his listeners that war had become terribly destructive and that aviation provided a means toward peace.[27] His peacetime strategy for the Empire was to maintain the Inter-Allied strategic reserve idea through an Empire civil air fleet that would be readily convertible into a strategic strike force if needed to supplement the Empire air force in emergency situations. Hence the development of civil aviation had to be accomplished with war in mind so that components could be standardized and proper routes, bases and types of aircraft constructed.[28] The key to the future defense of the Empire lay with sufficiently powerful military and civil air forces: 'In the next war, the existence of the British Empire will depend primarily upon its Air

Force. The giant aeroplane of today will evitably [*sic*] develop in striking power to something analogous to an aerial dreadnought.'[29]

Sykes recognized that warfare had become a war of nations rather than of armies and that it depended therefore on national output and civilian morale. He argued that, regardless of what international conventions tried to establish with resolutions and treaties, the reality of strategic bombing was unavoidable. Civilians and industries would be targeted. And while the First World War had ended with strategic bombing, the next war would begin with an immediate, long-range attack, so that the period of mobilization would be reduced substantially. Thus peacetime preparation for this inevitable situation was imperative.[30]

Again, Sykes maintained that civil air was the key to successful peacetime preparation. He reminded listeners that aerial attack was more effective than air defense and that the maintenance of a sufficiently large peacetime air service to provide defense was impossible. Large combat air forces during peacetime were impractical and unnecessarily expensive, and they could lead to another armaments race, reminiscent of the dreadnought preamble to the World War that had just ended.[31] Sykes also remembered his lesson of 1914 that a war might not end in a quick victory, and noted that a combat air force alone might not last long enough to sustain a war-winning effort.[32] On the other hand, a large civil air reserve, along with its industry, would fuel the necessary fire to defeat the enemy. Thus the only good preparation for the inevitable future air threat was to establish civil aviation.

In analyzing Sykes' concepts of air power one must acknowledge his ability to look to the future and anticipate a world where aircraft would be a dominant economic and strategic factor. His concepts of tactical and strategic air were appropriate, as was his focus on specialization and independence. By 1918 the air forces had hundreds of different types of aircraft. Sykes knew that army and navy commanders could not appreciate the diverse and sophisticated nature of air power and that to be effective it had to be flown and directed by specialists. Such specialists could not operate without an autonomous and independent service. Sykes had not initiated the independence of the RAF and the IAF, but he certainly maintained it when many of his comrades in arms were trying to return to former Army and Navy air organizations. Sykes' theories were courageous. They involved the confronting of a powerful military and political elite when his concepts ran contrary to tradition and appeared excessive. Air power costs threatened established programs and were unpopular with leaders who were trying to reduce expenditure. Sykes' policies pointed in new directions. While he argued for offensive action, much of the nation was preoccupied with air defense due to the loss of its insular invulnerability.[33]

Higham has noted that for air power to be effective it had to fit Mahanian principles: geographical location and conformation, territorial size, population, national character and character of government.[34] Sykes considered each of these issues while advocating air power to help the war effort and enhance the Empire. Britain's insular situation demanded the use of aircraft, both for defense and transport. Britain's population and industrial base accommodated production. The enterprising British nature and the government's desire to promote an integrated Empire also matched well with aerial expansion. The British environment was so well suited for an aerial revolution that Sykes became exasperated when faced with military ignorance and political reluctance.

He was naive, however, in thinking that the novelty of air power made it 'unhampered to a great extent by preconceived notions and therefore offering greater scope for individual thought'.[35] His individual thought was rebuffed by military and government friction and he eventually claimed that British sentiments against air power were simply 'blind prejudice'.[36] Sykes could conceive no possible rational or practical explanations for traditionalist reluctance to embrace air power with his level of enthusiasm. His romantic vision of air power was well conceived and perceptive, but his concepts were too far ahead of their time to be realistic. Later, however, once they lost their association with Sykes, they became an important influence in the formation of British air power doctrine during the post-war decade. As Malcolm Smith has stated, 'In spite of Trenchard's personal enmity for Sykes, it was in fact an approximation to Sykes' views of the aims of an independent air force, and the method by which that aim would be achieved, that formed the mainstream of RAF thinking by the end of the 1920s.'[37]

Interestingly, even though Sykes achieved less recognition as a theorist than the legendary Douhet, his ideas were remarkably similar to Douhet's and were conceived at about the same time. Douhet began writing about air power in 1909, and his principal ideas were published after the First World War: first, that there was no longer any distinction between combatants and non-combatants in war; secondly, that surface offensives were no longer possible; thirdly, that aerial warfare had now made war three-dimensional and that there was no defense against aerial bombing; fourthly, that war was now dictated by initial massive aerial bombardments with high explosives, incendiaries and poisonous gases; and lastly that the delivery of such amoral weapons of mass destruction would be performed by independent air forces of long-range bombers. The paramount concept behind all of Douhet's theories was the principle that national defense depended on 'command of the air' – the title of his influential book in 1921 and the very words Sykes used nearly a decade earlier to promote British air power.[38] The fact that Sykes went to Italy in 1911 to study the Italian air service and its organization makes it likely that he was influenced by Douhet. An equally valid assumption, however, is that Douhet may have been influenced by Sykes. Item by item, Sykes' pronouncements matched Douhet's nearly perfectly. Their only major difference was that Sykes never stated that long-range bombers were invulnerable, which they were not. Hence Sykes' perspective was more balanced in that he advocated a combined-arms approach to air power, rather than Douhet's more extreme position that command of the air was the singular key to victory. Sykes' vision of Empire air power was ahead of its time, and his implementation of policy was, at the least, a preamble to a revolutionary change in warfare.

SYKES AND THE AIR REVOLUTION

The air revolution was born in the heat of battle and baptized with fire; it was an ironic product of extremes. War had become more sophisticated and increasingly destructive, and the development of the aerial machine was another step in that process. Yet by the Armistice air technology was still young and its capabilities marginal. Hence a low aerial capability initiated a high level of sophistication in warfare – where the machine, rather than man, was the predominant factor. This, then, was the culmination of a firepower revolution that had begun with the adoption of gunpowder centuries earlier.[39]

Aviation required a sophisticated and professional service with a high degree of group and self discipline – the kind of organization that Sykes wanted. It necessitated specialization, advanced training methods and experimentation. It challenged the military tradition that victory depended mostly on the soldiers who fought. Although flown by courageous pilots, machines now fought machines, and the superior use of technology determined victory. In only four years developments in aircraft technology expanded exponentially in maneuverability, speed, payload, range, altitude capability, time-to-climb, armaments, armor, reliability, cockpit visibility and communications. Sykes correctly determined that the most significant applications of that technology were in ground and night fighting, torpedo attack and long-range bombing.[40] At the same time, under his management the air service went from the smallest auxiliary arm of the Army and the Navy to an autonomous and independent service.

A military revolution is a fundamental shift in the nature of armed forces and how they fight. This is clearly what occurred in the First World War with the RAF. Previously, warfare on land and at sea had been limited to sabres, bayonets and guns. Now it was fought with squadrons of aerial machines performing new missions that ushered in a new type of warfare. Air power was not simply an anomaly unique to the First World War. Thomas Kuhn has stated that the revolutionary process contains the following three steps: determination of facts, matching facts with theory and articulating theory.[41] Perhaps better than any other air service leader in the war, Sykes was able to assess the aerial situation, conceptualize effective uses of air power and articulate his ideas into organization and policy. He then fought traditional sentiments and differences of opinion within the military and political establishments to initiate the first phase of the air revolution.

As a revolutionary, Sykes fought the military establishment to bring about the organizational and strategic changes he believed were essential to achieve victory. This is a different interpretation from the idea that air power in the First World War was a rapid, chaotic and reactionary development that failed to meet expectations – or that the early evolution of air power was a slow and costly process plagued by trial-and-error methodology.[42] Both interpretations are valid to some extent, but they do not address a key issue that comes to light through a consideration of Sykes – that warfare had begun to experience a revolution in air power.

Experts describe revolution as a paradigm shift. Existing rules define the paradigm, and when those rules no longer work (which clearly occurred in the First World War), their failure signals the need for a new paradigm.[43] By the end of 1918 warfare had shifted from a war of fronts to a war of areas, and that change has been permanent.[44] For example, the *United States Air Force Manual 1-1* states 'The advent of air power, and later aerospace power, did not change the essential nature of war, but air power did change the way war is conducted.'[45]

Kuhn notes that the signal for revolutionary change is a crisis – when an anomaly occurs – but people are unwilling to renounce the traditional thinking that led them into the crisis.[46] Sykes certainly faced such a crisis in the First World War and had to overcome traditional thinking. Colonel John Capper wrote in 1909:

> Britishers as a rule have all the faults, as well as the virtues, of intense conservatism. We have little as a race of that valuable quality imagination, and in considering the importance of any new invention, we are apt to minimize, rather than exaggerate the purposes to which it may be adapted.[47]

Crane Brinton called such conservatism a 'conceptual scheme', which becomes an imbedded intellectual 'system in equilibrium' which most people are reluctant to question.[48] With regard to the British military in the First World War, such thinking was embodied in the Admiralty and War Office 'military mindedness' and its accompanying offensive-morale doctrine, misuse of technology and ineffective personalized command structure.

Yet, in any revolution, there are those who will stand against the system and its rulers in a movement that has been termed a 'desertion of the intellectuals'.[49] Thus when the 'air mindedness' ideas of revolutionaries such as Weir, Sykes, Montagu, Groves and Smuts contradicted traditional military mindedness, such a movement occurred. The desertion was not an external revolt but an internal one – a 'revulsion against misused authority'.[50] According to Chalmers Johnson, the precondition for such revolt is a condition of 'dysfunction' which occurs within a social system when it experiences disequilibrium.[51] This is precisely what occurred during the war when Sykes was consumed by the manpower shortage that had been caused by traditional military concepts and a stalemate at the front.

Revolutions require leaders. As mentioned throughout this study, Sykes was not a lone revolutionary but one of the most important and influential players in the process. Sykes challenged the Admiralty, the War Office, GHQ, Trenchard, Haig and other obstacles. Contrary to legend, Trenchard never grasped the 'air mindedness' concept during the war and he clearly did not promote revolutionary concepts of air power. To him, air was like ground – it had to be gained offensively and held at all costs. Trenchard believed air-service independence hampered that effort.[52]

Sykes' primary influence was in organization. He developed the RFC Military Wing in 1912 and re-established its structure twice again in 1914. Sykes' 'squadron' is still the fundamental building block of many of the world's air forces. He reorganized the RNAS at Gallipoli in 1915 and restructured the Air Staff in 1918. He helped to create the air force's strategic branch, the IAF. In addition, his revolutionary efforts did not cease after the war, for he established British civil aviation as well as international aerial navigation after 1918.

In addition to his organizational abilities, Sykes was a gifted and progressive technologist. He constantly desired efficiency and looked to technology for answers. He understood the dialectic between man and machine in war and appreciated technologies that could reduce the drain on manpower and help to break the frontal stalemate that technologies had produced when used according to old methods. Specifically, Sykes' ideas were visionary concerning combined arms, deep defense and limited offense. He rejected the idea of set-piece breakthrough battles. In 1914 he established the first RFC air policies, embodied in the RFC Training Manual and the official standing orders. He distinguished between tactical and strategic reconnaissance and established the intelligence gathering and dissemination system that thwarted an early German victory at Mons. As CAS in 1918, he commanded the Air Staff responsible for directing all RAF flying operations and promoted the use of aircraft in the most technically advanced roles possible at the time: tank support, night flying, artillery co-ordination, low-level ground attack, photographic reconnaissance, coastal patrol, escort and anti-submarine work. Most importantly, he more than any other individual fought to create the strategic strike force, organized as the Independent Air Force. His impact on aviation world-wide is still felt today in the size and structure of squadrons, the separation of tactical and strategic air, and air force independence. Air power today is not treated as a force auxiliary to armies and navies, and the long-range delivery of bombs and missiles has been an important part of the grand strategy of the world's major powers for 50 years. Sykes' concept of the economy of manpower by mechanical means has remained fundamental in Western warfare, where air forces have continued to pursue and capitalize on the latest technologies available.

It is popular today to portray early aerial technologies as unscientific inventions – *ad hoc* reactions to necessity where events shaped ideas rather than ideas shaping events. The idea is commonplace that the fighting aircraft simply emerged and was not the result of conscious planning. Such revisionist thinking ignores the fact that it took visionary thinkers like Sykes to make the aircraft effectively replace the cavalry horse.[53] Sykes brought about an intellectual awareness of what air power could do in war, and helped to implement the seminal change that catapulted it to its role on the modern battlefield.

Change did not occur instantaneously nor without problems. In fact it was a chaotic fight that produced marginal, immediate effectiveness. Sykes was often fighting uphill battles, and he learned expensive lessons, particularly at Gallipoli, when he failed to grasp the limits of air power in distant hostile territory. Yet many revolutionary leaders have blundered before succeeding, and great institutions have been born under tenuous revolutionary conditions.[54] Revolutions require leaders able to see beyond the immediate results, and the measure of Sykes' influence was seen as much during the recent Gulf War as in the slight destruction caused by fragile De Havilland bombers in 1918. Sykes fought not just to win the war, but to create a new service that would promote the political and economic future of the Empire during the next century.

He was a visionary and a revolutionary who concentrated on the mission at hand more than on career enhancement or popularity. His personal conservatism and sober demeanor placed him at odds with the social-club military establishment, and his overly ambitious view of air power made him appear unrealistic, which he clearly was at Gallipoli and after the Armistice. Sykes' unorthodox military background bothered him and drove him to prove to himself that he could accomplish as much, if not more, than those who had progressed through traditional routes. He entered the war as a staff college product who obediently conformed to established principles and procedures. He made mistakes and failed to predict certain events. Yet he was able to put the past behind him and, despite emotional setbacks, never resigned his post, always accepting commands and the tasks placed before him. Along with other innovative technologists, he struggled against traditionalists and the military system to promote his vision that warfighting machines – especially strategic bombers – could win the war. The history of Sykes' role in the First World War should not rest on unsubstantiated, anecdotal opinions which have led to his relegation to the margins. Rather it should be shaped by evidence showing the extent to which he initiated a revolution in air power that began conceptually during the First World War and has continued to shape warfare to the present day.

NOTES

1. Cooper, *The Birth of Independent Air Power*, 23.
2. Sykes, *Aviation in Peace and War*, 104. Sykes said that an essential part of air power development was that the 'man on the street' should acquire an air sense – an appreciation of aerial capabilities, confidence in air travel and comfort with the fact that aircraft were part of modern life.
3. Ibid., 7.
4. *Air Force Manual 1-1, Basic Aerospace Doctrine of the Unites States Air Force* (Washington, DC: Department of the Air Force, 1992), 2:272.
5. Ibid.
6. 'Review of Air Situation and Strategy for the Information of the Imperial War Cabinet', 27 June 1918, Sykes Private Papers.
7. Tim Travers, *How the War Was Won: Command and Technology in the British Army on the Western Front 1917–1918* (London: Routledge, 1992), 32, noted two schools of thought in 1918: 1. Haig's traditionalists and 2. the mechanical school, comprising men such as Lloyd George and Churchill. In this sense, Sykes and his mentor Wilson clearly aligned themselves with the mechanical school.
8. MacGregor Knox, 'Conclusion', in *The Making of Strategy: Rulers, States and War*, ed. Williamson Murray (Cambridge: Cambridge University Press, 1994), 638.
9. 'Review of Air Situation', Sykes Private Papers.
10. Sykes, *Aviation in Peace and War*, 7.
11. Ibid., 35.
12. Ibid.
13. Ibid.
14. Note on the Inter-Allied Bombing Force Problem, 13 July 1918, Sykes Private Papers.

15. Malcolm Smith, 53.
16. 'Review of Air Situation', Sykes Private Papers.
17. Ibid.
18. Webster and Frankland, 6.
19. Sykes to Lloyd George, 1 June 1918; and Draft of 3rd Session of Inter-Allied Aviation Committee Meeting, 21 July 1918, Public Record Office (PRO), Air 1/26/15/1/121.
20. Ibid.
21. CAS memorandum to War Cabinet [no date] July 1918, Air 6/17.
22. Draft of 3rd Session of Inter-Allied Aviation Committee Meeting, 21 July 1918, Air 1/26/15/1/121.
23. 'Notes by Chief of the Air Staff on the Independent Force', 7 Aug. 1918, Air 1/26/15/1/121.
24. Sykes, *Aviation in Peace and War*, 43.
25. Ibid., 98.
26. Ibid., 99.
27. Ibid., 7.
28. 'Review of Air Situation', 27 June 1918, Sykes Private Papers.
29. Ibid.
30. Sykes, *Aviation in Peace and War*, 100–1.
31. Ibid., 103, 138.
32. Ibid., 103.
33. Gollin, 96.
34. Higham, *Air Power*, 12.
35. Sykes, *Aviation in Peace and War*, 8.
36. Sykes, *From Many Angles*, 237.
37. Malcolm Smith, 56.
38. Douhet, 6–10, 30–4. Sykes and General Grierson spoke of command of the air during Sykes' speech to the Aeronautical Society of Great Britain in 1913.
39. J. F. C. Fuller, *Armament and History* (New York: Charles Scribner's, 1945), 109.
40. Sykes, *Aviation in Peace and War*, 96.
41. Thomas Kuhn, *The Structure of Scientific Revolutions*, 2nd edn (Chicago: University of Chicago Press, 1970), 34.
42. Liddell Hart, 355; and Higham, *Air Power*, xi, 5, 29.
43. Kuhn, 68.
44. Traditional frontal warfare involved defeating the enemy via breaking or outflanking his front. Air power, however, has introduced area warfare, where the ultimate outflanking movement is vertical. Aircraft, and now space assets, can attack the enemy area long before any surface movement across enemy borders.
45. *Air Force Manual 1-1*, 1:5.
46. Kuhn, 77.
47. Gollin, 105.
48. Crane Brinton, *The Anatomy of Revolution* (New York: Vintage, 1960), 10–16.
49. Brinton, 46, 66. See also Hannah Arendt, *On Revolution* (New York: Viking, 1963), 39.
50. Peter Calvert, *Revolution* (New York: Praeger, 1970), 133.
51. Chalmers Johnson, *Revolution and the Social System* (Stanford, CA: Hoover Institution on War, Revolution and Peace, 1964), 5. Specifically, the old military system was the dysfunction; the war was the 'accelerator of dysfunction'.
52. Collier, 76. Trenchard said that the government's hopes that the use of independent air power would hasten the end of the war simply showed that members of the Air Board were 'quite off their heads'.
53. Not only did aircraft take over the cavalry reconnaissance role, but they made

horses even more vulnerable. Tied to wagons or guns and located on roads, the horse was a large target that could not escape aerial attack. See Rudolph Stark, *Wings of War: A German Airman's Diary of the Last Year of the Great War* (trans. Claud W. Sykes) (London: Greenhill, 1988), 161; and James, sound recording, Reel No. 14, IWM sound recordings.

54. David Close and Carl Bridge (eds), *Revolution: A History of the Idea* (London: Croom-Helm, 1985), 8. Close and Bridge clarify the important point that revolution is not the new era but is merely the *prelude* to the new era. In the same way, the air power revolution in the First World War did not create new warfare; it simply initiated the process.

Epilogue

No prophet is accepted in his own country.

(Luke 4:24)

While many soldiers viewed the Armistice as a reprieve and a time to obtain leave, Sykes saw it as an opportunity for Great Britain to capitalize on a situation for which its soldiers had fought and died.[1] As the head of the British Air Section during the Peace Conference, Sykes fought to secure a lasting settlement that would ensure European stability but also facilitate the development of international air travel with an 'open sky' policy from which the British Empire could take advantage. Sykes recognized not only the defensive value of a strong air force but also the tremendous economic potential of an air service that promoted civilian aviation.[2] He fought against a dominant reactionary attitude that demanded drastic reductions during demobilization. Although the threat from Germany had vanished overnight, Sykes recognized potential problems with other nations, including France and the United States, and he viewed a threat to any of the dominions as a threat to the Empire. Since Sykes with Lord Weir had urged the development of civil more than service aviation, and in the light of Sykes' politically unrealistic approach to the post-war strength of the RAF, the new War and Air Minister Winston Churchill felt that Sykes could better serve the post-war air service as Controller General of Civil Aviation (CGCA) than as the CAS, the position Churchill offered to Trenchard.[3]

Churchill was aware of some animosity that had developed between Trenchard and Sykes, and the decision to place these two generals side by side in direct competition for scarce Air Ministry pounds was perhaps shortsighted. Churchill, however, was preoccupied with demobilization problems and War Office issues; as he wrote to Sykes about the CGCA position: 'It would be essential to the success of such an arrangement that you and Trenchard should be able to work together in goodwill and loyal co-operation.'[4]

As the new CGCA, Sykes played a key role in promoting techno-logical opportunities for Britain. He advocated world-wide wireless links, commercial air routes and weather services, and organized long-distance demonstration flights. His vision was of a prosperous, benevolent Empire connected by air.[5] His first months in Civil Aviation were promising and rewarding.[6]

Despite Sykes' visionary approach and strong support for commercial air transport, aviation technology was still in its infancy. On 3 May 1919 Sykes was involved in the most serious flying accident of his life: his pilot was killed and Sykes was badly shaken.[7] A brush with death was nothing new to him and he rebounded quickly. Yet it was a bad omen for his future in Civil Aviation.

Sykes' primary struggle as CGCA was financial. Adamantly arguing that Civil Aviation would provide the *matériel* and manpower foundation for the RAF, he fought the 'Geddes axe' Treasury cuts to obtain aviation industry subsidies. Sykes was too optimistic in his vision of commercial air capabilities, but he was convinced that without government help the industry would certainly die.[8] In addition, Sykes correctly feared that the War Office and the Admiralty were attempting to eliminate the Air Ministry, and he objected to the tremendous inefficiency presented by interservice rivalries and duplicated efforts. To some within air force circles, Sykes was a gadfly as he raised demands for a unified Ministry of Defence and published numerous articles about the ineffective RAF bureaucracy.[9] Sykes had left one war to enter a new, economic one. His continual fight for money in the Air Estimates appeared fruitless as Civil Aviation continued to shrink. After three frustrating years, he was unwilling to direct a poorly funded organization any longer. He resigned as CGCA in April 1922, in the same year his mentor General Wilson was assassinated.[10]

Free from any official obligations to the Air Ministry, Sykes began a media campaign for Imperial air defense that was reminiscent of his pre-war years. While most of the country was content to lick its wounds, Sykes called for action: to recognize that Europe could erupt again at any moment; to accept the British burden as Europe's badly needed rock of stability; and to avoid the chaos, bureaucratic inefficiency and wasted manpower that plagued all three services.[11] Like most strategists of the time, Sykes envisioned a period of peace that became established as a British planning concept; but Sykes' peace depended on a strong and effective air service – more civil than military. He condemned the Navy's attempts to reclaim its own air service and chastised the Cabinet's willingness to acquiesce on that point. Most importantly, however, Sykes was simply convinced that no organization could defend the Empire under the deleterious financial conditions that had compelled him to resign.[12]

Sykes had been consumed by work, yet his post-war efforts had not excluded an enjoyable social and personal life. During his tenure in

Civil Aviation Sykes had attracted widespread public attention by his marriage to Isabel Law, daughter of Andrew Bonar Law, the Conservative Leader of the House of Commons.[13] Before their engagement the future Lady Sykes had gained popularity by strongly supporting her father's politics and by helping the war effort in fund raising. Isabel was attracted to the excitement of flight. In fact, her introduction to Sykes was averted when, after she had persuaded someone to give her a flight in a service machine, she was hidden in a cabinet because of the arrival of a high-ranking officer – none other than Sykes. When Sir Frederick did finally meet Isabel, he became enamoured with her adventurous spirit and her conservative ideals that well matched his own. To Isabel, he was, literally, a gallant knight on a white horse – a former cavalry officer, war hero and aviation pioneer. The future Lady Sykes, whose mother had died in 1909, was a source of great support to her father and when he learned of her engagement to Sykes he exclaimed to Lord Beaverbrook, 'Something terrible has happened.'[14] He quickly recovered from the shock, however, and became devoted to his son-in-law. Following a brief courtship, the wedding took place on 3 June 1920 at St Columba's Church on Pont Street (Church of Scotland) and was described as 'The Politico-Aerial Wedding of the Week'.[15] During a reception for Sykes and his fiancée, parliament had adjourned so that Members could present their gifts to the couple. In his presentation speech, the Prime Minister Lloyd George received great cheers when he mentioned Sykes' high intelligence and the valuable service he had given to his country during the most trying moments of the war. The Prime Minister continued by wishing Sykes and his fiancée long life and happiness 'in a sphere where there will be no Speaker to keep order between them'.[16] The tremendous applause of approval marked this as a rare instance of party political unanimity. Wedding guests included the Prime Minister and Mrs Lloyd George; Lord Beaverbrook; Sir Edward Carson; Sir Robert Horne; Arthur Balfour; Rudyard Kipling and Major John Baird. After an official ceremony that looked like the Chelsea Flower Show, Sykes and his bride left No. 11 Downing Street and drove straight to Croydon, where they boarded a Civil Aviation aeroplane and flew to Newcastle for their honeymoon.[17]

Their marriage of 34 years was particularly happy, with complementary temperaments – his more reserved and hers more outgoing.[18] Their only son Bonar was born two years after the wedding. The major issue that stood between them, and one which caused Lady Sykes concern later in their marriage, was the great amount of work and consequent stress her husband imposed upon himself.[19] Lady Sykes was a loyal supporter, following Sir Frederick wherever his career took them, which at times was into less than comfortable environments. Isabel's friends tried to help Sykes on occasion, and her support underpinned his continuing career in politics, India, business and charitable work.[20]

Once out of aviation, Sykes aspired to enter politics. This decision no doubt resulted from the influence of his father-in-law, who had resolved to lead the Conservatives in the next General Election.[21] Because of Bonar Law's poor health, the Sykeses had not wanted to stray too far from England. An opportunity to serve the Empire in the House of Commons was the next best thing to serving in uniform, and it certainly provided another challenge for Sykes.

His other motives for entering the political arena involved a desire to promote the Conservative government and its program of reductions in bureaucratic growth, lower taxation and less government waste. Therefore Sykes' own political conservatism matched well with the Conservative ideology and platform, and he eagerly entered the race as a candidate for the Hallam Division of Sheffield. His campaign was an uphill struggle against the prevalent Socialist and Labour leanings in a blue-collar city such as Sheffield. He endured the ridicule and maintained his poise, arguing against indiscriminate public charity and for moderate protectionist trade policies. He maintained that lower taxes would boost employment and that the key to British prosperity and safety lay in Imperial co-operation. Aided by his knowledgeable and competitive campaign manager and a supportive organization of women, Sykes was able to defeat his opponent.[22] The Conservative Party won as well, so that Sykes was able to enter the House not as a freshman but as the son-in-law of the new Prime Minister.

The election was an important moral victory for Sykes. He had left the air service under bitter circumstances after years of dedicated service. With a calling to help the state and a personality which needed challenging adventures, Sykes needed new hope and a new horizon. The election bridged the gap from the past to the future.

Unfortunately for him, the great anticipations of a bright new beginning clouded over. Bonar Law was simply too ill to carry on. Sykes had the unpleasant task of delivering this news to the King, and shortly thereafter Stanley Baldwin was asked to replace Bonar Law as Prime Minister.[23] In addition, Sykes awakened to the realities of Commons procedures, which appeared 'unduly cumbrous' to a zealot of efficiency. He silently observed politics for a few months until in March 1923 a familiar subject surfaced. Sykes felt that he was perhaps the ultimate authority on the Air Estimates, and he now took advantage of a golden opportunity in the House to reaffirm the necessity for a unified fighting Air Force. Sykes condemned the one which Trenchard and the Air Minister Sir Samuel Hoare had created, saying that it was top-heavy and he emphasized the administrative and defensive advantages England could enjoy with a unified Ministry of Defence. After much debate, the House passed the Estimates, and Sykes had firmly established his reputation and ideology with his fellow Members of Parliament.

He might have assumed that finally he had snatched a small victory from the economic jaws that had defeated him in Civil Aviation, but the vote to re-create a defensive force of 52 squadrons was never fully implemented.[24] Over the next five years Sykes continued to sit on various sub-committees in the House of Commons and to work hard for Conservative and defense causes.[25] In journals and on the House floor he lashed out at the air service, noting how far it had diminished and how idle and over-staffed it had become when compared with the other services. Sykes wanted squadrons of aircraft and pilots to fly them, not new buildings.[26] He demanded more research, condemned the lack of government support for Civil Aviation, and published his opinions about the need for Imperial economic and defensive co-operation and the necessity for an effective Defence Ministry to deter potential aggressors. Sykes expected another European war and fought to help avert it.[27] Bureaucratic delays caused him great frustration, but he gained political maturity thereby. When the Second World War broke out ten years later, he was back in politics and blamed government inefficiency and short-sightedness for Britain's suffering at the hands of Hitler.

Sykes continued to embrace technology as a means to enhance the future of the Empire. He had seen how effective wireless communication had been in the war and, as chairman of the Broadcasting Board, he promoted radio broadcasting internationally and helped lay the groundwork for the British Broadcasting Corporation (BBC). Since he was sitting on several newspaper editorial boards at the same time, he naturally found himself at the heart of the debate between the radio and the newspaper industry. He had always stood against monopolies, but at the same time did not favor protectionism. Therefore Sykes tried to promote both industries, believing that there was room for both and that regulations for open competition and free enterprise would most benefit the country. He also worked to help to institute the first transatlantic wireless service, which the General Post Office and American Telephone and Telegraph completed in 1927.[28] To Sykes, this technological change was a monumental step in improving Imperial communications, since Canada would benefit from the service.

By the spring of 1928, Sykes had survived three elections without having to waver from his solid Conservatism; however, he needed a new quest. When the Secretary of State for India Lord Birkenhead offered Sykes the post of Governor of the Presidency of Bombay, he jumped at the chance to return to the land of his military roots. Sykes' enthusiasm did not blind him to the fact that India at the time was a hotbed of discontent and that he would be thrust into that turmoil and responsible for keeping Provincial peace.[29] Undaunted by the threat, Sykes entered another battlefield – this time with a wife and small son by his side.[30] They sailed for India in November 1928 aboard the mail steamer *Narkunda*.

Full of enthusiasm, and now a new member of the Privy Council, Sykes spoke like a crusader as he left England: 'We are glad to be allowed to take part in the great task of trying to help in India.'[31] He was confident that he could replace the successful and popular Governor Sir Leslie Wilson and eager to improve Indian prosperity and the standard of living.[32] 'In the widest sense he sought to maintain *Pax Britannica*, on which he believed British prosperity and world stability depended.'[33] The Governor's House on Malabar Point was opulent, and Sykes' duties included hosting and attending many gala events, including official obligations to associate with the Maharajahs.[34] His focus, however, remained on the Indian peasant.

Sykes' ambitions were too idealistic for the time. He spent most of his governorship quelling civil strife, not implementing progressive social changes. When he arrived in Bombay on 7 December 1928, he was greeted by a strike, a riot and murders.[35] Bombay was an industrial center with the best harbor in India, and it also was the heart of India's social upheaval. From Bombay M. K. Gandhi and Jawaharlal Nehru launched civil disobedience and the Youth Movement.[36] Sykes recognized Bombay as a testing ground for all of India and called it the 'trial of strength' between himself and anti-government forces.[37] He hoped that by maintaining a 'serene and friendly dignity', his mere presence would maintain peace.[38]

Thus Sykes had a battle before him that was no less dangerous than flying aircraft in war, and he approached the Indian crisis with the view that a military solution might be necessary. He ventured out into black flag demonstrations amid shouts of 'Frederick Sykes – Go Back', and he spoke of a better economic future where disenchanted youth could find employment. His visiting brother-in-law penned a vivid picture:

> There seems a kind of *Götterdämmerung* atmosphere about this place. The Princes and the British are the gods, and the nationalists Siegfried. Wotan begat Siegfried (or rather his parents) for the defense of Valhalha [*sic*]. So we have educated the Indians and they will bring us down as Siegfried brought down the gods. . . . I feel the sense of impending doom in the air. I can't help feeling that India is the battleground, not between East and West, but between the new and old world . . . there

are forces gathering here which will break out one day in fearful conflict the world over.[39]

To Sykes, the threat was real but impersonal. It was against the system; it was a product of social and political inefficiency that had caused economic distress.

Sykes had three major concerns: labor problems, commune agitation and Bombay's financial deficit. He wrote to the Viceroy Lord Irwin that he would cut expenses, face the labor extremists seriously and deal harshly with rioting and other violations of the law.[40] Irwin and Sykes had similar opinions of the Indian situation and worked well together. Sykes noted that civil disobedience was not the pacific movement its authors had intended.[41] Irwin expected 'being able to run a comprehensive conspiracy case against these men', and had decided to reintroduce helpful legislation in the form of a Public Safety Bill.[42] Sykes remained neutral in labor–owner antagonism, but he fought to prevent strikes and riots that inevitably ended in bloodshed.

He had political support, but the government he represented often exacerbated the hostility of his environment. Before Sykes' Governorship, the Simon Commission had created enemies throughout India, and seven days before Sykes arrived in Bombay police had beaten Nehru and his student followers for demonstrating against the Commission. As Governor, Sykes had the unpleasant task of trying to host the same Commission.[43] He tried to reduce its visibility and posted curfews and orders prohibiting assemblies of more than five people. Lord Peel, Secretary of State for India, was of the opinion that most of the Bombay rioting was due simply to a religious struggle between Hindus and Muslims.[44] At the focus of the unrest, however, Sykes disagreed. Economic decline had led to unsatisfied expectations and consequent public frustration in the form of terrorism caused by disenchanted workers and political revolutionaries. Regardless of the complex causes, Sykes had to answer to the government on the one hand and to himself on the other – for he still felt compelled to help India.

Sykes remembered the stalemate on the Western Front and tried to act swiftly, decisively and according to a plan of action in Bombay.[45] His political superiors, however, had no definitive answers to the civil unrest and Sykes had inadequate authority with which to carry out his responsibilities. Despite his constant pleas for effective laws and established procedures, he received only sympathetic apologies.[46]

Gandhi began his march of civil disobedience on 12 March 1930, and Sykes was convinced that the government could not treat him differently from any other Indian. Pinprick tactics without a publicly announced policy (strategy) would simply attest to Gandhi's success-ful influence.[47] The new Secretary of State, however, was eager to avert potential incidents, and he wrote to Sykes about the march:

> The enthusiasm caused at each stage of the journey seems to die down pretty rapidly when the Mahatma has passed on. If the whole escapade fizzles out in some ridiculous way, I shall be only too pleased and I devoutly hope that no strong measures will be required. The halo of martyrdom is obviously what he is after, and I hope it will be possible to avoid adorning him with it.[48]

Twenty days after the Secretary had written, communal riots broke out in Bombay and Calcutta. Gandhi was arrested on 4 May and by 2 December the Congress had been declared illegal. Sykes' problems had not 'fizzled out'.

Again he remembered the world war and looked to technology for an Indian solution. In the air service he had worked with wireless and later in Parliament he had promoted it as a way to link the Empire. He wrote to Irwin about establishing a wireless net across India to promote anti-Congress propaganda and to counterattack Gandhi's successful anti-government movement. By improving telephone communications, Sykes would enhance government security as well.[49] These measures could solve immediate problems as well as benefit India's long-term future.

Anti-government hostility remained and Sykes worked himself ill representing the government that was failing to support him.[50] Despite discomfort and warnings from doctors, he continued to work long hours until doctors ordered him home to London.[51] After delaying his departure until the turmoil over Gandhi had subsided temporarily, Sykes was replaced on 25 April 1931 by Sir Ernest Buttery Hotson, his senior Executive Council member.[52] By the time Sykes returned in November, the adjunct governor had had to be hospitalized through fatigue and stress.[53] Sykes now had a new Viceroy but was faced with the same old problems of civil unrest.[54]

Still abhoring an attritional battle, Sykes again stressed decisive action, even though he lacked government support. He wrote to the Viceroy:

> The point that I chiefly wish to emphasize is that if civil disobedience is to be resumed we must decide once and for all whether it is to be regarded as an all-India revolutionary movement intended to end the British Government in India: this is the declared aim of Mr Gandhi and the Congress itself, and does not appear to me to admit of serious doubt. That being so, I contend that our policy should be to declare war unequivocally upon the Congress, to take the offensive against it, and to adopt every possible measure to enable us to crush it in the shortest possible time.[55]

Sykes complained that the policy of remaining on the defensive had been unsuccessful, and he felt that they were doing India an injustice by not recognizing the enemy. As the ultimate governor of India, Britain had a moral obligation to create peace for Indians.[56]

Despite the fact that Indian social violence dissipated little during Sykes' tenure as Governor, he did accomplish some progressive reforms.[57] His *Manual for Village Improvement* established a long-term plan whereby Indians would organize administrative changes and the development of physical plant to improve the standard of living in the villages.[58] Sykes recognized the agricultural roots of the Indian economy, but he promoted efficiency and conservation within the agricultural industry to terminate the habitual practice of raping the land.[59] He supported the King Edward Memorial Hospital in Bombay as well as Bombay University, where he gave the commencement address as Chancellor in 1929.[60]

Sykes left the Bombay Governorship in 1933 with a mixed sense of failure and success. Although he had not been in military uniform as governor, he had returned to India as a soldier. He had fought another long battle in a thankless war. After five years Sykes' Indian adventure ended, but his love for the land and his affinity for the people remained with him for life. Whether in Ceylon, Quetta or Bombay, Sykes saw India as an important part of the Empire he was bound to serve and protect.

Sykes was now 57 years old and still full of zeal for new challenges. For the next 20 years he never stopped pushing himself – as politician, businessman, writer and land-owner. His public service far outweighed the private time he allotted to himself and his family. While society was busy forgetting the past, memories and lessons of war preoccupied his mind and compelled him to try to influence future events. British greatness was waning world-wide, and the threat of European war had emerged again. Sykes was convinced that he had the answers to these problems, if only someone would listen. He was haunted. He was driven. His prodigal Air Force had all but abandoned him and the country appeared as blind to his vision as it was plagued with bureaucracy. During these years Sykes called himself 'a voice crying in the wilderness', but he was too duty-bound to give up the noble effort.[61] He remained a recognized civic leader and former politician, but he slowly slipped into such obscurity that most flyers had never heard of him. Even many of his friends had no idea that he had once commanded the RAF. He was too proud to tell them.

Once back in England from India, Sykes filled his time with work in a variety of directorships. Most of these were in benevolent organizations such as the Miners' Welfare Commission and the British Sailors' Society. Mining and sailing both had elements as unfavorable as

India's social conditions and war's danger. Even when not at war, sailors lived a harsh life, and the annual death toll in the mines was 25,000. Sykes set out to improve the working conditions of miners in areas such as education, safety and cleanliness, and he helped to establish the first occupational training center for them. For Navy and merchant seamen he worked for improved facilities ashore. Sykes was a natural selection as Chairman of the Royal Empire Society in 1938, and in that capacity he traveled abroad to co-ordinate work with the Dominions, directing publication of the Society's journal as well as organizing speeches from dignitaries, such as Viscount Montgomery of Alamein, who spoke in 1947.[62] Montgomery demanded that his talk be strictly off the record as he wrote to Sykes, 'We do not want another war!!'[63] All his life Sykes had tried to enhance technology and link economies to bring together the Empire under common cause. He saw education as one key to that effort, and part of his campaign to wipe out Imperial 'placid ignorance' involved writing articles and making speeches, where he went so far as to suggest in 1939 that at least the war was finally helping to unite the Empire.

Sykes had warned of another potential war since November 1918. When Hitler's blitz hit London, Sykes and his staff at the Royal Empire Society were forced to run for cover. One person was killed and its new building was partly destroyed. Sykes was ready to serve again. At the outbreak of war, Sykes was 62 years old, but he enthusiastically caught the train to London to prepare his kit and to offer his services. The Air Ministry had notified Sykes to be 'in readiness'. He eagerly welcomed such a request from a part of his past, but the telegram was all he ever heard. He had been out of the air business for years, but he had strong ideas about air power and he knew war. The services, in their desperate situation, could have used a person with his experience and knowledge. Sykes was still a professional soldier at heart, and he needed to serve.

Sykes saw his opportunity back in politics and ran unopposed for the Central Division of Nottingham in 1940. In Parliament, Sykes remembered how lack of support from British society, industry and government had created his own critical predicaments during the previous war, and thus he fought strongly for the all-out effort against Hitler. Once again, he called for a supreme air force as the key to victory and constantly reminded his listeners and readers that he had been saying this for years.

Sykes also continued in his directorships and to write prolifically. The Royal Empire Society's Secretary described Sykes as 'a tower of strength to the staff . . . while he was at the helm all would be well and that difficulties however great would be overcome and wise decisions made by him.'[64] Sykes wrote articles for *The New English Review, The*

Times, the *Daily Telegraph* and *United Empire*, book reviews and forewords to books and his own work, *From Many Angles*.[65] Although he had intended to write an autobiography, he chose to write about what he considered was more important than the story of his life. His book is mainly a treatise on politics, economics, and defense – his personal opinions about the world situation and the Empire's responsibilities within it.

After the war Sykes remained consumed by the idea of a Commonwealth of English-speaking peoples and the qualities of life that he credited to the sacrifice of the Empire. He longed for a peaceful and tolerant world of liberty, Christian values and technological advancement. To achieve those objectives was the honorable quest, the 'Commonwealth challenge' he urged on his country, the Dominions and other English-speaking nations such as the United States.[66] As expressed eloquently by his son Bonar, 'Our [Britain's] demise as a great power, starting with the troubles of the twenties and ditherings of the thirties, and capped with the economic haemorrhaging of the post-war period, was a source of immense sadness to FHS – a sadness based on a noble vision, however faded and anachronistic.'[67] He maintained his vision and continued to work hard on various boards, including Atlas Electrical, Associated Commercial Vehicles and the Hong Kong and Shanghai Banking Corporation.[68] In retirement, he lived as he preached – a public servant. National sacrifice meant self-sacrifice.

Sykes never forgot his life as a soldier for the King and as a flyer with an infant air service. That service had cast him away as an unimportant remnant of the past: the RAF was Trenchard's legacy. The omission of Sykes was intended, obvious and successful. Sykes did not like the situation, but he learned to live with it and did not let it preoccupy his thoughts. Even in the privacy of his home he rarely reminisced about his days as a soldier.

Sykes' last years were spent in the country where he sought relief from hectic London and desired to work the earth. He had always abhorred the idea of debt and had saved for years to be able to purchase a farm. He bought one with an impressive manor house near Devizes. The previous owner had been another famous flyer R. R. Smith-Barry, whose name has been linked to the first progressive flying training program.[69] On Salisbury Plain, Conock Manor was not far from the aerodromes Sykes had created and commanded 40 years earlier. Many times he had flown over the soil he now owned. He felt at home.

Sykes' fervor for work never ebbed. He had always believed that hard effort deserved rewards and had never had much patience with laziness. In his last days he still inspected the gardeners' labors and criticized when he thought it was justified.[70] Sykes had been a man compelled to complete a task, even if that meant going without sleep. Despite Isabel's pleas to relax, he had a daily agenda and drove himself to keep it.[71] He liked poetry but rarely read a book for pleasure. Fishing was a bore and golf a waste of time. Earlier in life Sykes had played some tennis and had enjoyed shooting when it was popular, but now he had lost interest in both and had sold his guns. His work was his pleasure.

Sykes had preferred French when departing, and he bid his final *au revoir* to this world and to his Air Force in September 1954. He was not a young man, but he had lived and worked as one all his life. Although he had suffered two heart attacks, he had continued to raise a courageous smile and had attended to the work at Conock Manor. His closest friends agreed that Sykie could not have enjoyed life at a slower pace, and they were grateful that his passing went quickly.[72]

During his life of adventure, Sykes had scored impressive achievements. His awards and honors were many (see Appendices),[73] yet the one recognition that would have meant more to him than all the others combined never came: Sykes died knowing the air service had forgotten his accomplishments in the RFC and the RAF. Too modest to promote himself, he accepted his fate graciously.[74] Even though Sykes appreciated accolades he had never sought them. 'Surely no great man ever assumed so little.'[75]

NOTES

1. Trenchard telegram, 15 November 1918, Air 1/18/15/1/94. Schroeder, 213, mentioned that peace is for politicians, whereas armistice is the business of soldiers and does not necessarily imply peace. 11 November 1918 did not pacify Sykes, and during the Second World War he condemned British complacency that had failed to build up an Imperial Air Force to prevent the next war. See Sykes, *From Many Angles*, 3.
2. There is a sound argument that Sykes did not properly understand defensive aerial requirements. In analyzing Sykes' proposed RAF scheme in 'Air Power Requirements of the Empire', Mason notes: 'In other words, Sykes' Royal Air Force would have been prepared to implement an immediate bomber offensive, but not to withstand one.' See Mason, 40. On the other hand, there is a sound argument that Sykes wanted a defensive via the deterrent strength of a credible offensive force and saw more air power in the counter-offensive than an aerial defensive.
3. Sykes Papers, MFC 77/13/80. No doubt Churchill had decided that Trenchard was more politically in tune, and perhaps more militarily realistic as well (see previous note). To accept his appointment as CGCA on 26 May 1919 Sykes had to resign from the RAF. His resignation was effective from 1 April 1919, the birthday of the RAF. He was offered a three-year term at £2,500 a year, £500 of which was retirement pay from the RAF. Historians have suggested that

Churchill 'banished' Sykes from the RAF at this point; however, the former Air
Minister Lord Weir and Sykes had already discussed the option of Sykes' linkage
to civil aviation. Sykes clearly felt at this point that civil aviation, not service
aviation, was the future for flying. Sykes, of course, wanted to head both departments.

4. Churchill to Sykes, 9 February 1919, Churchill Papers, 16/4/73, Churchill
   College, Cambridge.
5. Interview with International News Service representative, Sykes Papers, MFC
   77/13/81; and Memorandum on long-distance flying, Sykes Papers, MFC
   77/13/84.
6. Sykes Papers, MFC 77/13/85. On 26 August 1919 the King appointed Sykes
   Knight Grand Cross of the Order of the British Empire.
7. Waterhouse, 170; and newspaper clippings, Sykes Papers, MFC 77/13/77.
8. Speech to the Australian and New Zealand Luncheon Club, Sykes Private Papers.
   Sykes told the club chairman Major-General Sir Newton Moore that he would be
   able to fly to Australia in five to six days, a virtual impossibility at the time.
9. Articles published in *Army Review*, *The Empire Review*, *Edinburgh Review*, *The
   English Review* and *Journal of the Royal Aeronautical Society*, 1922 to 1926, Sykes
   Private Papers.
10. Sykes, *From Many Angles*, 4–6. Sykes looked back upon Wilson's SWC and the
    Lloyd George War Cabinet as prime examples of efficient and effective systems.
11. Sykes, 'Imperial Defence and the Air', *The Empire Review*, 26 (April 1923),
    309–25. Sykes complained of interservice friction, money wasted on unnecessary
    facilities and instructors who did not teach. His solution was 'a correlation of
    defense policy, Home and Imperial', which could only be carried out by a radical
    amalgamation – a Ministry of Defence.
12. Speech to the Royal Aeronautical Society, December 1923, Sykes Private Papers.
13. 'W' (probably Weir) to Law, 6 April 1920, Bonar Law Papers, 103/5/4, House of
    Lords Record Office. He wrote to Law about his charming daughter and
    mentioned, 'she is marrying a right good fellow . . . [with] a big future before
    him'.
14. Bonar Sykes letter, 19 December 1995.
15. Society columns in *The Bystander*, 9 June 1920, 810 and *Daily Mirror*, 4 June
    1920, Sykes Private Papers.
16. Ibid.
17. News clippings, Sykes Private Papers. As a wedding present, a friend had
    arranged for them to stay at Lindisfarne Castle on Holy Island, off the coast of
    Northumberland.
18. William Sarum (Bishop of Salisbury) to Lady Sykes, 3 October 1954, Sykes
    Private Papers. Sykes was from a Unitarian background, but was not a practicing
    member. Isabel was raised a Presbyterian but became an Anglican. Although from
    different religious backgrounds, they worshiped together regularly, usually in
    Anglican churches. The Bishop of Salisbury mentioned that Sykes had been one
    of the most distinguished members of the Diocese, but also mentioned that he did
    not know Lady Sykes.
19. Interview with Bonar Sykes, 20 April 1994.
20. Bonar Law Papers, 12/2/47. In February 1923 the Prime Minister's friends were
    trying to find Sykes employment, in this case with the Phoenix Assurance
    Company. Through friends such as Lord Beaverbrook, Sykes joined newspaper
    boards and also obtained directorships of several transport companies, including
    Underground Electric Railways.
21. Sykes, *From Many Angles*, 305–9. The coalition government of Lloyd George and
    Bonar Law had been a sufficient compromise during the war, but now the

Conservatives decided to do political battle alone. The election took place on 25 November 1922.

22. Ibid. Sykes' electoral victory over a London barrister was by a margin of 4,232 votes.

23. Bonar Law was diagnosed with throat cancer in May and died on 30 October 1923.

24. See Graham T. Allison, *Essence of Decision* (Boston, MA: Little, Brown, 1971), 89. Allison notes how the implementation stage of politics can hamper decision-making. Also, Sykes, *From Many Angles*, 312–16. According to Sykes, Baldwin had demanded that the new program be completed 'with as little delay as possible.' In political vernacular, that turned out to be 12 years.

25. Sykes, *From Many Angles*, 319. Sykes worked with the Salisbury Commission on Imperial and National Defence; the Capital Ships Committee; the Imperial Communications Committee, where he was vice-chairman; the Wireless Sub-Committee as chairman; the Colwyn Committee on National Economy; a committee on public drinking houses that experimented with schemes to reduce drunkenness in society; and the Broadcasting Committee as chairman.

26. Sykes, 'Air Power and Policy', *The Edinburgh Review*, October 1925, 386. Sykes noted that flying was down to less than 0.5 hours per pilot per week. The Air Ministry had 50 employees for every aircraft, requiring 1,200 man-hours per hour of flight. He claimed that the Air Council had built up its size just to appear weighty when compared with the Admiralty and the War Office.

27. Sykes, 'Reduction of Armaments, Economy and Imperial Defense', *Army Quarterly* (April 1926), 13–28. He attacked the Air Minister's ideas, stating they did not need arbitration between the services, but rather amalgamation. Also, Sykes, 'Air Problems of the Empire', *The Edinburgh Review* (October 1926), 264–75; and Sykes, 'Air Power and Policy', 380–94.

28. Sykes, *From Many Angles*, 330.

29. In addition to ill feelings in India left over from the India Act of 1919, economic depression as well as ethnic and religious strife fueled social distress. Sir John Simon's Parliamentary Commission had recently arrived in India to study the failures of social reforms, but continual hostility hampered its work.

30. Sykes to Irwin (no date), Miss Eur F 150/3(b)/222, the British Library, Oriental and India Office Collections. Young Bonar Sykes remained in India from 1928 to 1931, at which time he was sent, in accordance with the normal customs of the time, to a preparatory boarding school at the age of eight and then on to Eton, where he detested the 'horrible collars'.

31. Undated and untitled news clipping, Sykes Private Papers.

32. H. C. Beere to Sykes, 14 May 1943, Sykes Private Papers. Against a prevalent world suspicion of British imperialism, Sykes wrote in *From Many Angles*, 53, that British accomplishments were quickly forgotten. They had wiped out small-pox, plague, cholera and other diseases; they had stopped famines, reduced child mortality and instituted peace.

33. Bonar Sykes letter, 19 December 1995.

34. 'Bombay Years' notes, Sykes Private Papers. Sykes described royal balls and banquets, official ceremonies and yacht racing, but he said that the rumor of Governors leaving India loaded with wealth was unsound. British law forbade his accepting gifts.

35. Irwin to Sykes, 15 December 1928, Miss Eur F.150/1.

36. 'Bombay Years' notes, Sykes Private Papers. Gandhi initiated civil disobedience from his home in the Bombay Presidency, at the ashram at Ahmedabad in Gujerat.

37. Sykes to Irwin, 26 January 1929, Miss Eur F.150/1.

38. He recalled his instruction at Quetta – that the loss of British military presence in India due to the Crimean conflict in the 1850s had led to the Indian Mutiny.
39. 'Bombay Years' notes, Sykes Private Papers.
40. Sykes to Irwin, 29 December 1928, and Irwin to Sykes 2 January 1929, Miss Eur F.150/1. Sykes wrote that the agitators were 'quite definitely out for trouble, and that we ought to seize the first and every opportunity of prosecution and of checking them in any way that may suggest itself'. Lord Irwin, who was Edward Frederick Lindley Wood, 1st Earl of Halifax and 1st Baron Irwin, said that the public would support any strong action Sykes took: 'take whatever steps you can to ensure protection being given to Labour wishing to work and so on.'
41. Sykes to Irwin, 5 February 1929, Miss Eur F.150/1. Owing to the deaths of ten people and many more injuries, Sykes cancelled a trip to Delhi to meet Irwin. He wrote the next day as well, 'Situation in Bombay is very serious, and Bombay Government consider it may be necessary at any moment to deal with Communist agitators.' He mentioned his authority under Regulation XXV of 1829, and on 10 February 1929 Irwin sanctioned the use of that regulation. Sykes wrote to the Secretary of State for India William Robert Wellesley Peel, 1st Earl Peel, on 10 February 1929, that the total casualties to date were 112 killed and 400 injured.
42. Irwin to Sykes, 18 January 1929, Miss Eur F.150/1. Irwin wanted a stronger police force and more power to convict. The Viceroy asked for Sykes' opinion regarding how to get better respect for ordinary law.
43. Sykes to Irwin, 7 February 1929; and Sykes to Peel, 6 March 1929, Miss Eur F.150/1. Sykes agreed that the agitators would achieve victory if the Simon Commission stopped passing through Bombay, but he also urged that their visits should be less 'official'. Peel agreed that the Commission should just pass through, going straight from the train to the ship. Also, Secretary of State Wedgwood Benn to Sykes, February 1931, Miss Eur F.150/3(a)/38.
44. Secretary of State of India (Peel) to Sykes, 8 February 1929, Miss Eur F.150/1.
45. Sykes to Irwin, 2 August 1929, Miss Eur F.150/1. He tried to get the Legislative Council to pass four Law and Order Bills: an Intimidation Act, a Security Act, a Picketing Act and a Land Revenue Bill.
46. Peel to Sykes, 21 February 1929, Miss Eur F.150/1. The Secretary of State apologized for Sykes' predicament and his inadequate support due to revenue problems. On 8 February he had said that he was glad such a good man as Sykes was there to handle such a difficult situation.
47. Miss Eur F.150/2. Sykes discussed civil disobedience with Irwin.
48. Wedgwood Benn to Sykes, 20 March 1930, Miss Eur F.150/2. William Wedgwood Benn, 1st Viscount Stansgate, replaced Peel as Secretary of State in 1929.
49. Sykes to Irwin, 23 March 1930, Miss Eur F.150/2. By 1932 the Secretary of State Samuel Hoare was praising Sykes for establishing wireless and effectively publicizing government information. Also, Hoare to Sykes, 9 September 1932, Miss Eur F.150/4(b)/252. Samuel John Gurney Hoare, 1st Viscount Templewood, became Secretary of State for India in 1931 and served in that capacity until 1935. This was the same man that Sykes had criticized in the House of Commons when Hoare had been Air Minister.
50. Miss Eur F.150/3(a)/38.
51. Sykes to Irwin, 5 April 1931, Miss Eur F.150/3(b)/143. Sykes was suffering from a duodenal ulcer and had been told to rest for three months.
52. *Who Was Who 1900–1980, Eminent Indians* (New Delhi: Durga Das, 1985), 384. While Sykes was away, an attempt was made on the substitute Governor's life, but a breast-pocket button prevented the bullet from carrying out its job.
53. Sykes to Irwin (no date), Miss Eur F.150/3(b)/222.

54. Freeman Freeman-Thomas, 1st Marquis of Willingdon, who as Viceroy actually assumed his position eight days before Sykes left for England.
55. Sykes to Willingdon, 14 December 1931, Miss Eur F.150/3(b)/229. Sykes' outburst was in response to a letter Lord Willingdon had sent to Sykes on 26 November 1931, where the former Bombay Governor and now Viceroy had condescendingly chastised Sykes' desire for additional powers and a program to deal with civil disobedience. Whereas Sykes wanted the extraordinary powers of a specific law to deal with a specific problem, Willingdon felt that each situation was too unique for that and wanted to handle all the incidents under ordinary law. Also, Miss Eur F.150/3(b)/210.
56. Miss Eur F.150/3(b)/229.
57. Miss Eur F.150/4(b)/207 and Miss Eur F.150 4(c). In open defiance of the police, there was serious rioting in Bombay in May, June and July of 1932, and Gandhi was still posing problems for Sykes during the winter of 1932–33.
58. Sykes, *Manual of Village Improvement* (Bombay: Government Central Press, 1933), 14–20. His systematic approach sounds like a modern Total Quality Management scheme. His main objectives were for better housing and public health to include sanitation and disease control. He promoted education, farming and industry, and a reduction in litigation that was hampering progress in nearly every area.
59. Sykes, 'Manual of Instructions for Government Officers in Connection with the Village Improvement Scheme', 39. In particular, Sykes strove to terminate deforestation, and local reaction to his program was 'overwhelmingly favourable'.
60. Sir Vithal N. Chandavakar to Lady Sykes, 4 October 1954, Sykes Private Papers.
61. ? to Lady Sykes, 1954, Sykes Private Papers. To this friend, Sykes' was the 'life nobly lived'.
62. Guden J. Jones to Isabel, 11 October 1954, Sykes Private Papers.
63. Montgomery to Sykes, 7 November 1947, Sykes Private Papers.
64. Gertrude Holloway to Lady Sykes, 30 September 1954, Sykes Private Papers.
65. Sykes, 'The Indian Political Situation', *The New English Review* (July 1945), 220–8.
66. Sykes had traveled to the USA and Canada before the war and had given informal speeches in both countries to support a united cause against repression. His unpublished 'Commonwealth Challenge' was a variation upon the theme he had created ten years earlier in works such as *From Many Angles* and 'Roads to Recovery'. Sykes saw the historical process as progress via economic, political and industrial power. It was the burden of the English-speaking peoples to carry on that progressive endeavor for the world. 'Commonwealth Challenge', 2–3, Sykes Private Papers.
67. Bonar Sykes letter, 19 December 1995.
68. A. Morse to Isabel (no date), Sykes Private Papers. Also, White to Lady Sykes, 9 October 1954, Sykes Private Papers. Thomas White, the High Commissioner for Australia, wrote that Sykes 'had such a rare quality of modesty which led to his achievements being less known than their great merit deserved'.
69. Maj. Archibald James, sound recording, Reel No. 6, IWM sound recordings. James stated that the big change in flying training came when the Irishman (Smith-Barry) figured out how to control a spin. Then it became a maneuver rather than certain death. The Sykes family still owns Conock Manor, where Bonar Sykes and his wife Mary now live. Smith-Barry had made improvements to the impressive eighteenth-century structure, and Sykes continued to improve upon the manor and the surrounding facilities. Locals remember Smith-Barry's using a shed in a nearby field to protect an aircraft in which he would give rides for sixpence each. He also used the machine to fly across the valley to rendezvous with

female friends. The shed still stands, as does an impressive carriage house. In its clock tower is a note tacked to the wall next to the clockworks. Smith-Barry had written in 1941: 'Placing one penny on the weight arm makes clock gain 6 seconds in a week.'

70. Interview with Bonar Sykes, 21 April 1994. Also, Margaret R. Akehurst (?) to Lady Sykes, 1 October 1954, Sykes Private Papers. She mentioned 'his sometimes despairingly stern judgements when other people's views and actions did not come up to his high standards!'

71. Instructions to hired hands, Sykes Private Papers. In September 1954 Sykes was busy tearing out trees, repairing cottages and replacing fencing. Also, A. Eland to Sykes, 15 April 1943, Sykes Private Papers. This friend, mentioning Sykes' devotion to whatever task was at hand, wrote that while Sykes was from many angles, he was 'but from one plane'.

72. Lord Blake to Isabel, 2 October 1954, Sykes Private Papers.

73. *Gazette Telegraph* listing of award recipients, Groves Papers, 69/34/1, IWM. Sykes, Brancker and John Salmond were inducted into the Order of the Bath at the same time, 1 January 1919. Trenchard, however, was not listed, and he openly resented the fact that Sykes got his KCB and GBE. Most of Sykes' decorations are on display at the Royal Air Force Museum, Hendon (see Appendices).

74. Lord Limerick to Lady Sykes, 3 October 1954, Sykes Private Papers. Many of Sykes' friends did not accept his lack of recognition. This friend from Parliament wrote, 'we – and no doubt a great number of others – had always felt that Sykie had never received the patriotic recognition that was his due'. He said that Sykes was too big to make anything of it, however.

75. George Lyttelton (Bonar Sykes' Housemaster at Eton) to Isabel, 5 October 1954, Sykes Private Papers. Words written by the housemaster at Eton. Lady Sykes received hundreds of condolences, many from distinguished friends. Viscount Weir wrote of 'my old friend', but the only senior airman to write was Arthur Longmore.

Appendices

Privy Council (PC) 1928
Knight Grand Commander of the Order of the Star of India (GCSI) 1934
Knight Grand Commander of the Order of the Indian Empire (GCIE) 1928
Knight Grand Cross of the Order of the British Empire (GBE) 1919
Knight Commander of the Order of the Bath (KCB) 1919
Companion of the Order of St Michael and St George (CMG) 1916
Knight of Justice of the Order of St John of Jerusalem (KJStJ) 1936
(Severely wounded) Queen's medal with 4 clasps 1901
Mentioned in dispatches five times
Ritter Kreuz (Germany) 1902
Croix de Comdr de la Légion d'Honneur (France) 1919
Croix de Comdr de L'Ordre de Léopold (Belgium) 1919
Order of St Vladimir (Russia) 1916
Distinguished Service Medal (DSM) (USA) 1919
Order of the Rising Sun (Japan) 1921
Grand Cross of the Order of the Lion (Persia) (date unknown)

APPENDIX 2: RECORD OF MILITARY SERVICE

Enrolled in Imperial Yeomanry Scouts, Irregular Forces, South Africa, Trooper No. 6060	26 March 1900
Discharged due to disbandment of unit	28 August 1900
Commissioned Lieutenant in Commander in Chief's Bodyguard, South Africa	9 November 1900
Discharged due to hospitalization and convalescence from wounds received in battle	6 March 1901
Commissioned 2nd Lieutenant, 15th Hussars, India	2 October 1901
Attached to West African Regiment	7 March 1903–21 September 1904
Promoted Lieutenant, 15th Hussars	29 July 1903
Promoted Captain, 15th Hussars	1 October 1908
Assigned General Staff Officer, 3rd Grade, War Office, London	25 February 1908–12 May 1912
Assigned Commander, Military Wing, Royal Flying Corps, and promoted to Temporary Major	13 May 1912
Promoted to Temporary Lieutenant-Colonel, 15th Hussars	9 July 1913
Assigned General Staff Officer, 1st Grade, attached to Royal Flying Corps in the field	5 August 1914
Assigned Wing Commander, Royal Flying Corps	22 November 1914
Reassigned General Staff Officer, 1st Grade, retaining rank of Temporary Lieutenant-Colonel	21 December 1914
Assigned Wing Commander, Royal Flying Corps	26 May 1915
Commissioned Colonel and 2nd Commandant, Royal Marines; also promoted to temporary Wing Captain, Royal Naval Air Service, Dardanelles	24 July 1915
Commission and appointment to Royal Marines and Royal Naval Air Service terminated	14 March 1916
Assigned Adjutant and Quartermaster-General, 4th Mounted Division, Colchester, Essex	27 March 1916
Assigned Temporary Assistant Adjutant General, War Office	9 June 1916
Promoted Temporary Brigadier General	8 February 1917
Assigned Director of Armaments and Quartermaster-General, War Office	27 November 1917
Resigned commission in Regular Army; Commissioned Major-General in the Royal Air Force as Chief of Air Staff	12 April 1918
Resigned regular commission and retired on retired pay from Royal Air Force	1 April 1919

APPENDIX 3: MAPS AND DOCUMENTS

SALVAGE ATT^{MT.} ETC.

GRAPNEL

Source: Balloon School Diary

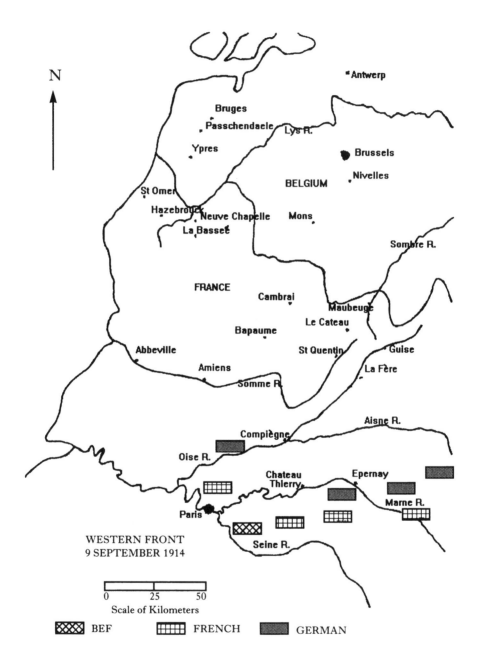

N

WESTERN FRONT
9 SEPTEMBER 1914

0   25   50
Scale of Kilometers

BEF   FRENCH   GERMAN

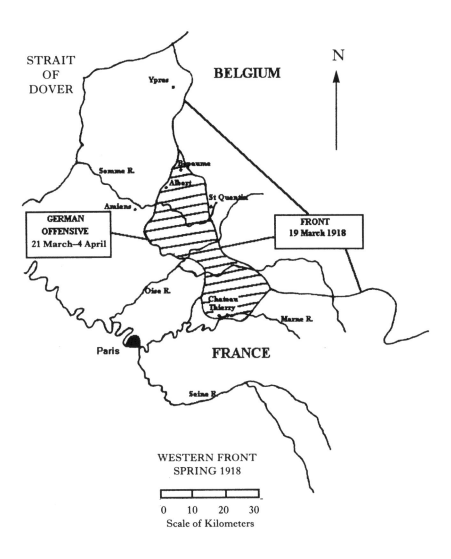

STRAIT
OF
DOVER

BELGIUM

N

Ypres

Somme R.

Bapaume

Albert

Amiens

St Quentin

GERMAN
OFFENSIVE
21 March–4 April

FRONT
19 March 1918

Oise R.

Chateau
Thierry

Marne R.

Paris

FRANCE

Seine R.

WESTERN FRONT
SPRING 1918

0   10   20   30

Scale of Kilometers

N

TURKEY

Gulf of Xeros

Samothrace

AEGEAN

SEA

Gallipoli

Salt Lake

Suvla
Bay

Chocolate
Hill

Anzac
Cove

Kephalos

Imbros

Helles

Lemnos

Tenedos

Mudros

GALLIPOLI PENINSULA
1915

0   10   20   30
Scale of Kilometers

Select Bibliography

UNPUBLISHED SOURCES

1. British Library, Oriental and India Office Collections, London
    Right Honourable Sir Frederick Sykes Papers
2. Bundesarchiv-Militärarchiv, Kriegsgeschichtliche Forschungsanstalt des
    Heeres, Freiburg
    General Oskar von Hutier Diary (Tagebuch v. Hutier, W-10/50640)
    General Hermann von Kuhl Diary (Tagebuch v. Kuhl, W-10/50652)
3. Churchill College, Cambridge
    1st Viscount Weir of Eastwood Papers
    Sir Winston Churchill Papers (Chartwell Collection)
4. Conock Manor, Devizes
    Sykes Private Papers
5. House of Lords Record Office, London
    Right Honourable David Lloyd George Papers
    Right Honourable Andrew Bonar Law Papers
6. Imperial War Museum (IWM), London
    Air Marshal Sir W. Sefton Brancker Papers
    Brigadier-General Percy Robert Clifford Groves Papers
    Field Marshal Sir Henry Wilson Papers
    Sound Records Archive
7. National Maritime Museum (NMM), Greenwich, London
    Admiralty letters, ADL 2
8. Public Record Office, Kew, London
    Admiralty Files, Adm 1 and 116
    Air Files, Air 1-9 and 19
    Cabinet Files, CAB 14, 16, 17, 19, 22, 23, 24, 25, 28, 29, 37, 38, and 45
    War Office Files, WO 32, 95, 106, 144, 153, 155, 157, 158, and 159
    Field Marshal Lord Kitchener Papers, PRO 30/57
9. Royal Air Force Museum, Hendon, London
    Miscellaneous Air Documents
    Moore-Brabazon, Lord Brabazon of Tara Papers
    Lieutenant-General Sir David Henderson Papers
    Air Chief Marshal Sir Cyril Newall Papers
    Marshal of the RAF Sir John Salmond Papers
    Sykes Papers
    Sykes Restricted Papers
    Marshal of the RAF Viscount Trenchard Papers

10. Royal Aeronautical Society, London
    Miscellaneous Air Documents
11. University of London, King's College, Liddell Hart Centre for Military
    Archives
    Air Chief Marshal Sir Henry R. M. Brooke-Popham Papers
    Major-General Sir Thomas Capper Papers
    Major-General Sir John E. Capper Papers
    Brigadier General P. R. C. Groves Papers
    General Sir Ian Hamilton Papers
    Lieutenant-General Sir Launcelot Kiggell Papers
    John Walter E. D. S. Montagu, 2nd Lord Montagu of Beaulieu Papers
12. Personal Interviews:
    Lord Blake
    Bonar Sykes
    Mary Sykes
    Officers at the RAF Staff College, Bracknell, Berkshire

PRINTED SOURCES

Air Force Manual 1–1, Basic Aerospace Doctrine of the United States Air Force, Washington, DC: Department of the Air Force, 1992.

Air Publications, RAFM

Air Pub 3, 'Instructions (transitional) to units as to their Accounting
    Procedure on the occasion of transfer to the Air Force'
Air Pub 7, 'Provisional Instructions Regarding Non-Technical Supplies and
    Services'
Air Pub 15, 'Quartering Instructions'
Air Pub 28, 'Wireless Stations'
Air Pub 38, 'Notes on Aerial Fighting'
Air Pub 72, 'Hints for Flyers'
Air Pubs 137 and 138, 'RAF Pay'
Air Pub 139, 'Royal Air Force Terms and Conditions of Service'
Air Pub 141, 'King's Regulations and Orders for the RAF, 1918'
Air Pub 143, 'Training Manual, Royal Flying Corps, Part I'
Air Pub 144, 'Training Manual, Royal Flying Corps, Part II'
Air Pub 156, 'Syllabus for a Six Weeks' Course at Schools of Aeronautics'
Air Pub 211, 'Demobilization Regulations for the Royal Air Force'
Air Pub 235, 'Notes for Equipment Officers, Mechanical Transport'
Air Pub 242, 'Notes on Aerial Bombing, Parts II and III'
Air Pub 381, 'Offence versus Defence in the Air'
Air Pub 956, 'Lectures and Essays from RAF Staff College'

Other Printed Sources

Henderson, David, *The Art of Reconnaissance*, 3rd edn, London: John Murray, 1914.

Murray, Archibald, 'Notes on Aerial Reconnaissance', BEF General Staff, 1915.

RAF Staff College 2nd Course, 'Development of Aeroplane Co-operation with the Army during the War', RAFM, Accession No. C/5/1/1.

Ranft, B. M., ed., *The Beatty Papers*, Vol. 1, London: Naval Records Society, 1989.

Roskill, S. W., ed., *Documents Relating to the Naval Air Service*, Vol. I, London: Navy Records Society, 1969.

Royal Aero Club Year Book 1915–16, London: Royal Aero Club of the United Kingdom, 1916.

Royal Air Force Communiqués 1918, ed. Christopher Cole, London: Tom Donovan, 1990.

Sykes, Frederick H., *Military Handbook of General Information on India*, Simla: Intelligence Branch, 1908.

Sykes, Frederick H., *Aviation in Peace and War*, London: Edward Arnold, 1922.

Sykes, Frederick H., 'Air Defence', *The Edinburgh Review*, 482 (1922): 209–27.

Sykes, Frederick H., 'Imperial Defence and the Air', *The Empire Review*, Vol. 37 (April 1923): 309–25.

Sykes, Frederick H., 'Some Aspects of Aeronautical Progress', *Journal of the Royal Aeronautical Society* (December 1923).

Sykes, Frederick H., 'Air Power and Policy', *The Edinburgh Review*, 242 (1925): 380–94.

Sykes, Frederick H., 'Air Problems of the Empire', *The Edinburgh Review*, 244 (1926): 264–75.

Sykes, Frederick H., 'Reduction of Armaments, Economy, and Imperial Defence', *Army Quarterly*, Vol. 13 (April 1926): 13–28.

Sykes, Frederick H., *Manual of Instructions for Government Officers in Connection with the Village Improvement Scheme*, Bombay: Government Central Press, 1933.

Sykes, Frederick H., *Manual of Village Improvement*, Bombay: Government Central Press, 1933.

Sykes, Frederick H., *From Many Angles: An Autobiography by Major-General the Right Hon. Sir Frederick Sykes*, London: Harrap, 1942.

Periodicals and Newspapers

The Aero
The Army Quarterly
Aeronautical Journal
Army Review
The Bystander
Daily Mail

Daily Mirror
Daily Telegraph
Edinburgh Review
The Empire Review
The English Review
Flight
London Gazette
Morning Post
The Quarterly Review
Sunday Express
The Times

Secondary Sources

Addington, Larry H., *The Patterns of War since the Eighteenth Century*, Bloomington: Indiana University Press, 1984.

Allen, H. R., *The Legacy of Lord Trenchard*, London: Cassell, 1972.

Allison, Graham T., *Essence of Decision*, Boston, MA: Little, Brown, 1971.

Arendt, Hannah., *On Revolution*, New York: Viking, 1963.

Arthur, Max, *There Shall be Wings: The RAF from 1918 to the Present*, London: Hodder & Stoughton, 1993.

Baring, Maurice, *Flying Corps Headquarters 1914–1918*, London: Blackwood, 1968.

Beaverbrook, Lord (Max Aitken), *Men and Power 1917–1918*, London: Hutchinson, 1956.

Bickers, Richard Townshend, *The First Great Air War*, London: Hodder & Stoughton, 1988.

Bidwell, Shelford and Graham, Dominick, *Fire Power: British Army Weapons and Theories of War 1904–1945*, London: Allen & Unwin, 1982.

Blake, Robert, 'Frederick H. Sykes', *Dictionary of National Biography 1951–1960*, ed. E. T. Williams and Helen M. Palmer, London: Oxford University Press, 1971, 948–50.

Blake, Robert R. and Mouton, Jane S., *The Managerial Grid*, Houston, TX: Gulf Publishing, 1964.

Bowyer, Chaz, *RAF Operations 1918–1938*, London: William Kimber, 1988.

Boyle, Andrew, *Trenchard*, London: Collins, 1962.

Brinton, Crane, *The Anatomy of Revolution*, New York: Vintage, 1960.

Bruce, J. M., *The Aeroplanes of the Royal Flying Corps*, London: Putnam, 1982.

Callwell, C. E., *Field Marshal Sir Henry Wilson: His Life and Diaries*, 2 vols, London: Cassell, 1927.

Calvert, Peter, *Revolution*, New York: Praeger, 1970.

Chamier, J. A., *The Birth of the Royal Air Force*, London: Isaac Pitman, 1943.

Chisholm, Cecil, *Sir John French: An Authentic Biography*, London: Herbert Jenkins, 1915.

Close, David and Bridge, Carl (eds), *Revolution: A History of the Idea*, London: Croom Helm, 1985.

Cole, Christopher (ed.), *Royal Air Force Communiqués 1918*, London: Tom Donovan, 1990.

Cole, Christopher and Cheesman, E. F., *The Air Defence of Britain 1914–1918*, London: Putnam, 1984.

Collier, Basil, *A History of Air Power*, London: Weidenfeld & Nicolson, 1974.

Cooper, Malcolm, 'A House Divided: Policy, Rivalry and Administration in Britain's Military Air Command 1914–1918', *Journal of Strategic Studies*, 3 (September 1980): 178–201.

Cooper, Malcolm, *The Birth of Independent Air Power*, London: Allen & Unwin, 1986.

Corum, James S., *The Roots of Blitzkrieg: Hans Von Seeckt and German Military Reform*, Lawrence: University Press of Kansas, 1992.

Dean, Maurice, *The Royal Air Force and Two World Wars*, London: Cassell, 1979.

de la Ferté, Philip Joubert, *The Third Service: The Story behind the Royal Air Force*, London: Thames & Hudson, 1955.

Divine, David, *The Broken Wing*, London: Hutchinson, 1966.

Donne, Michael and Fowler, Cynthia, *Per Ardua ad Astra: Seventy Years of the RFC and the RAF*, London: Frederick Muller, 1982.

Douglas, W. A. B., *The Creation of a National Air Force: The Official History of the Royal Canadian Air Force*, Vol. 2, Toronto: University of Toronto Press, 1986.

Douhet, Giulio, *The Command of the Air*, New York: Arno Press, 1972.

Escott, Beryl E., *Women in Air Force Blue: The Story of Women in the Royal Air Force from 1918 to the Present*, London: Patrick Stephens, 1989.

Ferris, John Robert, *Men, Money, and Diplomacy: The Evolution of British Strategic Policy, 1919–1926*, Ithaca, NY: Cornell University Press, 1989.

Fuller, J. F. C., *Armament and History*, New York: Charles Scribner's, 1945.

Futrell, Robert F., *Ideas, Concepts, Doctrine: Basic Thinking in the United States Air Force 1907–1960*, 2 vols, Maxwell Air Force Base: Air University Press, 1989.

Gamble, C. F. Snowden, *The Air Weapon, Being an Account of the Growth of British Military Aeronautics from the Beginnings in the Year 1783 until the end of the year 1929*, Vol. 1, London: Oxford University Press, 1931.

Gilbert, Martin, *Winston S. Churchill*, Vol. 4, London: Heinemann, 1977.

Gilbert, Martin, *First World War*, London: Weidenfeld & Nicolson, 1994.

Gollin, Alfred, *The Impact of Air Power on the British People and Their Government, 1909–14*, London: Macmillan, 1989.

Groves, P. R. C., *Behind the Smoke Screen*, London: Faber & Faber, 1934.

Hallion, Richard P., *Rise of the Fighter Aircraft 1914–1918*, Annapolis, MD: Nautical & Aviation Publishing Co., 1984.

Halpern, Paul G. (ed.), *The Royal Navy in the Mediterranean 1915–1918*, London: Royal Navy Records Society, 1987.

Higham, Robin, *The Military Intellectuals in Britain: 1918–1939*, New Brunswick, NJ: Rutgers University Press, 1966.

Higham, Robin, *Air Power: A Concise History*, London: Macdonald, 1972.

Higham, Robin, *The British Rigid Airship, 1908–1931: A Study in Weapons*

Policy, Westport, CT: Greenwood, 1975.

Higham, Robin, 'Air Power in World War I, 1914–1918', in *The War in the Air 1914–1994*, ed. Alan Stephens, Canberra: RAAF Air Power Studies Centre, 1994.

Holley, I. B., Jr, *Ideas and Weapons, Exploitation of the Aerial Weapon by the United States during World War I: A Study in the Relationship of Technological Advance, Military Doctrine, and the Development of Weapons.* Hamden, CT: Archon Books, 1971.

Hyde, H. Montgomory, *British Air Policy between the Wars*, London: Heinemann, 1976.

James, John, *The Paladins: The Story of the RAF up to the Outbreak of World War II*, London: Futura, 1990.

Johnson, Chalmers, *Revolution and the Social System*, Stanford, CA: Hoover Institution on War, Revolution, and Peace, 1964.

Kennett, Lee, *A History of Strategic Bombing*, New York: Charles Scribner's Sons, 1982.

Kennett, Lee, *The First Air War 1914–1918*, New York: Free Press, 1991.

Kilduff, Peter, *Germany's First Air Force 1914–1918*, London: Arms & Armour Press, 1991.

Kuhn, Thomas S., *The Structure of Scientific Revolutions*, 2nd edn, Chicago: University of Chicago Press, 1970.

Layman, R. D., 'Over the Wine-Dark Sea, Aerial Aspects of the Dardanelles/ Gallipoli Campaign', *Over the Front*, 9 (Spring 1994): 5–40.

Lewis, Gwilym H., *Wings over the Somme 1916–1918*, ed. Chaz Bowyer, London: William Kimber, 1976.

Liddell Hart, B. H., *The Real War, 1914–1918*, Boston, MA: Little, Brown, 1930.

Liddle, Peter, *The Airman's War 1914–18*, Poole, Dorset: Blandford Press, 1987.

Macmillan, Norman, *Sir Sefton Brancker*, London: William Heinemann, 1935.

Mason, Tony, *Air Power: A Centennial Appraisal*, London: Brassey's, 1994.

Mead, Peter, *The Eye in the Air: History of Air Observation and Reconnaissance for the Army 1785–1945*, London: Her Majesty's Stationery Office, 1983.

Middlebrook, Martin, *The Kaiser's Battle, 21 March 1918: The First Day of the Spring Offensive*, London: Allen Lane, 1978.

Millet, Alan and Murray, Williamson, *Military Effectiveness, Vol. I, The First World War*, Boston: Unwin Hyman, 1988.

Morrow, John H., Jr, *German Air Power in World War I*, Lincoln, NE: University of Nebraska Press, 1982.

Morrow, John H., Jr., *The Great War in the Air: Military Aviation from 1909 to 1921*, Washington, DC: Smithsonian Institution, 1993.

Mumford, Lewis, *Techniques and Civilization*, New York: Harcourt Brace, 1934.

Murray, Williamson, *Strategy for Defeat: The Luftwaffe 1933–1945*, Maxwell AFB: Air University Press, 1983.

Murray, Williamson (ed.), *The Making of Strategy: Rulers, States and War*,

Cambridge: Cambridge University Press, 1994.

Norman, Aaron, *The Great Air War*, New York: Macmillan, 1968.

Norris, Geoffrey, *The Royal Flying Corps: A History*, London: Frederick Muller, 1965.

Paret, Peter (ed.), *Makers of Modern Strategy from Machiavelli to the Nuclear Age*, Princeton, NJ: Princeton University Press, 1986.

Paris, Michael, *Winged Warfare: The Literature and Theory of Aerial Warfare in Britain 1859–1917*, Manchester: Manchester University Press, 1992.

Patrick, Mason M., *The United States in the Air*, Garden City, NY: Doubleday, Doran, 1928.

Powers, Barry D., *Strategy without Slide-Rule, British Air Strategy 1914–1939*, London: Croom-Helm, 1976.

Probert, Henry, *High Commanders of the Royal Air Force*, London: HMSO, 1991.

Raleigh, Walter and Jones, H. A., *The War in the Air: Being the Story of the Part Played in the Great War by the Royal Air Force*, 7 vols, London: Hamish Hamilton, 1922.

Reader, W. J., *Architect of Air Power: The Life of the First Viscount Weir of Eastwood*, London: Collins, 1968.

Schroder, Hans, *A German Airman Remembers*, trans. Claud W. Sykes, London: Greenhill, 1986.

Sinclair, Susan, 'Transactional Analysis', in *Communicating with Subordinates*, New York: Amacom, 1974.

Slessor, John, *The Central Blue: The Autobiography of Sir John Slessor, Marshal of the RAF*, New York: Praeger, 1957.

Smith, Malcolm, *British Air Strategy between the Wars*, Oxford: Clarendon Press, 1984.

Smith, Myron J., *World War I in the Air: A Bibliography and Chronology*, Metuchen, NJ: Scarecrow Press, 1977.

Stark, Rudolph, *Wings of War: A German Airman's Diary of the Last Year of the Great War*, trans. Claud W. Sykes, London: Greenhill, 1988.

Strachan, Hew, *European Armies and the Conduct of War*, London: Allen & Unwin, 1983.

Strange, L. A., *Recollections of an Airman*, London: Greenhill, 1989.

Taylor, John, W. R., *C.F.S.: Birthplace of Air Power*, London: Jane's Publishing, 1987.

Thetford, Owen, *Aircraft of the Royal Air Force, 1918–57*, London: Putnam, 1957.

Travers, Tim, *The Killing Ground: The British Army, the Western Front and the Emergence of Modern Warfare 1900–1918*, London: Unwin Hyman, 1990.

Travers, Tim, *How the War Was Won: Command and Technology in the British Army on the Western Front 1917–1918*, London: Routledge, 1992.

Van der Spuy, Kenneth Reid, *Chasing the Wind*, Capetown: Books of Africa, 1966.

Waterhouse, Nourah, *Private and Official*, London: Cape, 1942.

Webster, Charles and Frankland, Noble, *The Strategic Air Offensive against Germany, 1939–1945*, Vol. 1, London: HMSO, 1961.

West, Nigel, *MI6: British Secret Intelligence Service Operations 1909–1945*, London: Weidenfeld & Nicolson, 1983.
Who Was Who 1900–1980, Eminent Indians, New Delhi: Durga Das, 1985.
Winter, Dennis, *The First of the Few*, London: Allen Lane, 1982.

Unpublished Dissertations

Williams, George Kent, 'Statistics and Strategic Bombardment', Oxford University, 1987.

Index

aerial photography, 64, 73(nn119, 120)
Aerodrome Committee, 131
aerodromes: British bombing, 167, 168, 183(nn84, 86)
Aeronautical Ordnance Depot, 39
Aeronautical Society: address by Sykes (1913), 31–2
aeroplane competition (1912), 28–9, 46(n39)
Air Board, 93, 127, 149(n126)
Air Council, 117, 126–7, 178(n3)
Air Ministry, 112, 126–7, 130–3
air power: Sykes' theories, 216–28
air war: Sykes' role, 204–8
aircraft: Avros, 38; BE2 (Bleriot Experimental), 28, 34, 38; BE8, 38; Bristol Biplane, 23; DH4, 160; Farman boxkite, 19, 23; Farmans, 38; Fokker, 104; Fokker DVII, 134; Fokker DVIII, 135; Handley Page, 173; monoplanes, 30; seaplanes, 149(n126); Sopwith Camel, 134; Tarant Tabor, 173; Vimy bomber, 168
aircraft losses, 135, 164, 169, 172, 173
aircraft production, 139(n6); United States, 114, 140(n9), 159, 180(n27)
airships: Navy command, 30
Aisne, Battle of, 58
Allen, Wing-Commander H. R., 3, 190
American Air Staff, 130–1, 170
Amery, Leo, 98, 101
Amiens: German attack (1918), 101, 120–1, 144(n67)
Antwerp: Sykes' mission (1914), 59
Armistice (11 November 1918), 173, 231
Army: air service, 23; Navy rivalry, 34–6, 126–8; RAF relations, 131
Army maneuvers: (1911), 23; (1912), 28, 29–30; (1913), 37–8
Ashmore, Major-General E. B., 128, 129, 150(n137)

Bailey, Lieutenant G. C. G., 70(n53)
Baird, Major John L., 124
Balfour, Lord Arthur J., 89(n46), 168
balloon barrage, 129
ballooning, 14–15, 44(n1)
Bannerman, Sir Alexander, 26
Baring, Maurice, 191
Barrington-Kennett, Lieutenant B. H., 27, 37, 45(n29), 54
Beatty, Admiral David, 115
Belgium: bombing complaints, 166, 183(n75); Sykes' mission (1914), 59
Berlin: proposed bombing, 168, 184(n97)
bicycles: 4th Mounted Division, 93
Bliss, General Tasker H., 103
Boer War, 11–13, 44(n1)
Bolling, Major Raynal C., 114, 140(nn9, 10)
bombing: by IAF, 155–78, 178(n2); categories, 74(n139); daylight, 166; first missions, 59, 66, 71(n67); long-range, 113, 155–78; strategic, 5, 129, 130, 134, 155–78, 179(n15), 219–20; targeting debate, 165–8; training, 182(n62)
Brancker, Major Sir W. Sefton: aircraft debate, 38; Henderson relationship, 92–3; passed over as DGMA, 115–16, 141(nn17, 18); RFC reorganization, 61–2, 72(n92); Trenchard relationship, 60, 115–16
British Expeditionary Force (BEF): manpower reduction, 102; Mons retreat, 55–6; RFC relationship, 52, 54, 65, 69(n31)
Brooke-Popham, Major (later Air Chief Marshal Sir) H. R. M., 27, 29–30, 50, 52, 66
Bülow, General Karl von, 56
Burke, Major C. J., 27

Cadorna, General Luigi, 100

Canadian flyers, 131
Capper, Colonel John, 14, 32, 115–16, 225
Capper, Major-General Sir Thomas, 17–18, 32, 197
Carden, Major A. D., 27
Carleton, Brigadier-General F. R. C., 94, 95
casualties: reduction, 102–3, 109(n67), 134–5
cavalry: competition with aircraft, 29, 230(n53)
Cecil, Lieutenant Lord Hugh, 123, 143(n51)
Central Flying School (CFS): naval influence, 34, 36–7
Ceylon: Sykes' tea planting experiences, 10–11
Churchill, Sir Winston: Admiralty, 35, 77; appeal from Sykes (1915), 83–4; Munitions Minister (1917), 165, 180(n27); War and Air Minister (1919), 175–6, 231, 242–3(n3)
Civil Air Transport (CAT) Committee, 175
civil aviation, 174–5, 176–7, 231–2
Clausewitz, Carl von, 17–18, 21(n43)
Clemenceau, Georges, 100, 101, 136, 160–3
Cody, S. F., 29
Committee of Imperial Defence (CID), 23, 25
Commonwealth: Sykes' views, 241
Compiègne, 53
Conock Manor, 241, 246–7(n69)
conscription, 96–7, 106–7(n22)
Cooper, Malcolm, 4, 69(nn34, 35), 216–17
Cowdray, Lord, 115, 141(n16)
Crawford, Lady Gertrude, 148(n114)

Dardanelles *see* Gallipoli
de Havilland, Geoffrey, 1, 28, 29
de Robeck, Vice-Admiral J.M., 80, 81
De Wet, Christian, 11–12
demobilization, 173–5
Deperdussin, A., 29
Derby, Lord, 98, 107(n30)
Divine, David, 3, 23–4, 69(nn34, 35)
Douglas-Pennant, Violet, 148(n114)
Douhet, Brigadier-General Giulio, 24, 218, 223–4
Duval, Brigadier-General Maurice, 160

Edmonds, C. H. K., 82, 90(n53)
Edmonds, J. E. 'Archimedes', 22
Ellington, Major-General Edward, 3, 159, 170

Fisher, Sir John, 77
Fisher, Captain W. W., 150(n128)
flying circuses, 104
Foch, General Ferdinand: General Reserve, 100, 101; IAF control, 160–3, 168, 172, 181(n52)
Fokker scourge, 207, 214(n119)
France: non-cooperation with IAF, 159–62; RFC relocation, 51–4; Sykes' visit (1911), 24–5
French, General Sir John, 32, 37, 53; RFC reconnaissance, 54–7, 69(n33)
From Many Angles, 3, 241
Fuller, Lieutenant-Colonel J. F. C., 132
Fulton, Captain J. D. B., 24

Gallipoli: evacuation, 84–6; supply problems, 79–81, 83, 91(n64); Sykes' posting (1915–16), 66–7, 75–87
Gandhi, M. K., 236, 237–8
gas: use by Germans, 66
Geddes, Sir Auckland, 126
Geddes, Sir Eric, 115, 140(n14)
General Reserve, 99, 101
George V, King, 27, 119, 173–4
German XVIII Army Corps: observation by Sykes, 16–17
Germany: air superiority, 207, 214(n119); air tactics, 121, 145(n73); aircraft developments, 104, 134, 135; bombing missions, 128–9, 151(n142); combat arms, 99, 108(n40); industry vulnerability, 165–7, 182(n73); manpower shortages, 137; pilots' morale, 104, 110(nn75, 76); professionalism of air force, 200; spring offensive (1918), 120–2, 123–5
Gerrard, Wing-Commander E. L., 79
Gollin, Alfred, 4
Grantham: Machine-Gun Corps, 93–6
Green, Sir W. Graham, 115
Gregory, Lieutenant R., 25
Grierson, General James, 29–30
Groves, Brigadier-General P. R. C.: Gallipoli, 79; meeting Sykes in Sierra Leone, 14; RAF Director of Flying Operations, 125, 128, 135, 137, 153(n199); support for Sykes, 189;

writing, 3
Guest, Lieutenant L. V., 83
Gwynne-Vaughan, Mrs, 148(n114), 174

Haig, General Sir Douglas: air-power antagonism, 27, 29, 174; General Reserve antagonism, 99–102; Lloyd George relationship, 174; Sykes' opinion of him, 15; Trenchard relationship, 74(n136), 105, 188, 198–9
Haldane, Richard Burdon (Viscount), 117
Hamilton, General Sir Ian, 67, 76
Hamilton, Lady, 67
Hankey, Captain Maurice, 25
Harmsworth, Alfred Charles William (1st Viscount Northcliffe), 114, 115, 140(nn9, 10)
Harmsworth, Harold Sidney (1st Viscount Rothermere), 114, 115, 117–20, 140(n7), 142(n31)
Helles: evacuation, 85–6; landing, 76, 87(n4)
Henderson, Brigadier-General Sir David: aeroplane competition (1912), 28–9; Commander, 1st Infantry Division, 62, 72(n97); DGMA inefficiency, 93; ill health, 65, 66; RAF formation, 116–17, 141(nn23, 24, 25), 190; RAF resignation, 116–17, 141(n26), 141–2(n29), 195–6; RFC command, 25–6, 50–67, 195; RFC reorganization, 33–4, 39–40, 60–2, 71–2(n88); Sykes relationship, 62, 63, 66, 72(n95), 92–3, 141(n26), 194–6
Henderson, Ian, 116–17
Higham, Robin, 1, 42
historical studies, 3–4
Hoare, Samuel, 245(n49)
Holley, I. B., 48(n117)
Home Defence Squadrons, 128, 129, 150(n138)
home defense: RAF role, 128–30
Hotel Cecil (House of Bolo), 123–38, 198, 199
Hussars: 15th, 13

identification friend or foe (IFF) system, 37, 41
Imbros: RNAS location, 79–84
Independent Air Force (IAF), 155–78; creation, 113–15, 139(n4), 205; organizational problems, 156–63;

supply problems, 164–5, 207; Sykes' influence, 6; Trenchard's view, 190
India: machine-guns, 106(n15); Sykes with 15th Hussars, 13–14, 15–16; Sykes as Governor of Bombay (1928–33), 236–9
Inner War Cabinet, 109(n60)
Inter-Allied Aviation Committee, 157, 159, 161, 162, 220
Inter-Allied Bombing Air Force, 162
Inter-Allied IF, 156, 160–2, 168, 172–3
Irwin, Lord, 237, 245(n40)
Italy: Sykes' visit (1911), 24, 224

Jellicoe, Admiral John, 115, 143(n49)
Joffre, General Joseph, 57
Jones, H. A., 2

Kennett, Lee, 4
Keyes, Admiral Sir Roger, 80, 149(n116)
Kiggell, General Launcelot, 100
Kitchener, Lord Horatio Herbert: death (1916), 94, 198; Sykes' opinion of, 15; Trenchard relationship, 51, 60, 68(n7), 71(n74), 198
Kluck, General Alexander von, 56, 69(n33)

Lanrezac, General Charles, 55
Law, Andrew Bonar, 116, 143(n48), 197–8, 233, 234
Law, Isabel, 197, 233
leadership styles, 193, 211(n49)
Lewis, Gwilym, 3
Lewis, Lieutenant-Colonel P. E., 95
Lloyd George, David: French assistance requests, 136, 160; Haig relationship, 116; peace problems, 174; support for Sykes, 147(n98); SWC, 98, 99, 100, 160; Sykes' memorandum on manpower, 103; Trenchard's resignation, 103, 119
London: bombing, 166, 182–3(n74)
London Air Defence Area (LADA), 128
Longcroft, Captain Charles, 38
Loraine, Captain Eustace B., 45–6(n34)
Ludendorff, General Erich von, 143(n63), 165

M-5 Branch, 114, 140(n11), 170
Macdonogh, Lieutenant-Colonel George, 22, 26, 57
Machine-Gun Corps, 93–6, 103

MacInnes, Major Duncan Sayre, 26
Macready, Sir Nevil, 93
Maitland, Major E., 27
Man-Power Committee, 101–2
manpower: casualty reduction, 102–3,
    109(n67); replacement by technology,
    102–3, 122; shortages, 95–6, 97,
    98–100, 101–2, 134, 136, 146(n82)
Marne, Battle of the, 54, 56, 69(n34)
Mary, Queen, 27
Mason, Air Vice-Marshal Tony, 2
Middle East: RAF activities (1918),
    169–70
Milner, Lord Alfred, 98, 99
monoplanes: safety concerns, 30
Monro, Major-General Charles, 37, 84
Mons: 'protective reconnaissance', 41,
    69(nn33, 34); retreat from, 38, 55–6
Montagu, Lord John Walter Edward,
    109(n67), 110–11(n79), 195,
    211–12(n58)
Moore-Brabazon, Lieutenant John T.
    C., 64, 73(n120)
morale: Germany, 165, 169; Royal
    Flying Corps, 103–5
Morrow, John, 4, 54
Mukden, battle at, 18
Musgrave, Major H., 39, 64, 71(n67)

Nancy: IAF route to, 164, 182(n65)
Navy: airships, 30; Army rivalry, 34–6,
    126–8; flying operations, 127,
    149–50(n128); view of RAF formation,
    115, 126–7, 140(n14)
Nehru, Jawaharlal, 236, 237
Netheravon camp, 43–4, 48(n134)
Neuve Chapelle, battle, 65, 74(n136)
night flying, 164
Norman, Sir Henry, 119, 178(n2),
    179(n6)
Northcliffe, Lord *see* Harmsworth,
    Alfred Charles William
'Notes on the Economy of Man-Power by
    Mechanical Means', 102, 103, 122, 218

O'Gorman, Mervyn, 25, 32–3
Operation Michael, 6, 118, 120–2, 123–5
Organization Directorate, 96–8
Ottley, Rear-Admiral Sir C. L., 25

Paine, Captain Godfrey, 32, 34, 36,
    140(n14), 159
parachutes, 133, 152(nn172, 173),

153(n174)
Paris, Michael, 1–2, 4
Park, K. R., 78
Parliament: RAF debate, 119, 123
Passchendaele, 97
Patrick, General Mason M., 115
peace, 173–8
Per ardua ad astra, 28
Pershing, General John J., 115
personalized command structure,
    199–200
Pétain, General Henri, 96, 99, 101
Peyton, Major William, 13
pilots: training, 40–3, 147–8(n106),
    210(n34)
Powell, Major F. J., 110(n77)
Powers, B. D., 4

Quetta: Staff College, 16, 17–19

railways: British bombing, 167, 168
Raleigh, Walter, 2
reconnaissance: aircraft use for, 25,
    29–30, 45(n19); Gallipoli failure, 78–9,
    88(nn29, 30); Royal Flying Corps, 38,
    41, 54–7, 69(nn33, 34, 36);
    strategic/tactical, 70(n56)
Richthofen, Captain Manfred von, 124,
    147(nn103, 104), 152(n173), 206
Roberts, Lord, 11, 12, 20(n14)
Robertson, Field Marshall Sir William,
    100, 103
Rothermere, Lord *see* Harmsworth,
    Harold Sidney
Roure, Lieutenant-Colonel, 136
Royal Aero Club, 193, 210–11(n43)
Royal Aircraft Factory, 34
Royal Air Force (RAF): administration
    problems, 125–7; American
    involvement, 114–15, 130–1, 170;
    formation (1918), 112–16, 138–9(n1),
    190, 205; German offensive (1918),
    120–2, 124, 134–8; home defense role,
    128–30; peacetime role, 174–8; post-
    war reductions, 189, 209(n14); power
    politics, 116; social system, 196–201;
    Sykes as CAS (1918), 123–38, 169–78
Royal Flying Corps (RFC): aircraft
    destroyed by storms (1914), 58, 64;
    bombing missions, 59, 66, 71(n67);
    formation (1912), 25–6; Military
    Wing, 26–8, 33, 36; morale, 103–5;
    motto, 28; move to France (1914),

50–4; reconnaissance role, 38, 41, 54–7, 69(nn33, 34, 36); reorganization (1913), 33–4, 39; reorganization (1914), 60–2, 63, 71–2(n88); St Omer base (1914–16), 59; social system, 196–201; Standing Orders, 42–3; training, 59–60; Training Manual, 40–3, 48(nn113, 115); uniform, 28, 46(n35)

Royal Naval Air Service (RNAS): Gallipoli (1915–16), 75–87; RAF amalgamation (1918), 126, 148–9(n115); reorganization (1914), 63; split from RFC, 36; Sykes' reorganization (1915), 77–8, 79–81, 87–8(n15)

Royal Naval Armoured Car Division, 81

St Paul's Cathedral: Sykes' near collision, 160–1

Salmond, Major (later Air Chief-Marshal, Sir) Geoffrey, 64

Salmond, Major (later Marshal of the Royal Air Force, Sir) John, 117, 125, 142(n33), 144(n65), 147(n99)

Samson, Wing-Commander C. R., 25, 67, 76, 78, 80

Saundby, Sir Robert, 3

Scott-Moncrieff, Brigadier-General G. K., 25

seaplanes, 149(n126)

Seeley, Colonel J. E. B., 25

Serno, Hauptmann Erich, 87(n3)

Sierra Leone: Sykes' posting, 14

Simon, Major Sir John, 143(n51)

Smith-Barry, R. R., 241, 246–7(n69)

Smith-Dorrien, General Sir Horace, 16, 57–8

Smith-Pigott, Flight Commander J. R. W., 82

Smuts, General Jan Christian, 63, 73(n109), 113–15, 138–9(n1), 214(n109)

Somme: Battle of the, 94–6, 104, 110(nn74, 75), 207; bridge bombing, 135

South Africa: Boer War, 11–13, 19

squadron size, 25, 45(n15)

Staff College, 16, 17–19

Stopford, Lieutenant-General Frederick W., 78–9, 88(n29)

Strange, L. A., 3

Strategic Council, 156

Studd, Brigadier-General H. W., 98

Sueter, Commodore Murray F., 67, 76, 80, 83, 89(n46), 140(n14)

supply problems: IAF, 164–5, 207

Supreme War Council (SWC), 92, 98–101, 107(n27), 162

Suvorov, Alexander, 109(n61)

Sykes, Bonar, 244(n30), 246(n69)

Sykes, Ethel ('Number 2'), 9

Sykes, Major-General Sir Frederick: 15th Hussars (1901–08), 13–17; air-power theories, 216–28; autobiography, 3, 241; Boer War, 11–13, 44(n1); Brigadier-General promotion (1917), 96; CAS (1918), 112–13, 119–20, 123–38, 155–78; Ceylon, 10–11; childhood, 9–10; Controller General of Civil Aviation, 231–2, 242–3(n3); flying experiences, 14–15, 19, 22–3, 44(n2), 160–1; Gallipoli posting (1915–16), 66–7, 75–87; IAF, 6, 155–78; India (1928-33), 236–9; Machine-Gun Corps (1915–17), 93–6; marriage, 233–4; Member of Parliament (1922–28), 234–5; military training, 14–15, 17–19; offensive air policy, 42, 219; personality, 4, 10, 13, 36, 192, 193, 199–200, 201–4, 213(n93); post-war life, 231–42; retirement, 241–2; RFC command (1914), 62; RFC Military Wing command (1912–14), 25–44; Trenchard comparison, 1–2, 188, 193; War Office (1908–12), 22–5; War Office (1916–18), 92–106

Sykes, Henry (Guy), 9, 20(n2)

Sykes, Lady Isabel *see* Law, Isabel

Sykes, Mary, 9

Sykes, Stanley, 20(n2)

tanks: development, 95

technology: military approaches, 102, 228(n7); Sykes' views, 102–3, 122, 132–4, 218–19, 235

torpedo: first aircraft-delivered, 82, 90(n52)

training: bombing, 182(n62); pilots, 40–3, 147–8(n106), 210(n34)

Trenchard, Marshal of the Royal Air Force Lord Hugh M. (1st Viscount): assessment of his career, 187–91; bombing objections, 189–90; Brancker relationship, 60, 115–16; CAS

appointment, 105, 117, 142(n31), 242–3(n3); CAS resignation, 1, 103, 118–19, 123, 142(nn40, 41), 190–1, 210(n30); Haig support, 100, 188, 198–9; IAF command, 157–8, 160–2, 167–8, 190; morale policy, 103–5, 110(n77), 193; offensive policy, 42, 104–5, 110(n77), 188, 193; peacetime proposals, 176–7; post-war RAF command, 189; recollections of Sykes, 26, 36, 51–2, 66, 192–3; RFC reorganization, 61–2, 72(n92); Rothermere dispute, 117–20; Sykes comparison, 1–2, 188, 193; Sykes relationship, 51–2, 58, 62, 73(n103), 92–3, 123, 146(n93), 192–4
trench warfare, 58, 64, 97
Turkey: Gallipoli campaign, 75–87

United States: Air Force, 139(n3); aircraft production, 114, 139(n6), 140(n9), 159, 180(n27); enter war, 97–8; organizational failure, 48(n117); RAF link, 114–15, 130–1, 170

Vaughn-Lee, Rear-Admiral C. L., 80–1
Versailles: Supreme War Council, 98, 107(n27); Treaty of Versailles, 174

Wake, Brigadier-General Hereward, 98
war games: Versailles, 99, 108(n38)
Waterfall, Lieutenant V., 70(n53)

Waterhouse, Colonel Sir Ronald, 201
weather: meteorological office, 131, 137, 152(n160); problems for aircraft, 58, 64, 121, 124, 169
Weir, Lord: Air Minister, 114, 118, 139(n5); aircraft production, 139(n6), 156; bombing policy, 167–8; Henderson relationship, 116; IAF, 137, 159–63; RAF formation, 130–2; support for Sykes, 173; Trenchard relationship, 118
Weygand, General, 100
Whitgift School, 9
Wilson, Lieutenant-General Sir Henry: RAF formation, 129–30; support for Sykes, 22, 106, 196–7; Supreme War Council, 98–103; War Office, 22
Wilson, Staff Sergeant R. H. V., 45–6(n34)
Winter, Denis, 4
wireless communication, 65
Women's Army Auxiliary Corps (WAAC), 97, 107(n23)
Women's Royal Air Force (WRAF), 125–6, 148(nn113, 114), 174

Ypres: first Battle of, 56, 59

Zeppelins: bombing attacks, 128, 182–3(n74)
Zwehl, General Hans von, 70(n53)